SKIMPY COVERAGE

Cultural Frames, Framing Culture

Robert Newman, Editor
Justin Neuman, Associate Editor

SKIMPY COVERAGE

Sports Illustrated and the
Shaping of the Female Athlete

Bonnie M. Hagerman

University of Virginia Press • *Charlottesville and London*

University of Virginia Press
© 2023 by the Rector and Visitors of the University of Virginia
All rights reserved
Printed in the United States of America on acid-free paper

First published 2023

9 8 7 6 5 4 3 2 1

Library of Congress Cataloging-in-Publication Data

Names: Hagerman, Bonnie M., author.
Title: Skimpy coverage : Sports Illustrated and the shaping of the female athlete /
  Bonnie M. Hagerman.
Description: Charlottesville : University of Virginia Press, 2023. | Series: Cultural
  frames, framing culture | Includes bibliographical references and index.
Identifiers: LCCN 2022041058 (print) | LCCN 2022041059 (ebook) |
  ISBN 9780813949222 (hardcover) | ISBN 9780813949239 (paperback) |
  ISBN 9780813949246 (ebook)
Subjects: LCSH: Women athletes—Press coverage—United States—History. | Sports
  journalism—United States—History. | Human body in mass media—United States—
  History. | Sports illustrated. | Feminism and sports—United States.
Classification: LCC PN4888.W63 H34 2023 (print) | LCC PN4888.W63 (ebook) |
  DDC 071/.309—dc23/eng/20221130
LC record available at https://lccn.loc.gov/2022041058
LC ebook record available at https://lccn.loc.gov/2022041059

For Marc

And in memory of the graduate student volunteer Sports Illustrated *featured in 1963 who was my first coach. And my dad.*

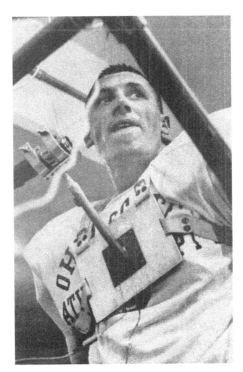

CONTENTS

Acknowledgments   ix

List of Abbreviations   xiii

Introduction: "How It All Began"   1

1   "The Big F"   17

2   "Girls Like That"   54

3   "An Odd Way to Even Things Up"   91

4   "The Frailty Myth"   126

5   "The Olympic Ideal"   159

6   "A League of Their Own"   193

Conclusion: "A Pretty Girl on the Cover"   229

Notes   247

Bibliography   287

Index   301

ACKNOWLEDGMENTS

WHEN A PROJECT spans two decades, like this one has, there are a lot of people to thank for moving it from a possibility to an actuality. It is my profound privilege and pleasure to do just that.

I would never have considered writing a book about sportswomen had I not been an athlete myself. That was made possible not just by Title IX, which Congress passed three years after I was born, but by a family who loved playing sports and made it a priority. My thanks, then, to my parents, Marge and Fritz Hagerman, and my brothers, Kris and Erik Hagerman, who as scholars and athletes themselves, inspired me to learn, to play, and to compete. They have always cheered me on in all of my academic and athletic endeavors, including this latest one. I owe a debt of gratitude, as well, to the many teammates and coaches who have passed through my playing life, one that has encompassed grade school recreational programs, high school varsity sports teams, collegiate crews, and adult tennis clubs. I am particularly thankful for the lessons I learned from coaches Malcolm Idleman, Willie Black, and Curtis Jordan and for the lasting friendships I have formed with teammates across time and sports. Thanks goes also to those athletes I coached at Westfield High School, and the coaches, administrators, and friends I worked with, including Jack Martin, Nancy Carpenter Babbitt, and Sandy Mamary.

This book was originally a master's thesis and then a doctoral dissertation, and I am grateful to my adviser, Katherine Jellison, for seeing the initial potential in the project, providing valuable guidance, and for encouraging me over the years to transform the dissertation into a book. Graduate school also yielded opportunities to work with professors and fellow graduate students alike whose questions, comments, and contributions have made this book better. My sincere thanks to Alan Booth, Alonzo Hamby, Joan Hoff, Steven Miner, Chester Pach, and Sholeh Quinn, as well as to Ray Haberski, Kimberly Little, and Jeff Woods.

I am especially indebted to my colleagues in the field of sports studies who offered incredibly detailed and helpful readers' reports. I am honored that Lindsay Parks Pieper and Derek Catsam saw such promise in *Skimpy*

Coverage and am grateful to them for their insightful comments and suggestions; they have unquestionably made *Skimpy Coverage* a better book.

I am fortunate to be surrounded and supported by colleagues, students, and staff from the University of Virginia. I am grateful to my home department of Women, Gender & Sexuality and the stimulating and supportive environment that encourages excellent teaching and innovative research. Many thanks to the support of friends and colleagues like Corinne Field, Charlotte Patterson, Farzaneh Milani, Allison Pugh, Doug Meyer, Lisa Speidel, Bridget Murphy, Lanice Avery, Andre Cavalcante, Matthew Chin, Tiffany King, and Denise Walsh. This project would have never taken its current shape without the many UVA students who have taken my classes on gender and sport since 2008. There are so many of you that it's impossible to acknowledge you individually, but know that your enthusiasm, passion, and insights contributed to this project and made it better; I am grateful every day to have been able to learn from you. A special thanks to the folks at UVA Library, including Director of Information Policy Brandon Butler and especially librarian Erin Pappas for hunting down resources that were crucial to the book's completion and for assistance above and beyond the call of duty. I wish also to acknowledge Mike Smith for his help in providing invaluable support and Jenny Lillich for sharing her indexing expertise.

A huge thank-you to my editor Nadine Zimmerli for her constructive criticism, patience, and firm belief that this was a project worthy of publication. Having *Skimpy Coverage* appear in book form has been a long-held dream, and it is only with her steady guidance that I have been able to transform vision into reality. I hope other authors are lucky enough to have an editor like Nadine in their corner. Many thanks, also, to everyone at the University of Virginia Press, especially Ellen Satrom and Ruth Melville.

While I have been lucky to have the amazing support of colleagues throughout my professional career, I am equally as fortunate in the friendships and relationships that have nurtured me throughout the (long) process of transforming *Skimpy Coverage* into a book. Amy Nolasco, Farrell Vangelopoulos, Adi Banavage, Larkin Mott, Lorri Bentch, and Andrea Larson provided boisterous encouragement, comic relief, and many much-needed study breaks. I'm also indebted to my in-laws, Harriet and Bob Selverstone, who have been both loving role models and indefatigable cheerleaders.

Finally, to the family I have made. It has been my greatest joy to be Jake and Alison's mom. They have never known me not to be working on *Skimpy Coverage,* and their wit, their laughter, and their love have both inspired and sustained me. And finally, to my husband, Marc Selverstone, who has seen this project in all its forms, and its author in all of hers, and still loves me anyway. For being my most favorite (if somewhat exacting) copy editor, my biggest supporter, and my greatest love, I dedicate this book to him and look forward to many more years of loving collaborations.

ABBREVIATIONS

AAGPBL	All-American Girls Professional Baseball League
AAU	Amateur Athletic Union
ABL	American Basketball League
ACL	Anterior Cruciate Ligament
AFL	American Football League
ATA	American Tennis Association
CAS	Court of Arbitration for Sport
DSD	Differences of Sex Development
IAAF	International Amateur Athletic Federation
IOC	International Olympic Committee
LGBTQ+	Lesbian, Gay, Bisexual, Transgender, Queer/Questioning, and Other Identities
LPGA	Ladies Professional Golf Association
MLB	Major League Baseball
MMA	Mixed martial arts
NBA	National Basketball Association
NFL	National Football League
NHL	National Hockey League
NWFL	National Women's Football League
NWSL	National Women's Soccer League
OCR	Office for Civil Rights
OPHR	Olympic Project for Human Rights

PGA   Professional Golf Association

SI   *Sports Illustrated*

USLTA   United States Lawn Tennis Association

USWNT   United States Women's National Soccer Team

USOC   United States Olympic Committee

USODC   United States Olympic Development Committee

USTA   United States Tennis Association

WBL   Women's Basketball League

WNBA   Women's National Basketball Association

WPGA   Women's Professional Golf Association

WTA   Women's Tennis Association

WUSA   Women's United Soccer Association

SKIMPY COVERAGE

INTRODUCTION

"How It All Began"

In 1964 *Sports Illustrated* was ten years old and finally in the black after a decade of losing money for its parent company, Time Inc. But its editors still had a problem: once the college football bowl games ended in January, the sports landscape was pretty bleak until spring training began for Major League Baseball in March. As a result, *SI*'s editors needed something to rouse the magazine and its readers from their winter doldrums. That something became known as the "Swimsuit Issue."[1]

Originally conceived as a means to "stir the pot a little," the Swimsuit Issue would consume increasingly greater amounts of *Sports Illustrated*'s creative energies and financial support. It first appeared on January 20, 1964, featuring Babette March having "FUN IN THE SUN ON COZUMEL."[2] By the late 1970s, "the sunshine issue" had become a *Sports Illustrated* institution, as well as, according to one reader, "an American tradition." During the 1980s, *Sports Illustrated*'s Swimsuit Issue was generating 10 percent of the company's yearly revenues, an advantage *SI* exploited by producing calendars with pictures from the issues' photo shoots.[3] By the 1990s, the Swimsuit Issue had become an issue unto itself that remained on newsstands for weeks. It no longer shared space with more traditional sports writing in the magazine's weekly edition, nor did it appear only in print form; coverage of the photo shoots was now available through videos (and then DVDs). By the twenty-first century, the Swimsuit Issue, which appeared in eleven languages in print and online, attracted tens of millions of consumers worldwide. *Sports Illustrated* further leveraged the issue by adorning it with trading cards and publishing two Swimsuit Issue-related coffee-table books. The magazine was clearly banking on expectations that "gorgeous women, encouraged by water to place their charms on display," would continue to resonate in an international market.[4] Given the Swimsuit Issue's spectacular history, it was a pretty safe bet.

Not everyone, however, was happy with the new addition to *SI*'s winter lineup. Letters opposing the Swimsuit Issue—many of which contained

Officially debuting in 1964, the Swimsuit Issue was designed to buttress *SI*'s meager winter sports news cycle and to "stir the pot a little."

demands for subscription cancellations—began arriving at *Sports Illustrated*'s offices as early as 1965. These grew in number and vehemence over the years, culminating in a record-high 339 cancellations following Cheryl Tiegs's 1978 appearance in a fishnet suit. Representing a minuscule percentage of the over three million who subscribed to *SI*—including the million or so who paid top dollar for the Swimsuit Issue at newsstands— it is not surprising that the magazine did not address those concerns until the twenty-fifth anniversary of the issue in 1989, and then only in jest. It refused to take seriously what some saw as the inordinate (and sometimes offensive) attention the magazine devoted to women whose only connection to sports was strolling—sometimes jogging—on a sandy beach in the tropics. Michael MacCambridge, who wrote an authoritative history of the magazine, contends that *SI* "might have deflected some of these complaints if it had done a better job of covering women in sports."[5]

This was, in part, the point Billie Jean King was trying to make when long-time *SI* contributor Frank Deford quoted the tennis great in that same twenty-fifth anniversary issue. Known for her activism on and off the court, King regarded the Swimsuit Issue as a distraction from the more pressing problem of the magazine's meager coverage of female athletes: "Women should stop screaming about that one issue and start screaming that SPORTS ILLUSTRATED doesn't carry enough women's sports. That's what's important. That's what's sexist." Deford sidestepped King's indictment, except to differ with her about the importance of the Swimsuit Issue. In "How It All Began," Deford noted that of the millions of readers who purchased the issue, some 40 percent were women. Far from "screaming about" the idea of beautiful women in swimsuits, female readers, according to Deford, actually wanted to be them. And this was not a bad thing. Deford quoted the *San Francisco Chronicle*'s Joan Ryan, who found that "all the SI bathing suit models are muscular and lean and authentic. They don't mind working up a good sweat. They're proud of the bodies they've worked into shape. There is nothing powdery or gushy about them. In other words, the women in the Swimsuit Issue are not the worst role models a young girl could have."[6] Perhaps, but the swimsuit models who have appeared in the Swimsuit Issue rarely appeared swimming—or engaged in any sport—in a magazine whose purported goal was to set the sports agenda. As role models for women in sport, Christie Brinkley, Kathy Ireland, and Elle MacPherson might have been athletic looking, but they were not, in fact, athletes.

The female athletes who did show up in *Sports Illustrated* were also "muscular and lean and authentic." But while the magazine spent huge amounts of money publishing and promoting swimsuit models, female athletes, as King complained, appeared infrequently in its pages—and when they did show up, they were often depicted as swimsuit model stand-ins. Thus, when the public was asked to think of women in *Sports Illustrated,* they thought of swimsuit models instead of sportswomen. This was hardly surprising and became even more understandable when *Sports Illustrated* began to include notable (and attractive) female athletes in the 1997 Swimsuit Issue—a trend it repeated in succeeding years.

Skimpy Coverage: Sports Illustrated *and the Shaping of the Female Athlete* argues that throughout *SI*'s decades-long history and dominant publishing performance, the magazine has conflated prevailing notions about swimsuit models and sportswomen, thereby constructing an image of the female athlete via the stories the magazine covered—and those it left unexplored. In presuming to set the sports agenda, *Sports Illustrated* thus provides a valuable lens for analyzing and assessing a history of female athletes. For *SI*, the idealized qualities of those athletes—highly feminine, good-looking, straight, white, able-bodied, and cisgender—mirrored those it prized in swimsuit models. This book, therefore, maintains that the female athlete and the swimsuit model, at least for *SI*, have been essentially one and the same.

This history of *SI* and its emerging archetype of the female athlete is worth telling if only for charting the distance sportswomen have traveled—both within *Sports Illustrated*'s pages and without—since 1954. That trajectory is at the heart of *Skimpy Coverage* and reveals an important story not only for sports history but for gender history as well. Numerous women, such as Billie Jean King, Serena Williams, and Megan Rapinoe, have used sports and the platform it offered to push for empowerment, freedom, equality, and acceptance in ways that have complemented, inspired, and challenged broader feminist agendas.

This, then, is a history of the female athlete according to *Sports Illustrated,* the first to explore *SI*'s rendering of sportswomen in a book-length treatment. *Skimpy Coverage* tracks those sportswomen from *SI*'s first issue on August 16, 1954, to the end of its weekly publishing schedule in 2018, and then into the 2020s as it appeared as a monthly print magazine. As a longitudinal study, *Skimpy Coverage* allows for a deeper and more sustained engagement with topics the magazine returned to again and again when reporting female athletes, including their femininity (or lack thereof), their access to sporting opportunities (or lack thereof), and their available professional prospects (again, or lack thereof). In addition, it incorporates reporting from *SI for Women* (and its various iterations), SI.com, and the Swimsuit Issue. Collectively, they offer a more nuanced appraisal of the *Sports Illustrated* sportswoman.

Before the *SI* sportswoman could appear, however, *Sports Illustrated* had to clear a number of hurdles to make it onto midcentury newsstands. The juggernaut that *SI* became was neither immediate nor assured and had its origins in a fairly practical and pedestrian twentieth-century decision.

"Muscles"

With $10 million either to invest or to lose to the government's taxmen, Henry Luce, the legendary founder of Time Inc., was looking to launch a new magazine in 1954. Even as company executives debated the pros and cons of numerous proposals, ranging from true crime to short fiction to intellectual discourse, Luce, though not a sports fan himself, could not help but notice the strong appeal of sports to the American public. The postwar boom had produced a variety of changes in American society, including the growth of a moneyed leisure class that liked to relax and was willing to pay for it. Indeed, Americans at this time spent some $18 billion on spectator interests and recreational sports, including table tennis, softball, bowling, golf, and boating.[7] Americans clearly were playing sports, but would they read about them on a regular basis?

Serious challenges faced those bold enough to even consider launching a weekly sports magazine in the early 1950s. The NBA and the NHL, as well as the AFL and the NFL, were all small outfits at the time. Major League Baseball, the most popular and significant of the professional sports organizations, had its own problems: its westernmost team in 1954 was the St. Louis Cardinals, and that team was experiencing a downward slide in its fan base. As for golf, only a dedicated few were interested in anything more than its major championships, while Jack Kramer's professional tennis circuit was still trying to gain its footing. And the undeniably popular sports of boxing and horse racing had to contend with charges of impropriety.[8] As a result, a sports magazine could not count on such struggling entities to provide consistent and newsworthy stories.

In addition, sportswriting was not considered a quality expression of the literary form, nor could magazine publishers conceive of a single magazine that would appeal to American fans with their varied and wide-ranging interests. The last successful general sporting magazine was a product of the mid-nineteenth century, when John Stuart Skinner, the "Father of American Sport Journalism," published *American Turf Register and Sporting Magazine* in 1829. Although other magazines had catered to Americans' interest in playing and reading about sports—by the 1890s, sports-minded Americans could choose among forty-eight periodicals for the latest news about a variety of sporting endeavors—many of those magazines failed within several years. Those that did survive met their ultimate demise following the stock market crash of 1929 and the ensuing economic depression that lasted until World War II. And why roll out a new magazine at all when television sets were becoming fixtures in Americans' homes? Television would allow fans to see sports competitions in real time, theoretically making sports magazines and newspapers obsolete.[9] Thus, by the onset of the postwar era, the prospects for publishing a successful sports weekly magazine were dim at best.

Despite this unfavorable environment, Luce moved forward with the project, one that insiders dubbed "Muscles." And that was the other problem: the new magazine did not have an official name. Luce wanted his new weekly to be titled *Sport*, but a journal by that name already existed, and its current owner wanted $250,000 for the rights to the title; Luce was willing to pay only $200,000. When talks stymied, Luce accepted "sportsman and entrepreneur" Stuart Scheftel's offer of his defunct title *Sports Illustrated* for $10,000 and a subscription to the new magazine.[10]

With a title in place, Luce challenged the American people to give the new sports weekly a try. He was confident that, given the chance, *Sports Illustrated* could make sports even more enjoyable. "And *that*," Luce contended, "could have consequences." As he put it, "At last, America will have a great National Sports Weekly."[11]

"The Accepted and Essential Weekly Reporter of the Wonderful World of Sport"

Even when *Sports Illustrated* was nothing more than "Project X," those at Time Inc. who supported Luce predicted that it "would not be A sports magazine. It would be THE sports magazine." To transform prophecy into reality, Luce marshaled and then applied the wealth generated by his publications *Time*, *Life*, and *Fortune* to promote, and later to sustain, his fledgling endeavor. He did this against the advice of company aides and in the face of criticism from *Business Week*, which predicted that *Sports Illustrated* would never top a million subscribers. Undaunted, Luce urged potential readers "to have a look at this new magazine of Sport. Not just one issue, please. Take a year's subscription and see how you get on together. You may find that it makes more enjoyable what you already enjoy." Henry Luce was successful in his salesmanship. When Time published its first issue of *Sports Illustrated* on August 16, 1954, new subscribers numbered 350,000, making *SI* the largest circulation launch at that point in magazine history. Publisher H. H. S. Phillips Jr. welcomed readers in the inaugural issue with the hope "that in some tomorrow you will no longer think of *Sports Illustrated* as Time Inc.'s newest baby, but as the accepted and essential weekly reporter of the Wonderful World of Sport."[12]

Longtime editor Andre Laguerre, who remained at the helm of *SI* for fourteen years (1960–74), adopted this philosophy and regarded *SI* as the authority that set the American sports agenda. The writers who worked for Laguerre and followed in his wake—most of whom were overwhelmingly white and male—also embraced the idea that *Sports Illustrated* alone determined which sports mattered and which did not.[13] Renowned *SI* writer Dan Jenkins told Michael MacCambridge that "the magazine was edited in those days from the standpoint of 'What we think is important is what you should think is important . . . and if you don't agree with it, that's your problem.' It was totally arrogant, but I think it was right." *SI*'s Bill Leggett reminded MacCambridge that many people watched certain games "because *Sports Illustrated* told them it was important." And most of those people—77 percent of them—were male. *SI*'s "target market" was—and has remained—men in their midthirties, even as the magazine shifted toward attracting "a younger and active demographic." With an editorial board, a stable of writers, and a list of subscribers that was overwhelmingly male, *SI* framed sportswomen, when they appeared at all, "as objects of the male reader's gaze."[14]

Thus, if *Sports Illustrated* has set the sports agenda, it was one that simply did not prioritize female athletes, often ignoring them completely or trivializing their accomplishments for a male readership. When it did include women, the magazine consistently prioritized whiteness—normalizing the white female as the athletic archetype—often relegating Black female athletes to its quadrennial coverage of the Olympic Games. Thus, by the early 1970s, thousands of Americans read *Sports Illustrated* every week, but they encountered female athletes in the magazine's pages only infrequently, and Black sportswomen even less so. When they did, the sports angle was often included only incidentally, a reality highlighted by two of *SI*'s own staff writers. In 1973 Bil Gilbert and Nancy Williamson, as part of their landmark three-part series on women and sport, had singled out *SI* for its substandard coverage of sportswomen. "Rather than describing how well or badly the athlete performed or even how the contest turned out," they noted, "writers tend to concentrate on the color of the hair and eyes, and the shape of the legs or busts of the women."[15]

Such a dynamic began to attract the attention of scholars during the 1980s when Mary Jo Kane argued that *Sports Illustrated* continued to overemphasize sportswomen's femininity while underemphasizing their athleticism. Angela Lumpkin and Linda D. Williams offered a similar critique in a 1991 study, asserting that the nature of *SI*'s coverage contributed to a general trend that focused on the attractiveness of female athletes first and their athletic ability second. In 1992 Gina Daddario asserted that the presence of models in the annual Swimsuit Issue "crowded" out female athletes in the magazine's pages both literally and figuratively. Ten years later, Janet S. Fink and Linda Jean Kensicki found that *SI* created a "false reality" in which female athletes were remembered for their sex appeal rather than their athletic aptitude. In 2011 Kim Kayoung, Michael Sagas, and Nefertiti A. Walker considered the portrayal of female athletes in *SI* Swimsuit Issues from 1997 through 2009, concluding that the athlete models were depicted as highly sexualized and without any relation to their sports.[16]

Other studies of sportswomen in *SI* have tended to focus on more quantitative concerns. Scholars have documented the frequency with which female athletes appeared in the magazine, the number of column inches devoted to features on female athletes, the number of times female athletes landed on the cover of *SI*, or the number of articles the magazine gave to sportswomen as opposed to sportsmen. These studies have offered significant insights into the magazine's marginalization of female athletes.[17] As journal articles, however, they are limited in the depth and breadth of their analyses. As a result, they fail to provide a comprehensive view of the varied challenges sportswomen have faced over the last six decades and how these concerns have been reflected in the pages of *Sports Illustrated*.

Skimpy Coverage builds on this early scholarship, as well as on more general works that chronicle the history of sportswomen. Ellen Gerber, Jan Felshin, Pearl Berlin, and Waneen Wyrick published the first historical account of the topic, *The American Woman in Sport*, in 1974. Since then, additional histories have appeared, including Susan Cahn's *Coming On Strong* (1994, 2015), Mary Jo Festle's *Playing Nice* (1996), Lissa Smith's *Nike Is a Goddess* (1999), and Jaime Schultz's *Qualifying Times* (2014). Although important works, none of these titles have addressed *Sports Illustrated* and the magazine's importance in shaping an image of the female athlete that was consumed by millions of readers.

In addition to expanding the literature on women and sport, *Skimpy Coverage* also adds to the conversation about gender and physical empowerment.

As early as 1792, Mary Wollstonecraft explored what scholars 150 years later would dub "the muscle gap," postulating in *A Vindication of the Rights of Woman* that no judgments could be made about a woman's physical capabilities until they enjoyed the same opportunities as men. While Wollstonecraft did not specifically address women's involvement in sport, she was ardent in her belief that both men and women should acquire strength of mind *and* body. Early feminists echoed Wollstonecraft and made entitlement to physical freedom a popular topic. For example, in 1895 suffragist (and cofounder of the Women's Christian Temperance Union) Frances Willard published *A Wheel within a Wheel: A Woman's Quest for Freedom,* in which she extolled the liberation associated with learning to ride a bicycle. Twenty years later, Charlotte Perkins Gilman's 1915 utopian work *Herland* described a female-dominated world in which women fully embraced their social, political, and physical freedoms, producing a society that was unparalleled in its level of sophistication and civilization. By 1954, Simone de Beauvoir had published *The Second Sex,* in which she promoted the importance of physical freedom for women, as well as the virtues of athletic competition—noting that women's contests were valuable in their own right and should not be compared with men's. She further acknowledged that athletic participation rewarded women with the means to battle the timidity and weakness society had tried to instill in them since childhood. Iris Marion Young built upon de Beauvoir's work when she explored the differences in feminine and masculine ways of moving, and the ways in which society valued that movement, in her 1980 essay "Throwing like a Girl: A Phenomenology of Feminine Body Comportment Motility and Spatiality."

Feminist scholars therefore have long prioritized a woman's right to physical expression as part of a larger discussion about equality. The translation to sports was a harder sell, however, as many second-wave feminists did not immediately embrace the transformative power of athletics and its use as a vehicle for promoting women's equality. In the final installment of their 1973 three-part series on the status of women in sport, *SI*'s Gilbert and Williamson asserted that "the women's liberation movement has stirred up interest in athletic equality even though the most active women's rightists have paid little attention to sport." They quoted the activist and radical feminist Robin Morgan as acknowledging the error: "We were slow getting into sports because many of us didn't know the field. But now the movement is becoming active in this area. We've become conscious of the body. It is a woman's right to control her body, be it wanting an abortion or wanting to strengthen it through sports."[18] Despite the delay, the activism of Billie Jean King, Serena Williams, and the U.S. Women's Soccer Team, among others, clearly showed that battles in the sports arena could advance women's rights outside of it and that issues of equality and social justice were concerns for *all* women. *Skimpy Coverage* illuminates this important connection and places the challenges and contributions of sportswomen—particularly *Sports Illustrated* sportswomen—within the broader history of gender and women's history.

This focus on *Sports Illustrated* underscores the importance of the magazine as the flagship of all general sports print media sources. Through 2016 *SI* enjoyed a subscription rate that was almost 30 percent higher than its nearest rival, *ESPN The Magazine*. With its long history, broad reach, and wide appeal—at its zenith, over three million people subscribed to *SI* and over thirty-four million people read it every week—*Sports Illustrated's* portrayal of females, both as athletes and as swimsuit models, is one that Americans have consumed on a regular basis.[19] Its treatment of sportswomen, in particular, delivered a clear message about how its readers should regard female athletes—and related issues of race, class, and sexuality—both in the magazine's pages and on the playing fields.

The simple fact is that *Sports Illustrated*, as the leading sports weekly in the nation, has contributed to the real-life rendering—and consistent selling—of the female athlete. If *Sports Illustrated* has set the sports agenda for the last six decades, or even just believes that it has, it is worth considering the place that sportswomen have occupied in its pages. Of particular note is the amount and type of attention they commanded, especially in comparison with what swimsuit models enjoyed. Throughout *Sports Illustrated's* history, it was the swimsuit models who invariably came out on top in such matchups. Rarely did the achievements of female athletes generate the hype the magazine devoted to its female swimsuit models. And when they did, it was often unrelated to their athletic prowess.

Media Circus

The case of "the righteous Scarlet Knights" encapsulates much of what *Skimpy Coverage* seeks to highlight. On April 3, 2007, the Tennessee Lady Vols defeated the Scarlet Knights of Rutgers in the women's NCAA championship basketball game. Fifteenth-ranked Rutgers—coached by the legendary C. Vivian Stringer—had surprised everyone by reaching the final, upsetting both number one–ranked Duke and perennial power-house UConn on its way to the championship game. It seemed an unlikely outcome for a team that had lost four of its first six games, but the Knights had regrouped to end their season with a 27–9 record. Although Rutgers failed to cap their Cinderella season with the title, they were poised for a strong return the following season. In fact, because the team's starting lineup remained fully intact for the 2007–8 season, *SI* ranked them third behind the University of Tennessee and top-ranked University of Connecticut.[20] It seemed that Rutgers had arrived, especially given the media frenzy that followed their participation in the 2007 championship game.

But the heightened interest surrounding the team had nothing to do with their play on the court. The morning after the final game, popular "shock jock" Don Imus took to his nationally syndicated radio show, *Imus in the Morning*, to describe the Rutgers players as "a bunch of nappy-headed hos." *SI* contributor Aditi Kinkhabwala noted that the incident "would plunge the Scarlet Knights into a maelstrom of media coverage and a nationwide race and gender debate." Throughout the "media circus,"

Rutgers's 2007 Cinderella season showcased some of the best qualities associated with sports, even as it highlighted the dismal media coverage female athletes often endured.

Sports Illustrated found that "the players were universally applauded for being eloquent and dignified" in the many news conferences, phone calls, and television appearances that ensued. But the reason for all the media attention was not lost on them: junior Essence Carson wondered, "Where were these major networks when we were making history [on the court] for a prestigious university?"[21]

It was an excellent question for both major television networks and major sports magazines like *Sports Illustrated*. Rutgers was a compelling story. Not only had the team overcome a dismal start to make it to the championship game, but the players had earned back the respect of their coach, who was so disappointed in their behavior during the early part of the season that she barred them from their locker room for an entire month and took away their practice gear.[22] But their resilience, their ability to overcome and win against all odds, failed to merit a story in *Sports Illustrated*, which explored (and condemned) Imus's racist comments but ignored the quality of play that put Rutgers in the path of Imus's ire in the first place.

For decades, the media has alternately praised or punished sports-women for displays of traditional, white femininity or the lack thereof. As a result, female athletes have had to contend with sexism as well as racism and homophobia, all the while battling assumptions that they are the weaker sex, unable to deal with the attendant injuries that result from transgressing a male preserve. Even in such an environment, American females have participated in competitive sport in increasing numbers at the high school and collegiate levels, thanks in large part to the passage of Title IX in 1972, and have enjoyed a growth in Olympic and professional opportunities that emerged during the twentieth century. Over the last twenty years, sportswomen have increasingly used these platforms to advocate for change for themselves and their teams, criticizing a media that has often treated them and their concerns as an afterthought or as tabloid fodder. These are issues that crystallized around the reporting of the Scarlet Knights in 2007 but have dominated *Sports Illustrated*'s coverage of female athletes since the 1950s.

ORGANIZED THEMATICALLY, *Skimpy Coverage* addresses the issues *Sports Illustrated* revisited time and again when addressing female athletes in its pages, many of which were raised by the magazine's own Gilbert and Williamson in their landmark series. Their work is a touchstone for my own, with an important caveat. Although Gilbert and Williamson focused important attention on the sexism women confronted in sport, they failed to explore the overlapping oppressions of sexism and racism experienced by sportswomen of color, thus further prioritizing and normalizing whiteness in their reporting. *Skimpy Coverage* seeks to correct that oversight through a comprehensive account of the *Sports Illustrated* sportswoman.

Chapter 1, "The Big F," examines how issues of femininity have long bedeviled female athletes, especially in the pages of *Sports Illustrated*. Susan Brownmiller's 1984 classic, *Femininity*, which *Sports Illustrated* specifically referenced, informs this chapter, which includes discussions of how women strove to be uniformly and perfectly feminine and the benefits that accrued from those displays. This examination reveals the ways in which femininity remains a goal for female athletes in the twenty-first century.

The staying power of this ideal reflects, in part, stubborn stereotypes that a sportswoman's "masculine" interest in sport reflects a corresponding "masculine" interest in other women. Thus chapter 2, "Girls Like That," begins with Billie Jean King's then-shocking 1981 announcement that she had had an affair with a woman, making her the first American athlete to admit publicly to such a relationship while still actively competing. Although "innuendoes about lesbianism" dominated the early years of organized sport for women, more recent controversy has focused on the rights of trans women and women with Differences of Sex Development to compete in sport. This chapter concludes with the selection of Megan Rapinoe, an out lesbian and vocal social activist, as *Sports Illustrated*'s 2019 Sportsperson of the Year and the progress such an award represents—or fails to represent—for the magazine, LGBTQ+[23] sportswomen, and female athletes regardless of their sexuality or gender expression.

Chapter 3 explores the passage of Title IX and the conflicting messages *Sports Illustrated* transmitted in describing the law's guidelines and impact. While all *SI* writers regarded Title IX as a momentous paradigm shift in American women's sports—it guaranteed equity for females in institutions that received any kind of federal funding—they could not agree whether such a change portended good or ill effects. "An Odd Way to Even Things Up" reflects *SI*'s mixed messaging as well as its focus on what it deemed Title IX success stories, regardless of whether those stories had anything to do with the concrete effects of Title IX. *SI*'s focus on those successes, in fact, shifted the focus away from the need for more structural and sustained change.

Title IX resulted in a significant increase not just in the number of females playing sport but in the number of females becoming injured as a
result of that play. Consequently, age-old concerns about women's innate
physical and mental weaknesses resurfaced, allowing critics to portray
women as unsuitable for sport. This is the subject of chapter 4, "The Frailty
Myth," which examines the staying power of the belief that female athletes
are unequipped for the strains of sport—always the victims of their biological destinies, instead of victors determining their own futures.

Concerns for sportswomen's health, however, seemed to dissipate every
four years—and then every two years starting in 1994—as female Olympians became visible symbols of their countries' soft power. During the Cold
War, countries used their sportswomen's achievements to boost the all-
important medal count in an effort to influence hearts and minds at home
and abroad. As essential ambassadors for advancing their nation's athletic ambitions and international aspirations, female athletes both promoted and embodied "the Olympic ideal," the topic of chapter 5.

Women's Olympic glory not only enhanced their countries' international
profiles, it also allowed female athletes the rare opportunity to take center stage. Such a position was in stark contrast to professional sportswomen, many of whom were anonymous players in leagues that were
athletic afterthoughts. A midcentury attempt to launch the LPGA is often
considered the debut of women's professional sport, but women had played
for pay before 1950. Although more recent attempts to launch (and then
sustain) professional leagues in soccer and basketball have dominated the
sports pages, it is the women's tennis tour that has emerged as the model
to emulate with media coverage and earnings that mimic those of their
male counterparts. But even with such advantages, female tennis players
continue to battle assertions that they don't play as much, nor as well, as
the men and thus should not reap the same benefits. Chapter 6, "A League
of Their Own," traces *SI*'s portrayal of the challenges professional sportswomen have faced in selling their leagues to paying customers, and their
qualified success in doing so.

Skimpy Coverage concludes with "A Pretty Girl on the Cover," which
considers how Andre Laguerre's famous query to then *SI* staffer (and future
Swimsuit Issue editor) Jule Campbell—"Jule, my dear, how would you like
to go to some beautiful spot and put a pretty girl on the cover?"—guided
not only publication of the Swimsuit Issue in 1964 but *Sports Illustrated*'s
inclusion and portrayal of female athletes throughout its subsequent

history.[24] Which "pretty girls"—who were also athletes—ended up on the *Sports Illustrated* cover, and perhaps more importantly, which did not, go a long way toward informing the ideal *Sports Illustrated* sportswoman. Moreover, the appearance of actual sportswomen in the Swimsuit Issue, a trend that began in 1997, encapsulates the story *Sports Illustrated* told its readers about the women it covered—and uncovered.

The goal of *Skimpy Coverage*, then, is to use *Sports Illustrated* as a lens to examine the history of female athletes and the evolution of trends that have influenced their empowerment. Although the intended scope of *Skimpy Coverage* is broad, it is by no means exhaustive. Since 1954 *Sports Illustrated* has published hundreds of features on female athletes (compared with the thousands on their male counterparts) and reported on iconic moments in women's sport history, but not all of them are addressed in this work. Instead, *Skimpy Coverage* explores those topics that have recurred in *SI*'s coverage of sportswomen and have informed the magazine's publishing arc from the mid-twentieth into the twenty-first century. In the process, and in setting the sports agenda, *Sports Illustrated* established a set of criteria for the female athletes who appeared in its pages. It was one that mimicked what *SI* prized in its swimsuit models—attractive, often scantily clad, and, above all, traditionally feminine.

1

"The Big F"

In 1984 *Sports Illustrated's* Kenny Moore used his *Sports Illustrated* track and field beat to feature Tiina Lillak, a Finnish javelin thrower and world record holder. Moore regarded Lillak not only as the best in the history of her sport but as "an athlete who evoke[d] a longer look" at the issue of femininity. The blonde-haired, blue-eyed Lillak was "compellingly beautiful" at "nearly 6 feet tall, 160 pounds, with broad shoulders and a sprinter's tapered legs." Such a description, according to Moore, was not meant to reinforce general stereotypes about female javelin throwers or beautiful blondes, but to highlight that Lillak's "beauty ha[d] little in common with traditional feminine attraction" and that she was actually helping to do away with conventional notions of beauty and femininity. Moore also wanted to clarify what kind of femininity he was discussing: "traditionally defined femininity . . . the sweet, fragrant, demure kind of womanhood" that he dubbed "the big F."[1]

Susan Brownmiller had explored "the big F" and its facets earlier that year in a book titled, simply, *Femininity*. She had asserted that "the struggle to approach the feminine ideal, to match the femininity of other women and especially to outdo them, is the chief competitive arena (surely it is the only sanctioned arena) in which the American woman is wholeheartedly encouraged to contend." To lose in this arena, according to Brownmiller, meant a woman was "viewed as a failure in core sexual identity" and that society would appraise her as "mannish or neutered or simply unattractive, as men have defined these terms." Moore referenced *Femininity* in his article, invoking Brownmiller's thesis that "men have consistently and systematically found alluring only those aspects of female gesture, dress, speech, shape and motive that require women to be, or seem weak and dependent." But Moore also asserted that there were a few women, and "more all the time, who attract by being capable, bright, healthy and tough."[2]

This new definition of femininity seemed to embrace traditionally masculine attributes of strength and vigor expected of male athletes. Historically, masculinity and athleticism were seen as mutually reinforcing; such

In 1984 *SI*'s Kenny Moore maintained that Finnish javelin thrower Tiina Lillak was helping to do away with conventional notions of beauty and femininity, which he dubbed "the big F."

an association emerged, according to sports sociologist Michael Messner, in the 1890s when men found that, owing to greater mechanization, their jobs no longer prioritized physicality. Sports thus became a dependable way for men to prove their masculinity, as it set them apart—and above—women. As sports participation became an acceptable, and even required, expression of manliness, the opposite was true for women. According to Messner, "female athleticism was viewed as conflicting with the conventional ethos of femininity." But Messner also noted that the female athlete had become, by 1988, "contested ideological terrain," which demanded, according to the scholar Jennifer Hargreaves, a recognition that the ideology associated with femininity was not "fixed," and thus in constant need of "reassessment."[3]

Brownmiller had acknowledged that the ideal feminine shape was "subject to change" over time, but her focus on "the feminine body in the Western World" privileged whiteness and ability as universal experiences.[4] Despite these shortcomings, *Femininity* offered such mainstream accessibility that even a *Sports Illustrated* sportswriter could refer to it and confidently assume his audience was familiar with its arguments. However, while Brownmiller's was the first explicit examination of femininity from a scholarly viewpoint, *Sports Illustrated* had been engaging the issue implicitly since 1954.

The infamous Swimsuit Issue is a case in point. Even before the Swimsuit Issue officially appeared in 1964, *SI* had seemingly defined a set of parameters for the feminine form when it featured attractive women in swimsuits on its cover. In 1954 "pretty Pamela Nelson" was the "girl in the surf," while former "top models" Betty di Bugnano and the Countess Consuelo Crespi (née Gloria O'Connor) assumed cover turns in 1955 and 1957, respectively. Teen swimmers Chris von Saltza, Becky Collins, and Donna de Varona appeared on the magazine's cover in 1958, 1959, and 1962. Smiling, pretty, and scantily clad, these attractive, white females embodied Moore's definition of "Big F" femininity. So did Babette March when she appeared on the first official cover of the Swimsuit Issue in a leather bikini and pigtails. By 1978, however, the magazine had decided to market a more sexually charged version of femininity, one that featured Cheryl Tiegs in a fishnet bathing suit that showed her nipples and, in the words of *SI* managing editor Mark Mulvoy, "vaulted the Swimsuit Issue into the consciousness of America."[5] By 1999, the progression from girl-next-door to sexpot was complete when the magazine dispensed with featuring only swimsuits, opting for body paint as well. By then, the Swimsuit Issue had also included cover models of color when Tyra Banks appeared with Valeria Mazza in 1996 and then earned a solo cover turn in 1997. Its premium on sex appeal was clear by the beginning of the twenty-first century, when the magazine regularly described the models as "hot." In 2002 Yamila Diaz-Rahi and her pals were "red hot in Latin America"; the "hottest models" appeared in 2003; the Swimsuit Issue got "hotter" in 2005; and by 2010 Brooklyn Decker was downright "sizzling."[6] An evolution in femininity that Moore predicted in 1984 had arrived, but it had more to do with a sensual eroticism than muscled athleticism.

That same development is evident with sportswomen in *Sports Illustrated*. In the early years, the magazine offered a femininity that was lovely and pure; titillation was permitted—a glimpse of satin shorts or lace-edged underwear—but there was a respectability and an expectation of proper female behavior: hair ribbons, ruffles, and whiteness. Come the 1980s, femininity was no longer "sweet" and "fragrant," but erotic and aerobic, and in the 1990s, some sportswomen were featured as both athletes and swimsuit models. By the twenty-first century, *Sports Illustrated*'s depictions of sportswomen were filtered through a lens of femininity seemingly shaped by the magazine's heavy reliance on the hugely successful Swimsuit Issue. As *SI* swimsuit models moved from one-piece bathing suits to body paint, its athletes traveled a similar path. In both cases, the ultimate effect was titillation. Thus the magazine's readers were encouraged to ogle not just the models in the Swimsuit Issue but the athletes as well, which became easier to do when sportswomen like Jenny Thompson appeared topless—with some well-placed hands—in 2000.[7]

Using aspects of Brownmiller's approach, but adopting a more racially inclusive analysis, this chapter will consider how *Sports Illustrated* presented the femininity of its sportswomen in discussions about their body, emotion, clothes, hair, and skin—with skin offering an explicit opportunity to explore femininity, whiteness, and race—and how those portrayals evolved over time. The conception of femininity that *SI* offered was one that female athletes generally embraced, looking to make the case that femininity and sports could "go together"; rarely did they acknowledge or challenge the idea that femininity was, in the words of Susan Brownmiller, "an unreliable goal." *Sports Illustrated* thus reflected prevailing ideas about femininity, even as it contributed to its own rendering of them, pushing expectations about what sportswomen should wear, when they should show some skin, and how they should best showcase their bodies.

"A Hot Body Can Count as Much as a Good Backhand"

In 1961, *SI* introduced "the world's loveliest sportswomen," eight female athletes from a variety of disciplines, including golf, water skiing, and riflery, who "represented . . . the many lovely women throughout the world who bring grace and beauty as well as skill to the rugged world of sport." Balancing the masculine nature of sport with a woman's femininity was a standard ploy for *Sports Illustrated*, which accentuated a sportswoman's attractiveness as much as, or even sometimes more than, her athletic prowess. In 1976, for example, *SI* described professional golfer Jan Stephenson as a "little Australian dumpling . . . who went around looking more like a starlet than a professional athlete." The magazine acknowledged that Stephenson would probably "not rewrite any LPGA records, but she has won a tournament and she will win more, and meanwhile she was a very feminine person in Palm Springs. She even had a ladylike golf swing, but mainly she had her looks and manner."[8] In *SI*, a sportswoman's femininity—whether in the form of chaste loveliness or erotic sex appeal—was the achievement that mattered most.

Such an approach obviously privileged those female athletes who embraced the qualities—and measurements—of a Hollywood starlet. These were traits that were synonymous with "the Big F." But what about the female athlete for whom "the Big F" had nothing to do with femininity and everything to do with food? In 1979 *Sports Illustrated*'s Kenny Moore featured shot-putter Maren Seidler, who found that she had to discuss her size "way out of proportion to my concern about it, because so many people are interested in that aspect." But Seidler understood that "people's ideas about femininity crystallize when they're faced with the issue of lady shotputters," since "most Americans" were not necessarily comfortable with "the presence of this large and powerful woman in their midst." It was a concept she had grasped a decade earlier when, as she prepared for the 1968 Olympic Games, she sought to allay readers' fears by rejecting comparisons with her hypermasculine Soviet rival and touting her own special "competition earrings." Despite being a "curiosity," Seidler avowed that she had "always been comfortable being big." Was this part of the new type of femininity that Moore would predict in another five years? In 1979 Moore concluded that the "powerful" Seidler had "solved the problem of being a Big Person in a grand way," but it seemed Seidler herself was not so sure: "For years when people would write about me and about my blue eyes, I would say, 'Why put that muck in?' But secretly I was pleased. So there must be an internal dichotomy at work here." It was one that sportswomen and *Sports Illustrated* would continue to grapple with: how to redefine femininity in an arena that "call[s] for muscle."[9]

Muscles had moved to the center of the femininity debate for *Sports Illustrated* in 1982 when the magazine asked: "Are large muscles feminine, does that matter, and what does 'femininity' mean anyway?" These were important questions, not only for an article about female bodybuilders but for a conversation about female athletes, and American women more generally. Indeed, bodybuilding icon Arnold Schwarzenegger claimed that women's growing interest in bodybuilding paralleled the evolution of second-wave feminism: "More women were feeling secure about doing things that only men had done. They were going to gyms and asking how to build bigger biceps, and some of them were entering contests. They could never have gotten away with it 10 years earlier." One female body-builder was hopeful for a future in which society not only accepted her sport but also considered well-muscled women as legitimately feminine: "I guess [officials] don't think muscles are feminine, but that will change as we become more familiar with what athletic women look like."[10]

Alas, such a future eluded most female athletes, especially during the early 1980s when sportswomen were increasingly encouraged to ditch competitive opportunities for getting fit. It was a time, according to sports historian Jaime Schultz, "when public culture emphasized the aspirational body culture of aerobics, often at the expense of serious women's sports." It was indicative of an era marked by a "general backlash against the social, political, and economic gains women made in the preceding decades" in the board room and in the gymnasium. Aerobics ultimately went the way of disco, but an emphasis on—and the expectation of—a well-toned, active body that was attractive to a male gaze transcended the 1980s and continued to inform women's fitness and women's sports for decades to come.[11]

Whether the ideal female body was slender or curvy, muscled or toned, one of its features was consistent: it was visibly abled. *Sports Illustrated* addressed disabled athletes in 1995, noting that they had "been consigned to sport's netherworld, where most of the attention they . . . get is unflattering and maddening." Such depictions tended to focus on the inspiration disabled athletes provided, as opposed to the skill, passion, and dedication they possessed. Although *SI* heightened disabled athletes' visibility, it did not address the ways in which their experiences were gendered. In 2000 the sports sociologist Jennifer Hargreaves found that sport was an environment that prized "physical perfection and slenderness," which caused disabled women to "experience a very real sense of alienation from their bodies because of the constant reminders through popular body imagery of what they are not." Indeed, while sport served as a way to shore up disabled men's masculinity, it presented a challenge for disabled women; sports scholars Hélène Joncheray and Rémi Richard found that disabled women who played powerchair football "face[d] a contradiction: opposing a dominant discourse in sport that requires athletes to be feminine, and in parallel facing another discourse that presented disabled women as asexual." Although the authors noted that "disabled women's relation to femininity is not uniform," for many disabled female athletes, their status as asexual and nongendered meant that there was no femininity for them to defend. They simply did not figure into the discussion.[12]

Female bodybuilders were also consigned to the margins of the femininity debate well into the twenty-first century. Scholar and bodybuilder Leslie Heywood attributed her sport's continued liminal status to long-held beliefs about femininity and what women are supposed to look like: "People expect women to look soft, and if they don't it messes with old stereotypes." In her article for *SI for Women*, Carmen Renee Thompson agreed, finding that "in a sport that's supposed to be all about muscles, men can go all out, but female bodybuilders struggle to keep up with society's changing definitions of femininity." Women could now "look athletic or have small muscles and still look sexy," but female athletes, and especially female bodybuilders, needed to achieve "a softer look," combining their muscles "with more feminine touches for the sport to survive."[13] Thus, a well-muscled femininity was possible, but it still needed to be associated with a certain amount of sex appeal.

For Black sportswomen, not even sex appeal could always bolster their femininity. In 1998 sports scholars Patricia Vertinsky and Gwendolyn Captain found that Black women contended with enduring stereotypes that conflated "depictions of black womanhood and 'manly' athletic and physically gifted females." Indeed, the image of the powerful Black woman, a holdover from the days of slavery, was one of strength, independence, and endurance—qualities often associated with masculinity. Twenty years later, a Morgan State study revealed that not much had changed in media depictions of Black sportswomen, and that stereotypes about Black women's "natural brute strength" continued to hold sway.[14]

That was evident in 2015 after Serena Williams had won Wimbledon, her third Grand Slam tournament in a row. Following that victory, *SI* reported on the "body image controversy" ignited by a *New York Times* article attributing Williams's success to her "large biceps and a mold-breaking muscular frame, which packs the power and athleticism that have dominated women's tennis for years. Her rivals could try to emulate her physique but most of them choose not to." SI.com's Elizabeth Newman rightly noted the racial dimensions of the story, especially since it compared Williams with her white rivals. Newman asserted, "Make no mistake—Serena is neither thin, nor demure and she makes no excuses for it. Nor is she blonde or white, which often causes a racial divide when social commentary about her beauty and femininity are brought up." And it had been brought up a lot. Newman noted that "the controversy over body image is nothing new in the Williams household. Ever since Serena and older sister Venus burst onto the tennis scene in the late 1990s, they have been condemned for both their muscular physiques and crushing physicality on court." It was a combination that netted multiple tour titles for both sisters in singles and doubles but resulted in fewer endorsement opportunities than their white peers.[15] Even hyperfeminine spreads in the Swimsuit Issue (Venus appeared in 2005, and Serena was featured in 2003 and 2017) could not overcome the sisters' impressive musculature and the meanings it invoked.

Seeking to redefine a femininity that was more inclusive of well-muscled bodies was an ambitious project and, according to sports scholar Helen Lenskyj, a flawed one. In 1986 Lenskyj asserted that "equating muscle with femininity and eroticism was not necessarily progressive; it could easily be distorted and co-opted as yet another measure of heterosexual glamour among competing women." Take *Sports Illustrated*'s coverage of the 1999 U.S. Women's World Cup soccer team. *SI*'s Rick Reilly marveled that the "goal-goal girls" had successfully managed to combine "Amazonian ambush and after-prom party" with their "bright-red toenails" and "diaper bags. The U.S. women's soccer team is towing the country around by the heart in this Women's World Cup, and just look at the players. They've got ponytails! They've got kids! They've got (gulp) curves!"[16] These were women with multiple feminine bona fides.

And the team doubled down on them in the run-up to the 1999 Women's World Cup soccer final. Star player Mia Hamm had endorsed a Soccer Barbie and was one of *People* Magazine's "50 most beautiful"; team captain Julie Foudy had appeared bikini-clad in *Sports Illustrated*'s Swimsuit Issue playing soccer on the beach with her husband; and the entire team had played along with David Letterman's description of them as "soccer babes." Then Brandi Chastain struck the winning penalty kick to secure an American victory before an audience of 90,000 fans and "whipped off her jersey and celebrated with abs bared and biceps cocked." In doing so, she initiated a firestorm.[17]

Sports Illustrated viewed Chastain's action to be a strong statement of the modern female athlete and a new kind of femininity, especially when paired with "the fact that Chastain had just posed in *Gear* magazine, proudly baring her buffness in, well, the buff. Women aren't supposed to

When Brandi Chastain whipped off her jersey in victory after winning the 1999 World Cup, *SI* viewed her action to be a strong statement of the modern female athlete and a new kind of femininity.
Not everyone was convinced.

have muscles, are they? If they do, they aren't supposed to show them off,
right? Wrong. Today's female athletes are challenging society's perceptions
of femininity and the ideal female body type." Chastain asserted that her
pose in *Gear* relayed the pride she had in her well-muscled physique: "I ran
my ass off for this body . . . I have biceps and shoulders as big as my dad's.
I'm not going to hide it." A year later, Olympic swimmer Jenny Thompson
added additional fuel to the fire when she smiled up from the pages of

Sports Illustrated wearing red boots and a pair of star-spangled shorts—and nothing else. *SI* noted the swimmer's impressive physique and Thompson defended her pose in the November/December issue of *Sports Illustrated Women:* "My stance in the picture was one of strength and power and *girls rule.* It's nothing sexual. I wasn't pouting or giving a sexual look. It was like, here I am. I'm strong." Both Chastain and Thompson represented a host of sportswomen who took pride in showing off their athletic bodies in as little clothing as possible, viewing (and defending) their actions as displays of strength and empowerment. Why then, wondered *SI*'s Rick Reilly, did "some women have their girdles all in a wad?"[18]

According to author Mariah Burton Nelson, "There is still a struggle about who's going to define female beauty, who's going to define what women should wear and how they should behave. Women's sports will not have arrived until [women] are writing those rules for ourselves." Former Women's Sports Foundation president Donna de Varona believed that women were always at a disadvantage when they were forced to defend their athleticism by proving their femininity, which in de Varona's opinion was code for sex appeal: "We always have to prove that we're feminine and sexy. We can be tough and sweaty and a sex symbol; if we do that we're acceptable." Yet she noted that for men to gain recognition as athletes, sex appeal was not a requirement: "Michael Jordan," she asserted, "didn't have to take off his clothes." Some sportsmen did, or almost did—Joe Namath, Jim Palmer, and David Beckham, for example—but it was optional. For women, an ultrafeminine, ultrasexy image was both compulsory and essential for acceptance.[19]

But was a sportswoman's sex appeal necessarily a bad thing? In 1997 professional beach volleyball star (and top fashion model) Gabrielle Reece joined her bikini-clad teammates in debating the importance of sexual attractiveness with *SI*'s Michael Silver in that year's Swimsuit Issue. Silver found that "sex appeal is women's beach volleyball's greatest selling point," as well as "its biggest headache inducer and its greatest source of debate." Player Angela Rock wondered why the sport had to be "about sex appeal at all." She lamented that "other sports have attractive women in skimpy uniforms, but ours is the one that gets stereotyped as a skinfest, and that's not the image we're trying to project." But her teammate Holly McPeak had no problem using sex to sell beach volleyball: "If people want to come check us out because they're scoping our bodies, I don't have a problem with that, because I guarantee they'll go home talking about our athleticism."

Player Linda Hanley rejected the either/or poles represented by Rock's and McPeak's perspectives, asserting that "there doesn't have to be such a complete division between 'You're beautiful and sexy' and 'You're athletic and strong.' The Reeboks and Nikes are starting to realize that the athletic body is sexy, and Gabrielle Reece has a lot to do with that."[20]

So did tennis player Anna Kournikova. In 2000 the eighth-ranked Kournikova peered out from the cover of *SI* with nary a tennis ball or racquet in sight; the only indication she was even remotely associated with the sport was the tagline: "Advantage, Kournikova." But Frank Deford openly admitted in the accompanying article that any benefits the young player enjoyed would not necessarily be associated with her athletic prowess: "She won't win the French Open, but who cares? Anna Kournikova is living proof that even in this age of supposed enlightenment, a hot body can count as much as a good backhand." For Kournikova, it actually counted more. Having won exactly zero singles titles on the Women's Tennis Association tour, she was, nevertheless, her "sport's highest earner off the court," even eclipsing her doubles partner and five-time Grand Slam singles champion Martina Hingis.[21]

It was Kournikova, according to *SI*, who defined "the career blueprint" for others on the tour, including "dozens of other young players from the former Soviet Union" like Simonya Popova. L. Jon Wertheim featured the "strikingly attractive," unbelievably athletic, and ultrafeminine seventeen-year-old Popova in 2002. In addition to her 125 miles per hour serve and "murderous intent," the 6'1" Popova had "pulchritude and attitude in equal measure. Her midriff-baring outfits, so small they appear to come from Gap Kids, highlight her ample decolletage. She has already agreed to pose for the tour's annual swimsuit calendar." Here was the perfect feminine athlete: she had the muscled power of the Williams sisters, the court craft of Martina Hingis, the political acuity of Billie Jean King, the swimsuit chops of Steffi Graf, and the body of Anna Kournikova. It seemed too good to be true, and of course it was: Popova was a computer-generated creation with an equally bogus biography. While some saw the piece as one in which *Sports Illustrated* parodied itself and its emphasis on female attractiveness over athleticism, the magazine had seemingly defined its ideal of athletic femininity, one that embodied "strength, attitude and sex appeal" in equal measure.[22]

At the beginning of the twenty-first century, then, cultural norms still held that female bodies needed to be above all feminine. And if you pushed the boundaries of acceptance by being too big or too muscled, you needed to affirm your feminine credentials, particularly in the pages of *Sports Illustrated,* with earrings, sex appeal, or a spread in the magazine's Swimsuit Issue. Despite Moore's predictions of a new kind of femininity that was "capable" and "tough," conventional notions continued to hold sway; perhaps dainty and demure had been swapped out for sexy and hot, but the need to comply with "Big F" femininity was paramount. And it was now commodified. As beach volleyball player Gabrielle Reece acknowledged, "Women's sports need something else to sell, and if that's women who are incredibly fit and attractive, so be it."[23] In the end, many sportswomen felt like they were either buying into the idea of selling their sport with sex appeal—at least initially—or waiting until they could safely take up athletic space without first validating their feminine credentials. Until that time, a sportswoman's acceptance hinged on showcasing a feminine body. And if she could shed a few tears in the process, then so much the better.

"Girl Enough to Cry"

In 1970 *SI*'s "girls from the mountain next door" were accustomed to making their way down the slopes at speeds in excess of 20 to 30 miles per hour and were "full of fire and ferocious" while doing it. "Still," as *Sports Illustrated* assured its readers, "inside every girl ski racer there hides a real live girl who can change quickly into her wistful, it's-poor-little-old-me disguise and disarm men for miles around. Glamour is not their game and chic is for all those elderly ladies in their 20s. Instead, girl racers are made of steel and spice and everything nice—like Canada's gamin Betsy Clifford . . . who was tough enough to enter the world championship giant slalom . . . and girl enough to cry just a little bit when she beat everybody else to win a gold medal."[24] After alpine ski racer Rosi Mittermaier claimed her own gold medal at the 1976 Olympics, she "went directly to her mother, handed over the bouquet of roses she had been given, and said, 'Mummy, I can't help it. I have to cry.'"[25] Despite the athleticism, toughness, and skill of these athletes, the magazine's focus was on their ability to be "girl" enough—read feminine enough—to cry when they got that gold medal.

According to Susan Brownmiller, emotion was a quality all humans experienced, but the acceptability of its expression varied according to gender. She noted that it was "commonly agreed that women are tossed and buffeted on the high seas of emotion, while men have the tough mental fiber, the intellectual muscle, to stay in control." Crying and its variations—bawling, sobbing, weeping—were a loss of control that was decidedly feminine.[26] While it might be gendered, it was not, in Brownmiller's account, specifically racialized. It was for author Michelle Wallace, however, who addressed the issue in her 1978 book, *Black Macho and the Myth of the Superwoman*. Wallace noted that owing to "the intricate web of mythology which surrounds the black woman, a fundamental image emerges," one in which a Black woman did "not have the same fears, weaknesses, and insecurities as other women, but believes herself to be and is, in fact, stronger emotionally than most men." She was also "less of a woman in that she is less 'feminine' and helpless."[27] As a result, crying was the emotional province of white women, while Black women were noted for their anger.

Take the case of Serena Williams. In 2009 *Sports Illustrated* recounted her fuming frustration with a line judge and "graphic meltdown" during the semifinals of the U.S. Open. Williams expressed her rage and "unleashed a cascade of profanity" against a lineswoman for calling a foot fault. *SI* recounted the scene for readers: "'You'd better be f---ing right!' Serena Williams yelled. 'You don't f---ing know me! I swear to God I'm going to take this ball and shove it in your f---ing throat!'"[28]

Angry tirades were nothing new in tennis—John McEnroe was famous for them throughout the 1970s, and even tennis phenom Martina Hingis "threw an epic tantrum" at the French Open in 1999. But instant replay and current personalities on both the men's and women's tours, according to *SI*, had "conspired to give tennis a kinder, gentler face." Until Serena Williams went off on a line judge. In response, the match umpire halted play immediately, while the tournament referee assessed a point penalty (effectively giving Williams's opponent, Kim Clijsters, the win because it was match point) and fined her $10,500. Williams issued a "grudging apology" in which she took ownership of her "inappropriate outburst." Two years later, at the 2011 U.S. Open finals, she "brandished her racket at chair umpire Eva Asderaki and snarled, 'I hate you!'" putting a "a face on a tennis fortnight that for sheer negativity had no equal."[29] Regardless of whether there was an apology following an outburst of fury, anger was an emotion that was simply not feminine. According to Susan Brownmiller, it just wasn't "nice." For men, anger was "often understood, or excused, as reasonable or just," and "may even be cast in a heroic mold—a righteous response to an insult against honor that will prelude a manly, aggressive act." But a woman who "seethes with anger" is "unattractive," and more, "she is hard, mean and nasty; she is unreliably, unprettily out of control."[30]

That woman seemed to be Serena Williams, who at the 2018 U.S. Open was again furious. During the championship match, the chair umpire Carlos Ramos charged Williams with two violations—the first for coaching and the second for breaking a racquet; in response, Williams called the umpire a thief for taking a point from her, before Ramos docked her an entire game for verbal abuse. *Sports Illustrated* knew that for many, "Nothing could be easier than lumping Williams's most recent Open tempest" with her outbursts in 2009 and 2011. But, according to Williams, she "was fighting for women's rights and for women's equality and for all kinds of stuff. For me to say 'thief' and for him to take a game, it made me feel like it was a sexist remark. He's never taken a game from a man because they said 'thief.'" *SI* also acknowledged the sexist undertones, noting that the altercation had "highlighted [the sport's] double standard regarding men's and women's comportment." The CEO of the WTA, Steve Simon, did as well, insisting: "There should be no difference in the standards of tolerance provided to the emotions expressed by men versus women."[31] But there were differences in both the acceptance and treatment of Williams's various incidents, not only because of her sex but because of her race.

For Brittney Cooper, author of *Eloquent Rage: A Black Feminist Discovers Her Superpower*, both Serena and Venus Williams have created a "kind of alchemy that uses their physical strength and strategic prowess on the court, together with all the racial slurs and insults they have endured over the years—being called the N-word, being called ugly, being told their bodies were too manly—to create something that looks magical to the rest of us." For Cooper, "watching Serena play, particularly when she's beating white women, is like watching eloquent rage personified."[32]

Serena Williams's anger was definitely on display, but there was little acknowledgment of its elegance or its context in *Sports Illustrated*. In "Black Women Have Never Had the Privilege of Rage," journalist Kimberly Seals Allers noted that "what's been blatantly missing from mainstream dialogue is a nuanced understanding of how rage is perceived by and received from black women." While tennis fans seemed taken aback by Williams's actions on the court, Seals Allers noted that Black women's "anger has never been viewed as legitimate or warranted due to unfair treatment; instead, it's been twisted into a pathology." While Seals Allers did not reference

Serena Williams or the fallout following her 2018 outburst, she certainly could have; within days of Williams's altercation with Ramos, the Australian cartoonist Mark Knight portrayed Serena Williams with exaggerated lips, body, and hair jumping on her racket in outrage, while the umpire speaks to Naomi Osaka, asking whether she would just allow Williams to win. In addition to the racist stereotypes associated with Williams's physicality were the sexist and racist stereotypes associated with her anger. The illustration certainly seemed to confirm Seals Allers's assertion that "being labeled as angry and harsh ensures black women aren't seen as real human beings with a full suite of emotions, including fear, fragility, and vulnerability." Williams was caricatured as a petulant child throwing a tantrum, thereby stripping her of purpose, respect, and agency. As a result, she was part of a history that Sears Allers traced back to the days of slavery, when Black women's rage, hatred, and outspokenness were punished and thus had to be hidden from view and masked with smiles and acquiescence. Giving voice to and being accepted for displays of such raw anger was not a privilege the enslaved woman enjoyed, and Sears Allers made a compelling case that it still eludes Black women today.[33]

Love was a safer and far more appealing emotion in women than anger. Love, according to Brownmiller, "confirm[ed] the feminine psyche," especially since it involved compassion, nurturing, and "amorphous, undifferentiated caring"—particularly of others and almost always in heteronormative, nuclear associations that confirmed traditional patriarchal patterns. Such loving expressions were kindhearted and affectionate—literally the opposite of the angry tirades so disparaged in (Black) sportswomen like Serena Williams. As a result, *SI* often portrayed its (white) female athletes in love—with boyfriends, fiancés, and husbands—implying that one's attractiveness to men was powerful proof of one's femininity. And it was. However, the romantic love associated with an intimate partner could ebb and flow; having a child was important and permanent proof of a sportswoman's femininity.[34]

As early as 1955, *Sports Illustrated* discussed the challenges of women being both athletes and mothers in its feature on fencer Louise Dyer, whose sport was often dogged by spotty performances as expectant mothers were constantly leaving and then returning to competition after their pregnancies.[35] But mixing sports and motherhood was nothing new; Olympic sprinter Fannie Blankers-Koen had won four gold medals at the 1948 London Olympics as a mother of two. In the 1970s and 1980s, tennis players Margaret Court and Evonne Goolagong both continued successful professional tennis careers after having children.

Motherhood was, for some women, the ultimate competitive advantage. In 1988 *Sports Illustrated*'s Shannon Brownlee had referenced a number of female athletes who had "equaled or exceeded their best feats after giving birth," including track stars Mary Decker Slaney and Valerie Brisco, golfer Nancy Lopez, and diver Pat McCormick. Although some sportswomen cited the physical benefits that resulted from pregnancy—enhanced strength and an increased pain tolerance—Brownlee also focused on the psychological advantages. She found that in 1988 many of the current "top female athletes [had begun] their careers when competitiveness was considered less than feminine." As a result, "psychologists suspect that having a baby allows some women to reach their athletic potential by reassuring them of their femininity." It was an important bona fide given a 1985 poll that found 58 percent of the 1,700 people surveyed believed that "women often must choose between being athletes and being feminine."[36] This attitude had already informed Emily Wughalter's 1978 theory of the "Apologetic." According to Wughalter, most females recognized that sports was a male arena and thus refused to pursue such gender inappropriate behavior; for those who did, they needed to engage in compensatory behavior by offering overt displays of femininity: wearing "ruffles and flounces," talking about their boyfriends, and having babies. By 2020, more females were engaging in athletics than ever before, but the Women's Sports Foundation found that "pressures to adhere to narrow gender norms and gender-role stereotypes" remained a challenge.[37] Females might not have to forgo athletics entirely, but the pressure to remain feminine while playing sports remained an obligation, and having a child seemed to reduce that burden.

This was the stuff of "Big F" femininity. Who could be threatened by a tearful female athlete who had so clearly stamped her feminine credentials by having a baby? Even the seemingly ever-angry Serena Williams gained major kudos for her "mothering" not only of daughter Olympia but also of Naomi Osaka amid the boos from a pro-Serena crowd during the U.S. Open final in 2018. In their never-ending quest for feminine validation, *Sports Illustrated* sportswomen could neither undervalue the power of maternal love nor overlook the importance of those "ruffles and flounces."

"A Little Lace Goes a Long, Long Way"

In 1949 "Gorgeous Gussie" Moran played Wimbledon wearing a pair of lace panties under her tennis dress, shocking officials and fans alike with the titillating display. Moran recounted the scandal for *Sports Illustrated* in 1954, remembering that the "lace panty stir" focused "more attention" on "my backside than on my backhand." The man behind the "lacy unmentionables" was fashion designer Ted Tinling, who advocated for a woman's freedom of movement on the tennis court "without spoiling the appearance of a dress." Tinling was Wimbledon's worst nightmare as he delighted in challenging the staid Wimbledon establishment with an "arsenal of teasers" that included not only lace but also gold lamé panties and pink petticoats. Tinling's creations resulted in various Wimbledon "bans on color," which forced him to "search for something else demonstrably feminine"—hence, the emergence of Gussie's lace-trimmed underwear. As *SI*'s Gwilym S. Brown noted in 1969, "a little lace goes a long, long way." This was true for all women's sports, but particularly women's tennis, which had a long history of testing the boundaries of acceptable sporting attire.[38]

In 1919, for example, the great French player Suzanne Lenglen abandoned long skirts and corsets for a mid-calf dress, while Americans Helen Jacobs and Alice Marble adopted shorts during the 1930s. Gorgeous Gussie Moran then displayed her lace-trimmed backside in 1949. In all cases, tennis players looked to blend freedom of movement with fashionable flair; however, as Susan Brownmiller correctly surmised in the 1980s, "The right to move freely has always been a dangerously unfeminine issue; the right to be titillating has greater appeal." But not at Wimbledon. In 1985 American Anne White competed in her first-round Wimbledon match wearing the requisite white in the form of a bodysuit that plunged from "neckline to twinkling toes." Dubbed a "latter-day Gussy [*sic*] Moran" by *SI* writer Curry Kirkpatrick, White would later assert that she had worn the suit because of the cold weather. However, her functionality defense held little sway with the Wimbledon establishment. The All England Club banned White's "sexy attire" for not being traditional enough. With this ruling, the American returned to the court in a white skirt and top, but White insisted she had shown "'a lot of guts'" in choosing to wear the unconventional bodysuit; Kirkpatrick agreed and noted she also showed "some dynamite something elses."[39] Titillating indeed.

Thus, the goal of athletic clothing for females, while providing the required freedom of movement so desired by sportswomen, was to insulate female athletes against an unfortunate association with masculinity and all the qualities such a correlation suggested. Clothing—particularly the right kind—could help a sportswoman combat long-held and unfavorable assumptions, especially in *Sports Illustrated*. In 1958 the magazine introduced "champions in fine plumage," six "lovely" sportswomen who "demurely" modeled haute couture better suited to a cotillion than a field of play. Such depictions belied the "old canard that girl athletes are nice kids though nothing to look at." Two decades later, the designer gowns were gone, but *SI*'s Frank Deford still marveled at tennis player Chris Evert's ability to rise above what had remained the dominant thinking at the time: "a male is considered more of a man if he's an athlete, but a woman athlete is perceived to be less of a female." Evert admitted to being well acquainted with the paradox and realized that "right from the start I was sort of different from the stereotypical athlete. . . . I probably helped bring some femininity into a sport that was pretty masculine at the time. I think the public liked that."[40]

That's for sure. The fans, the media, and corporate sponsors all loved Evert's "girl next door" image, which included "her lovely feminine way of moving, her impeccable grooming," and the twenty outfits she traveled with to every tournament. Although the media portrayed her at times as a haughty "Ice Queen," Evert seemed to have achieved that enviable and elusive state of being both feminine and athletic, a claim *SI*'s Jon Wertheim validated in 2006 when he noted that Evert was the "poster girl for femininity in sports" and represented "proof that a girlie-girl could still be an elite athlete." Evert admitted that she had previously "thought of women athletes as freaks," even hating herself, "thinking I must not be a whole woman. The nail polish, the ruffles on my bloomers, the hair ribbons, not wearing socks—all that was very important to me, to compensate. I would not be the stereotyped jock."[41] Evert was also a poster girl for the Apologetic, literally resorting to ruffles to prove her femininity.

Other tennis players opted for outfits that dispensed with ruffles but still showcased their femininity. In 2002 Serena Williams shocked fans by wearing a skin-tight, micro-shorted black catsuit for the 2002 U.S. Open, and followed up two years later with a denim tennis outfit complete with cropped top and black "boots." Her sister Venus's self-designed outfit for the 2010 French Open was a lacy, corseted, red and black number complete with flesh-colored underpants that smacked of lingerie. Those fashion choices stunned and disturbed fans, the media, and officials alike, and in 2018 they ultimately elicited official action. That year, the French Open establishment banned Serena's full-length catsuit, an outfit that made her feel like a superhero and evoked comparisons with the block-buster film *Black Panther;* more importantly, the outfit offered the necessary compression to reduce embolisms, to which she was prone following the difficult birth of her daughter. In response, French tennis officials instituted a dress code that would ban similar kinds of outfits moving forward. "It will no longer be accepted," they said. "One must respect the game and the place."[42] It was an interesting choice of words, especially when a health decision prompted the outfit. Moreover, it ignored other players who had pushed the boundaries of acceptability and respectability, regardless of gender; Andre Agassi, for example, made a memorable debut at the French Open in 1990 wearing neon pink spandex short tights under his denim cutoffs, and female tennis players have been constantly reducing their hem lengths. What made those choices respectable—and acceptable—and a Wakanda-esque full-body suit unacceptable? French officials did not elaborate, but it is hard not to wonder whether it was the body within the catsuit that was really the problem.

Women's tennis has always pushed boundaries where feminine clothing is concerned. According to sports historian Jaime Schultz, "From the moment women first picked up their rackets, their attire inspired questions of decorum, social distinction, physicality, and femininity." But it was not just tennis players who enjoyed "conspicuous and controversial fashion moments"; other sports also allowed women "to wear costumes that inspired extreme public and media attention." During the 1940s, the All-American Girls Professional Baseball League opted for a short-skirted dress with satin underpants. In 1964 female Soviet speedskaters adopted "costumes" that allowed them to display "themselves at their shapely best." And "six-girl" beach volleyball teams donned their "bikini uniforms" as they took to the sand in 1968.[43]

Beach sports, in fact, highlighted just how much had changed for sportswomen, and how much still remained the same. By 1996, beach volleyball was an Olympic sport and players viewed it as a "model for the 21st-century sports movement" because of a professional tour that combined both sexes and paid them equally. Perhaps because of those similarities, the difference in uniforms was even more striking: the men wore tank tops and shorts, while the women were required to wear bikinis. Thus, the "skinfest" aspect that Angela Rock had acknowledged in 1997 was still evident in 2012 when *SI* attributed the popularity of women's beach volleyball to the "excellent" play as well as the "semi-naked-glistening-otter aspect," even as the International Volleyball Federation now allowed women to choose among a variety of uniform options with varying degrees of coverage.[44] For its part, *SI* discussed neither the original justification for the difference in men's and women's kits nor the subsequent rule change.

Instead, *SI* left it to its website to insist that "there's more to beach volleyball than just the bikini," even as other sports have continued to require it of their female athletes. Most recently, the International Handball Federation fined the Norwegian women's beach handball team for refusing to play in the required bikini bottoms during the Euro 2021 tournament. The federation had rejected repeated petitions since 2006 to allow additional uniform options, affirming the importance of bikini uniforms in "helping athletes increase their performance as well as remain coherent with the sportive and attractive image of the sport." Although the federation finally acquiesced and allowed females to wear tank tops and shorts like the men, only the women were instructed to "wear short tight pants with a close fit."[45] The femininity of women's uniforms continued to be codified.

Nowhere was that more necessary than on the women's professional golf tour. Throughout the 1960s, as the LPGA struggled to gain in popularity, officials sought to convey a decidedly feminine image of the women pros to ensure adequate prize money and secure television coverage. To that end, as early as 1963, LPGA tournament director Lennie Wirtz "sweetly, kindly, quietly and firmly ordered the girls to improve their personal appearance on and off the golf course. The chubby ones were asked to slim down a little or, if they could not to refrain from wearing shorts. Frequent permanent waves were suggested, and playing outfits were to be kept neat and well-pressed." Far from embracing a new kind of femininity, Wirtz's directives, as relayed by *SI*, were reminiscent of the "Rules of Conduct" that regulated player behavior in the All-American Girls Professional Baseball League from 1943 to 1954. Cubs owner Philip Wrigley had conceived of the league as a way to encourage civic patriotism during World War II and "to develop a level of play that fans would pay to watch while also emphasizing femininity." In addition to those short-skirted uniforms, the league mandated charm school and instituted a rule that required that players "ALWAYS appear in feminine attire when not actively engaged in practice or playing ball." While the AAGPBL fined its players for a lack of feminine appearance (looking unkempt resulted in a fifty-dollar fine), the LPGA relied on its players taking the hint.[46] Many of them did.

In 1968 LPGA golfer Carol Mann "rate[d] femininity first, golf second," insisting on wearing the new-fangled fashion of culottes with matching tinted hose. Mann accepted the risks associated with her choice: "One stop near a bush with those babies and there goes a run and four dollars, but I don't care. We all should try to look more feminine out here. Being thought of as anything other than a woman absolutely frosts me." Curry Kirkpatrick reminded *SI* readers that Mann's "fine sense of femininity . . . [was] not always easy to find on the women's tour."[47]

Thus, regardless of the sport or the decade, a female athlete's choice of clothing was an important means of proving her femininity, both on and off the field of play. In 1986 *SI* found that Louisiana Tech's women's basketball team was "required to be ladylike," since they lived in Ruston, Louisiana, "where there [was] no great tradition of Women's Lib [and] the team carrie[d] an almost antebellum image." Such a perception was further bolstered by the magazine, which pictured the team's racially diverse "five leading Lady Techsters" as twentieth-century Scarlett O'Haras, sporting hoop skirts, beribboned hats, and long gloves. Four years later, tennis player Steffi Graf had won nine Grand Slam singles titles, including the Golden Slam in 1988, but she had, as a result of her on-court dominance, "pick[ed] up all sorts of baggage along the way—masculine baggage." In an attempt to soften her image, Graf's father and manager finagled a spread in *Vogue,* in which she wore "(more or less) a black Norma Kamali maillot dress, adjusting her high heel and aiming her décolletage lensward."[48] The magazine layout left little to the imagination and, as a result, left little doubt that while Graf may have been the best women's tennis player on the professional tour, she was first and foremost a woman—a very feminine one.

Securing the right kind of clothing became its own competitive challenge. In 2002 *Sports Illustrated for Women* gave "Olympic moguls medalist and fashionista Shannon Bahrke five hours and $500 to shop in New York City's trendy SoHo district." Writer Anne Fulenwider reported that Bahrke, who had "skied onto the world stage wearing red-white-and-blue hair ribbons and nail polish," knew what she was looking for: "I want frilly, feminine clothes. I love sparkles and pink things and ruffles." Two years earlier, *Sports Illustrated for Women* had featured Felicia Zimmerman, a fencer "who embodied femininity and sport" as she embarked on a "shopping spree of Olympic proportions," readying herself—and her wardrobe—for the Sydney summer games in 2000. Her guiding philosophy included the idea that "a woman's best attribute is that she can look tough and athletic as well as elegant and beautiful."[49]

Shopping sprees for frilly clothes? Corseted tennis outfits that smacked of lingerie? Culottes and hoop skirts? Where was the focus on athletic achievement? While some sportswomen might have appreciated a play-by-play recap of their actual athletic dominance, many understood that it was comments on their fashion style, both on and off the field of play, which allowed them to craft and maintain a carefully calibrated feminine image.

By the late 1990s, however, some female athletes decided to dispense with most of their clothing altogether. In 1999 high jumper and part-time model Amy Acuff used "her attire—or lack of it—to attract attention to her sport." Wearing a halter top made of fur at one meet, she also donned an Anne Klein–designed flesh-colored uniform that gave the illusion of nudity at another. No illusion was required when Acuff appeared in a calendar with eleven other female track athletes—Acuff wore body paint and little else. She regarded her choices as "entertainment" and justified her clothing decisions by declaring: "Too many people hold fast to the old image of female jocks. They have a problem with seeing female athletes as feminine and beautiful. Something unique has to be done to bring the public to the table. After that, they can see what great athletes we are."[50]

As sportswomen moved into the twenty-first century, they still had to contend with the "old canard" that female athletes are less feminine than female nonathletes. Clothing—the right kind, the right amount, and on the right body—could help sportswomen portray themselves as truly feminine. But sportswomen could never discount the importance of a nice-looking hairdo and a full can of hair spray.

"Bouffant Belles"

In 1964, armed with "a can of Rayette's The Young Set hairspray," coach Margaret Ellison of the Texas Track Club "pioneer[ed] a new glamorous look in women's track." Ellison's athletes, dubbed the "Bouffant Belles" by *Sports Illustrated*, took to the track with their hair in "either bouffant or flip if at all possible." Coach Ellison asserted that she was "trying to change the stereotyped image of the track girl." And the best way she knew to do that was with attractive uniforms, required cosmetics, and "majestic hairdos."[51]

SI allowed that the style might not have been "aerodynamically sound and may be 'out' east of the Hudson," but it was "an unqualified sensation at a track meet." Aerodynamics aside, one runner asserted that the team's "trademark" look gave them an edge over the competition, and not just because judges could easily distinguish them at the finish line: "Bouffant is easier to run in because the wind doesn't blow your hair in your face." It wasn't the only competitive advantage; not only did it enhance the girls' beauty, a strategic perk in any competitive arena, but the team's weekly beauty shop appointment also helped reduce tension. Moreover, such an emphasis on appearance reduced attrition rates; Ellison "found that girls lose interest in track . . . if you don't make a game of it. That's why we have different uniforms every year and go in for makeup and hairdos."[52] A feminine look was crucial not just to a female athlete's performance but to her acceptance of sports as a desirable activity.

A bouffant style required not only numerous salon appointments and a substantial volume of hairspray but also a fair amount of hair. Long hair thus was crucial to achieving an overall feminine effect whether one opted for bouffant or not. Track star Marie Mulder was a case in point. In 1967 *Sports Illustrated* noted that Mulder had "done some image remaking. Her soft, brown hair, once cut in a boyish bob, now hangs down to her shoulders, flowing behind her when she runs, like Batman's cape." According to Mulder, "I got sick of people who saw me running in my sweat suit and yelling, 'Hey, boy, you better get a haircut,' says Marie. Now they know for sure I'm a girl."[53] And here was the bottom line: sports supposedly masculinized its participants—why exacerbate an already perilous situation with a short, masculine haircut? Hair length was a variable that most females could control.

For many sportswomen, then, short hair seemed the stuff of utopian dreams or of feminist crusades—or both. In 1915 the author and feminist activist Charlotte Perkins Gilman published *Herland,* which detailed an all-female society whose members were athletic and, coincidentally, wore their hair short, "some few inches at most . . . all light and clean and freshlooking." Gilman so believed in the "sensible and sanitary" benefits of short hair that she took to the lecture circuit in the 1910s to convince women to cut their hair as a way to enhance their health and their quest for equality. Scholar Karen Stevenson relates that Gilman saw women's short hair as a step toward "the disruption of feminine ideals which did not serve women's interest" and an androgynous world that would "reject 'femininity' in favor of humanity." What she did not bargain for was that women would seek to compensate by shoring up their feminine credentials through other means and that the ruckus over a woman cutting her hair would continue, especially when bobbed hair became popular.[54]

In addition to upsetting this accepted power structure, the "bob" joined speakeasies and Devil Rum in the 1920s as indisputable evidence that American society was not only immoral but sliding into degradation. It was not until 1976 that Dorothy Hamill's signature "wedge cut" belied such claims when the wholesome skater sparked a new short-hair craze with what would become one of the most classic short hair styles ever. Thousands of American females of all ages flocked to the salon to acquire their own "Dorothy Hamill Do," encouraged by the likes of Clairol, which featured the skater in a series of advertisements for their "Short and Sassy" hair care products, including a 1977 ad campaign in which Hamill explained why she loved her hair short.[55]

Even though Hamill made shorter hair fashionable, longer cuts remained de rigueur for most female athletes, who often used ponytails to corral their tresses. The ponytail had become so ubiquitous by the late twentieth century that it was virtually synonymous with women's sports: the 1999 U.S. Women's World Cup team was dubbed "the ponytail posse," while SI's Alexander Wolff referred to NBA assistant coach Becky Hammon as "the ponytail express." The hairstyle was incorporated into the logos for various women's sports leagues, including the National Women's Soccer League, the Women's Tennis Association, and the National Pro Fastpitch League, as well as various leagues for cricket, volleyball, and rugby. The ponytail even came to denote Title IX compliance; Jaime Schultz found that the law's "measure for proportionality has been (incorrectly) reduced to 'counting ponytails,'" just as it had been used wrongly to signify an entire group of women regardless of race. Schultz asserted in "The Politics of the Ponytail" that there is "a racial dimension to the ponytail that warrants acknowledgment," as it is a hairstyle that "constructs and normalizes a particular version of femininity"—one that is heterosexual and white. Such an association was not lost on various sports leagues like the WNBA, which had plans to "refresh" its logo for the 2020 season, substituting its 2013 version of "a player with a ponytail going for a layup" with one who "is also going toward the basket [but] her hair is in a bun"—a hairstyle more universal to sportswomen, regardless of race. Player input was essential in the decision to become, according to WNBA chief operating officer Christy Hedgpeth, "much more culturally relevant than we are."[56]

Cultural relevance was lacking in the late 1990s when journalists, onlookers, and fellow players alike tried to make sense of the early hair styles of tennis players Venus and Serena Williams. In June 1997, fifty-ninth-ranked Venus "made her debut at the All-England Lawn Tennis Club with the subtlety of a crashing space station," particularly because of "her clattering headful of beads—green, purple and white, in honor of the tournament." With her upbringing on the tough streets of Compton, California, and her beliefs as a Jehovah's Witness, Venus Williams "was like nothing Wimbledon had ever seen."[57]

Perhaps not for the tea-and-scones set, but the "clattering" hairstyle had already made quite a stir in Hollywood. In 1979 "the blonde and perfect 'Ten'" Bo Derek, wore them for the movie of the same name and, as Susan Brownmiller observed, "was widely copied for her beaded braids." Derek had adopted the style "from Cicely Tyson and some sophisticated black models who found the initial inspiration in African motifs."[58] But it was Derek who made the braids a hit, while for Black women, it was another example of their culture being co-opted by the privileged class.

Beaded braids might have been popular in Hollywood, but not at Wimbledon and certainly not on a tour that was very white in skin tone and overly blonde in hair color. Described as "shocking" and "daring," the Williams sisters' hair elicited varied reactions on the court. In an early match in 1997, Martina Hingis, on the brink of becoming number one on the women's professional circuit, dismantled Venus in a tournament, "after which a tennis official handed [her] one of the colored beads that had fallen from Williams's braids and said she should tell people it was a souvenir. Hingis scoffed, 'I'll say something better than that.' She walked into her press conference, flung the bead into the crowd like a brave tossing a fresh scalp and said with a giggle, 'I have a nice present for you. One of Venus's pearls.'"[59]

By 1999 both sisters were feared entities on the tour, and the eventuality of them "battling in Grand Slam finals, their hair beads and gargantuan groundstrokes whipping through the wind," was, according to *SI*, "beyond the delicious fantasy stage." As "the beaded divas of tennis," both sisters had talked big and promised that "someday they would alter the sport's complexion, dominate the field, and run neck and neck as the two best players in the world." By 2002 they had made good on their predictions and, according to SI's L. Jon Wertheim, had entered "a new phase": "The beads are gone. Their dresses and tresses no longer have much shock value. . . . The novelty appeal has faded. Instead, the sisters are perceived—and they perceive themselves—first and foremost as tennis players, a grim reality for the rest of the field." SI's focus on the Williamses' beaded braids, while "othering" the sisters, also overlooked the ways in which "hair issues" were emotionally fraught for all Black sportswomen. Indeed, ESPN writer Lonnae O'Neal noted that Black women's hair was "closely tied to feelings of identity, public perception and how you feel about yourself on a daily basis. Many black women don't grow up hearing about bad hair days; they hear about having 'bad hair.'" And while "all women are victimized by a tyrannical beauty industry . . . black women are the ones with the specific twist of black women's hair," which was further complicated by their participation in sports.[60]

For all female athletes, their hair—whether it was bouffant, braided, or beaded—was, according to Brownmiller, "central to the feminine definition."[61] That was especially true for the Williams sisters, since most of the early SI articles about them referred in some way to their beaded braids. Venus and Serena Williams may have been the hardest hitters the women's tennis tour had ever seen, but their hair garnered as much space in the magazine as either their strength or any discussion about their future success on the tour. Reflections on their hair and their skin served to exoticize the Williams sisters as racial "others." It was a reality familiar to many sportswomen of color.

"Exotic Beauty"

In 1956 Sports Illustrated touted the arrival of tennis sensation Althea Gibson, calling her "the most interesting contender at the pinnacle of world tennis." The "lanky, dark, courageous" Gibson possessed "great strength and grace" and was emerging as the sport's "most exciting prospect" despite her many crises over the years, which, according to the magazine, "have largely been crises of self-confidence."[62] Such a description completely overlooked the racism that had prevented her from participating in tournaments sanctioned by the United States Lawn Tennis Association until 1950; Gibson had become the first Black player to break into the exclusively white world of competitive tennis—one that had systematically prevented players of color from competing, thereby effectively banning them from participating in any of the major Grand Slam tournaments. Although Gibson might have been a "new" prospect for the USLTA, she had dominated the Black American Tennis Association and its tournaments for well over a decade.

Sports Illustrated's description of Gibson was in sharp contrast to how it described her white rivals. "Former model" Karol Fageros "contribute[d] high fashion and glamour" to the tour; she was joined by "attractive blonde, Shirley Bloomer" and Darlene Hard with her "vibrant personality." Meanwhile, the "awkward" Gibson, who was "grimly determined" and wielded a "powerful serve," was exotic simply because she was the first Black player accepted by the USLTA. In addition, she possessed an aggressive serve and volley game when most of her opponents employed a conservative, baseline strategy. Decades later, SI would assert that Gibson had "played a masculine game."[63] With her Blackness, her aggression, and her strength well publicized, Gibson represented both a curiosity on the women's tour and a stereotype in American society. Indeed, many in the white establishment believed that Black women could participate in sport with less stigma than their white sisters, since Black womanhood was already defined by "masculine" qualities such as power and strength. In effect, Black women had nothing to lose by playing sports because they were already defined by these nonfeminine qualities.

Track star Wilma Rudolph had begun to explode such ideas in the early 1960s, with help from legendary coach Ed Temple, who guided not only the women's track and field team at Tennessee State but was head coach of the American women's Olympic track and field team in both 1960 and 1964. Like Coach "Flamin' Mamie" Ellison, Temple placed a premium on femininity, famously insisting: "I don't want oxes; I want foxes." Temple contended, "Our girls are just as feminine as any. We teach them to be young ladies first and track girls second. They work hard out on the field but after practice they put on their powder and lipstick just like everyone else." It was a lesson Rudolph learned well. She had grown up in an environment where the assumption was that "you couldn't be a lady and a good athlete at the same time." Girls opted out of sport because they feared being tagged as tomboys; instead, they participated in fashion shows and dance, doing "it for show, and to make sure they were considered

feminine and not masculine." Rudolph seemed to transcend such limitations. The "beautiful Olympic medalist, Wilma Rudolph" was "gracefully
available for interviews" and was "poised [and] friendly." The "grimness"
that attended descriptions of Althea Gibson in the 1950s and that characterized the Williams sisters in the early 2000s was absent; in its place
was the incomparable elegance of Wilma Rudolph. Her biographers Rita
Liberti and Maureen M. Smith note that the sprinter's "palatable identity
markers" allowed her to offer a nonthreatening version of athleticism. This
was particularly important for the Black community, since "Rudolph's
physical appearance in its proximity to hegemonic beauty standards" represented "an opportunity to resist dominant ideologies, which dismissed
black women as uncivilized and beyond the bounds of ladyhood."[64]

As the "Glamour girl" of the 1960 Rome games, Rudolph transformed
discussions about femininity and Blackness, but her feat was situational
and limited. Indeed, Liberti and Smith regard Rudolph as a "change agent,"
but only up to a point. Portrayals of the sprinter, particularly in *Sports Illustrated,* as beautiful and graceful served to diminish the talents—and the
femininity—of other Black sportswomen like shot-putter Earlene Brown
and remained in contrast to white female athletes like swimmer Chris
von Saltza, whose feminine depictions "negated" those of Rudolph's.[65]
Wilma Rudolph might have possessed some feminine attributes, but
she was regarded as an exception, and thus her performance, while noteworthy, did not necessarily upend stereotypes about female athletes, track
and field competitors, or Black sportswomen more broadly.

In 1975 track star Willye White insisted that the "femininity thing" remained an issue for all sportswomen, regardless of color. White explained
to *Sports Illustrated,* "All female athletes have the same problem . . . there
is the femininity thing. As an athlete you take on certain masculine qualities on the field. Off the field you have to be feminine." She concluded that
"a female athlete is always two different people . . . a male athlete can be
the same all the time. He doesn't have to defend his masculinity." The only
difference for Willye White, as a Black female athlete, was that in addition
to the "femininity thing," she also had to contend with issues of race. If,
as a female athlete, White was concerned about being feminine, her race
demanded other obligations: "Being black, I have to be on my toes, to
state what I want in a positive way. Whites respect intelligence, authority.
I do not like this approach, but society does not allow me to be any different. I would much rather have society make offers than for me to make

demands." Giving voice to the unique oppressions she encountered as a Black woman in sports in 1975, White vocalized what legal theorist Kimberlé Crenshaw would later describe as an intersectional analysis of her predicament.[66] It was an issue *Sports Illustrated* failed to explore, choosing to focus on the exoticism of Black female athletes instead.

In 1979, for example, *SI*'s Kenny Moore described sprinter and Olympic hopeful Evelyn Ashford as "an arresting beauty in repose as well as flight, her eyes liquid and large, with something of an Egyptian cast." Moore's description was clearly othering, and he used similar signifiers to describe Ashford's successor, Florence Griffith Joyner, praising her "exotic beauty" and the "elaborate stylishness" of her racing attire. Moore and other journalists diligently inventoried Flo Jo's looks: at the 1987 world championships she ran "in a hooded, starred-and-striped skin suit"; a year later, at the Olympic trials, she wore "apple-green" for the initial round of the 100 meters, while for the second round, she opted for an "electric plum bodysuit" that she accessorized with a turquoise bikini brief. She also modeled other bodysuits, including a white lace number, as well as her signature one-legged outfits throughout a successful sprinting career that ultimately garnered three gold medals at the 1988 Olympics in Seoul, South Korea, and several *Sports Illustrated* covers.[67]

Flo Jo thus balanced her "exotic"—read Black—beauty with a feminine fashion sense that produced media-worthy commentary as well as lucrative endorsements. She represented, according to *SI*'s Moore, "a cultural phenomenon" and "a cross-over triumph"—appealing to fans of all ages, sexes, and races. Moore argued that Flo Jo had been able to strike that elusive equilibrium between femininity and athleticism, a feat no less impressive, as history shows, because she was Black. His explanation is worth quoting at length:

> The lesson seems to be that pure sporting attainment is not enough to make a black woman a star: athletic achievement must be accompanied by something else. Over the years the idea that sport is unfeminine was only slowly worn down, first by comely tennis players, swimmers, gymnasts and—almost by sequined definition—figure skaters. Later, runners and basketball players expanded the range of sports that didn't necessarily kill femininity. Aerobics helped. Yet as 1988 began, plenty of that old tension between traditional demure ladyhood and high performance remained imbedded in the American consciousness. Then Griffith Joyner

JULY 25, 1988 $2.25

Sports Illustrated

U.S. OLYMPIC TRIALS

FASTEST WOMAN IN THE WORLD

371

FLORENCE GRIFFITH JOYNER
SMASHES THE
100-METER RECORD

Florence Griffith Joyner's combination of sporting achievement and trendsetting fashion proved that athleticism and femininity were not mutually exclusive, regardless of race.

painted her nails, put on a white lace body stocking and won the Olympic trials 200 in 21.85.

Because Flo Jo had successfully balanced athletic achievement with trendsetting fashion—not unlike Chris Evert—Moore proclaimed her as "a heroine to all women who struggle[d] to reconcile feminism and glamour."[68]

A decade after her Olympic triumphs (and following the occasion of her premature death just shy of her thirty-ninth birthday), Tim Layden asserted that Florence Griffith Joyner "was alone in her sport," having "melded athleticism and glamour like no other woman." Nearly thirty years after Wilma Rudolph had presented an image of a graceful and feminine Black sportswoman, Florence Griffith Joyner had managed the same. But was Flo Jo just one more exotic exception? Not according to sports historian Amira Rose Davis, who asserted that Flo Jo had "created a playbook for Black female athletes who later built brands in their own image." Davis found that "it was a brand that insisted Black femininity was not antithetical to athletic success. And it was a brand that sold."[69] That was true for Florence Griffith Joyner, and even more so for Serena Williams.

By 2015 Serena Williams was *SI*'s Sportsperson of the Year and had, according to the magazine, "hit this rare sweet spot, a pinch-me patch where the exotic became the norm." *SI*'s Christian Stone noted that in addition to her dominance on the court, the magazine was "honoring Serena Williams too for reasons that hang in the grayer, less comfortable ether, where issues such as race and gender collide with the games." While Stone failed to acknowledge the tangible results of intersecting oppressions of race and gender, other journalists, like Juliet Spies-Gans, noted how Serena Williams had been likened to a gorilla and criticized for a body that was "too masculine, too large and powerful." Stone did acknowledge that Williams's outspokenness on and off the court allowed her to be "a difference-maker in other areas, speaking out against body shamers in both words and actions." Indeed, according to Stone, the idea for the *SI* cover was "her inspiration, intended . . . to express her own ideal of femininity, strength and power." But according to Spies-Gans, Serena's femininity was defined within a crucible of "prejudice, both of the racist and misogynist variety, on and off the court." Because Serena had "been bullied time and time again over her appearance," Spies-Gans now praised the tennis great's courageous decision "to embrace her previously mocked femininity." Thus the cover shot allowed Serena to "mak[e] one of her most important statements yet: That femininity and athleticism can meet and meld, and that the notion that beauty and brawn are mutually exclusive is inane and simply outdated."[70] Williams, with her dark skin, muscles, and outspokenness, certainly represented changing notions of femininity and seemed to confirm that even if femininity was an elusive goal, female athletes nevertheless sought to achieve it as persistently as any athletic accolade, even in the twenty-first century.

When *Sports Illustrated* chose Serena Williams as their Sportsperson of the Year in 2015, she was the first Black woman to earn the honor. The magazine made it clear that the cover shot was her idea and was designed "to express her own ideal of femininity, strength and power."

"Do Competitive Sports Tend to Make Women Less Feminine?"

Throughout the 1950s, Jimmy Jemail used his "Hotbox," then a regular feature in *SI*, to ask provocative, sports-related questions of well-known athletes, celebrities, and prominent figures in the sporting community. He then published a selection of the answers, which were often as compelling at the queries themselves. In October 1954, Jemail tackled the issue of women, sports, and femininity when he asked, "Do competitive sports tend to make women less feminine?"[71]

Answers to Jemail's question varied widely. "Marilyn [Monroe] DiMaggio, movie star," envied women champions' "nice muscles," but found herself wondering: "Would a man rather take a lovely bit of femininity in his arms or a bundle of muscles? I'm perplexed. I don't know." Her husband, Joe DiMaggio, was less confused: "I've seen many of the best women stars in competition. And I've talked with them at social functions. They are as feminine as most women." The Yankee great particularly singled out Babe Didrikson as "the greatest all-around woman star" and "one of the finest women I have ever met. She has great courage, a feminine quality."[72]

Other responses included one from a Rhode Island sports arena owner, Louis Pieri, who believed female athletes in general tended to be less feminine. He maintained that "femininity thrives on masculine protection." When a woman could meet a man as an athletic equal, he argued, then she was not "exactly a clinging vine." Dan Ferris, secretary of the Amateur Athletic Union, disagreed with Pieri only in that he believed female athletes could be clinging vines: "Most girls in track and field events are small and cute. They can cry as readily as the clinging vine, particularly when they lose." Former golf star Estelle Hoagland had some choice words for Pieri, Ferris, and their ilk: "You men are old-fashioned. You think the clinging vine who stays at home is the true feminine type. Today American women compete with men in business, politics and sports. This doesn't lessen physical charm. It heightens women's zest for things, giving them more feminine appeal."[73]

When wrestling champion June Byers responded to Jemail's question, she asked one of her own: "What is femininity?" Byers declared that she doted on her young son, was a loving wife and a good cook, wore expensive furs, drove expensive cars, and wore $30,000 in diamonds each day. Byers followed up, asking, "Am I feminine?" Neither Jemail nor *Sports Illustrated* answered Byers, but it was a query that Susan Brownmiller would find inherently flawed: "The problem is not that some women are feminine failures, but that femininity fails as a reliable goal."[74] *Sports Illustrated* continued to sidestep the issue; neither Kenny Moore in his *SI* feature on femininity in 1984, when Brownmiller's book first appeared, nor writers since have questioned the assumption that sportswomen needed to foreground their femininity to be successful. Neither have sportswomen themselves. The focus was on a new kind of femininity, one that embraced athleticism and dispensed with old notions of sweetness and modesty and heralded a new reality in which women could attract by being "capable" and "tough."

By 1998 the future was now when *SI*'s Rick Reilly noted a paradigm shift in the way society viewed sportswomen's femininity. Reilly reported the story of Katie Hnida, homecoming queen and kicker for her high school's football team. He announced that Katie had to be among the top ten sports stories of the 1990s as she "wriggl[ed] her sash over her shoulder pads," and then headed back to the locker room. Reilly gushed, "Is this a great time or what? We're past the 1970s, when girls had two options in sports: cheerleader or pep squad. We're past the '80s, when girls had two options in life: to be a jock or a girl. Now we're into the Katie Era, when a young lady can kick the winning field goal on Saturday afternoon and look drop-dead in her spaghetti-strap number on Saturday night. Hnida's take on a 'Katie Era'? 'I guess what I want to show is that it's O.K. to be athletic *and* feminine.'"[75]

That shift became a transformation when women's World Cup fever took the United States by storm and placed women's sports and the issue of femininity at the forefront of a national discussion that captivated millions. *SI* praised superstar Mia Hamm for providing "the femininity, the beauty and the naked passion that the sport and the camera need." But Hamm was not the only one with feminine bona fides. The '99ers might have played superbly competitive soccer, but they also appeared naked in men's magazines, mothered young children, and were, according to cocaptain Julie Foudy, "booters with hooters." Brandi Chastain told *SI*'s Erika Rasmusson that she was "much more comfortable because society has finally accepted the notion that women can be athletic and feminine."[76] These were sportswomen who embodied *Sports Illustrated*'s ideal of athletic femininity, showcasing the "strength, attitude and sex appeal" which *SI*'s fictional Simonya Popova would make famous in 2002.

SI's constant evaluation of sportswomen's feminine credentials—and indeed, their defining of an athletic feminine ideal—contributed to, even as it was reflective of, larger cultural pressures that celebrated and rewarded feminine displays by all women. But those displays had evolved over time, from showcasing a shy loveliness to openly celebrating and marketing sex appeal. *Sports Illustrated* and sportswomen alike showcased women's bodies. Both understood that "sex sells" and could market women's sports when mainstream America—the media and would-be fans—was slow to accept and appreciate sportswomen's athleticism. Muscled bodies could be sexy, particularly when they were unencumbered by lots of clothing, or any clothing at all. But while a hot, abled body was ideal, it was not enough. Expressing maternal love was a plus, and shedding tears of joy either in victory or defeat confirmed stereotypical ideas about femininity. But anger was not a luxury that sportswomen could afford, especially if it was expressed by women of color. From the beginning, femininity in *Sports Illustrated* was racialized. In all respects, Black women were at a disadvantage; their well-muscled bodies, angry reactions, "elaborate" outfits, beaded braids, and exotic skin color all served to other them, especially in the inevitable comparisons with their white counterparts.

Perhaps the one issue that has transcended race, and even time, is a required femininity in sportswomen's uniforms, even as expectations about the volume and type of the clothing has drastically diminished and changed. In the 1940s, the All-American Girls Professional Baseball League required its players to wear a hyperfeminine dress on the field; in 2021, beach handball players were required to wear bikinis. Femininity was not just encouraged but policed and codified as well. And if a sportswoman transgressed? In both cases the leagues levied fines on the offending athletes, mandating an overt display of femininity—regardless of how that display had changed and how much female athletes had challenged such regulations.[77]

As a result, many female athletes, regardless of their sport or their level of play, have continued to pursue femininity with the energy, time, and passion better suited to achieving Olympic gold than to acquiring an elusive set of attributes associated with quintessential womanhood. They not only pursued it but sought to protect it—in a court of law if necessary. In 2000 biathlete Myriam Bedard was horrified when she realized that her image had been used by Wrigley's gum without her permission and that it had been altered so that it "stripped her of her femininity." Bedard, according to *Sports Illustrated*'s Shane Peacock, filed suit against Wrigley's, arguing that "her femininity is an asset threatened by the ad." Bedard contended that she had "always made a point of remaining feminine in a sport that is very demanding and very masculine," and that the ad, which showed her "grimacing" and "shorn of her blonde hair," had "infringed upon what is dearest to me after my loved ones—my integrity as a woman and the integrity of my image."[78]

By the twenty-first century, Bedard and others believed that an athletic femininity was an achievable goal. Throughout the previous century it had been an elusive objective, one that only a select few—Wilma Rudolph, Chris Evert, Flo Jo—had fully realized. In 1997 Frank Deford acknowledged that "woman athletes have always had to deal with the negative image of being too mannish. This is how jealous men have put down athletic women: Denying them their femininity, making them neuter. . . . Nevertheless, in contradiction, there has always been a vein of accepted pulchritude that has cut through the mass of antagonism toward women in sports. It is almost as if, despite themselves, men deign to give special dispensation to a select few gorgeous athletes." Two years later, the American women's soccer team had not only won the World Cup but had secured Sportswomen of the Year honors (in both *Sports Illustrated* and *Sports Illustrated for Women*), in part for teaching "an attentive country that female athletes are buff, aggressive, proud, smart, feminine and not afraid to take a cleat to the face."[79]

It appeared that sportswomen had finally arrived. They could balance athletic prowess with hair ribbons and offset dark skin with lacy uniforms. Some female athletes, however, by the very nature of their sport, had an easier time balancing their athletic prowess with feminine niceties than others. Diminutive gymnasts and figure skaters could "prove" their femininity, even as they vaulted and double-axeled their way to victory, with less difficulty than well-muscled bodybuilders and shot-putters. But regardless of their sport, sportswomen needed to validate their feminine credentials.

Even as sportswomen praised a new era in which glamour and athleticism could coexist and in which they worked to uphold the integrity of their feminine image, few questioned, as Donna de Varona had, the need for women to work so hard to achieve this balance, and the sacrifices it meant in terms of a more basic human integrity, as well as the time, energy, and money that could have been directed to other endeavors. Was the cover that honored Serena Williams as Sportsperson of the Year, featuring her in a black, lacy leotard with legs bare except for black heels slung over a gilded throne, "fierce or sexist?" Spies-Gans acknowledged that in 2015 it still "depend[ed] on who you ask." While many weighed in with their views on Williams's photo op, too few considered the ways in which an athletic femininity—especially one that was Black—could be oppressive and used to circumscribe certain behaviors in favor of others. In 2020 Amira Rose Davis acknowledged Florence Griffith Joyner's pioneering efforts "to be unabashedly Black, feminine, and athletic—all at the same time," but found that "her legacy offers broader lessons. While the box built around Black women athletes has expanded in places, there is still a box."[80]

It is a reality that female athletes, regardless of race, seldom seem to question, either consciously or subconsciously, instead looking to adapt old ideas of the "Big F" even as they offer new modes of thinking about femininity. But think about it, pursue it, and embody it they do, unfailingly. Perhaps because the advantages of a feminine display are worth the price of presenting an acceptable version of their bodies, emotions, clothes, hair, and skin. Those benefits include lucrative endorsements, increased media coverage, and, perhaps most importantly, insulation against associations with lesbianism. Susan Brownmiller did not include sexuality among the concepts she addressed in *Femininity*. She did, however, note in her epilogue that "the fear of not being feminine enough, in style or in spirit, has been used as a sledgehammer against the collective and individual aspirations of women since failure in femininity carries the charge of mannish or neutered, making biological gender subject to ongoing proof."[81] Without card-carrying feminine credentials, sportswomen could be subjected to a lesbian stigma.

2

"Girls Like That"

FOR SPORTS ILLUSTRATED in the 1960s and 1970s, women's tennis *was* Billie Jean King. She had dominated the sport and used her visibility to condemn inequities in prize money and to establish an independent women's tour. King's actions transformed women's sports as she showed female athletes and women's rights activists alike that athletics could be both the site and the vehicle for the advancement of women's equality. As a result, her success on the court and her outspokenness off it ensured that *Sports Illustrated* regularly chronicled her sporting as well as her feminist achievements.

It was therefore not surprising when, in May 1981, King's name once again appeared in *SI*. This time, however, *SI*'s Jerry Kirshenbaum was not singling her out for Sportswoman of the Year honors or recounting her victory in another "Battle of the Sexes." On May 11, 1981, Kirshenbaum considered the ramifications of King's admission that she had engaged in a sexual affair with a woman.

It was not the first time *Sports Illustrated* had addressed King's sexuality. In 1975 the magazine reported that King had "been asked point-blank if she [was] a Lesbian. She denies it." According to *SI*, this line of questioning was nothing out of the ordinary, and indeed was standard protocol for male journalists writing about female athletes: "Most of the interest in the sex lives of Billie Jean and the other women players seems to be of the healthy boys-will-be-boys variety previously devoted to movie queens."[1] Six years later, however, denials had given way to a declaration in which the married King became the first American athlete, male or female, to admit publicly to a "homosexual liaison" while still engaged in competitive sport.

Kirshenbaum placed King's admission in perspective. He explained that tennis great Bill Tilden, Olympic decathlete Tom Waddell, and NFL running back Dave Kopay had acknowledged same-sex relationships—albeit after they had retired—and gay men competed in other sports, including figure skating and boxing. But according to Kirshenbaum, homosexuality "has been far more of a factor in women's sports. It is generally agreed that homosexual relations among women athletes tend to be more open, more enduring and, at the top level of certain sports, more widespread than among their male counterparts." Homosexuality was also presumed to be far more prevalent in sportswomen than in sportsmen because the attributes necessary for peak performance—speed, power, and strength, all of which were associated with traditional masculinity—were presumed to be absent among gay men, yet prevalent among top female athletes. The outcome of such an equation, then, was that sport—especially the elite sport that *Sports Illustrated* regularly reported—was populated by straight men and lesbian women.[2]

Kirshenbaum's article appeared at a time when scholars like Pat Griffin were beginning to examine the lesbian experience in sports and to question such long-held assumptions. In 1989 *Sports Illustrated*'s Jaime Diaz quoted Griffin in a piece that explored the struggling LPGA golf tour and the "whisper campaign" that tagged many of the female pros as lesbians. Diaz wondered whether women's sports saw a higher incidence of lesbians than in the general population. Griffin believed "getting accurate data would be impossible" because "we live in such a homophobic society." It was also beside the point, since the issue, according to Griffin, was not the number of lesbians in women's sport but pervasive homophobia, which hurt all female athletes, regardless of their sexual orientation.[3]

Kirshenbaum had alluded to homophobia in his 1981 article, citing the enormous pressure on all female athletes to emphasize their femininity in order to avoid the lesbian stigma. But as early as 1973, *Sports Illustrated*'s Bil Gilbert and Nancy Williamson had found that sportswomen walked a fine line: too much of an emphasis on dating and boyfriends meant you were a "heterosexual wanton." Not enough, and you were a mannish, "homosexual pervert"—arguably the worse of the two options. Between the "jokes and warnings" and "good fun," there were "a great many girls [who] simply avoid[ed] sports completely."[4] Such an outcome, according to Gilbert and Williamson, was in the "best interest of the male athletic establishment," especially if it quieted demands for female equality and generally deterred female participation in sport. If a vibrant women's sports movement represented "a formidable threat to male pride and power," then a powerful tool to curb the menace was the stigmatization of sportswomen as masculine and abnormal.[5]

It would be a device that proved powerful—both in American society and, crucially, in *Sports Illustrated*—for diminishing and marginalizing all sportswomen, regardless of their sexual orientation or sexual identity. Expecting sportswomen not just to showcase their femininity but to prove their femaleness burdened them in real and significant ways that became more onerous over time. Female athletes struggled with lesbian innuendoes throughout most of the twentieth century, but by the 1970s they also had to battle transphobic policies mandating that the only acceptable sportswomen were those who had been assigned female at birth. By the twenty-first century new rules about how women needed to verify their sex led some sports organizations to create entirely new categories for those (female) athletes identified with Differences of Sex Development. At every turn, the number of female athletes who were required to confirm and convince athletic federations, the public, and *Sports Illustrated* that they were "real women" only increased. It was a troubling history that *Sports Illustrated* at first simply reported—engaging in some innuendo of its own—before charting a more inclusive course that traced the problems associated with validating an athlete's femaleness and highlighted the damage inflicted on all sportswomen when authorities imposed a narrow definition of sexual identity.

"Don't Be a Muscle Moll"

At the end of the 1920s, the medical community, particularly the new field of psychology, regarded women who possessed sexual desire for other women as suffering from a "total inversion of gender role." Americans at the time were particularly fascinated with the theories of Havelock Ellis and Sigmund Freud which emphasized the importance of an individual's sexuality to his or her social and psychic life. An inevitable focus on defining normal and deviant sexual expression ultimately paved the way for a lesbian taboo, which associated a deviant sexual identity with outward displays of gender dysfunction manifesting in displays of male dress and an interest in athletics. Indeed, lesbianism and women's sports became increasingly conflated when tests conducted during the 1930s revealed that the only women who scored as "more masculine" than lesbians were "superior women college athletes." In scientifically "proving" that female athletes were "more masculine" than lesbians, psychologists also guaranteed that sportswomen would be considered less than "real" women.[6]

By the 1930s, then, society had made a connection between the female athlete, who had a "mannish" interest in sports, and the lesbian, who had a "mannish" interest in sex with other women. As a result, supporters of women's sport looked to minimize the expected fallout, as when female Texas physical education teachers "posted signs on school bulletin boards reading: DON'T BE A MUSCLE MOLL." Those teachers had a specific example in mind: Babe Didrikson, whose masculine physique, clothes, and hair, as well as her athletic aptitude, had become synonymous with "lesbianism." Indeed, Dr. Belle Mead Holm, who was "dean of the women's physical-education department at Lamar University in Babe's hometown of Beaumont, recall[ed] . . . : 'My mother used to cry when I played soft ball. She'd say, 'I just don't want you to grow up to be like Babe Didrikson.'"[7]

As "a rawhide kid of 18," Babe Didrikson dominated the National Women's AAU Track and Field Championships and Olympic tryouts in 1932. Legendary sportswriter Paul Gallico extolled her exploits when she won the team title as a one-woman squad. Babe's 30-point score, accumulated by winning five of the eight events she contested, showcased those qualities with which she became synonymous: her "natural aptitude and talent for sports, as well as her competitive spirit and indomitable will to win."[8] While Gallico remembered her impressive ability and the records she amassed, others remembered her short hair, long pants, and brash boasts. The androgynous Didrikson became an object lesson to girls everywhere of how sports could corrupt a woman's femininity, and by extension her sexuality.

By the 1950s, Babe had learned that lesson only too well. As a cofounder and player on the LPGA, she retained her cocky demeanor and a hunger to win but had dispensed with the short hair and the long pants, replacing them with a more feminine look that she bolstered with perfume bottles, a "lovely pastel mink stole," and a heterosexual marriage. As Babe Didrikson Zaharias, she dominated the LPGA circuit, but her accolades were not limited to the greens alone. Her husband proudly touted her domestic triumphs in *SI*, announcing that she "sew[s] like a demon and makes dresses and drapes and everything." Yet even when a female athlete prominently displayed her feminine achievements, she was still suspect—as Babe was until her death in 1956—since she was often unmarried, childless, or working full-time. Such women hardly embodied the image of "normal" American femininity in the 1950s. Sportswomen, with "their masculine bodies, interest and attributes . . . were visible representatives of the gender inversion often associated with homosexuality."[9]

Some female athletes, however, seemed able to evade a lesbian stigma—at least for a time. Before the 1950s, the heterosexuality of African American female athletes was rarely questioned—either by their Black communities or by a Black press. An association between sport, Blackness, masculinity, and lesbianism only emerged, according to sports historian Susan Cahn, "when African American athletes were becoming a dominant presence in American sport culture."[10] Thus, at a time when Black sportswomen were finally able to overcome barriers to sport associated with sexism and racism, homophobia became a powerful tool to control their behavior and limit their success.

Tennis player Althea Gibson, for example, endured veiled references to her sexuality as early as 1957 owing in part to her aggressive serve-and-volley game and her reluctance to marry. According to scholar Ashley Brown, Gibson "diverged from the standards of heteronormativity and respectability that had long formed the litmus test for African American womanhood."[11] In the 1970s, five-time Olympic sprinter Willye White recognized that the sporting world demanded certain behaviors of all its female athletes, regardless of race. According to White, there was "a stigma attached to being a female athlete. If you wear your hair too short and you are always in jeans, the fellows say you are funny. That is why I like to wear short dresses and lots of makeup."[12] Thus, by the late 1950s, the lesbian label had begun to proscribe the conduct of all female athletes, regardless of race.

With *Sports Illustrated*'s emergence in the mid-1950s and its dedication to the general (and most usually male) sporting scene, it is not surprising that the magazine rarely addressed the issue of lesbianism in sport. When it did, *SI* used innuendo to avoid a frank discussion of why homophobia and not lesbianism was the real problem in women's sports.

"Innuendoes about Lesbianism"

In 1956 *Sports Illustrated* assured readers that exercise guru Bonnie Prudden, whom *SI* had featured in a number of issues, was "the complete opposite of the classic caricature of the unattractive gym teacher." Six years later, *SI* featured billiards player Marian McKibben, who realized that her participation in a collegiate pool tournament meant that "people looked at me as much as to say, 'Mother told me there would be girls like that when I went away to college.'"[13]

From "unattractive gym teachers" to "girls like that," *SI*'s regular use of veiled references when discussing lesbianism in women's sport continued throughout the 1970s. In 1971, for example, *SI* writer Dan Jenkins "knew" that the lady golf pros "had a tour of their own, but [he] also knew what most guys felt about it: you would've bet that every one of 'em out there on the women's pro tour could overhaul a diesel truck if she put her mind and energy to it." A year later, *SI* featured bowler Paula Sperber and encouraged readers to rethink their image of a female bowler: "Those who think of the finals of a women's professional bowling tournament as a heroic clash between the Goodyear blimp and a 247-pound lady truck driver from Boise, Idaho obviously haven't yet caught Paula Sperber in her act." Both features used analogies to acknowledge a potential lesbian presence before dismissing it with lengthy descriptions of their subjects' femininity.[14]

And it wasn't just sportswriters who used lesbian euphemisms. Sportswomen did, too. Willye White had alluded to the need to wear feminine clothes and cosmetics to offset any chance of being considered "funny" in 1975. Two years earlier, members of the Radcliffe crew team were "conscious of the stereotypical female athlete but were scarcely hung up about it." In using such euphemisms, *Sports Illustrated* and its reading public did not have to face the issue of lesbians in sports directly. Such a refusal by journalists and female athletes alike to address the issue openly reinforced societal attitudes about lesbian athletes based on myths, stereotypes, and fears.[15]

This began to change, especially for *Sports Illustrated*, when in 1978 Frank Deford candidly discussed the damage that lesbian innuendoes had visited upon the LPGA—which had been dubbed the "Lesbian Professional Golf Association." Deford reported that professional female golfers had suffered "personal, abusive forms of criticism," and that "innuendoes about lesbianism wounded the LPGA the deepest, especially since [the tour had to] depend upon country-club venues and values." Although Deford had dispensed with veiled references to lesbianism in his own article, he failed to consider why lesbian innuendoes should have been so damaging to female athletes and such a deterrent for country clubs. Indeed, the problem for Deford was not that lesbian innuendoes had been used to describe female athletes; it was just that, in this particular case, they had been misapplied. Deford wondered how the LPGA could be associated with lesbianism when it showcased the sultry Bauer sisters, the physically well-endowed Jan Stephenson, and the dazzling Nancy Lopez.[16]

As a result of such reporting, lesbianism in sport, whether subtly implied or openly addressed, remained the problem. And this was not unique to sport in the 1970s. Prominent feminist groups, like the National Organization for Women, were reluctant to discuss—and even more reluctant to accept—lesbian liberation as part of their overall platform, fearing that such support might threaten the future of feminist organizations and any success their agenda might have with mainstream Americans. The costs of such homophobia fell heavily on lesbians throughout American society, but especially in the world of sport, as female athletes risked not just personal condemnation but financial ruin with many thousands of dollars lost in endorsements.

Nevertheless, change was in the offing as a gay and lesbian movement—one that could trace its roots back to the 1920s—was reinvigorated and expanded with an activism that emerged not just with the famous Stonewall resistance of 1969 but with the Compton's Cafeteria Riot in 1966. Both demonstrations served to draw national attention to the struggle of people with diverse sexual identities and gender expressions during the 1970s. By the early 1980s, gay and lesbian communities were headline news as HIV and AIDS placed both their health and legal struggles, finally, on a national agenda. Less well-known were efforts by former Olympic decathlete Tom Waddell to openly recognize and celebrate the athletic aspirations and accomplishments of lesbian, gay, bisexual, and transgender athletes. Although they were originally conceived of as the "Gay Olympic Games," proposed legal action forced Waddell to call them the "Gay Games" instead.[17] Such a combination of sport and what would become known in the late twentieth century as the LGBTQ+ experience was reflected in sports studies, as scholars began challenging the belief that a lesbian presence harmed women's athletics.

"Being Gay Has Hurt"

In 1983 Mary A. Boutilier and Lucinda SanGiovanni wrote in *The Sporting Woman* that to ignore lesbians in sport was to misunderstand the many issues, including homophobia, affecting and limiting women's sporting interests. In 1985 a special issue of *Women's Studies International Forum*, edited by M. Ann Hall, included several articles that explored lesbianism in sport and the problem of homophobia. One group of contributors found that the "verbal abuse" associated with lesbian baiting was an effective control mechanism in maintaining the patriarchal order: "The female in sport is described as mannish, muscle-bound, unpretty, unhappy, having hormone problems, having menstrual problems, hating men, loving women. She's called a jockette, a butch, a dyke, a lezzie. Like all slander, this communicates two messages: the target is as she is alleged to be; it is unnatural and undesirable to be that way. The implication that skillful women are not women is one of the strongest devices in the patriarchal bag of tricks for keeping women from movement competence."[18] In the same issue, Helen Lenskyj explored the media's treatment of lesbianism in women's sports. While citing some progress, her conclusion was sobering: "Although there have been recent instances where mainstream media have taken a neutral or even supportive stand on issues of discrimination against lesbian athletes, homophobic attitudes continue to prevail."[19]

Such reporting was evident in *Sports Illustrated*, especially when it addressed Martina Navratilova's rise in women's tennis. In 1981 *SI* reporter Sarah Pileggi discussed Navratilova's number 3 ranking, her recent triumph over Andrea Jaeger, and her relaxed confidence as she spent time with "her companion, novelist Rita Mae Brown." A year later, Pileggi again featured Navratilova, describing her dominance on the tennis circuit and her private triumphs and tribulations. Pileggi made no comment criticizing, excusing, or explaining Navratilova's sexual orientation, noting only that the tennis star was "through talking about the subject, at least for the time being."[20] In neither article did Pileggi measure Navratilova's athletics by the yardstick of sexuality or refer to her sexual orientation with disparaging euphemisms; Pileggi treated Navratilova like any other athlete, discussing her athletic achievement and providing information about her personal life, like sportswriters did for any feature subject, male or female. But was that the right approach to pursue? Navratilova was not like every other athlete; she was the only professional sportsperson living openly with another woman while still active as a professional athlete.[21] Pileggi did not take advantage of an opportunity to explore the difficulties Navratilova experienced because of her sexuality or to confront Americans' fears about lesbian sportswomen. It was a lost opportunity to educate an American public sorely in need of understanding that homophobia was the problem in women's sport.

Navratilova was the subject of a less neutral story in *Sports Illustrated* in 1984, when Frank Deford addressed the attendant publicity Navratilova encountered when she brought "her newest traveling companion" with her to Wimbledon. Deford recounted the harassment Navratilova endured from the "scandal reporters and paparazzi" who camped out on her lawn and woke her at all hours of the night, finding that much of the reporting "violated basic human decency as much as it did journalistic canons." But Deford felt that Navratilova was generally naive in her expectations, given her recent actions: "Her very valid claims that her privacy is invaded are diminished because she flaunts her private life. One doesn't fight innuendo with coyness. Besides, she selects generally newsworthy friends—professional athletes, a lesbian writer of *romans a clef*—and now the blonde Texas mother of two . . . [who] once actually sent a note to Navratilova in the middle of a match. On another occasion she blew kisses to her while seated in the press gallery." In other words, while Deford did not necessarily approve of the harassment Navratilova endured, she had it coming. Her actions, and those of the women with whom she was involved, amounted to "titillation," which "only made the naturally curious unnaturally so, and the insensitive vile."[22] Ten years earlier, Deford had not accused Chris Evert of "titillation" or "flaunting her private life" when she conducted a very public relationship with fellow tennis player Jimmy Connors. But then, Chris Evert was involved in a heterosexual relationship and, even more importantly, had seemed to accomplish the impossible in women's sports: attaining athletic success while maintaining her femininity. In effect, Chris Evert had achieved immunity from the lesbian stigma.

For Deford, it was an impressive feat, especially since in sports "a male is considered more of a man if he's an athlete, but a woman athlete is perceived to be less of a female. The really extraordinary accomplishment of Christine Marie Evert Lloyd is that she has risen to such heights in the face of the self-consciousness engendered by that thinking." By that time, Evert—with her ruffles and ribbons—was "safely settled" as Mrs. Lloyd. Rival Martina Navratilova lacked the husband but understood the importance of a feminine presentation. In her 1985 autobiography, *Martina*, Navratilova shared her realization that

> people judge you by appearances, and since I was all woman underneath, I finally figured I might as well start dressing the part. . . . I don't feel masculine on the court. I know I'm stronger than other women and faster than most, but I'm not bigger than a lot of them. I was working out and eating better and I felt confident and healthy and feminine. Put it this way:

I like standing out there in front of 18,000 people in my bright new orange and gold outfits, with a touch of blusher on my cheeks. I felt good about myself, better than I ever had.

Despite Navratilova's professed femininity and impressive on-court success, public acceptance and lucrative corporate sponsorships eluded her. In 1992 *SI* questioned Chris Evert about her rival and friend's lost opportunities. In response, Evert acknowledged, "Being gay has hurt [Navratilova] with endorsements. That's just the way it is. It's difficult, because in terms of her being a role model, I would tell my child to look at the way she conducts herself on the court. Look at how she fights for every point. And look how honest she is with people. I guess a lot of parents aren't ready

Regardless of Martina Navratilova's on-court dominance and colorful new outfits, pervasive homophobia prevented her from earning the corporate sponsorships her peers enjoyed.

for that yet."[23] Evert might have found it unfortunate that homophobia had imposed limits on Navratilova, but she simply accepted the fact that because Navratilova was an out lesbian athlete, she paid a price—in lost endorsements, public approval, and hero worship.

While Navratilova's tennis prowess was acceptable, her lesbianism was not. Although she might have tried to compensate, presenting a traditionally feminine image, her lesbianism seemed to trump any display of traditional femaleness she might muster.[24] Both Evert and Navratilova found displays of feminine behavior necessary, but only Evert was successful in combining athleticism and femininity. Once a sportswoman's homosexuality had been established, homophobia assured that the lesbian athlete would never be considered a normal woman and, indeed, might even be a danger.

"Speculation and Anxiety about Lesbianism"

In their 1973 three-part *SI* series "Women in Sport," Gilbert and Williamson sought to enlighten an American society woefully ignorant about female athletes. The writers found that "behind the myth that participation in sports will masculinize a woman's appearance, there is the even darker insinuation that athletics will masculinize a woman's sexual behavior." Despite the authors' attempts to prove otherwise, many people were convinced that a female's participation in sport would give rise to confusion about her "proper role." For example, in 1974 Little League officials committed to upholding sex discrimination in youth baseball leagues enlisted the aid of psychologists who argued that "sex mixing early in life [was] dangerous because it [led] to 'role-blurring.'"[25]

The results of role blurring as it related to sexuality could be particularly threatening, especially for the unsuspecting straight athlete. In 1985 tennis player Pam Shriver attributed "homosexual relationships" to the loneliness of the tour and the time and distance between heterosexual women and their male partners. Shriver maintained that all athletes were vulnerable to something; for the men's tour, the "problem" was alcohol or drugs; on the women's tour, it was "another woman—maybe an older one who's already had some homosexual relationships. So they become friends. And the comfort and convenience of that leads to a sexual relationship." Shriver insisted that she was not passing judgment and maintained that "there's not nearly as much of that stuff as people think."[26] Maybe not, but Shriver's point seemed clear: not only was lesbianism in women's sports a problem, it was a potential threat.

And dangers lurked not just in potential lesbian relationships between athletes. In February 1982 *Sports Illustrated* reported that South Carolina's women's basketball coach, Pam Parsons, had engaged in a sexual relationship with one of her players. In their article, *SI*'s Jill Lieber and Jerry Kirshenbaum maintained that "such an accusation would be no less unsettling if it involved a male-female or male-male liaison between coach and athlete." However, both authors admitted "that speculation and anxiety about lesbianism are common among women basketball players and parents who fear that their daughters will be compromised by lesbian coaches. Not all women basketball coaches, certainly, are homosexual, nor do those who *are* necessarily get involved with, or impose their sexual preferences on, their players."[27] The authors' assurance did little to de-emphasize the supposed threat lesbianism posed to female athletes, contributing instead to an atmosphere of homophobia. Lieber and Kirshenbaum not only stressed the lesbian nature of the incident but seemed to confirm presumptions that lesbians in sport represented a presence that was both threatening and predatory.

Such an approach was reinforced in 2001 when *Sports Illustrated* published a "Special Report" by Grant Wahl, L. Jon Wertheim, and George Dohrmann which found that coach-athlete relationships represented "one of sport's biggest taboos," especially when they were of the same-sex variety. The authors quoted Mary Jo Kane, who asserted that such heterosexual relationships were bad enough, "but because of homophobia in and around women's sports, if it's a lesbian relationship, the negative perception is exacerbated—it quietly moves from the arena of poor judgment to the arena of deviance and immorality."[28]

Pat Griffin addressed that dynamic in 1998. In *Strong Women, Deep Closets,* she found that parents and their athlete children did not automatically think that male coaches would pursue sexual relationships with their athletes but did assume that lesbian coaches would, "usually without any information to justify these fears." Reporters were keen on ferreting out information about lesbian coaches and their sexual abuse of female players, even as the evidence showed that improper sexual relations between a heterosexual coach and his female player happened more often.[29] As a result, when those abuses did occur, they were front-page news, both in the tabloids and the sports columns.

Such accounts distracted from academic efforts to show how the lesbian label policed and constrained all female athletes in ways that effectively diminished their athletic success and power in the sports world. By the 1990s, then, the issues of homophobia and lesbianism in women's sports were no longer consigned to the dark shadows of sports scholarship. But fears about lesbians, particularly in sport, remained endemic. This was in contrast to a national LGBTQ+ movement that had started securing important legal gains on the state and national levels by prohibiting discrimination based on sexual orientation. Throughout the mid-1990s, women's sports increasingly reflected this broader cultural change as several sportswomen came out—using *SI* as their platform to do so—unapologetically discussing their lesbianism without innuendo, concealment, or evasion.

"Coming Out Party"

In 1993 Pat Griffin wondered why, "despite the progress made in women's sport over the past 20 years, the association of athleticism with lesbians and the use of the lesbian label to intimidate women in sport [was] so powerful."[30] As the new millennium approached, Griffin found that while American society could at least discuss a gay and lesbian presence in various professions and among family, the same was not true for sports. Griffin asked, "How can we think that athletics is exempt from this growing demand that we come to grips with integrating openly lesbian, bisexual, and gay people into U.S. culture? How can we think that athletics will evade the call to address the broad gap between our professional ideals of fairness and justice and our treatment of lesbian, gay, and bisexual athletes and coaches?" Griffin urged a transformation of sport to accept all women and their various sexual orientations. Such a development included tolerance but moved beyond it as well; Griffin desired institutional protection against discrimination and an affirmation of the lesbian presence in sport.[31]

Such an avowal was slow to appear in the 1990s, especially in *Sports Illustrated*. Indeed, in 1999 a member of the Australian women's national soccer team declared that she and her teammates were "not big, butch masculine, lesbian football players."[32] Two years earlier, *Sports Illustrated Women/Sport* had published a "First Person" article by Olympic softball gold medalist Dot Richardson in which she asserted "that the stereotyping of female athletes as lesbians has been one of the biggest hindrances to the development of women in sports." Richardson believed the day was coming "when women athletes would be judged on accomplishment, not sexuality," but until that time, she was frustrated that all female athletes were "painted with that brush." And it was a damaging one; Richardson maintained that "most" of her "friends got out of athletics because of the whispers." In both cases, the need to "prove" that not all sportswomen were lesbians was palpable throughout the 1990s as lesbianism remained the problem. It was indicative of what scholar Pat Griffin described as the lesbian bogeywoman concept, which "cast [lesbians] as a threat not only to 'normal' women in sport, but to the image and acceptance of women's sport altogether." Such a depiction effectively policed female athletes by imbuing a lesbian label with the power of "marking the boundaries of acceptable (nonthreatening) sport participation."[33]

The power of the lesbian bogeywoman was on full display in 1995, when CBS golf commentator Ben Wright, at the LPGA's Championship in Wilmington, Delaware, urged local reporter Valerie Helmbreck to "face facts here. Lesbians in the sport hurt women's golf." Wright spoke with Helmbreck about how "lesbianism was paraded" on the women's tour, and he maintained that "when it gets to the corporate level, that's not going to fly. They're going to a butch game." Wright's comments ignited a controversy, and as Wright (and CBS) engaged in denials, LPGA commissioner Charles Mechem "took the statesmanlike position that sexual orientation shouldn't be an issue in women's golf," even as he denied that lesbianism existed on the women's tour.[34] But *SI* thought it was "disingenuous to suggest that open homosexuality wouldn't be an issue to the corporate world on which the women's tour depends. If there are closet lesbians on the tour, it's in the best interests of the LPGA that they remain so in light of the way sponsors cravenly shunned tennis's Billie Jean King and Martina Navratilova when their lesbianism became public." The magazine wondered why, in this environment and amidst this controversy, "no one on the tour used the incident to step forward and say what should have been said: There are gays among us. Deal with it."[35] Yet such a statement, according to *Sports Illustrated,* and to the then widely admired Ben Wright, almost ensured corporate hostility to the LPGA, thus placing the tour's future in doubt. Was it really any surprise that at first no one heeded such a call?

Despite the risks, someone soon did. In 1996 Muffin Spencer-Devlin became the first golfer in the LPGA's forty-six-year history to "come out," using *Sports Illustrated* as her chosen platform. In a series of interviews that culminated in the article "No More Disguises," *SI*'s Tim Layden found Spencer-Devlin to be "at peace with the most momentous decision of her . . . life," as were others who were peripherally affected by the situation. LPGA commissioner Jim Ritts remarked, "I don't think I'm naïve about this. I know there are still individuals who have problems with diversity, but we've come so far as a society that I don't see this as a topic that really moves people." Spencer-Devlin's sponsors had similar reactions: "The division head at MET-Rx [a manufacturer of food supplements] simply shrugged. Callaway's president, Don Dye, [was] more voluble. 'As far as we're concerned . . . if it doesn't interfere with her ability to hit a golf ball and she continues to show the kind of integrity that she clearly does, she's our kind of spokesperson.'" While some fellow players worried that her announcement would not "help the LPGA," others, like Swedish golfer Helen Alfredsson, contended, "If you dare to be happy, people should accept that." Such reactions were in stark contrast to the reception Navratilova experienced when she came out in 1981 and was met with censure from officials and fellow players, millions of dollars in lost endorsements, and a media more interested in innuendo than straight talk.[36]

Three years after Spencer-Devlin's announcement, Tim Layden explored the ramifications of another athlete's "coming out party." During the first week of the 1999 Australian Open tennis tournament, Amélie Mauresmo introduced her girlfriend to the media and then proceeded to dominate the competition with a hard-hitting style that elicited some notable responses. After Lindsay Davenport lost to Mauresmo in the semifinals, she commented at the post-match press conference: "A couple of times, I mean, I thought I was playing a guy out there, the girl was hitting it so hard, so strong." Layden found that Davenport's words might have gone "largely unnoticed" if Mauresmo's next opponent had not conflated a hard-hitting style with lesbianism in derisive comments. Defending champion Martina Hingis "said of Mauresmo, 'She's half a man; she's here with her girlfriend.' With that, a cause celebre was born."[37]

But the nature of the response to this brouhaha was a lesson in the pervasiveness of homophobia as well as transphobia, as athletes and reporters alike had a tendency to conflate same-sex sexuality and trans identity. While Davenport "was appalled at the tempest her statements had helped stir up" and had a note of apology delivered to Mauresmo before the final, Hingis took a different tack. "Everyone makes her own choices," Hingis said, "but you don't have to show it in everything you do. They are hugging and kissing each other all the time, and I'm just, 'O.K., there is a limit.'" Layden reported that Hingis apologized for her remarks after she defeated Mauresmo in the championship match, but the reporter found that Hingis had been less than genuine: "I'm not regretting anything I said about her," Hingis later stated, "but I have to see [Mauresmo] for many years, and I don't want to have to look into the wall every time I see her coming." Layden concluded the article by congratulating Hingis, even as he turned a few of the champion's words around on her: "Too good, Martina. As the loser might have said—but didn't—it was almost like playing a guy."[38] While Layden clearly opposed Hingis's homophobic behavior, he nevertheless used her homophobic (and transphobic) remarks to call out her bad form; it was a missed opportunity to dispense with the prejudice altogether.

In a follow-up article for *Sports Illustrated for Women* later that spring, Layden described Mauresmo's "disclosure" as "remarkably brave." In addition, he wondered "why no player came to her defense or why Women's Tennis Association officials did nothing to defuse a controversy that turned Mauresmo into tabloid fodder." Good questions, but answers were not forthcoming. Despite the silence, Layden predicted that the incident would "test both Mauresmo and the women's tour. The last prominent openly gay player was Martina Navratilova. 'Martina chose not to live in the closet, and there were consequences in terms of endorsements and business,' says Pam Shriver, who won 20 Grand Slam doubles titles with Navratilova. 'That's unfortunate, but that's the way it is.'" But Mauresmo's situation signaled an important shift: Layden found that in response to Mauresmo's announcement, "Nike and Dunlop reaffirmed their support for Mauresmo, who sealed deals with two more companies after Melbourne."[39]

But not all lesbian athletes enjoyed a positive reception to their coming-out announcements. In the December/January 2002 issue of *Sports Illustrated Women*, Michael Silver introduced readers to the Philadelphia Liberty Belles, one of ten teams in the National Women's Football League. Even as he discussed the growing popularity of women's football in general, Silver focused on fullback Alissa Wykes and wrote that if the sport ever took off, "Wykes might be remembered as a rugged pioneer." Like Muffin Spencer-Devlin, Wykes used Silver's *SI* article as an opportunity for coming out and asserting that a strong woman playing sports should not have to risk stereotyping: "It's not right for people to assume that because a woman is strong, self-assured and independent, she's a lesbian. . . . She should be able to play sports without being stereotyped." Wykes pauses for a beat and starts to laugh. "Of course I *am* a lesbian," she says. "I've had a partner for the last six years, and it's been awesome. I guess you can call this my coming out party." Perhaps it was a celebration for Wykes, but not for the owner of the NWFL, Catherine Masters, who insisted, "Our league is not a soapbox for anyone's personal agenda."[40]

Other leagues were likewise reluctant to showcase their players' non-heteronormative personal lives. According to L. Jon Wertheim, the WNBA seemed to promote only straight players: "Team media guides . . . unfailingly list players' spouses and offspring. Despite a sizable contingent of gay players in the league . . . no 2002 media guide mentions a player's girlfriend or domestic partner." A similar policy was in effect for fans as a number of WNBA franchises looked to push a "family-friendly" marketing strategy that was designed to mitigate a prominent lesbian fan base. Although Wertheim found that "some teams, such as the Los Angeles Sparks and the Miami Sol, have recognized gay women as a core demographic," it remained "a thorny subject around the league." In 1999, scholar Sarah Banet-Weiser had found that "the WNBA has strategically represented itself in such a way as to counteract the American public's fear about the players and thus, by association, the sport—being homosexual. Fans and sponsors are encouraged to see basketball as a sport to be played not only by those women labeled as deviant by dominant ideology but also by those who follow normative conventions of heterosexual femininity." Three years later, the feminist sport scholar and WNBA consultant Mary Jo Kane found that the WNBA power structure "believe[s] that if they're ever truly going to make it, they need to emphasize traditional femininity because the institutions that have power and control will find it more palatable." Nonetheless, the New York Liberty's Sue Wicks had felt comfortable coming out in 2002 in response to a reporter's question, and asserted in *SI* that same year, "You're a wife, a mother, a lesbian, who cares? The real victory will come when people just view us as athletes."[41]

Jennifer Hargreaves regards such acts of "coming out" by Spencer-Devlin, Mauresmo, Wykes, and Wicks as absolutely crucial.[42] In speaking up, these lesbian athletes were fighting for inclusion even as they battled homophobia and the assumption that heterosexuality was natural. It was a hope for a future that, by the twenty-first century, seemed possible—especially in *Sports Illustrated*.

"Pro-Gay"

In 2005 *Sports Illustrated* reported that WNBA superstar Sheryl Swoopes, the most dominant woman in her sport, had announced she was gay. Devoting less than 150 words to what the magazine described as Swoopes's self-outing, *SI* clearly did not delve into the importance of her revelation. Instead, it was left to *ESPN The Magazine*'s LZ Granderson to correctly acknowledge Swoopes as "the most recognizable athlete, male or female, to come out in a team sport." She was also the first prominent Black athlete to come out, and she told Granderson, "You don't have your well-known gay African-American who's come out. Not to my knowledge. I know it's not accepted in the Black community. I know I'll probably take a lot of flak. But in all honesty, that's not my biggest concern." What was distressing to Swoopes was that people might "look at my homosexuality and say to little girls—whether they're white, Black, Hispanic—that I can't be their role model anymore." Swoopes's anxiety was not about lost endorsements, but a lack of acceptance.[43] She need not have worried.

Eight months after Swoopes's groundbreaking announcement, *SI* found that she was enjoying support that had been "phenomenal" and "very emotional." And it had come not only from the gay community. Swoopes reported that NBA stars Shaquille O'Neal and Kevin Garnett had expressed their love and support. For Swoopes, "To hear that from two of the biggest guys in the NBA did so much for me and my confidence." *SI* virtually ignored the racial significance of Swoopes's coming out, much like it would do when Brittney Griner came out in 2013.[44] However, these announcements were especially notable given that Black lesbian athletes faced overlapping oppressions of race, gender, and sexuality. Black sportswomen could never escape sexism and racism, and the daily discrimination associated with their visible marginalized status often deterred them from adding yet one more burden of living as an out lesbian.[45] But Swoopes and Griner showed that change was evident for Black lesbian sportswomen, both in popular support and from sponsors as well; Swoopes retained her deal with Nike following her announcement, while Griner became the first openly gay athlete signed by the footwear and sportswear behemoth.

It was representative of a nationwide change that had Americans recoiling in response to the 1998 murder of University of Wyoming student Matthew Shepard—regarding it as a hate crime—and extending the rights and benefits of marriage to gay and lesbian couples, and even validating same-sex marriage in some states. Such acceptance was particularly clear in *Sports Illustrated* when the magazine openly opposed the homophobic legislation signed into law by Russian leader Vladimir Putin as the 2014 Winter Olympics in Sochi neared. *SI*'s Jack Dickey described the penalties (which included fines and possible detention) for peddling "gay propaganda," criticized the country for the law's recent origins, and took the International Olympic Committee to task for its ineffectiveness: "The IOC said it had been assured by Russian higher-ups that the law would not affect anyone traveling to Sochi for the Games—but, naturally, other Russian officials said the law would be enforced as usual." Alexander Wolff followed up in a similar vein in *SI* only days before the games began, criticizing Vladimir Putin for his conflation of homosexuality and pedophilia and praising the West's condemnation of the "New Russia" and its "targeting of what it calls 'propaganda of nontraditional sexual relations' ostensibly to protect young people."[46]

The magazine became a platform for gay acceptance at home and abroad when it featured Brian Burke's article "To Russia, With Love." Burke, the director of player personnel for the U.S. men's Olympic hockey team and father to an openly gay son, used the magazine to encourage those in the "Olympic movement" to "speak up" against Russia's antigay laws. While Burke wasn't calling for a boycott of the games, he was hoping that "athletes of all sexualities and nationalities will recognize the injustices being perpetrated upon innocent people in Russia. I hope they realize that if they join voices, they can effect change. So, Olympians, when you pack your skates, pack a rainbow pin. When you practice your Russian, learn how to say, 'I am pro-gay.'" And Burke encouraged athletes, sporting organizations, and *SI* readers to remember that "the pressure to do what's right shouldn't end with the closing ceremony."[47] This was an impressive call to arms, one almost unimaginable even two decades before. But by 2015 it seemed all but assured that gays and lesbians throughout the United States would achieve the right to marry, and that the last barriers preventing their full acceptance in all areas of society would surely fall.

Such was not the case for trans folk in the United States. By the twenty-first century, they had gained crucial visibility—trans activist Laverne Cox had appeared on a 2014 cover of *Time* magazine, which described trans rights as "America's next civil rights frontier." But while visibility was important, acceptance eluded trans sportswomen as they looked to dispel damaging stereotypes, rewrite Draconian rules that limited their participation, and change repressive attitudes that insisted an athlete's femaleness was determined at birth.

"The Transgender Athlete"

As early as 1976, *SI* had featured tennis player Renée Richards, who, asserting that she was "'anatomically, functionally, socially, emotionally and legally . . . a female,'" sued the WTA to play in the U.S. Open. *Sports Illustrated's* Ray Kennedy acknowledged that readers might have been confused: "At first, it seemed like a put-on. A transsexual tennis player? A 6'2" former football end in frilly panties and gold hoop earrings pounding serves past defenseless girls? A 42-year-old Yale graduate, Navy veteran, devoted father and respected eye surgeon reaching the semifinals of the $60,000 Tennis Week Open in South Orange, N.J. and demanding to play in the U.S. Open at Forest Hills? In *women's* singles? Who ever heard of such a thing?" Lots of people had by the time the article appeared in *Sports Illustrated.* Even as Richards fought for a chance to compete at Forest Hills, she realized she had "embarked on a crusade for human rights, a quest 'to prove that transsexuals as well as other persons who are fighting social stigmas can hold their heads high.'" While Kennedy understood that tennis might have been "a rather fragile or inappropriate vehicle for carrying such a weighty message, it nonetheless provides, as Richards is well aware, the kind of exposure that attracts disciples."[48]

Perhaps, but not everyone was convinced. When Richards won the right to compete in the Tennis Week Open, twenty-five of her female competitors dropped out in protest, and the U.S. Tennis Association subsequently required all women entrants in the U.S. Open to pass a sex chromosome test, thereby barring Richards from participating. Members of the WTA were split over Richards's right to play: Gladys Heldman, regarded as "the founding mother of the women's pro circuit," believed Richards had "all the rights of a woman" and should be allowed to play, while player Rosie Casals considered Richards a "threat" to the women's tour because she was still "physically a man and that gives her a tremendous and unfair advantage."[49]

Others questioned why she was pursuing such a tack. Was this about tennis at all or about media exposure instead? Kennedy pointed out that Richards's "Hollywood lawyer" was "peddling" her autobiography—perhaps a WTA win might help sell a few more copies? According to Richards, money was not the issue: "I make $100,000 a year as an eye surgeon. Would you change your sex for $1 million?"[50] It was a query that deserved a thoughtful response, but none was forthcoming. Instead, the assumption prevailed that transgender persons would change their sex for some kind of gain and then change back again on a whim. There was a serious information gap between what the transition process entailed and what the cisgender community understood to be true.

What this came down to was what Richards had already conceded: her transsexual status was "mind-boggling" to the majority of Americans who, in 1976, lacked an awareness about trans persons in American society, and even less in sports. But in an attempt to enlighten and inform, Kennedy worked to educate *SI* readers; he cited both the legal and medical research that supported Richards's claim to compete as a woman, recognized that her lawsuit "could have an impact on all sports," and rejected the idea of "Richards as a self-promoting exhibitionist."[51] Although the New York Supreme Court ruled in Richards's favor in 1977, the battle for acceptance of the transgender athlete was really just beginning, and Kennedy's coverage of the Richards case offered *SI* readers an important primer about the issues facing trans athletes. Not only did Kennedy give Richards the opportunity to share her own voice about being a female both emotionally and legally, but he also addressed the particularly controversial issue of a trans athlete's—particularly a trans *female* athlete's—supposed unfair advantage in sport.

Yet twenty-five years after Richards combated accusations that she had enjoyed an unfair advantage on the women's tennis tour, Michelle Dumaresq was fighting the same battle in cycling. After years of psychotherapy and hormone treatments, as well as gender-affirming surgery, Dumaresq began competing in downhill cycling. *Sports Illustrated*'s Austin Murphy noted that "after just three races, her license was suspended by the sport's international governing body, the UCI [Union Cycliste Internationale], which was responding to complaints that she had an unfair physical advantage." Following a subsequent review and reinstatement, the battle really began. Murphy noted that two of Dumaresq's Canadian teammates made the "surreal suggestion" that she should have to compete in "a separate transgender category." That idea was rejected by the Canadian Cycling Association, which also affirmed Dumaresq's legal status as a woman. However, neither ruling stopped the French champion Anne-Caroline Chausson, who had placed first at World's, from lamenting the unfairness of the situation and maintaining that Dumaresq, who finished twenty-fourth in the same race, was the stronger of the two women—a peculiar claim given the results. Even as *SI*'s Murphy sought to educate readers, he admitted to a learning curve of his own: "Compassion was not my initial response to the news that a transgender mountain biker was creating a stir in Canada. My initial response was gratitude, as in, Thank you, God, for the easiest column I will write this year. Sure, there would be a few gray areas with pronouns. But here was a column whose kicker practically composed itself. Whether you agree with her or not, you have to admit: What she did took balls." Despite the crude joke that simultaneously acknowledged and derided Dumaresq's gender-affirming surgery, Murphy acknowledged that his interview with Dumaresq ultimately left him "enlightened and sympathetic," and he found that her presence on the tour in 2002 was in fact celebrated by some of her peers and regarded as a sign of progress.[52]

By the time *Sports Illustrated* published "The Transgender Athlete" a full decade later, coauthors Pablo Torre and David Epstein had dispensed with the bad jokes to explore important questions: "What happens to the athletes whose physiology doesn't match their gender identity? Against whom do they compete? What obstacles do they face? And how are they being treated by sports' governing bodies?" Torre and Epstein also used their article to educate readers about what it means to have gender dysphoria: "For transgender men and women, the physiological traits that distinguish them as male or female don't conform to how they feel about themselves. Some have undergone sex reassignment surgery or hormone therapy to make their biological and gender identities match. Others ... have not." The authors described the "staggering degree of victimization" that trans students still faced in 2012 and the continuing debate over transgender athletes and how long it takes to negate the athletic advantages of a former gender, particularly those athletes who transition from male to female.[53]

Torre and Epstein noted that it was "only now," in 2012, "that transgender athletes are gaining sustained recognition from sports' governing bodies." That was due, in part, to the efforts of Lana Lawless, who successfully sued the LPGA in 2010 when it denied her application to compete in qualifying tournaments because of its "female at birth" bylaw. The same year, George Washington University basketball player Kye Allums became the first openly transgender Division I athlete, patiently explaining to reporters, "Yes, I am a male on a female team. And I want to be clear about this: I am a transgender male, which means, feelings-wise . . . I feel as if I should have been born male with male parts."[54]

While Allums's case for some was perplexing and provocative, it was not contentious, since Allums had not yet begun hormone treatments. And trans men seeking to compete against cisgender men was equally uncontroversial. It was the transition from male to female—as in the cases of Richards, Dumaresq, and Lawless—that challenged sports' governing bodies at all levels, and indeed athletes in general, to define, and accept, a policy that produced competition that was fair for all athletes, regardless of the sex assigned to them at birth. The IOC took a first pass at this thorny issue in 2004 when it issued the Stockholm Consensus, in which any trans athlete who wanted to compete in a category not of their birth sex had to undergo gender-affirming surgery and two years of hormone therapy and legally change all personal identification papers before competing.

Initially regarded as a progressive policy focused on inclusion, the Stockholm Consensus codified guidelines based on the "advantage thesis," which essentially laid out rules that mitigated any unfair advantage, especially physical advantage, transgender athletes—particularly trans women— might have over their cisgender competitors. As such, it was more restrictive than inclusive, as it contributed to a narrow definition of femaleness that was quantifiable and provable. Indeed, sports scholars Sheila L. Cavanagh and Heather Sykes argued that the policy was "symptomatic of a refusal to recognize self-identification with respect to gender" with a "priority . . . given to sex-testing regimes and narrow, medically governed, definitions of sexed bodies."[55] With its Stockholm Consensus, the IOC perpetuated a strict gender binary that othered trans athletes and ignored intersexed athletes altogether.

The NCAA took a different tack. Its 2011 Inclusion of Transgender Student Athletes, coauthored by Pat Griffin and Helen J. Carroll, included only one requirement: trans female athletes needed to complete one year of hormone treatments to become eligible. This policy was based largely on the authors' 2010 publication "On the Team: Equal Opportunity for Transgender Athletes," which offered recommendations to colleges and universities for including transgender student athletes in its programs and for implementing inclusion policies.[56]

Even as some of the most prestigious governing bodies of sport were issuing guidelines allowing (and regulating) the participation of transgender athletes, trans sportswomen still had to contend with questions about their unfair advantage. While trans women observed the loss of strength and speed as early as three weeks after beginning hormone treatments, Torre and Epstein asserted in their *SI* article that no amount of estrogen shots could "undo certain physical characteristics" and cited the case of Lindsey Walker, a 7'1" trans female who transitioned after college and hoped to compete for a spot on the 2016 U.S. Women's Olympic basketball team. The authors noted that Walker's "size, almost unheard of in women's hoops, would test the delicate balance between inclusion and competitive equity."[57]

SI's David Epstein addressed the issue of unfair advantage in 2013 when he featured Fallon Fox, a transgender mixed martial artist, who had transitioned from male to female, undergoing testosterone-suppression therapy and gender-affirming surgery in 2006. According to NCAA and Olympic rules, Fox's eligibility was not in doubt; Fox had also met the requirements for the Association of Boxing Commissions, which required proof of at least two years of hormone therapy before a trans woman could compete. Nevertheless, the Florida State Boxing Commission placed Fox's fights on hold, "presumably," according to Epstein, "to verify that she [has] transitioned appropriately and has undergone sufficient testosterone suppression." Regardless of her eligibility, the familiar argument of an unfair advantage dogged Fallon, as it had Walker, Richards, and other trans sportswomen. In May 2015 mixed martial arts star Ronda Rousey announced that there was no "undo button" on having experienced puberty as a male, and that Fox retained an unfair advantage due to the bone structure she had acquired during male puberty.[58]

Neither Torre nor Epstein identified exactly how Walker's height and Fox's bone structure would guarantee a competitive advantage in sport, and indeed the predictions about the athletes' dominance never materialized: Walker failed to make the 2016 Olympic team, and Fox amassed a record of 5–1 before retiring—impressive but not exceptional. While it was clear that there was a fair amount of misinformation and misunderstanding about the transgender athlete, *Sports Illustrated* was engaging the issue—and so were its readers. Letters written in response to the article questioned the fairness of allowing "athletes who were born male" to participate in women's events and the NCAA's policy regarding hormone treatments; but another letter acknowledged the piece as "both enlightening and thought-provoking. Not only did it address the issue of equality in sports, but it also exposed the type of discrimination and malice that some of these athletes encounter. I'm glad people are beginning to acknowledge this often disrespected group."[59] While transgender athletes enjoyed progress as evidenced by increased media coverage, prominent endorsements, and athletic scholarships, some of the same concerns that Renée Richards confronted in the 1970s remained contentious issues in the 2010s.

Indeed, in February 2019 Martina Navratilova asserted in an op-ed for the *Sunday Times* of London that trans women should not compete against cis women and that to do so was "insane." The piece was Navratilova's response to the fallout she had received when she tweeted the previous December that "you can't just proclaim yourself a female and be able to compete against women. There must be some standards, and having a penis and competing as a woman would not fit that standard." Putting aside that there were, in fact, standards for trans men and women to compete—and had been since 2004, including mandated hormone therapy under the care of a medical professional—Navratilova was not "prepared for the onslaught that followed," particularly from transgender cycling champion Dr. Veronica Ivy, who challenged what she considered to be Navratilova's transphobic comments. In response, Navratilova apologized and committed herself to becoming more educated "on this issue." Two months later, her "views" had only "strengthened": "To put the argument at its most basic: a man can decide to be female, take hormones if required by whatever sporting organization is concerned, win everything in sight and perhaps earn a small fortune, and then reverse his decision and go back to making babies if he so desires. It's insane and it's cheating. I am happy to address a transgender woman in whatever form she prefers, but I would not be happy to compete against her. It would not be fair."[60]

Navratilova challenged the widely accepted practice of regulating trans athletes' hormone levels, arguing that it didn't "solve the problem." She asserted that athletes who were assigned male at birth enjoyed greater muscle, bone density, and red blood cells, and the training they pursued before their transition "only increased the discrepancy." The only way to eliminate any advantage was for the trans sportswoman to start hormones before the onset of puberty to neutralize the aforementioned advantages, which was "unthinkable" to Navratilova. But the bottom line for the former tennis great was what she viewed as "a critical distinction between transgender and transsexual athletes": Navratilova considered the latter—those who had surgically "done the deed"—as having fully committed to changing their gender, being "few in number," and, most importantly, "rarely enjoy[ing] a competitive advantage." Surgery seemed to represent the point of no return. But on the topic of how it mitigated increased muscle, bone density, and red blood cells, which would have been the same regardless of surgery, Navratilova was silent.

Many were stunned by Navratilova's comments, given that she had long been a pioneer for LGBTQ+ rights and other activist causes. Even more curious was that Renée Richards, who coached Navratilova to two of her nine Wimbledon championships (and whom Navratilova acknowledged in her editorial), had already addressed this idea of "switching" for financial compensation back in 1976. Veronica Ivy weighed in again and clarified what "changing your sex" actually entailed for the transgender athlete who opted out of surgery and mocked the ludicrous idea that cisgender men would do it simply to make a few bucks on the women's tour. Ivy asserted that Navratilova (along with other critics of trans athletes) "imagines a nonexistent cisgender man who will pretend to be a trans woman, convince a psychologist and a physician to prescribe hormone therapy, undertake the process for legal changer [sic] recognition, then wait the minimum 12 months of testosterone suppression required by the current IOC rules, compete, and then change his mind and 'go back to making babies'? No such thing will ever happen. This is an irrational fear of trans women." Irrational though it was, such concerns dominated the media coverage—except in *Sports Illustrated*. The magazine simply acknowledged Navratilova's comments in a brief two-hundred-word statement. There was no discussion of Navratilova's characterization of prepubescent trans teens engaged in hormone therapy as being "unthinkable," nor was there conversation about the differences between transgender and transsexual athletes and what advantages they might enjoy, respectively, in sport.[61]

While *SI* was generally silent about Navratilova's op-ed and her comments about trans athletes in 2019, the magazine dedicated an online "daily cover" to "the most controversial athlete in America" in 2022: University of Pennsylvania swimmer Lia Thomas. *SI*'s "exclusive interview" provided Thomas with a platform to share her story, but the choice to describe Thomas as "the trans swimmer dividing America" indicated that she was the problem and not American society's transphobia. Owing to Thomas's dominance in the pool, she was at "the center of a national debate—a living, breathing, real-time Rorschach test for how society views those who challenge conventions." In 2022 the outlook was grim. Despite rules governing trans participation in sport at the collegiate and Olympic levels, there was a growing movement toward exclusion of trans athletes: eighteen states had passed legislation preventing transgender students from participating in high school sports consistent with their gender identity, and both the NCAA and the IOC had dispensed with their own rules about trans athletes, opting instead to allow individual sporting federations to decide rules for compliance. Both organizations made it seem like this was progress, but it was actually the reverse, since a number of sports federations, like the International Amateur Athletic Federation (IAAF; now World Athletics), had already adopted exclusionary policies regarding sportswomen. In this time of retrenchment, Thomas endured accusations that she, and other trans women, "had larger hands and feet, bigger hearts and greater bone density and lung capacity," and thus enjoyed an advantage in sport that was enhanced by having undergone male puberty. As a result, trans sportswomen threatened Title IX and "the integrity of women's sports." Despite opposition from other teams, Penn teammates, teammates' parents, and USA Swimming, the University of Pennsylvania, the Ivy League, and ultimately the NCAA insisted on Thomas's right to swim, while *SI* regarded Thomas's "poise in the face of debate over transgender athletes" as "a lasting statement for equality."[62] These were small victories in what was shaping up to be a protracted war over what really defines a woman in sport. And attacks against trans sportswomen were only the opening salvo.

"A Difference in Sex Development"

In 2009 Caster Semenya won the 800-meter race in the World Championships, beating the second-place finisher by over two seconds. Over a decade later, the sports world continued to deal with the fallout from that long-ago race in Berlin, partly because Semenya crushed her competition and partly (mostly?) because, according to the *New Yorker,* Semenya had been so "breathtakingly butch" while doing it.[63] Questions about whether Semenya was a "real woman" materialized almost immediately, leading the IAAF to suspend the South African runner until her status could be confirmed. *Sports Illustrated* picked up the story two weeks after that eventful race and followed it with all its twists and turns for the next ten years.

Shortly after the race, *SI*'s David Epstein got to the heart of the controversy surrounding Semenya's epic win: "Should she really have been running against women?" Epstein briefly reviewed the IAAF's history since the 1960s of looking to prove that female entrants "were not men masquerading as women." From visual inspections (in which a panel of doctors inspected female athletes' genitalia) to buccal smears (a scientific test to confirm XX chromosomes in women), Epstein outlined the "demeaning process" that testing involved and the fact that science is not objective, insisting, "The human body isn't engineered to always fit neatly into MALE and FEMALE categories." That was clear in 1990 when the IAAF "convened an international group of experts—geneticists, a psychologist, and endocrinologist—to answer the question of how to determine once and for all, if a woman is a woman." The group's recommendation? Stop trying . . . and stop testing. Shortly thereafter, the IAAF ceased mandatory testing (the IOC would follow suit in 2000) but "reserved the right to conduct tests in suspicious cases." Caster Semenya, it would seem, was such a case. Yet it was unclear as to what exactly was so "suspicious" and what they were actually testing. In 2009 Epstein speculated that it had something to do with her elevated hormone levels, but even if this were true, it would not represent "anything near a smoking gun. Hormone patterns vary tremendously among people and can fluctuate throughout the day. And any number of conditions—a birth defect, ovarian disease, a hormone-producing tumor—could cause a woman to have unusually high testosterone."[64]

Epstein concluded that unless sports authorities were prepared to organize competition according to "arbitrary competitive hormone classes," then what was left were the guidelines proffered by the 1990 panel. "If [sportswomen] believe they're female and they're raised as female, they should be allowed to compete as females." Epstein asserted that unless the IAAF could prove that Semenya was pretending to be a female (which the IAAF did not contend) or "it wants to set a standard the medical community says would be arbitrary," then Semenya should keep her 800-meter world championship title, and thus be recognized as the woman she said she was. Perhaps most powerfully, Epstein concluded with a question for his readers: "Who's to tell her any differently?"[65]

Since 2009 Caster Semenya has
been at the center of a conversation
about athletic success, gender
norms, and sex verification.

There were plenty of medical professionals, athletic figures, and sports
officials who were more than happy to do just that. Although the IAAF
permitted Semenya to return to competition (almost a full year after it had
suspended her), there was some suggestion that because of her reported
hyperandrogenism, she would either need surgery to correct an overpro-
duction of testosterone or undergo hormone replacement therapy to offset
high testosterone levels. Semenya returned to competition under a cloud
of controversy. She raced, but submitted slower times; she participated
in the 2012 Olympic Games, but earned silver.[66] Perhaps she was taking
estrogen supplements that impaired her speed? But the more important
question, the one that Epstein asked back in 2009 as to who has the authority to tell someone what sex they are (and based on what information),

got lost in the mix until the IAAF sought to suspend yet another runner for hyperandrogenism. Once again, the story dominated the headlines, but in this case for different reasons.

In 2014 the Athletic Federation of India dropped sprinter Dutee Chand from its national team roster for both the Commonwealth Games and the Asian Games. Chand had recently been identified with hyperandrogenism and was thus ineligible to compete. According to IAAF regulations, Chand had four options: undergo surgery, receive hormone treatments, compete with the men, or retire. Chand chose to fight the IAAF instead. In 2015 she appealed to the Court of Arbitration for Sport and asserted that the IAAF's policy (and by extension the IOC's as well) on hyperandrogenism was unfair. The CAS suspended the policy, citing a lack of evidence substantiating a correlation between testosterone levels and female performance. The CAS gave the IAAF two years to produce the evidence. Until then, Chand, and all female athletes suspected of having hyperandrogenism, were permitted to race in all upcoming competitions, including the 2016 Olympic Games.

That included Semenya, and as the Rio games neared, *Sports Illustrated*'s Tim Layden made some predictions. It was "likely," he wrote, that Caster Semenya would win gold in the 800 meters, and that "her performance [would] be stunning: She is 5′10″ and weighs 161 pounds, with muscular arms, broad shoulders and narrow hips. She has a severe jawline, hard and strong, and a competitor's unflinching eyes." For Layden, it was not Semenya's actual competition itself which would be stunning, but her overall "butch" body image. And that led to another prediction: "Her races in Rio will trigger an emotional debate on gender and sports, one that is far more challenging than the comparatively simple issue of doping." This was as much (or more) about the way Semenya looked while crushing her competition as opposed to the actual outcome of the race.[67]

It was also, according to Layden, about what many believed to be Semenya's intersexuality, "in which a person has anatomical sex characteristics of both males and females. That causes her to be hyperandrogenous—her body produces much higher levels of testosterone than most other females. And that in turn builds greater muscle mass and allows her to run faster." Layden acknowledged that such a supposition had yet to be substantiated and was based on "the assumptions of journalists and competitors . . . connecting a series of dots." Nevertheless, it didn't stop comments like those of the American 800-meter runner Phoebe Wright, who disliked the idea of excluding people but insisted "we have to keep our sport fair, which means deciding where the genetic and performance advantage is too much. It sucks to ask a person to alter herself in order to compete. It's not Caster's fault she was born the way she is; some may even consider it a talent. But would you watch the Super Bowl if you knew who was going to win?"[68]

Wright touched on one of the hot-button issues associated with Semenya's case: was it still sport if the outcome was guaranteed? Curiously, no one had any reservations about Katie Ledecky's performance in her 800-meter freestyle swim at the Rio Olympics, also in 2016. For that race, the biggest question was not whether Ledecky would win, nor whether she would break a world record—for both questions, it was simply by how much. So why the difference in treatment? Ledecky clearly had advantages outside the pool that Semenya did not enjoy, embodying a traditional femininity (read white and Western) that clearly marked her femaleness. This was a privilege the Black, South African Semenya simply did not possess.

Perhaps the biggest issue in the Semenya controversy, and one Layden did not address, was that while various athletes, the IAAF, and the IOC paid lip service to the idea of fairness and ensuring a level playing field, the reality is that elite sport is anything but level and fair. There's no limit to how much countries can spend on their athletes; because of generous budgets, some teams reward medal winners with huge bonuses, and their athletes have access to the latest technological developments in sportswear, equipment, and nutritional supplements. In addition, some athletes have conditions—polycythemia, enlarged lung capacities—that grant them competitive advantages; where are the rules governing their competitions? The question no one was asking was why the focus was on hyperandrogenism as the *only* condition that needed to be regulated.

Nevertheless, Layden's 2016 article "Engendering Debate" sought to educate and inform and was successful not only in introducing basic terms and concepts but in defining them as well. Two years later, Layden revisited the subject of his original article, admitting that he had felt somewhat detached from a subject who granted only the rare interview. That changed when he attended Semenya's press conference following the ruling by the CAS upholding the IAAF's policy of having athletes with hyperandrogenism either undergo corrective surgery or hormone treatments; opt out of races between 400 and 1600 meters; or, if refusing treatment, run with the men. Layden found that in meeting Caster Semenya "the murky and divisive science melted away, and a person remained behind." It was someone who was going to suffer from what the *SI* writer called "a flawed solution to a complex problem—that is, if it can be considered a problem at all." One of the biggest takeaways from the 2018 article was that Layden asserted that the "new ruling on gender eligibility appears targeted."[69]

This was not news to Caster Semenya. In an online piece for SI.com, Chris Chavez included her statement about the most recent ruling and the IAAF's treatment of her over the previous decade: "I know that the IAAF's regulations have always targeted me specifically. For a decade the IAAF has tried to slow me down, but this has actually made me stronger. The decision of the CAS will not hold me back. I will once again rise above and continue to inspire young women and athletes in South Africa and around the World." Having reviewed the CAS's ruling and the logistics of what it would mean in terms of testing for sportswomen and also the research that both supported and opposed the position, Chavez concluded his article with a statement from Semenya: "I just want to run naturally, the way I was born. It is not fair that I am told I must change. It is not fair that people question who I am."[70]

Again the issue of fairness, this time with a different twist. Chavez stayed with the story, reporting on Semenya's supposed last race before the policy took effect and her subsequent challenge of the CAS's ruling in the Federal Supreme Court of Switzerland. While the Swiss court considered the runner's appeal, it ordered the IAAF to suspend its controversial policy regarding "athletes with a difference in sex development." Chavez included the governing body's entire statement, but the gist of it once again revolved around what the IAAF considered fair competition: "The IAAF considers that the DSD Regulations are a necessary, reasonable and proportionate means of protecting fair and meaningful competition in elite female athletics, and the CAS agreed. The IAAF will seek a swift reversion of the superprovisional order moving forwards so that the DSD Regulations apply to all affected athletes in order (among other things) to avoid serious confusion amongst athletes and event organizers and to protect the integrity of the sport."[71] The IAAF was successful in its efforts and the CAS reinstated DSD regulations in 2020.

However, if the IAAF's goal is "fair and meaningful competition," why the focus on one condition and not the myriad other ways in which athletes are privileged? The IAAF and *Sports Illustrated* declined to discuss this aspect of the controversy, just as they failed to consider the race of those who have been suspended by the IAAF's policies in the pursuit of "integrity." While the Chand and Semenya cases are different, they both involve women of color who hail from developing countries and do not necessarily represent white, Western expectations of femaleness and womanhood. And in the end, defining femaleness has been the IAAF's ultimate goal all along. The IAAF's current policies represent simply another chapter in an already long and damaging tale of trying (and failing) to definitively identify what makes a female athlete a true female. Perhaps it is time to honor the suggestions of past medical professionals and the growing chorus of current ones to simply abide by a sportswoman's claim that if she's a female, she's a female.

"Tipping Point"

On May 6, 2013, Jason Collins appeared on *Sports Illustrated*'s cover as the face of "the gay athlete." An NBA veteran, Collins had not "set out to be the first openly gay athlete in a major American team sport. But since I am, I'm happy to start the conversation." *SI* extolled the bravery of Jason Collins for "shattering . . . one of American sports' and society's thickest barriers," as did Billie Jean King, who recognized the value of the incremental progress represented by Collins's announcement: "You've got to push—one by one by one by one. You've got to just push all the time to get a little bit of movement. And then eventually there's that tipping point where, finally, it's more of a cascade. From glacier to flood."[72]

It was a major moment for the LGBTQ+ athlete, but there were other transformative occasions that were of similar import, particularly for the lesbian sportswoman. In 1994 *SI* marked its fortieth anniversary by honoring "the 40 individuals who have most dramatically elevated and altered the games we play and watch"; at number 14 was Martina Navratilova, who, when she was "confronted with the accusation that she had an unorthodox sexual preference—and that's what it still is in the mainstream world of sport, an accusation—she decided to tell an inquiring reporter the truth." *SI* realized the importance of that moment when Navratilova came out in 1981: this was not a big reveal after an entire athletic career had concluded; this was not explained away as a one-time mistake or dalliance. In being outed, nine days after she became a U.S. citizen, Navratilova committed to a passion for justice at "the forefront of the U.S. gay-rights movement."[73] The fact that in 1994 *Sports Illustrated* singled out Navratilova not only for her on-court prowess but also for her off-court bravery for telling and living the truth of her sexual orientation marked a significant moment for the magazine and the sports world.

Important as such a celebration was, *SI*'s failure to consistently address, and to denounce, homophobia in women's sports has hindered its ability to deal with lesbians in sport in the constructive manner *SI*'s Jerry Kirshenbaum had called for after Billie Jean King's 1981 press conference. Following King's admission, Kirshenbaum was convinced that "for better or worse, the subject of lesbianism in sport will undoubtedly be receiving greater attention."[74] Attention, perhaps, but not necessarily acceptance, particularly in *Sports Illustrated,* which leaned heavily on euphemistic catchphrases and homophobic language throughout much of its decades-long discussion about lesbian athletes.

Of shorter duration was the magazine's inclusion of trans athletes, but a major moment for *Sports Illustrated* came in its 1976 article on Renée Richards. *SI*'s first serious treatment of a trans sportswoman made the issue visible to its millions of readers, and Ray Kennedy's balanced reporting educated them about the issues facing trans sportswomen. But such visibility was short-lived. Not until the early twenty-first century would *Sports Illustrated* again devote a feature article to the challenges experienced by trans athletes, publishing "The Transgender Athlete" in 2012. A "tipping point" of sorts, Pablo Torre and David Epstein's reporting was reminiscent of Jack Olsen's five-part series on the Black athlete in 1968 and Bil Gilbert and Nancy Williamson's three-part series on the female athlete in 1973, which also sought to feature groups of marginalized athletes. Like Kennedy decades earlier, Torre and Epstein sought to educate *SI*'s readers, even as they encouraged them to think about questions that Kennedy had not considered in the mid-1970s. Two years before Laverne Cox appeared on the cover of *Time Magazine* personifying "the transgender tipping point," *Sports Illustrated* had contributed some notable reporting about what *Time* would refer to as "America's next civil rights frontier."[75] But as in society more broadly, the sports world was slow to move past narrow, restrictive, and exclusive definitions of gender, and female athletes continued to be constrained by ideas introduced in the early 1980s that "skillful women are not women." Not *real* women anyway.

As a result, intersex athletes were also targets of sports policies that focused on theories of "advantage" instead of inclusion. Discussions about intersex athletes appeared for the first time in *Sports Illustrated* in 2009 and disproportionately focused on women of color. Unlike lesbian and transgender sportswomen, who have seen policies increasingly—albeit unevenly—promote acceptance, intersex athletes have experienced institutional discrimination that limits their participation and polices their womanhood. A "tipping point" is sorely needed for intersex athletes, but remains elusive.

Time will tell if sport can move past restrictive definitions of femaleness for all sportswomen. Certainly no one leaving Billie Jean King's press conference in 1981 could have expected that in 2019 an out soccer player would become the undisputed star of the Women's World Cup both on and off the field. Megan Rapinoe had come out publicly as the London Olympics approached; open about her sexuality with those around her, the crafty midfielder recognized in 2012 that using her platform and her voice could be a powerful agent for change: "We live part of our lives in the media, and there's something to be said for saying, 'This is who I am, and I'm proud of it.' The more people who do come out, the more, I guess, normal it becomes." Tipping point indeed, and one that was only underscored when Rapinoe won *SI* Sportsperson of the Year honors in 2019 for being "a galvanizing force on a team that is now looked up to by any woman who doesn't want to be told she's come far enough, who's taking matters into her own hands." The figurative became literal when *SI* featured her on the cover wielding a sledgehammer, "smashing the patriarchy" with its traditional feminine ideas that had long been, according to Susan Brownmiller, the sledgehammer. Deemed a "change agent," Rapinoe was only the fourth woman to win *SI*'s annual award "unaccompanied" and the first to do so as a visible member of the LGBTQ+ community. In July 2019, following the American World Cup triumph, *SI*'s Grant Wahl acknowledged that "rarely have we seen an athlete at the highest level talk the talk—and did Pinoe ever, demanding equal pay for women players, increased investment in the women's game and greater respect for the LGBTQ+ and other minority communities." Cocaptain. Outspoken activist. Unparalleled athlete. Out lesbian. "American icon."[76] By 2019, all of those aspects of Megan Rapinoe's identity were equally featured—and celebrated—in *Sports Illustrated*.

When Rapinoe came out in 2012, Pat Griffin applauded her decision, averring the need for the "visibility" of LGBTQ+ athletes "to help change the sports world top to bottom." And change was still crucial in 2012 given the discrimination against lesbian athletes and coaches, incidents of negative recruiting, and homophobic slurs by fans, coaches, and teammates which contributed to a hostile environment for all athletes, regardless of their sexual orientation. It was because of those issues that Griffin believed "Megan Rapinoe's coming out matters. We still have prejudice and discrimination to fight in women's sports."[77]

That statement is as true now as it was a decade ago. Transformative change is still needed both in women's sports and in *Sports Illustrated*. But the magazine clearly forged new ground for the gay athlete, the transgender athlete, and the athlete with differences of sex development, having at

Megan Rapinoe was named SI Sportsperson of the Year in 2019—the first visible member of the LGBTQ+ community to be so honored.

least made visible the challenges they have faced and the barriers they have yet to break down.[78] It represents important progress for all athletes, but particularly for Billie Jean King, who in 1981 had been outed and as a result had lost all her endorsements—some two million dollars within 24 hours. But King's 1981 outing, while significant, is often overshadowed by her spectacular 1973 win in the Battle of the Sexes, which made her an American icon. That glittery, sporting spectacle, which encapsulated the zeitgeist of a nation, was also one that *SI* later positioned, misleadingly, as having "saved" women's sports by ensuring the future of a 1972 Congressional Act called Title IX.

3

"An Odd Way to Even Things Up"

ON SEPTEMBER 20, 1973, over 30,000 fans descended upon the Houston Astrodome to watch Billie Jean King take on Bobby Riggs in the Battle of the Sexes. The twenty-nine-year-old King had finally succumbed to the fifty-five-year-old Riggs's badgering, agreeing to the tennis match only after the self-described hustler and "male chauvinist" had beaten the number-one ranked women's player, Margaret Court, in the first (although usually overlooked) Battle of the Sexes. While Riggs had been a champion in his day, he was well past his prime in 1973 and plying a seniors circuit that garnered little attention and very little money. The women's professional tour, on the other hand, was starting to enjoy both, thanks in large part to the efforts of Billie Jean King. Thus, in Riggs's mind, his biggest competition was the women's tour—and King herself. And what better way to prove that the women's tour deserved neither attention nor money than for an old male champion to beat the top women's players?

The festivities began with a smiling King entering the Houston Astrodome in a sequined tennis dress atop a beplumed Egyptian litter carried by loincloth-wearing "gladiators," while Riggs arrived in a Chinese rickshaw drawn by women wearing short skirts and t-shirts emblazoned with "Sugar Daddy." Curry Kirkpatrick reported the match for *Sports Illustrated* and tried to focus on what little athleticism there was in an affair that seemed more parody than sporting event. He praised King's aggressive play and her ability to dictate the tempo of the game, which forced Riggs "to match her net play, her speed and movement" and to "abandon his kit bag of drop shots and chicanery." Once it became an athletic contest, it was clear to Kirkpatrick, to spectators, and to the millions more who watched on television that Riggs was overextended and outclassed. King won in straight sets (6–4, 6–3, 6–3), proving to many that women needed to be taken seriously as athletes and competitors. Indeed, Kirkpatrick maintained that because "of Billie Jean alone, who was representing a sex supposedly unequipped for such things, what began as a huckster's hustle in defiance of serious athleticism ended up not mocking the game of tennis

Billie Jean King's victory over Bobby
Riggs in the 1973 Battle of the Sexes
was a glitzy affair that represented a
seminal moment in American sports
history and gender history, but one
that had no direct impact on Title IX.

but honoring it. This night King was both a shining piece of show biz and
the essence of what sport is all about."[1]

But this was not just about sport. King was, according to Riggs, "the sex
leader of the revolutionary pack," and as a result, the match took on greater
significance for many Americans, serving as a referendum on women's
equality in American society more broadly.[2] That equality was to be enhanced by Title IX, the landmark legislation that Congress had passed in
1972, which offered unparalleled access to education, and by extension to
sports, for millions of females. Because of its sweeping breadth—it applied
to all high schools, colleges, and universities that received federal funding

of any kind—it is not surprising that Title IX has been synonymous with gender equity in athletics.

More curious is the association of Title IX with Billie Jean King's triumph over Bobby Riggs. The outcome of a match between professional tennis players had no bearing on a law that applied only to "members of the underrepresented sex" at institutions that received federal funds. The Battle of the Sexes was simply not germane to Title IX: King's loss would not have scuttled the law, and her win did nothing to promote compliance. Yet it was hard not to conflate the two, especially when *Sports Illustrated* often chose to celebrate Title IX anniversaries by focusing on Billie Jean King and other sportswomen whose achievements were culturally significant, yet legally irrelevant to Title IX. Such a focus detracted from the gains women made when real, transformative, and long-lasting change was in the offing.

Through the years, *Sports Illustrated*'s rendering of Title IX—its passage, potential drawbacks, and immense significance—has served as a primer for its readers. If *Sports Illustrated* was the authority that set the American sports agenda, as its editors and reporters touted, then the magazine's overall depiction of Title IX is significant, for it failed to consistently support the measure in its pages. Some writers were jubilant, presenting Title IX as life changing and long overdue, even if there were those who regarded its scope as too broad and its timetable too swift. Others portrayed the law as damaging to men's sports and to institutions forced to comply with "unfair" regulations, while still others ignored, trivialized, or vilified those individuals who demanded its enforcement. And then there were those who marked Title IX's milestones by reveling in Billie Jean King's triumph over Bobby Riggs, effectively distracting *SI*'s readers from the reality that even with the passage of Title IX in 1972—and King's victory a year later—full gender equity continued to elude women in sport well into the twenty-first century.

"Too Far, Too Fast"

Title IX of the Education Amendments of 1972 sought to supplement the Civil Rights Act of 1964, which had outlawed discrimination in the work force but had not included education in its purview. Because Title IX encompassed not only academics but extracurricular activities as well, *Sports*

Illustrated realized that the law would require school administrators to rethink the way they addressed issues of gender equality, particularly in terms of financial disbursements to women's athletic programs. In 1974 *SI*'s Andrew Crichton observed that Title IX was nothing short of a paradigm shift in redressing inequities in sport: "Obviously if the fairness test is used, more will be expended on women's athletics as directors ask themselves such questions as is it fair that men have locker rooms and women do not; that men can use the field with artificial turf and women cannot; that men fly to the big game and eat steak the night before while women hold bake sales to pay for their bus tickets and brown-bag lunches? Finally, women directors and coaches should receive equal pay and responsibilities and enjoy equal working conditions."[3] The grim reality of women's sports—which were underfunded and underrepresented—was clear to everyone, but the way forward to promote a level of fairness was not.

Congress passed Title IX in June 1972, but it took three years to iron out the regulations. During that time, elected officials debated (1) whether Title IX actually applied to athletics (it did); (2) whether football and other revenue-producing sports should be exempt from its purview (they weren't); (3) whether women would compete for spots on men's teams or if a "separate but equal" approach would prevail (it was the latter); and (4) whether the emphasis would be on equal expenditures or equal opportunities for women's sports (again, it was the latter). Title IX's opponents were neither happy with the new guidelines nor shy about sharing their opinions about them: Walter Byers, the executive director of the NCAA, predicted that "impending doom is around the corner if these regulations are implemented."[4]

Title IX's opponents regarded anticipated expenditures on women's sports as a "big bugaboo," but Crichton also noted their distress about the pace with which the anticipated changes were to be enacted. He acknowledged that an equality of opportunity was now not only legally required but morally correct; yet he urged caution: "It would be a mistake . . . to push for it too fast." University of Kansas athletic director Clyde Walker could not have agreed more: "Most colleges are trying to establish women's programs any way they can. That was the way men's programs began. Colleges felt their way. The necessity for women's programs is here. But the government must understand we need time."[5]

While the focus was on the haste with which Title IX was being implemented, few sportswriters in *Sports Illustrated* actually addressed the fact that women had endured decades of inequality. As early as 1894, women from Stanford and Berkeley had played each other in the first women's intercollegiate basketball game, so a 1970s government mandate requiring equity in women's education and sports was not so much a rapid shift as it was a gradual evolution almost a century in the making. Even in 1978, after an additional three-year grace period, *Sports Illustrated* continued to wonder whether the changes Title IX had wrought in women's sports were simply "too far, too fast."[6]

Despite trepidation about the law, *Sports Illustrated* hailed the release of its guidelines in 1975. Robert Creamer proclaimed that the new rules "meant that for women in most schools the need to hold cake sales to raise money to support second-rate athletic programs in third-rate facilities is finally a thing of the past." He celebrated the enlarged budgets for women's sports and the increased number of female participants (up 342 percent among high school athletes), noting that the effects were not just immediate but widespread: "Even the Justice Department's gymnasium in Washington, once an all-male sanctuary, is now open to women." But with all the impressive changes, Creamer realized that "the most significant advance in 1975 was widespread public awareness that women were increasingly active in sports and an acceptance, even approval of the fact."[7]

It was a sharp departure from the pre-Title IX era in terms of access, opportunity, and funding, when sportswomen enjoyed few competitions, no scholarships, and very little organizational assistance, regardless of the sport and their own level of competition. It made the magazine's support of Title IX even more notable, especially when John Underwood reported that a hard sell about Title IX's ill effects was on in 1975: "What we are encouraged to feel for college football this fall is pity. We have been reminded by college administrators and ministers of the NCAA that these are indeed hard times, that football programs are not making enough money, that various fiscal wolves are at the door (some in skirts demanding equal time)." But the *SI* reporter was not buying into the gloom and doom scenario, not in the way of financial deprivation, nor the new and "cruel" reality facing football coaches and players, which necessitated a reduction in the total number of football scholarships from 105 to 95 and eliminated a $15 per month laundry allowance. Underwood cautioned *SI* readers to "hold your flowers. College football ain't down yet."[8]

Yet the drumbeat from opponents of Title IX was unceasing. By the end of the 1970s, the controversy surrounding Title IX had come to a head. The

U.S. Department of Health, Education, and Welfare had assumed responsibility for enforcing Title IX and announced that it would deny funds to
federal institutions that were not in compliance. Athletic directors across
the country considered the situation a "momentous crisis" of "unprecedented magnitude," while *Sports Illustrated* referred to the Department of
Heath, Education, and Welfare compliance guidelines as "an odd way to
even things up."[9]

Clearly there were some mixed messages coming from *Sports Illustrated* about Title IX. Crichton's depiction of Walter Byers's apocalyptic
vision of a bleak sports landscape with the decimation of college football
stood in stark contrast to Creamer's celebration of a law that would finally elevate women's sport and bring some much-needed equity. It was
a matchup that echoed mainstream American society's hopes and fears
about wholesale change demanded by marginalized communities that for
some was simply too much, too fast, and came at too great a price. It was
also a matchup that *SI* reporters—and their readers—would recycle in the
years to come. The players would change, but for the next few decades
the arguments—especially about Title IX causing the demise of men's
sports—would remain distressingly the same, even after *Sports Illustrated*
exposed the many inequities facing women in sport.

"Sport Is Unfair to Women"

Female athletes had long experienced unfairness in sport, but many *SI*
readers did not discover the extent of that discrimination until *Sports Illustrated* emblazoned "Women Are Getting a Raw Deal" across its May,
28, 1973, cover. That issue saw the first of a three-part series by Bil Gilbert and Nancy Williamson which explored the status of women in sport.
The authors' introduction is worth quoting at length:

> There may be worse (more socially serious) forms of prejudice in the
> United States, but there is no sharper example of discrimination today
> than that which operates against girls and women who take part in com-
> petitive sports, wish to take part, or might wish to if society did not scorn
> such endeavors. No matter what her age, education, race, talent, residence
> or riches, the female's right to play is severely restricted. The funds, fa-
> cilities, coaching, rewards and honors allotted women are grossly inferior

to those granted men. In many places absolutely no support is given to women's athletics, and females are barred by law, regulation, tradition or the hostility of males from sharing athletic resources and pleasures. A female who persists in her athletic interests, despite the handicaps and discouragements, is not likely to be congratulated on her sporting desire or grit. She is more apt to be subjected to social and psychological pressures, the effect of which is to cast doubt on her morals, sanity and womanhood.[10]

In 1973 *Sports Illustrated* published a three-part series on women in sport detailing the extensive discrimination female athletes encountered at all levels of play.

Gilbert and Williamson went on to list the ways in which female athletes of all ages encountered prejudice and discrimination. Minuscule to non-existent athletic budgets in schools, a paucity of athletic scholarships, small purses for professional tournament wins, and a total absence of girls' sports programs were not unusual. In general, American female athletes encountered less opportunity and enjoyed fewer benefits than their male peers, resulting in lower participation rates for women. But for many Americans, this reflected the reality that females were not as interested in playing sports as males: the demand simply did not exist.

Gilbert and Williamson attempted to dispel this myth in part 2 of their series. In particular, they noted that the eagerness of American females to engage in athletics "despite discouragements and humiliations indicates a fundamental and real interest."[11] In effect, they shifted culpability from women to institutional sexism as the barrier to full participation and thus flipped the script; instead of seeing the low numbers of female athletes as proof of their general lack of interest, Gilbert and Williamson enumerated the many obstacles to their play and saw participation numbers—low as they were—as evidence that women wanted to play despite a lack of funding and facilities. Females were interested in sports participation regardless of the many impediments that had been thrown up to deter them.

Gilbert and Williamson predicted that Title IX would have a huge impact on the lives of female athletes: "In time, women's sports will attract greater public interest. The press will cover women's athletics more frequently and seriously." The authors were correct—mostly. As a result of Title IX, American sports was absolutely and almost immediately transformed as women's participation soared—at the collegiate level the numbers doubled within five years alone—forever changing the American athletic landscape. But the obvious and immediate uptick in women's participation numbers did not see a concomitant rise in the press coverage of women's sports, and certainly not in *Sports Illustrated*. Gilbert and Williamson's prediction of more frequent and serious press coverage raises the question: more than what? In 1971 *Sports Illustrated* devoted a total of eight articles to women's sports, including one on "Stewardess Week" when "airline hostesses" not only "skied" but "swam, skated and danced."[12] With that kind of reporting, increasing the frequency of articles that featured female athletes would not be a particularly difficult challenge.

Despite this lack of media coverage, Gilbert and Williamson assessed the impact of Title IX a year after publishing their groundbreaking series and found increased participation levels, athletic budgets, and scholarships for females, as well as a greater respect for women's sports in general. This was good news in 1974, but concern remained about Title IX's full implementation by the 1978 deadline. According to Gilbert and Williamson, "the substantive matter is whether the inevitable will be accepted with good or ill grace, whether the accommodation will be pleasant and constructive, as it appears it can be, or bitter and divisive which would be regrettable."[13] There would be considerable regret and bitterness, particularly on behalf of institutions that saw females not only embrace gender equity in sport but fight for it as well, using the significant heft that Title IX provided them.

"A Considerable Weapon"

Four years after Congress passed Title IX, the Yale women's crew team was still not fully benefiting from the law's provisions. Day after day, the women's crew team had to wait on the bus—"sweating and stinking and cold"—for the male rowers to finish showering because, unlike the men, they had no access to similar facilities at the boathouse. The women also confronted a hierarchical system of privileges that benefited the heavyweight men's team and subordinated the women to the lowest rung of the athletic feeding chain, regardless of how they performed on the water. In response to such inequities, the women settled on a course of action that was both direct in its expression of their complaints and audacious in its delivery.

On March 3, 1976, nineteen female rowers, led by team captain Chris Ernst and accompanied by a stringer for the New York Times, "marched into the office of Joni Barnett, the director of women's sports, and made a bold political statement that would resonate around the country." That statement was both visual—the women stripped, revealing naked bodies with TITLE IX written on their chests and backs—and verbal. Ernst delivered a speech that began, "These are the bodies Yale is exploiting." Such a brash protest garnered the attention of the administration, fellow students, and alumni and forced the school into action. The basic demand for facilities and the embarrassment that resulted worked wonders: the women got their showers and a measure of respect as well. But the real legacy of the protest was underscored by SI's Michael Bamberger on the fortieth anniversary of Title IX: "The legal, social and political ramifications were clear: Yale, which first admitted women in 1969, needed to comply with federal law."[14]

Sportswomen had to fight for the enforcement of Title IX, in some cases literally using their bodies to make their case. But particularly curious was the coverage of the Yale protest in *Sports Illustrated*. While celebrated in its fortieth anniversary coverage as part of "nine stories that reflect the spirit of IX," the incident had gone unreported in *SI* at the time it played out. Such silence can be attributed to the fact that *SI* was then covering the Winter Olympics in Innsbruck and showcasing the impressive feats of American speed skater Sheila Young, who was the first American athlete to win three medals at a single Winter Olympics. And although "Yale Women Strip to Protest a Lack of Crew's Showers" did make it into the *New York Times* in March 1976, it was buried on page 33; it was a small ripple in a minor woman's sport. Nevertheless, it was one of the first examples in which Title IX was used successfully to combat gendered inequities in sport and to effect material change, and *SI* chose not to mark the occasion until decades after the event.

By 1979 it was impossible to ignore the power of Title IX. *SI*'s Jerry Kirshenbaum regarded it as "a considerable weapon," one that women were threatening to wield in the courts. That year, Kirshenbaum reported that female athletes at Michigan State University were suing the administration for alleged discrimination:

> Sixteen months ago, MSU's women athletes began to complain that they were being treated less favorably than the men. While the men were issued three or four pairs of gym shoes, the women received only one. A doctor was present at men's games, but not when the women played. The women had to wash their own uniforms. What is more, they practiced in a gym with a warped floor and inadequate heat and returned to their dorm so late they had trouble getting a hot meal. And, oh yes, they had ample time to talk over these grievances during all-night drives home from games in station wagons. The men traveled by bus and plane.

In response, Michigan State made some improvements, but, according to Kirshenbaum, turning on the heat and providing laundry facilities were not enough to forestall legal action. Indeed, MSU sportswomen filed a formal complaint and then brought suit, asserting that the university had violated Title IX due to the numerous inequities, which Kirshenbaum had cataloged for *SI* readers.[15] It was clear that Title IX had heightened awareness and recognition of the pervasive inequalities sportswomen had long endured, and had both inspired and enabled them to fight for their rights, refusing to settle for quick fixes at the expense of systemic change.

That activism, for Gilbert and Williamson, was a cause for celebration. In 1974 they recognized that it had been "women—not big league commissioners, rule changers, labor negotiators or moneymen—[who] have been the most formidable movers and shakers of the athletic world. In courts of law and on the playgrounds of America they have been demanding and doing things that have altered long-standing policies and prejudices." They also acknowledged that it was this "two-pronged pressure—from the government and coeds—that is inducing change."[16] By the 1980s, such activism would become even more critical, as Title IX's effectiveness, and indeed its very existence, was in jeopardy.

"A Law That Needs New Muscle"

In 1974, Gilbert and Williamson believed the idea that "there should be equal opportunity in sport" was so well established that opponents were "becoming increasingly rare," especially since "sexual discrimination is no longer regarded as fashionable, rational or politic." Their hopeful optimism was possibly naive but definitely premature; ten years later, *Sports Illustrated* noted that Title IX was "a law that needs new muscle."[17] A series of challenges to Title IX, beginning in the early 1980s, reflected a general turn to the right in the United States during the Reagan years, which resulted in a backlash to the gains made by the women's movement in American society and especially in American sport.[18] Playing out in both the court of law and the court of public opinion, Title IX was under attack.

While disputes regarding the law had emerged even as it was conceived, the first major setback to Title IX occurred in 1984. That year, the U.S. Supreme Court essentially stymied the law's effectiveness in its *Grove City College v. Bell* ruling. Craig Neff succinctly summarized the case for *SI* readers:

In '78, Grove City (Pa.), a small coed school affiliated with the Presbyterian Church and staunchly resistant to government regulations that it felt interfered with its independence, refused to fill out a form stating that it had complied with Title IX. When the U.S. Department of Education cut off financial aid to Grove City students, the college filed suit. Grove

City claimed that it was not bound by the provisions of Title IX because while some of its students received federal funds, the college had never accepted direct financial aid.

The Supreme Court ruled that Title IX applied only to those programs that actually received financial assistance. As Neff noted, "This was a crucial distinction," because until the Supreme Court's ruling on Grove City College, "the common interpretation of Title IX had been that it applied to all of the activities at a school that received federal assistance for any purpose." While the outcome of the lawsuit did not eliminate the law altogether, it drastically reduced its purview, as athletic departments rarely received federal funding directly. It was a serious blow to Title IX, one acknowledged at the time by *Sports Illustrated*: "the shelving of 40-odd cases" investigating Title IX violations was a serious concern, but "worse still is the possibility of gains in women's programs being reversed." In the wake of Title IX's passage, most schools had not only increased opportunities for women to play sports but also "claim[ed] to be morally committed to parity for women's athletics. But without a strong Title IX to prod them, even the best-intentioned athletic directors may be tempted to deal with future budget crunches by cutting back on women's programs." Even as *SI* recognized the potential fallout from the *Grove City* decision, the magazine noted that there was "strong bipartisan support ... in both houses for the proposed Civil Rights Restoration Act of 1985," which would affirm Title IX's broad application, effectively neutralizing the *Grove City* decision.[19]

Congress did pass the Civil Rights Restoration Act—but not until 1988— with big enough margins that *SI* was confident that it would "restore fair play for women's athletics." Neff noted that even though "the women's sport movement has shown resilience," with colleges adding teams for its female athletes even without compulsion from Title IX, "not all the news has been good. Some women's sports programs have suffered from budget reductions that weren't imposed upon men's teams—and that might not have been allowed had Title IX been in force."[20]

But even when Title IX *was* in force, colleges and universities looked to cut women's sports programs, often justifying the move by eliminating men's programs as well. *SI* addressed such a case in 1991 when the College of William and Mary moved to cut its women's basketball program, "'the most expensive and the least successful' of the school's nonrevenue-producing teams." In addition, William and Mary sought to reduce overall costs by getting rid of men's wrestling and men's and women's swimming. Even with the cuts, the college would still be offering twenty-one varsity sports, eleven for men and ten for women; yet the women's basketball team saw the decision as violating Title IX and hired a lawyer with experience in winning similar kinds of Title IX complaints. In the end, the case was not even filed; eleven days after W&M announced its "cost-cutting plans," the school restored all of the sports as a result of "a very impressive and overwhelming response from athletes, their families and alumni—and after the teams found some serious 'commitments' for outside financial support."[21]

Despite a growing archive of legal precedent supporting sportswomen's rights, renewed government commitment to Title IX, and the willingness of female athletes to fight for their Title IX rights in court, discrimination persisted.[22] It was a fact Sports Illustrated recognized when Alexander Wolff offered a muted celebration of the law's twentieth anniversary in 1992, noting that "two decades have elapsed since Title IX banned gender discrimination in federally funded schools, yet equity for women in high school and college sports remains elusive." Elusive was an understatement, especially when Wolff enumerated the many ways women continued to experience inequities in sport: "Women make up more than half of all college students in the country, yet they make up only a third of athletes in Division I colleges, and not much more in other schools. And they receive only one in three athletic scholarship dollars. Look at operating budgets of college athletic departments, and women get only one in every five dollars. Look at recruiting budgets, and it's even less than that." While dispelling the myth (once again) that football was unfairly hampered by Title IX regulations because it paid not only for itself but for women's sports as well, Wolff noted that even if such a fallacy were true, "the Department of Education's Office for Civil Rights . . . has ruled that a sport's ability to produce revenue is irrelevant." Moreover, Wolff exploded yet another myth when he dismissed the idea that a winning football program resulted in increased alumni donations, citing multiple studies that had proved "no correlation between success in football and alumni giving."[23]

The bottom line was that federally funded institutions still sought to avoid compliance with Title IX for myriad reasons, but especially to save money during economic downturns. They also sought to challenge what they viewed to be the unfair demands that Title IX compliance placed on

schools even when they had demonstrated a real commitment to an investment in women's sports. Brown University was at the vanguard of such
Title IX defiance in May 1991 when it cut four sports—men's water polo
and golf and women's volleyball and gymnastics. *SI* noted that, even with
the cuts, "given the Title IX compliance landscape, Brown stacks up fairly
well, offering 13 varsity sports for women, 14 for men. Still, men make up
61 percent of Brown's athletes but only 51 percent of its students." Like
William and Mary, even with the reduction in programs, Brown University still offered a vibrant athletics program for women; also like W&M,
Brown University backed down, but only after the women's teams successfully sued under Title IX—an outcome regarded as a bellwether by other
universities and schools.[24]

For the defendants in *Cohen v. Brown University*, the crux of the issue
was expressed by lead counsel Maureen H. Maroney in a 1997 article for
Sports Illustrated titled "The Numbers Don't Add Up." She asked readers,
"Does a fair-minded university where half the students are women have an
obligation to try to fill its varsity rosters with equal numbers of men and
women even if far more men than women want to participate?" The basis
for Brown's legal fight was that Title IX was essentially demanding that the
university abide by quotas: "Women now constitute 53% of the Brown student body, but Brown doesn't want to count heads and set aside 53% of its
varsity positions for women because it believes that equal opportunity can
be afforded through a broad array of teams that reflect the relative interests and abilities of both sexes." It seemed a shame, especially for a school
that had been "at the forefront of the women's athletic movement when it
established 14 women's varsity teams shortly after it became coed in 1971."
It also seemed unfortunate that if "substantially more men than women"
have "the desire and ability to compete on the varsity level," they should
"have to duke it out among themselves to get the slots that are left after all
the women have been accommodated." After questioning whether women
"will naturally participate in athletics in numbers equal to men," Maroney
offered what she considered to be the essential point: "Women don't have
to have 50% of the varsity positions to succeed as athletes. They need equal
opportunity, and you don't get that from a numerical formula."[25]

The counsel for the plaintiffs took issue with Maroney's characterization of the case, particularly the emphasis on Title IX as a quota system.
Lynette Labinger and Arthur H. Bryant argued that "Brown can comply
with Title IX by doing any of the following: 1) providing participation

opportunities 'substantially proportionate' to undergraduate enrollment of men and women, 2) expanding its program in a manner 'demonstrably responsive' to the developing interest and abilities of the underrepresented gender or 3) 'fully and effectively' accommodating the interests and abilities of the underrepresented gender with its present program. Brown has done none of these things." Labinger and Bryant made an important point: while Title IX critics lambasted the law for imposing a quota system, it was just one of three ways to comply with Title IX. Schools could also show a history of adding sports for the underrepresented sex or prove that they had accommodated the interests of the underrepresented sex. Furthermore, the lawyers took issue with Maroney's opposition to offering opportunities for participation without proof of interest and countered with their own forceful statement: "Unless we know women really don't have the interest or the ability, how can we possibly justify offering them less? After 25 years Brown should stop making excuses and comply with the law."[26]

It was a legal exchange more suited to a law review than a sports magazine, but SI's treatment of the dispute underscored the emerging importance of Title IX and women's athletic equality in American popular culture. But the terms of the debate were far from even: Maroney's argument appeared as an opinion piece in the magazine's "Point After" section with a tagline that described Brown as "fighting to ensure Title IX benefits all students."[27] The rebuttal occurred not in the same section, or even in the next issue, but over a month later in the "Letters" section. As a result of its timing and placement, the magazine—whether it meant to or not—lent greater credence to the equation of Title IX with a quota system simply by the greater visibility of Maroney's article. At the very least, Sports Illustrated missed an opportunity to moderate a fair debate. It prioritized what Brown University stood to lose if Title IX was enforced, as opposed to what sportswomen might gain if the law was strengthened and supported.

Despite these optics, the ruling against Brown University was significant because several Title IX cases promoting the "quotas are unfair" argument were abandoned. As a result, colleges and universities now faced tough decisions regarding their budgets, and men's "minor" sports—those that are non-revenue producing—disproportionately felt the sting. In 1998 Sports Illustrated relayed that Providence College was terminating three men's programs in an "effort to comply with Title IX, the federal antidiscrimination law that requires, among other things, that athletes representing a college reflect the female-male ratio of the student body." Not only was the statement inaccurate in light of Title IX's compliance requirements, it also cited cuts to men's sports as the only solution to satisfy Title IX and ensure the "ladies first" requirement.[28]

Sports Illustrated's Ivan Maisel looked to combat this line of thinking in 2000. He assured college administrators that "Title IX need not be a death sentence for men's minor sports": "The way to enhance women's sports without killing men's programs is as obvious as it is politically unpalatable: arms control talks. Football coaches insist that the 85-scholarship limit is their absolute minimum. They might be believed if their predecessors hadn't said the same thing when the number was 105 and again when it was 95. . . . If football's limit was 75, those 10 extra scholarships could pay for two swimming coaches." Maisel's solution was not new. Almost two decades earlier, Alexander Wolff had suggested making changes to college football, including reducing the number of roster spots. He argued in 1982 that devoting 100+ slots to football players was ludicrous, especially when only sixty-five could travel to away games, and particularly in comparison with NFL teams that were limited to rosters of only forty-seven. Both Wolff and Maisel encouraged institutions to rethink their current priorities and sought to show how Title IX could be enforced without functioning as a death sentence to men's "minor sports" like wrestling. SI Women's Susan Casey reinforced that idea in 2002: "While it is depressingly true that more than 170 men's wrestling programs have disappeared in the past 20 years (along with other lower-profile men's programs), Title IX didn't cause their demise. Title IX does not tell universities how to spend their sports budgets, it just says that both sexes must get equal access to the resources."[29] Regardless of such strong and oft-repeated statements, cutting college football expenses—the number of scholarships, coaches' salaries, roster spots, and the funding given over to facilities—was simply a nonstarter for most institutions. Having failed to exempt college football from Title IX when Congress passed the legislation in 1972, its supporters would remain committed to protecting the popular behemoth, no matter the cost.

Part of their defense involved controlling the narrative, and they got an assist from Sports Illustrated. Even when the magazine found that the decline in men's minor sports resulted from athletic departments and budgets prioritizing football and urged a reexamination of athletic budget dispersals, popular columnists like Rick Reilly resorted to familiar tropes that Title IX "has caused brutal cuts in men's sports over the past 30 years." In response, an exasperated reader took him to task: "For the umpteenth time, let's set the record straight. Reilly states that 'Title IX has caused brutal cuts in men's sports over the past 30 years.' Not true. It's the men who run athletic programs who make the decisions to cut men's programs in order to protect the sacred cow of football. Title IX merely assures that women have the opportunity to participate. Nowhere does the law say that men must have diminished opportunities in order for women to play. Please keep the two issues separate."[30] But like Reilly, most Americans could not separate them even in the 2000s, when the early and consistent messaging held that the law represented a harbinger of doom for men's sports.

This was even more notable because, in the same issue that he conflated Title IX and the decline in men's sports, Reilly was the rare reporter who acknowledged that female athletes had "suffered for 100 years without [Title IX]." Nevertheless, political opponents, fixated on Title IX representing a quota system, felt that the rights of a few females who *might* want to play sports were being prioritized over thousands of males who *did* want to play. Once again critics ignored the reality that there were three ways to comply with Title IX, including an option that allowed schools to show that it had accommodated "fully and effectively" the interests of the underrepresented sex; if indeed fewer females wanted to play sports than males, institutions merely needed to prove it. But even as participation rates among females have soared in the three decades since Title IX, males also experienced an increase in their participation levels— 15 percent at the high school level and 31 percent at the collegiate level. Far from drumming men out of the athletic arena or killing men's sports altogether, Title IX has enabled the continued expansion of men's participation rates, even as it made space for sportswomen. But instead of focusing on compliance flexibility and the growing participation rates of both male and female athletes, the emphasis remained on Title IX causing the destruction of men's minor sports and the potential weakening of college football programs.[31]

Despite continued opposition to Title IX, *Sports Illustrated*'s Alexander Wolff celebrated its twentieth anniversary in 1992, characterizing it as "supremely reasonable. It doesn't frown on differences in interest, only on disparity in accommodation. Title IX mandates *equity,* not *equality.*" And whether or not you agreed with such an explanation, "It's the law, and it's backed by a threat to withhold federal funds from schools that flout it." Wolff went on to admonish those who would oppose Title IX, asking, "Isn't it kind of pathetic that we need any prodding to provide women with the same educational opportunities we provide for men?" This was especially true given the astronomical rise in participation rates among females, which showed, according to Wolff, "how overdue Title IX was."[32] While a quantitative measure was important—and the numbers were impressive—there were other, equally significant qualitative measures of the law's success. Some were felt immediately, while others became apparent as the years passed by.

"Bearing the Fruit of the Passage of Title IX"

By the time the thirtieth anniversary of Title IX rolled around, female participation rates in sport were simply staggering. *Sports Illustrated*'s Susan Casey reported that "in 1972, 1 in 27 high school girls participated in sports. That number has now risen more than tenfold, to 1 in 2.5." What was particularly remarkable was that the number of females playing sports reached and then exceeded the two million mark by 1977—five years after Congress first passed the law, and two years after the rules and regulations had been ironed out.[33] Such a dramatic rise in such a short period of time belied the assertions of some Title IX detractors who had insisted that the issue was not about female access to sport—it was that females did not want to play in the first place.

And the news was just as impressive on the collegiate front. According to Casey, "There are 3,714 more distaff programs at university campuses across America then there were 20 years ago," providing opportunities for almost 167,000 women to play at the collegiate level. More women were thus participating in more sports in college than ever before, but some sports benefited more than others.[34] In an effort to comply with Title IX, a number of colleges and universities added varsity women's crew programs as well as teams in golf, ice hockey, and wrestling. But perhaps the greatest beneficiary of Title IX was women's soccer.

In 1971, a mere 700 girls played high school soccer. By 1990, that number was approaching 150,000 and *SI* was referring to the University of North Carolina women's soccer team as a "major minor"—a sports dynasty in a non-major collegiate sport. Five years later, *Sports Illustrated* acknowledged Michelle Akers as the "best female player in the world," but she was relatively unknown; that didn't change even after Akers led the

U.S. women's team to a victory in the inaugural Women's World Cup in 1991. Yet their achievement received zero coverage in SI. In fact, it was not until the 1996 Summer Olympics in Atlanta that the magazine recognized the sport and its athletes, describing the first women's Olympic soccer final as "a red-letter date," especially given that 76,481 spectators looked on, "the largest [crowd] ever to see a women's sporting event in the U.S."[35]

While the Americans won the coveted Olympic gold medal in 1996, it was their performance in the 1999 Women's World Cup that exploded expectations and stereotypes associated with a woman's team sport. Over 90,000 people attended the Women's World Cup soccer final in the Rose Bowl, but perhaps just as important were the 2,100 media personnel who covered the tournament—or, according to SI, "2,099 more than greeted the team in 1991." The magazine concluded that the United States was now "women's soccer country. Every other sport . . . is just trying to keep up." Eight years earlier, that women played soccer at all on the national level had barely registered with the American people and the sports media; by 1999, Sports Illustrated was calling the women's play "breathtaking," and Americans were taking pride in a team that "had gone from near obscurity to a national conversation piece in just three weeks." Fans and journalists alike had been captivated by the play of both the Americans and the Chinese in the final. After ninety minutes of regulation time and two fifteen-minute overtimes, the game remained a scoreless tie. When the American team won the match on penalty kicks, the country was smitten, and Sports Illustrated was jubilant. And SI was not alone. Steve Rushin noted that the women's team had netted not only an SI cover but ones for Time, Newsweek, and People as well. Curiously, Rushin saw this as worrying, since "this tidal wave of coverage . . . threatened to drown out any and all other women in sports."[36] Given the paucity of media attention focused on female athletes, that was an unintended and troubling consequence, but of far greater concern was that women's soccer would not be able to sustain such coverage.

Yet even after the World Cup had concluded, Sports Illustrated continued to celebrate the team's achievements, placing them among their twenty favorite teams of all time—the only all-female squad included—and celebrating them as their choice for Sportswomen of the Year. In the accompanying article, SI's Michael Bamberger wrote: "The Women's World Cup was competition at its most vibrant and the final took your breath away. It fused two often ignored elements of American sports, women and soccer, into one transformative moment, and held a nation in thrall. What will forever be remembered about the match at the Rose Bowl is the intensity and spirit with which the American and Chinese women played. The U.S. team, with its spellbinding victory, reminded us of the highest purpose of sport: to inspire." And they had inspired many. Over 650,000 fans attended the three-week tournament, and over 40 million Americans watched the games on television. *SI*'s mail also reflected the personal impact that the World Cup had had on its audience. One male reader from Colorado wrote: "Before the Women's World Cup, I did not pay much attention to women's sports, but the U.S. team showed me why women's sports deserve more respect."[37] It was a paradigm shift of simply mammoth proportions. Women's sports had entered the American mainstream thanks to a women's national soccer team that played fabulous soccer and did so with a poise and passion (and a femininity) that corporate sponsors, American sports fans, and *Sports Illustrated* could not ignore. Here was a team that garnered increased visibility and respect for all women's sports, even as it transcended gendered distinctions altogether. The big question, of course, was whether the sports media, Madison Avenue, and American sports fans would continue to invest in women's soccer and women's sports more broadly, or if this was a one-off, never to be repeated.

The American soccer players who won the 1999 World Cup and charmed a nation represented a Title IX generation that had come of age. Since its passage in 1972, Title IX has guaranteed thousands of women access to athletic opportunities. Yet, *SI* ignored the effects of the law on the '99ers' triumph, and its readers noted the omission: "Thanks for your cover story on the U.S. Women's World Cup soccer victory. I was surprised that you made no mention of the role Title IX played in this victory or the fact that Title IX became law the same year that Mia Hamm was born (1972). It is important to remember that while it was the teams' [sic] outstanding play that brought home the World Cup, it was Title IX that opened the door to make it all possible." *SI*'s Bamberger corrected the oversight when he honored the team as *SI*'s Sportswomen of the Year. He viewed the team's success as the ultimate legacy of Title IX, comparing it to the night when Billie Jean King defeated Bobby Riggs:

> It was the most significant day in the history of women's sports, bearing the fruit of the passage of Title IX in 1972 and surpassing by a long shot that burn-your-bra night in '73 when Billie Jean King beat Bobby

The "'99ers" seemed to embody a Title IX generation that had come of age.

Riggs, the late goofball showman, in a made-for-TV tennis spectacle at the Houston Astrodome. That night's drama, of course, required the services of a man. The three-act play performed at the Rose Bowl—the game, the overtime, the shootout—required nothing but women, 40 of them (44 if you want to include the match's four officials). In the final summer of the 20th century, the era of the woman in sports finally arrived.[38]

Even as *SI* celebrated the '99ers and the impact of Title IX on women's sports, its juxtaposition of King's triumph and Title IX conflated the two.

Yet those events were dramatically different, especially in their connection to Title IX. The '99ers were Title IX babies; they had grown up during an era of Title IX protections and directly benefited from the funding that high schools and colleges invested in their sports programs. But if Brandi Chastain's game-winning penalty kick "was an iconic expression of the ideals behind the law that sparked a women's sports revolution," Billie Jean King's straight-sets win over Bobby Riggs was inconsequential where Title IX was concerned. Indeed, historian Susan Ware has noted that "Title IX was never mentioned in all the voluminous coverage the match received"; it simply did not feature in the media devoted to the King-Riggs hoopla, of which there had been much. That was particularly true for *SI*, which devoted several articles to the pre-match festivities but did not frame a King victory as proof of Title IX's merit. In addition, while King had to play—and win—in a sequin-studded sports spectacle against a man, the '99ers could engage in "vibrant" and "breathtaking" competition against other women, with nary a sequin in sight, underscoring the many serious opportunities females now enjoyed to contest sport. No longer, it seemed, did women have to "worry about" competing with men to gain visibility and admiration in what *SI* deemed "gender-bending sideshows."[39] The '99ers' achievement conveyed an acceptance of women in American sports and American society that was made possible by Title IX.

"Unique in Its Focus on Women in Sports"

Although *Sports Illustrated* was slower than some readers would have liked in making the connection between Title IX and the '99ers' success, *SI* was quick to highlight the importance of the law when it launched a magazine specifically tailored to women. *Sports Illustrated Women/Sport* appeared on newsstands in April 1997 and was *Sports Illustrated*'s "response to both the explosive growth of female participation in sports since the passage of Title IX 25 years ago—in 1971 one of 27 girls participated in high school sports; today, one of three does—and to the burgeoning popularity of women's sports among fans." Title IX had created both the reason and the audience for the new magazine, and in some ways the career arc of its editor, Sandra Bailey: "As a member of the pre-Title IX generation," *Sports Illustrated* president Donald M. Elliman Jr. noted, "Bailey shied away from covering women's sports when she began her career as a sportswriter." But

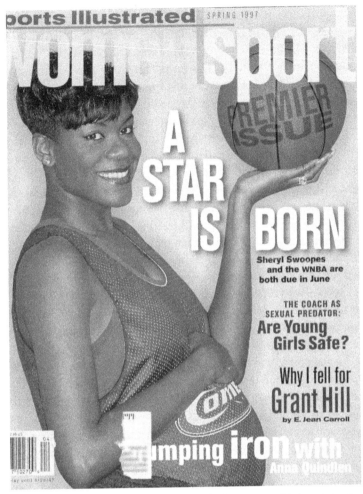

As a result of Title IX, millions of females had participated in sports by the law's twenty-fifth anniversary. *Sports Illustrated* viewed them as the perfect audience for a new magazine that specifically targeted sportswomen.

it was clear that "Bailey's attitude, like that of society at large, has changed." The result was *Sports Illustrated Women/Sport*, and Elliman asserted that the change in attitude—and seemingly the new magazine itself—were both "long overdue."[40]

While the president of *Sports Illustrated* saw the creation of the new magazine as "unique in its focus on women in sports," *Sports Illustrated*

Women/Sport was not a new idea. Billie Jean King's magazine *womenSports* had appeared in 1974 in direct response to the dearth of female athletes appearing in *SI*. But if *SI Women/Sport* was not necessarily "unique" in focusing on female athletes, it was unlike anything *Sports Illustrated* had published before. That was true not just in its content and the centering of sportswomen but in its approach. According to Bailey, it prioritized what women wanted to read, which she characterized as "the human side of the story." The actual layout of the magazine looked different as well. The first issue of *SI Women/Sport* was taller and wider than *SI*, with a glossy cover that piqued the curiosity of its readers with articles entitled "Why I Fell for Grant Hill." Its *Cosmo*-like quality was not lost on pundits; a week after the magazine first appeared, *New York Times* columnist Robert Lipsyte called the new publication a "proud fanzine" that was "slick, smart and heterosexual enough" to keep the men happy without being threatened.[41]

Yet after just two "test issues," publication of *SI Women/Sport* was suspended without explanation despite plans to move to a monthly publication in 1998. Two years later, *SI* introduced *Sports Illustrated for Women*, which retained both Sandra Bailey as editor and a glossy cover. Appearing quarterly and offering readers their athletic horoscope, the magazine sought to appeal to a wide range of women who wanted to enjoy "what is best about sports . . . whether you are trying to make the cut for the high school basketball team, playing college soccer or staying fit by running or playing tennis on weekends." While *SI for Women* (later renamed *SI Women* in September 2001) ultimately enjoyed a circulation rate of 400,000 subscribers and was hailed as progress, questions that Robert Lipsyte had asked upon the release of *SI Women/Sport* in 1997 were still relevant for *Sports Illustrated for Women* in 1999. Lipsyte had considered the ramifications of a sports magazine that was exclusively about and for women and wondered: "What does it all mean? That women have entered the mainstream sports consciousness or that they are being ghettoized? And is it possible that the ghetto is better?" Sports sociologist Michael Messner addressed this issue in 2002, noting that while *Sports Illustrated for Women* "can be viewed as a sign of progress for women's sports," it also left *SI* "off the hook in terms of any obligation its publishers and editors might otherwise have felt to incorporate more and better women's sports reporting."[42]

While *Sports Illustrated for Women* allowed writers to focus on the issues, concerns, and needs relevant to sportswomen, the magazine *did* marginalize sportswomen and set them off as "the Other." For decades, the achievements of female athletes have been qualified because of their gender, with the assumption being that sports were masculine activities unless otherwise noted. In schools across the country, women's teams and leagues have had to qualify their titles by adding "lady" in front of team names or "ettes" following them, yet their male counterparts have no such modification; likewise, *Sports Illustrated*'s women's magazine, *Sports Illustrated Women*, needed to be qualified.[43] In addition, sportswomen's coverage in *Sports Illustrated*, which was already meager, now declined even further. In 2001, for example, when *Sports Illustrated Women* enjoyed its highest production rate to date of eight issues per year, *Sports Illustrated* included just five articles that solely focused on women in sports, including one that followed up with the original 1972 Dallas Cowboy cheerleaders. The cheerleaders were on the cover of that issue—just one of two covers that depicted females in 2001; the other featured Elsa Benitez "Heat[ing] up Tunisia" in that year's swimsuit issue.

The shunting of female athletes by *SI* into a separate magazine, instead of simply increasing the number of pages in the original to include more coverage of sportswomen, underscored *SI*'s begrudging coverage of sportswomen. That was particularly the case in 2002 when Time Inc. decided to shutter *Sports Illustrated Women*, citing a particularly "lousy economic climate." By that time, *SI Women* had shifted its focus from covering amateur and professional female athletes to becoming a fitness magazine. Thus, what seemed to serve as evidence of Title IX's success—a separate *SI* magazine specifically for sportswomen—was more a confirmation of the antagonism toward female athletes who were taking up greater percentages of athletic budgets and demanding additional space in sports media. It also exposed the limits of Title IX. While the law could mandate athletic equity in terms of teams, coaches, and facilities, it had no control over the amount, or the type, of media coverage sportswomen received. It was an issue that *SI*'s Rick Reilly had acknowledged in his usual garrulous style in 2003: "If you are a woman, there are only three ways to get the sports world to notice you: 1. Strip down to your panties and bra and wrestle over beer. 2. Play crappy tennis but look hot pulling the second ball out of your briefs. 3. Tweak Hootie's nose. Break records? Win at unthinkable rates? Push the envelope of female athletic achievement? Forget it, sweetheart! How 'bout a boob job?"[44] Reilly provided numerous ways in which the sports media—including *Sports Illustrated*—continued to marginalize and ignore sportswomen. And there were other drawbacks that, unintended or not, served to limit Title IX's goal of promoting gender equity in sport.

"Still, There's Work to Do"

In addition to mandating equality of opportunity in sports for women, Title IX also required equitable facilities, competition schedules, and coaching. As the law increased women's participation, it did the same for coaching opportunities and coaches' salaries. Gilbert and Williamson had noted that, before Title IX, "with few exceptions, women who coach girls' sports in secondary schools receive between one-third and one-half the salary of men who coach comparable sports for boys." In addition, "the woman coach often is expected to supervise candy sales, cooking contests and raffles to raise money to purchase the girls' uniforms and pay travel expenses." It was a situation the legendary Pat Summitt had known only too well; having signed on to coach the University of Tennessee women's basketball program in 1974, she not only coached the team but "taped ankles, washed uniforms and drove the team van." *SI* deplored the unfairness, asserting that coaches of women's teams should "receive equal pay and responsibilities and enjoy equal working conditions."[45]

Title IX guaranteed the end of a second shift for coaches of women's teams. But, as *SI* noted in 1988, "ironically, the growth of women's programs hasn't resulted in a proportional increase in jobs for female coaches." In fact, it had inadvertently caused the opposite outcome; due to an increase in salaries and in prestige, men were now much more interested in coaching women's teams. And the results of such a shift were dramatic. In 1972 women accounted for 90 percent of the coaches of women's college teams; twenty years later, they accounted for only 48 percent. *Sports Illustrated* described collegiate female coaches' coaching prospects at this time as "especially bleak," noting that one of the "surprising results of Title IX has been the gradual disappearance of women from the ranks of college coaches." The forecast was that "if the trend continues, in another 20 years there may be *no* women coaches at the college level." While that dire prediction did not play out, *SI* acknowledged on the fortieth anniversary of Title IX that, even with all of Title IX's gains, "still, there's work to do." This was particularly true for coaching, both in terms of increasing the number of women coaches at the collegiate level and the salaries of coaches for women's teams.[46] And it was especially true for coaches of color.

In 2020 Black women represented only 2 percent of head coaches and athletic directors. It was in sharp contrast to white women, who represented 21 percent of all NCAA coaches, and 19 percent of athletic directors—and to men, who represented 77 percent of all NCAA coaches and 79 percent of athletic directors. And the numbers were not much better for collegiate Black sportswomen, who enjoyed prominence in Division I outdoor track and field (42.7 percent) and basketball (66.5 percent) but were essentially invisible in lacrosse, swimming, and soccer.[47] It was not a new issue.

As early as 2005, scholar Jennifer E. Bruening had found that "while Title IX has provided countless opportunities for White women in sports like rowing, soccer, and lacrosse, increases in the representation of Black women has not happened." In 2012 William C. Rhoden investigated the impact of Title IX on Black sportswomen for the *New York Times* and echoed many of Bruening's findings. In sharing the results of a 2007 report by the U.S. Department of Education, Rhoden observed that except in Division I basketball, where Black women made up 50.6 percent of the athletes, and in indoor and outdoor track and field, where they represented around 27 percent, they were underrepresented in most varsity sports: "They are all but missing in lacrosse (2.2 percent), swimming (2.0), soccer (5.3) and softball (8.2)." According to Dionne Koller, director of the Center for Sport and Law, "race [was] by far the most debilitating limitation of Title IX," and as a result the law was "not the effective tool it has been made out to be for leveling the playing field for all girls. There is unfinished business, but we're not talking about it."[48]

That changed in 2012 when, as Rhoden reported, "20 African-American women with various connections to athletics" convened a forum "to tackle the vexing issues of gender and race. The topic was 'What's Not Being Said About the Title IX Anniversary.'" While Rhoden noted that Title IX had "been monumental in women's and girls' sports participation," the focus of the law had been "gender equity, not racial equity in women's sports," with "the most glaring outcome of the legislation" being that white women "have been the overwhelming beneficiaries." The symposium attracted Benita Fitzgerald Mosley, an Olympian and chairwoman of the board of the Women's Sports Foundation, who wanted to explore the "widening gap of opportunity separating white women and nonwhite women." Also in attendance was Tina Sloan Green, cofounder and president of the Black Women in Sport Foundation and the first Black head coach in women's lacrosse, who wanted to use the occasion to "make sure" that Black sportswomen "tell our own story." Black women needed to be their own advocates, and she insisted that "we have to be the first ones at the table. We have to have some proactive measure for making sure there [are] increased numbers of African-Americans. We've got to take charge of our agenda."[49]

While both women had similar goals, their conclusions were different. Fitzgerald Mosley determined "that the inequality of opportunities was an unintentional blind spot that could be corrected with good will." For Sloan Green, "there was a sense . . . that the gap was in some ways a moat designed to protect white privilege, opportunity and power." Sloan Green believed the gap was no "accident," especially because "the value of sports is not only the physical and the mental, but it's also valuable in terms of preparing you for an administrative opportunity, especially with sport being a multibillion-dollar business." Regardless of their stance, both women drew important attention to the fact that Title IX was not, in the words of scholar Jenny Lind Withycombe, "colorblind." Building off the work of renowned sociologist Patricia Hill Collins, Withycombe asserted that "the more blind we are to the ways race functions in US society, the more blind we become to white privilege and the more we silence the voices at the margins to reinforce the idea that gender, race, sexual orientation, and/or class do not affect people's opportunities and experiences."[50]

There was no question that Black female athletes derived value from Title IX. Fitzgerald Mosley acknowledged as much when she credited the law with granting "a whole host of African-American women" college scholarships, thereby enabling them to earn college degrees. But she also asserted that white female athletes, particularly white suburban female athletes, disproportionately benefited from the law. It was a reality that leading '99er Brianna Scurry—one of two women of color on a national team that was, according to the goalie, "historically as white as a bedsheet"—acknowledged when she noted the lack of diversity in U.S. women's soccer. "The two biggest obstacles" to achieving racial equity in women's sport, she maintained, were "accessibility and cost."[51]

Ignoring the importance of race was, according to Dionne Koller, "an old way of thinking about inequality, in which gender was the model. The only model." She asserted that such an approach was indicative of second-wave feminism, which was "stuck in a 1970s version of the equality axis of oppression, especially as experienced by women and girls of color. In the work force, we've moved on; in our equality thinking, we've moved on. But in the sports construct, we've stayed at the 1970s thinking that it's one way, it's gender inequality, and that's it." This stance represented a feminist agenda that did not consider other kinds of oppressions such as sexuality and, most importantly, race. While some Black women like Pauli Murray and Florynce Kennedy figured prominently in the women's liberation movement, it was opposition to a middle-class, straight, white woman's agenda that inspired other Black women to explore a feminism that was uniquely their own; the Combahee River Collective statement in 1977 and Alice Walker's expression of "Womanism" in 1979 are examples of Black women seeking to assert the importance of their experiences and voices. As second-wave feminism gave way to third-wave feminism in the early 1990s, feminists prioritized the different experiences of women, embracing intersectionality—a term coined by Kimberlé Crenshaw in 1989 to express the overlapping oppressions particularly experienced by Black women which, because of their sex and race, uniquely affected the societal barriers they faced.[52]

It was an angle that *Sports Illustrated* simply did not address. In 1968 *SI* had devoted five consecutive issues to sussing out the inequalities that Black sportsmen encountered at all levels of sport, but that series did not address the plight of the Black female athlete. In 1973 the magazine devoted three consecutive issues to exploring the discrimination sportswomen encountered, but, likewise, the unique oppressions experienced by Black women were not discussed. The last time *Sports Illustrated* addressed issues of equality where Black sportswomen were concerned was in 1956 when the magazine relayed Althea Gibson's struggle to break the color barrier in amateur tennis in 1950.[53] But in that instance, Gibson was a Black athlete breaking a color barrier in sport in the mold of Jackie Robinson, not a Black woman experiencing discrimination because of both her race and her sex. Black women and the unique challenges they encountered were all but invisible.

As Rhoden intimated, that conversation was long overdue, especially when the unchallenged assumption about Title IX was that its effects—at least for female athletes—had been uniformly positive. As Title IX moved from the late twentieth into the early twenty-first century, and feminism moved from second wave into the third wave, the demand for an intersectional approach to feminism in all its guises was more important than ever.

"A Watershed Moment"

On the fortieth anniversary of Title IX, *Sports Illustrated* celebrated by releasing a cover with the law's famous thirty-seven words emblazoned across it. In addition, *SI* once again remembered "when Billie beat Bobby." L. Jon Wertheim found that the "made-for-TV referendum on gender equity" was "at once, a cultural touchstone and a bit of cultural schlock, a watershed moment that came wrapped in gold lame and glitter." Wertheim noted that King won not only on the tennis court but "in the court of

Sports Illustrated celebrated the fortieth anniversary of Title IX with a cover devoted to it—literally. The law's first thirty-seven words were emblazoned across the May 7, 2012, edition.

public opinion." Curious as that might seem to sports fans four decades later, King reminded Wertheim that "you have to remember where we were as a society."[54] It was an America that had just started to see the effects of the women's movement emerge in laws that would allow a measure of reproductive freedom, protections against domestic violence, and access to equal credit and equal pay.

But while King's win in the Battle of the Sexes was hard fought and well publicized, it had very little to do with Title IX.[55] And the focus on the King-Riggs match as a "watershed moment" in Title IX history detracts from the actions of those who made sure that the law was enforced and remained on the books. With over fifty articles dedicated to Title IX's guidelines, challenges, and successes, *SI* did provide important facts and commentary and became an important venue for readers to share their support for and their opposition to the law. But a focus on the Battle of the Sexes as an important moment in Title IX history served to diminish a long history of activism in women's sports and to distract from an ongoing need for Title IX's enforcement.

Indeed, it was a form of "symbolic annihilation," a term coined by George Gerbner in 1976 to describe the absence of representation, or the underrepresentation, of certain people in the media. Gerbner noted the ways in which the media promoted stereotypes about groups and denied them specific identities as a way to marginalize them based on their race, sex, class, and sexual orientation; it resulted from a conscious decision designed to maintain social inequalities. Two years later, Gaye Tuchman expanded on the concept, seeing symbolic annihilation as marginalizing communities in three different ways: trivializing or vilifying their achievements, or simply making them invisible. *SI*'s Bil Gilbert and Nancy Williamson had seen symbolic annihilation at work several years before the term was coined. In 1973, in the first installment of their three-part series exploring how sport was unfair to women, Gilbert and Williamson asserted that "the amount of coverage given to women's athletics is meager and the quality is atrocious. Most of the stories that do appear are generally in the man-bites-dog journalistic tradition, the gist of them being that here is an unusual and mildly humorous happening—a girl playing games."[56]

Gilbert and Williamson singled out *Sports Illustrated* in particular for focusing on sportswomen's attractiveness as opposed to their athleticism. Rick Reilly would return to that issue thirty years later when he called out the media, including *SI*, for ignoring the noteworthy achievements of female athletes. It was a trend that only continued in the magazine's coverage of Title IX, when it sought to marginalize the law's effects by conflating it with Billie Jean King's Battle of the Sexes victory, which simply had no bearing on Title IX. Indeed, Susan Ware has noted that "when Billie beat Bobby, she wasn't carrying the banner for Title IX precisely because the law was not yet associated with women's sports in the popular mind." And Billie Jean King was not the only sportswoman whose accomplishments *SI* conflated with Title IX. On the thirtieth anniversary of the law, *SI* regarded it as "a fitting time to catch up with a foursome who went where no woman had gone before," focusing on Roberta Gibb, who competed in the Boston Marathon unofficially in 1968 and 1969; Kathryn Massar, who played Little League baseball; Pam Postema, who became the first female umpire to call a Triple A Minor League Baseball game; and Manon Rheaume, the first woman to play in an NHL preseason game.[57] Like Billie Jean King beating Bobby Riggs, these were impressive feats—and they had no bearing whatsoever on Title IX compliance.

When the Yale women's crew actually carried that Title IX banner—on their own persons no less—*SI* failed to cover the women's demand for shower facilities. But while showers were the catalyst, the Yale women wanted more than just basic amenities. They used their Title IX protest to assert that they were "not just healthy young things in blue and white uniforms who perform feats of strength for Yale in the nice spring weather; we are not just statistics on your win column. We're human and being treated as less than such."[58] It was a powerful statement about the power of Title IX to transform in ways that transcended equitable facilities, coaching, and scholarship dollars, but a point that *Sports Illustrated* simply did not recognize until decades after the fact.

While the magazine ultimately acknowledged the Yale women and the ways they had confronted sexism, *SI*'s record in detailing the unique condition of Black sportswomen who battled both sexism and racism was downright dismal. Years after Crenshaw first coined the term "intersectionality" in 1989, the magazine has yet to explore the ways in which Title IX has disadvantaged female athletes of color. Indeed *SI*'s anniversary celebrations have privileged the achievements of white women—be they relevant or not. From Billie Jean King to the 1976 Yale women's crew team to the 1999 World Cup–winning women's soccer team, white women were overwhelmingly the stories and faces of Title IX. By the fortieth anniversary,

Black female athletes appeared in the magazine's photo spread, and Lisa Leslie joined Mia Hamm and Summer Sanders as the "Spirits of '72," but a focus on the support provided by "Father Figures" figured more prominently in *SI*'s coverage than the challenges faced by Black sportswomen.[59]

Finally, *Sports Illustrated* often served as a platform to condemn Title IX and its main beneficiary: women's sports. It gave space to Title IX critics who associated the law with "impending doom" and frequently made the assertion that women's sports were brought into being at the expense of men's sports—particularly men's minor sports.[60] Title IX and female athletes were the evil villains in a plot in which males who *did* want to play sports were deprived of the ability to do so on the premise that females *might* want to play sports. In the pages of *SI*, the quotas Title IX required for compliance—at least according to the lawyers for Brown University—were roundly castigated. And then there was football, which some members of the U.S. Congress and the executive director of the NCAA tried to exclude from Title IX's purview, believing that the sport's ability to generate revenue (although not necessarily a profit) meant that it should be exempted from having to settle for an equitable dispersal of funds which still allowed millions of dollars to be spent on 100-person football rosters. As late as 1995, the College Football Association and the American Football Coaches Association were lobbying Speaker of the House Dennis Hastert for preferential treatment that would free them from having to comply with Title IX guidelines.[61]

As *Sports Illustrated* celebrated the fiftieth anniversary of Title IX, reporter Maggie Mertens found that the old trope about Title IX "killing men's sports" is a "fear that is still well worn, with athletic directors and coaches from 1972 to today claiming that big moneymakers for schools like men's football and basketball shouldn't have to share money with less profitable (read: women's) sports." Mertens found that most people still regarded Title IX compliance as "a zero-sum game": any allocations to women simply meant less for men. But in June 2022, Mertens earmarked encouraging signs of progress. College football players have certainly benefited the most from name, image, and likeness deals, but it's women's college basketball players who have snagged second place, suggesting that "women's teams may be worth more than we've been led to believe." When Sedona Prince's TikTok video of the women's "weight room" at the 2021 NCAA women's basketball tournament went viral, it evoked Title IX violations of years past. "But," according to Mertens, "this time people cared."

She acknowledged that "though not universal, maybe it's these shifts in how women are viewed that are the truly celebratory results of Title IX."[62]

Occasions for celebration are important, but vigilance and activism remain essential, especially when Title IX is in constant need of defense and enforcement—decades after it was first enacted. In 2013 Quinnipiac University had to commit to "significant" improvements, including identifying two women's teams as "sports of emphasis," adding more coaches of women's sports, offering more scholarships to female athletes, and providing better facilities. Also in 2013, the University of Southern California committed to providing equal facilities for the women's crew team after a fourteen-year investigation by the Office for Civil Rights, the government agency tasked with policing Title IX compliance. In both cases, the plaintiffs prevailed but only after protracted, multiyear battles. This was indicative of Title IX lawsuits—while plaintiffs often won their cases, verdicts were rendered long after those who had brought the suit had graduated; Amy Cohen brought her suit against Brown in 1991, only to see the Supreme Court rule in 1997—five years after she had graduated. Justice could be had, but most claimants realized that their activism would benefit not themselves but future generations of women.

Also, while direct action is necessary to hold institutions accountable for Title IX noncompliance, a similar kind of activism is needed to pressure the Office for Civil Rights to withhold funds from institutions that are not Title IX compliant. And there are many. As of 2021, some 75 percent of colleges and universities receiving federal funds have not satisfied the parameters of Title IX, yet the Office for Civil Rights has never withheld funds from any institution as a penalty for their failure.[63] It seems clear that not only do colleges and universities need to be held accountable, but the federal government also needs to be pressured to discipline these institutions when appropriate. The failure to do so has allowed schools to believe that there will be no reprisals for their actions. As Title IX celebrates its golden anniversary, a new generation of activists is needed to demand enforcement and to require penalties when appropriate.

Some of those activists will come from the most unexpected places. WNBA star Lisa Leslie recognized in 2012 that "'going to college on a full scholarship, playing in the Olympics might never have happened for me without [Title IX]. I was lucky to have it in place during my era. I don't consider myself an activist, but it's important I try to help other young women the way that the people who pushed for Title IX helped me.'" After a short pause, she added, "'Maybe I am an activist.'" Born in 1972, Lisa Leslie was a Title IX baby who recognized that "Title IX has made the biggest difference of all."[64]

The effects of Title IX were experienced in a number of unintended and unexpected ways, including the decline in women's coaches, and in the increase in injuries sportswomen suffered. Indeed, because more females were now playing athletics than ever before, they were becoming susceptible to a concomitant rise in injuries related to their participation. Such a consequence resulted in greater concern about whether women could survive the rigors of sport or whether they were victims—if not of their biological limitations, then of cultural constructions that regarded them as lacking the strength, both physical and mental, that for male athletes was both innate and intrinsic.

4

"The Frailty Myth"

In the September/October 2000 issue of *Sports Illustrated for Women*, contributor Meesha Diaz Haddad reviewed what she considered two "required readings" for subscribers: *Chamique*, an autobiography written by college basketball star (and future WNBA great) Chamique Holdsclaw, and *The Frailty Myth*, by best-selling author Colette Dowling. Haddad regarded Holdsclaw's story, published the year after she graduated from the University of Tennessee, as "top-notch inspiration for the college set," and found that *The Frailty Myth* "convincingly debunks" the centuries-old "myth that women are the weaker sex."[1]

Those books garnered another tandem review almost simultaneously in *Sports Illustrated*, but Charles Hirshberg's assessment was more mixed. While both Holdsclaw and Dowling offered insights into "women and sports," they represented contrasting interpretations. Hirshberg found Holdsclaw's optimism about the current state of women and sport to be inspirational; women were accepted and respected as muscled athletes and even desired, not just by the opposite sex but by Madison Avenue as well. As a result, it was "a surreal experience" for Hirshberg to then read *The Frailty Myth*. Dowling insisted that women were still not welcome in sport, and that men took every opportunity to undermine them so that they appeared physically inferior to their male counterparts. Hirshberg was not impressed. He asserted that Dowling relied too much "on gender studies from the 1980s and early '90s, well before the explosion in women's athletics at the end of the century," and that she was downright "paranoid" about the media intentionally diminishing sportswomen. Overall, she had written a "boring" book in which she "drones on, asserting what almost everyone knows: 'that the difference between boys' and girls' performance levels may be greatly influenced by societal expectations.'"[2]

It was hard not to agree with Hirshberg, at least as far as Holdsclaw was concerned. Chamique Holdsclaw had dominated college basketball during her time at Tennessee. During her four years, she had won the NCAA championship three times, rewriting the Tennessee record books with her scoring and rebounding talents. She won both the Naismith and Sulli-van Awards for the most outstanding female college basketball player and the most outstanding amateur athlete, respectively, and secured what was perhaps an even greater prize: a multiyear, multimillion-dollar deal with Nike that had her poised to become the highest paid female athlete ever.

There was no question that Holdsclaw had been successful, but some-thing was keeping other sportswomen from fully realizing their potential. According to Dowling, it was a cultural belief, centuries in the making, that associated women with weakness and incompetence. She insisted, "The myth of women's frailty has been so systematically entrenched that it could fairly be called a hoax. But a hoax is a conscious deceit, while myths are believed in as truth. What propels them is complicated and in-visible." *SI*'s own Bil Gilbert and Nancy Williamson had recognized such a situation in their 1973 groundbreaking three-part series. The authors con-cluded that "most people, if they think about it at all, consider sport risky and inessential for girls." Because such deep-seated attitudes were just then being questioned, Gilbert and Williamson found it "difficult to assess how good American female athletes might be if they were offered athletic facilities, support and encouragement even roughly comparable to what men receive."[3] It was an idea Mary Wollstonecraft had raised back in the eighteenth century, when she asserted that women's physical capabilities could not be fairly evaluated until they enjoyed the same opportunities as men. Thus Dowling's reference to the long-standing notion of female inferiority being unfairly assumed was historically accurate, but decidedly unpopular.

Hirshberg was not alone in preferring Holdsclaw's story, one of Title IX dreams fully realized, as opposed to a litany of remaining barriers that prevented women's physical equality. But the struggles Dowling de-scribed, sadly, were not so different from those experienced during the late nineteenth and early twentieth centuries. At that time, medical profes-sionals regarded women's participation in sport as harmful and injurious. Fainting couches and rest cures became de rigueur, especially for (white, wealthy) women whose feeble constitutions included irritable nervous systems that threatened not only their immediate (reproductive) health but the future of a (majority-white) America.[4]

Thus, the "frailty myth" that had held sway during the Victorian era had, according to Dowling, remarkable staying power and remained evident in twenty-first-century sport. And it was especially apparent in

Sports Illustrated throughout its publishing arc. In her book, Dowling recounted specific instances in which *SI* upheld a "male-female hierarchy" that defined male athletes as "real" athletes and particularly successful female athletes as neither "real" athletes nor "real" women. Such a characterization helped "make the myth viable" as "society constructed elaborate ways of keeping women cut off from their strength; of turning them into physical victims and teaching them that victimhood was all they could aspire to." The frailty myth, then, was one that *Sports Illustrated* sustained, and which contributed to an understanding of sports as an activity that was inappropriate or downright unsafe for women.

Particularly important in this discussion was Dowling's reference to women athletes as victims. Michael MacCambridge, who wrote a history of *SI,* has noted that when the magazine featured a female athlete on its cover, she was attractive, had suffered a tragedy, or both. For example, Monica Seles had won eight Grand Slam tennis championships by April 1993, but did not earn an *SI* cover until she had been stabbed; Nancy Kerrigan had won the 1993 U.S. Figure Skating Championships, but did not appear on the cover until she was clubbed on the knee a year later.[5]

On the whole, *Sports Illustrated* tended to portray sportswomen as victims to its largely male readership. Although *SI for Women* was inclined to an opposite approach, its impact was diminished. *SI* enjoyed a weekly subscription rate that was close to five times that of *SI Women,* which appeared only every other month and ceased publication after just five years. As a result, the predominant message *Sports Illustrated* readers received about sportswomen for over a half century was an updated version of the "frailty myth": that female athletes experienced physical debilitation and mental anguish because they were ill suited to withstanding the pressures and vagaries of the sports world. The aforementioned attacks on Monica Seles and Nancy Kerrigan are illustrative on this count; not only did they occur within a year of each other but both incidents garnered extensive coverage in *Sports Illustrated* as reporters tried to make sense of the attacks and what they meant both physically and psychologically to the sportswomen who endured them.

"Savage Assault"

In 1989, at the age of fifteen, Monica Seles joined the professional women's tennis tour, won her first career title, and concluded her first year on the

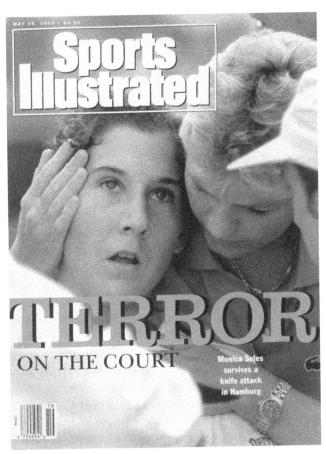

By 1993 Monica Seles had won eight Grand Slam tennis singles
titles, but the nineteen-year-old did not garner a *Sports Illustrated*
cover until she was stabbed during a changeover at a tournament in
Hamburg, Germany.

tour ranked number 6 in the world. Seles was nothing less than a tennis
phenom, and for the next three years she dominated the women's tour,
defeating veterans like Chris Evert and Martina Navratilova, as well as
young stars like Steffi Graf and Arantxa Sánchez Vicario. The numbers
were simply astounding: from 1990 to 1993, she enjoyed a winning percentage of 92.9 percent and, even better, 98 percent at Grand Slams, where
she amassed eight championship titles.[6] As 1993 began, there was talk of
a rivalry with Steffi Graf, but Graf had managed to best Seles in a Grand

Slam championship final only once, doing so at Wimbledon in 1992. Following that defeat, Seles responded by beating Graf at the Australian Open in an epic three-set match in January 1993. It would be the last time Seles would play a Grand Slam tournament for two years.

Three months after her win Down Under, Seles was the victim of a "savage assault" by a "deranged" Steffi Graf fan who, at a tournament in Hamburg, Germany, stabbed Seles in the back during a changeover. "Although the 19-year-old Seles was not seriously injured," *SI* reported, "there was nothing superficial about the wound inflicted on her psyche." Seles had already been "wary of a physical attack," and given that her worst fears had materialized, *Sports Illustrated* asked an important question: Would Seles, following the projected four-week recuperation, be interested in playing again? Graf urged Seles to return to the tour as quickly as possible, noting that the threat of obsessive fans committing violence was "something we all live with. It's the price we have to pay." While *SI* acknowledged that "athletes have been used as pawns by politicians, abused by mobs and taken hostage and slain by terrorists," the magazine observed that "rarely, if ever, has an athlete of Seles's stature been so savagely attacked purely for reasons related to sport."[7] There was no standard playbook for recovery, and for the next two years, the women's professional tennis tour had to manage without its most dominant player.

By 1995 Seles was ready to discuss "her harrowing two years away from tennis" and contemplate a comeback. When her reappearance on the tour failed to materialize, talk of a return gave way to rumors: Seles was not playing to collect an insurance payoff; she was faking it; she was paralyzed with fear when her assailant received a two-year suspended sentence for the attack; she suffered from severe depression. The psychological trauma was very real, as stepping on a tennis court triggered memories of the assault. Seles revealed that "nobody could tell me it would be O.K. because there is no guarantee. The one place I felt safe was a tennis court—and that was taken away from me. . . . And now, this is the place I feel least safe."[8]

Despite her reservations, Seles "made a triumphant return to the court" in August 1995, winning her first tournament in over two years. Five months later, she earned her fourth Australian Open title. With those victories, *Sports Illustrated* reported that Seles's "greatest gift is overcoming tragedy." In truth, however, she remained a shadow of her former self. Although Seles retired officially in 2008, she did not play another tournament after 2003 and did not win another Grand Slam title after her 1996 Australian triumph. For many tennis historians, Seles would always be a victim, if not of her assailant Gunter Parche, then of the "what if?" game that dogged talk of her career, as she was literally struck down in her prime.[9]

As Seles contemplated her comeback in 1995, *SI* insisted that "never has such a dominant athlete been derailed in so bizarre a fashion." But Seles had some unfortunate competition in that regard from figure skater Nancy Kerrigan, who appeared on the January 17, 1994, cover of *SI* after having been "brutally attacked at the Olympic trials." Only weeks before the Olympic Games in Lillehammer were to begin, Kerrigan had become a "victim" when she was "felled by one savage blow to her right knee by a bludgeon-wielding assailant." *SI* wondered whether Kerrigan's attacker was "a demented Tonya Harding fan."[10]

A week later, it was Harding herself, her ex-husband, and her bodyguard who came under suspicion for planning and initiating the assault. As law enforcement officials and prosecutors investigated what role, if any, the "embattled" Harding had played, the U.S. Olympic Committee considered whether she should be removed from the team. As deliberations on all fronts continued, Harding's camp tried "to stem the rising tide of opinion and speculation implicating her." Her coach, Diane Rawlinson, "went so far as to suggest there had been two victims of the assault. 'Nancy first, of course, but I think Tonya's also a victim. Tonya will not be in line to make the type of money from endorsements that she would have been in line to make.'" It was a claim designed to elicit sympathy, but with its heavy emphasis on the financial fallout, it did not win many fans for a person whose hardscrabble approach, which *SI* had admired in 1992, now offered cause for concern.[11]

SI realized that Americans now would watch the 1994 Winter Olympics just "to see Nancy as Snow White and Tonya as the wicked stepmother in a battle to the death." Harding's tough, "bad-girl" persona and Kerrigan's good, girl-next-door quality offered stereotypical and contrasting representations of femininity that smacked of an athletic catfight just waiting to happen. Case in point was the excessive media interest in the Olympic practice session that would reunite the skaters for the first time since the assault. According to *Sports Illustrated,* "400 journalists were assembled in a holding pen overlooking the ice, while Olympic officials filled a bank of bleachers." Their biggest talking point? "What was the closest the two skaters ever came to touching each other on the ice? Swiftly and inexplicably, the journalists agreed on an answer: 31 inches. The world had a right to know." This was crucial information, especially if Harding and Kerrigan closed such a paltry distance with a war of words or, better yet, a flurry of fisticuffs. None of that occurred, but the possibility was ever present as the "soap opera" continued to dominate media coverage of the Olympics. *SI* reported that Kerrigan's camp suggested she "might wear goalie pads" to her first shared practice with Harding; instead, Kerrigan opted for the same outfit she had been wearing when attacked. Journalists viewed the fashion choice as carefully calculated and designed to knock Harding off balance. Kerrigan was clearly the winner, if not of a catfight, then of psychological one-upmanship which was equally compelling.[12]

That *SI* and other media liked a good tussle between women was not news. As media critic Susan J. Douglas found in 1995, "the absolute importance of the catfight was to demonstrate as simply and vividly as possible that sisterhood was, in fact, a crock of shit."[13] Reducing a debate, a disagreement, or an athletic competition between women to a catfight and a soap opera trivialized the issue, minimizing the real trauma Kerrigan had endured as well as the serious criminal charges Harding confronted. Even as E.M. Swift, the author of *SI*'s articles on the drama, emphasized the latter, he seemed more peeved that the case had "dragged an ostensibly refined sport into a gutter of violence, greed and sensationalism." The real victim, then, was the sport of figure skating, as the Harding/Kerrigan "sideshow" stole "the limelight from some of the most famous names in the history of figure skating. . . . And it [left] a cavity of despair for the more uplifting stories that now might never be told."[14] Of course, the sideshow was a product of the media's own making, and helping sustain the circuslike atmosphere was Swift's own reporting. There was a sense of blaming the victims for a media firestorm entirely beyond their control—especially in the case of Kerrigan, whose own story was of the inspiring variety Swift had feared was consigned to oblivion.

Indeed, despite the injury, the resulting media circus, and early predictions of only a fifth-place finish, Kerrigan nabbed the silver medal. Swift acknowledged her inner fortitude, asserting "that this beauty had more than a small measure of grit and fight and moxie in her." But the most forceful statement about Kerrigan's state of mind came shortly after she was attacked, when her sports psychology consultant, Cindy Adams, declared, "Nancy Kerrigan's not a victim; she's a survivor." Adams allowed that Kerrigan did not "understand" what had "happened or why, but she's not going to let this get in the way of what she's set out to do."[15]

Both Seles's and Kerrigan's assaults garnered covers and multiple articles in *Sports Illustrated* in which both athletes were depicted as overcoming adversity and returning to elite competition with impressive results. Though they might have been victims at one time, these women were clearly survivors. Indeed, Kerrigan's camp had actively rejected the "victim" moniker, clearly staking a survivorship claim, while Seles's 1996 Grand Slam seemed proof positive of her full recovery. But in important ways, both remained victims of the media, which sensationalized their stories. In particular, *Sports Illustrated* contributed to coverage that kept *SI* readers focused on Seles's stabbing, not her Grand Slam record, and on Kerrigan's clubbing, instead of her silver medal. As a result, their entire careers became encapsulated by a moment that neither could control and that only highlighted their vulnerability as female athletes, a hallmark of the frailty myth. The assaults had one more important element in common: both underscored just how closely the physical and the psychological were intertwined.

"There's a Delicacy to Greatness"

Ronda Rousey first appeared in *Sports Illustrated* in March 2008 as part of a feature on Olympic athletes preparing for the summer games in Beijing. While Rousey became the first American woman to medal in judo, it was not her bronze-winning performance that intrigued *Sports Illustrated*. It was Rousey's post-Olympic career in mixed martial arts and her sheer dominance in the sport that singled her out for attention and netted her multiple feature articles as well as appearances in two swimsuit issues.[16]

By 2012 Rousey was "remaking the MMA landscape," thanks in part to her signature armbar move that forced her opponents into a quick and often injurious submission. But she also had an uncanny ability to convert doubters into devotees. "MMA kingmaker" Dana White "had repeatedly declared that no woman would ever compete" in the Ultimate Fighting Championship, until he encountered Rousey and then decided to add a women's division. Rousey attracted thousands of fans to the sport and captivated *Sports Illustrated,* which by 2015 referred to her as "the world's most dominant athlete, (arm)bar none." Her impressive record—she was undefeated in eleven fights, seven of which lasted less than a minute—coupled with the lack of a serious challenger seemed to confirm Rousey's hegemony.[17]

That was until she was defeated in 2015 by Holly Holm. *SI*'s Jon Wertheim noted that "Holm didn't just beat the crap out of Rousey, she beat the invincibility out of her." And she did it in fifty-nine seconds. Rousey's fall had been not only rapid but precipitous; "only two years ago [Rousey] wasn't merely a superstar, she was a superhero. Wonder Woman with no headband but a complement of black belts instead." But losing in the MMA was part of the sport, and fellow MMA champion Demetrious Johnson reminded *SI* readers that it was less about the loss and "all about how you deal with it." A year and a half after the bout, Wertheim found that

> in Rousey's case the dealing has not gone well. Once omnipresent, she was suddenly nowhere. Once omnipotent, she was, by her own reckoning, stripped of power. In one of the few interviews she's given in the last 18 months, she told Ellen DeGeneres that after her first loss, "I was down in the corner, and I was like, *What am I anymore if I'm not this?* I was literally sitting there and thinking about killing myself, and that exact second I'm like, *I'm nothing. What do I do anymore?* And *No one gives a s--- about me anymore without this.*"

The utter devastation of Rousey's loss—particularly psychologically—was, according to Wertheim, "a reminder that sports celebrity has its own set of thermodynamics" and that "There's a delicacy to greatness."[18]

It was an issue that Wertheim had explored in 2003 in the first notable effort by *Sports Illustrated* to address mental health in sport. Wertheim relayed that one in every six Americans suffered from depression, which along with bipolar disorder and social anxiety disorder were the three most common kinds of mental illness. And because athletes in particular were part of "a culture suffused with testosterone and seldom characterized as either sensitive or progressive, mental illness remains largely stigmatized—and, not surprisingly, largely undiagnosed." Wertheim found that mental illness did not discriminate on the basis of class, affecting people from all socioeconomic levels, but it was gendered: "In the U.S. more than twice as many women as men suffer from depression. Since there is little evidence that brain chemistry is markedly different between genders, many believe that women are simply more attuned to their emotions and more likely to seek treatment." Although the vast number of professional athletes were men, Wertheim found that "some of the most

high-profile jocks to speak openly about their struggles have been women."
He surmised that the difference could be attributed to the idea that "males
in general (and alpha males in particular) are much less likely than women
to acknowledge their mental illness . . . because of the enduring misconception that mental illness somehow indicates inner weakness."[19] It was
another example of the frailty myth—despite the similarities in brain
chemistry and in being exposed to the same risk factors that increased
the incidence of psychological struggles, mental illness remained more
stigmatizing for men whose masculine toughness would seem to mitigate
such issues than for women, for whom feminine weakness in all areas
was supposedly a given.

Regarding mental health as a weakness was a fallacy that was both
gendered and racialized. Wertheim pointed out that the National Mental
Health Association had found "the enduring misconception that mental illness somehow indicates inner weakness" to be "particularly common in
the African-American community, from which a disproportionate number of athletes hail." It was a reality echoed by basketball star Chamique
Holdsclaw, who in 2009 used *Sports Illustrated* to "open up on her battle
with depression." Given Holdsclaw's dominance on the court, her abrupt
departure from the WNBA in 2004 was all the more shocking. Holdsclaw
used her platform to be candid about her own battle with depression,
drawing important attention to the fact that even athletic superstars were
not immune to mental health struggles. Previously she had been reluctant to discuss the issue, seeing her "situation as embarrassing. There's
a stigma, especially in the African-American community. We're such
prayerful people, the answer is always, 'Let's go and pray.'"[20]

Holdsclaw was not wrong in identifying religion as a deterrent to mental health treatment in the Black community, and the belief that prayer
would prove a successful therapy. But there were additional factors causing a reluctance among Black American athletes to reveal their struggles
with mental health. For example, although Black athletes encountered the
same risk factors as their white counterparts, including the stresses associated with a nomadic lifestyle and expectations of success, the trauma
associated with systemic racism compounded an already taxing reality.
As a result, some 20 percent more African Americans reported serious
psychological distress but were reluctant to consult medical treatment,
given not just an abiding faith but a long history of mistreatment and exploitation by medical professionals. Such a past caused Black athletes to

wonder whether those professionals would regard mental health struggles as an inherent weakness—much like intellectual abilities had once been diagnosed. Despite such obstacles, Black athletes were increasingly discussing their mental health struggles. In addition to Holdsclaw, *Sports Illustrated* shared NFL star Ricky Williams's battle in 2003, NBA player Ron Artest's public acknowledgment in 2010 (after winning the NBA title no less), and Royce White's openness about the issue in 2012. This was progress, to be sure.[21]

Wertheim had anticipated that development as early as 2003. He asserted that "the wheels of change do turn in sports, however slowly. In interviews, nine mental health experts who treat athletes unanimously asserted that disorders of the mind are gradually shedding their stigma in sports." "Gradually" was the operative word. *Sports Illustrated* drew attention to "a recent rash of suicides" in 2011, and while the issue had been "radioactive" for decades, "the fortress appeared to be giving way." A year later, golfer Charlie Beljan proved that it was possible for an athlete to "have a mental-health issue and still go out and beat the world." But in 2014, when SI.com caught up with Chamique Holdsclaw, contributor Andrew Lawrence took the opportunity to point out that "mental illness still carries a stigma, especially for athletes."[22]

Nevertheless, real change was discernible in 2015 with *SI*'s reporting of Michael Phelps's mental health struggles. In the article "The Rehabilitation of Michael Phelps," the decorated swimmer bluntly discussed his state of mind following the 2012 Olympics and the six gold medals he won in London: "I was in a really dark place. Not wanting to be alive anymore."[23] It was a stunning revelation from an athlete whose name is inextricably linked with Olympic greatness. Although his performance at Beijing inspired much of his legend, Phelps reported that "After '08, mentally, I was over. I didn't want to do it anymore. But I also knew I couldn't stop. So I forced myself to do something that I really didn't want to do, which was continue swimming." After treatment in 2014, Phelps was preparing for the Rio Games, not "to fulfill historical imperatives but for his own, rediscovered joy."[24] It was a startling admission from one of the greatest athletes of all time—made all the more so by the absence of similar admissions from other male athletes of his stature.

The experiences of Rousey, Holdsclaw, and Phelps helped to draw important attention to mental health issues in sports regardless of an athlete's win-loss record. Those discussions set the stage for tennis player Naomi Osaka to withdraw from the 2021 French Open in an effort to protect her mental health, and for Simone Biles to reduce her Olympic schedule in Tokyo for the same reason. In his article for SI.com, Wertheim praised Osaka for putting "a spotlight on mental health" and expressed "profound empathy" for the "vulnerable athlete" whose "wellbeing ought to be our first priority." Robin Lundberg echoed those comments when Biles withdrew from the team gymnastics competition at the Olympics in 2021, asserting that "Simone Biles doesn't owe anyone anything. She needs to take care of herself first."[25] But the frailty myth helped shape sportswomen's stories, particularly in comparison with their male counterparts. If mental health was at first regarded as a weakness, it was one that was easier for female athletes to bear and to discuss. Given the overall assumption that they were physically weaker than men, it stood to reason that women were not mentally as tough either—an assumption that reflected entrenched notions not just of femininity but of masculinity as well. As mental health gained greater traction in the pages of *Sports Illustrated* in the early 2000s, women's mental health struggles figured more prominently because of their limited presence in the magazine. This was also true for the physical challenges sportswomen sustained, not only in terms of causation, incidence, and treatment, but more importantly in how they affected the very future of women in sport.

"No Shortage of Scars"

In 2018, Tim Layden noted that "becoming the greatest U.S. skier ever takes a toll," and Lindsey Vonn's vast catalog of injuries was as well known as her seventy-eight World Cup victories. Layden recounted Vonn's grim tally as she prepared for the 2010 Vancouver Olympics: "There was the 70-mph downhill training crash two days before the 2006 Turin Olympics, which left her to contest four events with back and pelvic bruises. . . . There was her nearly severed right thumb, injured while she was opening a champagne bottle. . . . There was the bloody tongue, chomped open when her knee bounced up into her chin as she won a World Cup downhill. . . . And there was the deep bone bruise in her left wrist after a scary giant slalom crash." It led Layden to conclude that Vonn had "no shortage of scars, some more lasting and more meaningful than others; some barely noticeable; some still healing." And some still to come. Following a training mishap that ended any hope for medals in 2006, Vonn sustained additional knee injuries over the next several years, ultimately tearing her anterior cruciate ligament and missing the 2014 Olympic Games entirely.[26]

Vonn's ACL injury was one that has bedeviled athletes for decades, regardless of their sport or their gender. *Sports Illustrated* had drawn attention to the issue in 1991 when Richard Demak discussed "the NBA's most feared injury." While other torn ligaments could be repaired, the ACL could not, which was why most surgeons opted to use either a patellar tendon from the patient or a harvested cadaver tendon. Adding to the difficulty of the injury was the duration of the rehab, which was often a year-long process, and the unpredictability of an injury that often came without warning. Finally, although players could return to their sports after ACL surgeries, surgeons cautioned that "their knees [would] never be the same." All of this was particularly troubling for women, who experienced ACL injuries at higher rates than men.[27]

Despite what *SI*'s Jack McCallum called an "epidemic of torn knee ligaments" among women, he acknowledged in 1995 that "if past is prologue, nothing that happens to female athletes—outside of one of them wearing a clinging body suit or dunking during a game—is likely to cause a major ripple in the sports world." There was simply not enough urgency to spur research that explored why women were four to six times more likely than males to suffer an ACL injury. Yet McCallum realized that because sportswomen experienced a higher incidence of ACL injuries than men, their opportunities to play sports were in jeopardy, since some would use such an incidence to "prove" that female bodies were physiologically not suited to such a strain.[28]

It was an example of the frailty myth in action. In 1991 Demak believed that a higher incidence of ACL injuries among NBA players could be attributed to the fact that their "shoes [were] too good" or that "players [were] bigger, stronger and faster." Four years later, McCallum's reasons for a higher incidence of ACL injuries among collegiate female basketball players were similar; he noted that the women's game had "become decidedly more up-tempo" and was "also more physical," while "the footwear factor" meant chances were better "of sustaining a deceleration injury like an ACL tear." But while some of the reasons for an ACL tear were similar among men and women, the responses to the injuries were decidedly different. Demak stressed the need for new innovations like braces, improved surgical techniques, and rehabilitation procedures to get men back on the floor as quickly as possible. There was no question that men should continue playing the game; medical science simply needed to catch up. For women, however, McCallum insisted that "it is entirely reasonable to wonder whether the game has, in some respects surpassed the physical ability of women to withstand it." And he was not alone. Surgeons and coaches alike wondered whether "women [were] pursuing an on-court style that may be deleterious to their health."[29] In terms of ACL tears, then, male athletes survived the injury to play another day while female athletes became victims of an injury that reflected a wider societal concern about the suitability of women playing sports just like men. Such a presumption threatened to curtail not only women's progress but their very presence in sport.

Such ideas were reminiscent of late nineteenth-century medical theories which postulated that vigorous exercise compromised female physical and especially reproductive health. Such arguments clearly had staying power, since in 1973 SI's Gilbert and Williamson found it necessary to underscore the fact that "the almost unanimous medical opinion [is] that no sport per se is more harmful for a girl than for a boy." Regardless of the athletic activity, there was no "higher incidence of injury" among girls "than in boys' programs, nor [were] girls being injured or exhausted for reasons that appear to be directly connected with their sex." Nevertheless, Creighton Hale, the president of Little League Baseball, adamantly opposed admitting female players owing to his belief that girls would develop breast cancer if they got hit in the chest. SI correctly surmised that "the real dispute" regarding girls being allowed to play Little League baseball was "neither physical nor cosmetic nor medical. The real dispute is social: what identity do we perceive for the sexes in America?"[30]

McCallum echoed this sentiment when he offered "a somewhat more complicated theory about women's ACLs, one that speaks to changes in the women's game, training methods (or lack thereof) and society's view of women athletes." He quoted University of Iowa trainer Alex Kane, who asserted that "girls are not being exposed to motor learning skills at critical periods in their early development, and the consequences of that are manifest in these injuries." The bottom line for Kane was that "girls aren't taught" and "aren't encouraged to learn" the necessary skills and exercises to prevent such injuries.[31] Such a comment reflected the enduring power of the frailty myth with its perennial supposition that society still viewed sports as more natural—and more appropriate—for boys than for girls.

SI for Women took a different tack, particularly in its depiction of female athletes as survivors rather than casualties. The magazine's Dana Sullivan acknowledged potential ACL risk factors that were unique to women, but touted the benefits of strength training and exercises that "could prevent as many as 80% of female ACL injuries." That number would bring women's incidence of ACL injuries into parity with men's. In addition, Sullivan provided a list of "dos and don'ts" to avoid general knee pain and enlisted the help of WNBA star Rebecca Lobo, who had torn her ACL in 1999, to demonstrate a prevention program readers could begin at home.[32] The message was clear: although women might suffer ACL injuries as a result of their athletic endeavors, with proper coaching and training, such injuries did not have to occur at a greater rate than men, nor did they have to be career ending.

By 2017 that was truer than ever before, as an ACL tear was "no longer" a "giant-slayer." *Sports Illustrated* reviewed innovations in knee care, including the growth of arthroscopic surgery, advances in the regenerative capacity of the body, and a new emphasis on presurgery conditioning and strengthening. Such improvements meant a "return to full activity, including contact" six and a half months after surgery. What's more, the treatment timeline was not sport specific, nor was it gender specific. It was one for "athletes."[33]

Thus by the 2000s both male and female athletes who suffered an ACL tear were unquestionably survivors as they returned to play. But perhaps most important was that women had survived the broader debate as to whether women's bodies and their "unique" susceptibility to injuries disqualified them from certain sports or indeed sport altogether. But the frailty myth nonetheless continued to affect the way *SI* depicted female athletes as they battled everything from injuries to eating disorders.

"Losing to Win"

In 1977 *SI* featured athletes who literally "hunger[ed] for success." Looking to lose weight, the athletes had used drastic means: a football player drank nothing but fruit juice during the week, giving up his fast on the weekends to eat "'everything that wasn't tied down,'" while some jockeys subsisted solely on sunflower seeds or resorted to "flipping," a euphemism for purg-ing.[34] Although the article explored the pressures on male athletes to make and then maintain weight, it never referred to their tactics specifically as binge eating, anorexia, or bulimia.

This was not surprising, since most male athletes did not experience disordered eating behaviors as a serious issue with long-lasting repercus-sions and were rarely depicted as having to contend with eating disor-ders or a negative body image. In contrast, *SI* reported that by the 1990s, eating disorders had "easily" become "the gravest health problem facing female athletes." It was yet more proof that when women played sport, they risked their health and well-being in ways that men simply did not. In a 1994 special report for *SI*, Merrell Noden found that 93 percent of the programs reporting eating disorders were in women's sports, particularly "appearance" and endurance sports, and that 30 percent of women on the tennis tour and 70 percent of female runners had "dabbled in it in its many hideous forms."[35]

In his report, Noden was deliberate in explaining the difference be-tween anorexia and bulimia, since at the time there was a tendency to conflate the two. He defined bulimia as "a binge-purge syndrome in which huge quantities of food—sometimes totaling as much as 20,000 calories in a day—were consumed in a short period of time and then expelled through self-induced vomiting, excessive exercise, the use of diuretics or laxatives, or some combination of those methods." Although the jockey that *SI* had interviewed in the 1970s insisted that he did not experience any long-term ill effects from his twenty years of "flipping," there were real health concerns associated with such behaviors: "Stomach acids rot the teeth of bulimics and, if they are sticking their fingers down their throats to induce vomiting, their fingernails. Electrolyte imbalances disrupt their heart rates. But since bulimics are usually of normal weight years may pass" before they are found out. Anorexia—or self-starvation—was more easily detected and according to Noden, was "driven by a distorted per-ception of one's appearance. It is not unusual for an anorexic who is 5'8" to weigh 100 pounds or less—and still think she's too fat." And long-term effects like amenorrhea and osteoporosis were "catastrophic." But both an-orexia and bulimia offered an important, competitive advantage in a num-ber of sports, especially gymnastics, as females could better maintain the slim, boyish bodies that were better suited to the tricks demanded of elite gymnasts. As Noden observed, "In the Lilliputian world of gymnastics, arrested development seems to be an occupational necessity."[36] Eating disorders seemed to be just part of the job.

That had been true since the 1970s. Cathy Rigby, who sought to emulate the diminutive Olga Korbut in 1972, battled bulimia for twelve years. Christy Henrich, who missed out on the 1988 Olympic team by .118 of a point, died from multiple organ failure due to complications from anorexia at the age of twenty-two.[37] Clearly, the effects of eating disorders were dire and devastating, and Noden's article drew important attention to what was then an underreported condition that affected primarily female athletes. But even as Noden educated *SI* readers about anorexia and bulimia, his emphasis remained on the vulnerability of female athletes in general and the tragedy of Henrich in particular. The frailty myth remained in effect.

Kelli Anderson's 2001 article on eating disorders for *Sports Illustrated for Women* echoed some of the significant points Noden had made in 1994, including that "an alarming number of female athletes and coaches are buying into the dangerous idea that you can never be too thin." In addition, the "same societal pressures that affect all young women—to be beautiful, to be thin, to be feminine," are magnified by sports participation because of "the belief that reducing body weight and/or body fat will enhance performance." Although many athletes regardless of gender are often interested in reducing body fat, the consequences are very different. While males can reduce their body fat, even drastically, "with little apparent systemic dysfunction," most females become amenorrheic when their body fat drops below 17 percent. This is particularly problematic. When the menstrual cycle is interrupted, "the female body stops producing the estrogen necessary to build and maintain bone density," which makes women more susceptible to fractures and to osteoporosis.[38]

Although both Noden and Anderson discussed warning signs that might indicate anorexia or bulimia, Anderson offered readers sidebars that highlighted organizations that could provide help ("Where to Turn") as well as recent innovations in preventing eating disorders ("An Ounce of Prevention"). But perhaps the biggest difference was the titles of the articles themselves. In contrast to Noden's "Dying to Win," which appeared in *SI* and began and concluded with references to Christy Henrich's death, Anderson's "Losing to Win" in *SI for Women,* while also referencing Henrich's story, started by introducing readers to an athlete recovering from anorexia and closed with a discussion about the messaging around

body image. The emphasis for Anderson was not on female athletes succumbing to eating disorders but on their successfully overcoming them.

Female athletes' battles with eating disorders were often featured in
both magazines, and by the early 2000s the focus for both *SI* and *SI for
Women* had shifted to survivorship. It was a notable departure for *Sports
Illustrated,* which had previously emphasized sportswomen's suffering
more than their resilience. In 1999 basketball player Shelley Garcia had
battled bulimia successfully, UConn cager Shea Ralph's "recovery" from
anorexia was "ongoing," and Dutch cyclist Leontien Sijlaard-van Moorsel had "fought her way back from anorexia to become the most decorated female cyclist at a single Games." Overcoming such eating disorders
often required ignoring triggering comments from coaches, judges, and
teammates. A Dutch cycling official gave Sijlaard-van Moorsel "a tip";
a teammate told Ralph that "she looked 'a little thick'"; a judge informed
Christy Henrich that she "would have to lose weight if she wanted to make
the Olympic team"; a coach told swimmer Tiffany Cohen, "Imagine how
much faster you would have swum at the Olympics if you had been a
lighter weight." For other athletes, their biggest critics were themselves:
Shelley Garcia "looked at her teammates—many of them sculpted upper-
classmen who had shed the baby fat that still clung to her frame—and
decided she had to . . . lose 10 pounds."[39]

Only rarely did an athlete ignore external stimuli and quiet inner criticism. In 2007 Serena Williams had returned to tennis after months away
from the tour. With her ranking at "a lowly 81" and her fitness and match
preparation widely viewed as "lacking," Williams defeated six seeded players on her way to the Australian Open championship title. *SI* acknowledged that, with Williams, "looks can deceive. For all the cracks about
her physique, Williams never fatigued, even when playing three-setters in
sweltering heat. Nor was her movement lacking." Williams herself pushed
back against her critics: "I'm definitely in better shape than I get credit for.
[It's] just because I have large bosoms and I have a big ass. . . . I was just
in the locker room staring at my body, and I'm like, 'Am I really not fit?
Or is it just because I have all these extra assets that I look not fit?' I think
if I were not to eat for two years, I still wouldn't be a size two. . . . I'm just
not built that way. I'm bootylicious, and that's how it's always going to
be."[40] Such a comment from arguably the best player in the game of tennis
underscored the battles other sportswomen waged to gain a measure of
confidence in and about their own bodies that allowed them to survive the

In 2007 Serena Williams defied critics who found her fitness lacking by winning the Australian Open. Her questions about her physique underscored the battles other sportswomen waged against eating disorders, and the ways in which race complicated such struggles.

ravages of eating disorders. It also provided insight into the ways in which race complicated such struggles.

Although historically eating disorders have been viewed as a problem predominantly for white women, research has exploded such long-held suppositions. Not only are Black teenagers 50 percent more likely than white teenagers to suffer from bulimia, they are significantly less likely than their white peers to receive help and thus more likely to be victims of the disease than survivors. As early as 1989, *Sports Illustrated* related that tennis player Zina Garrison, "lonely and depressed" on tour, had begun "food binges, devouring bags of cookies, boxes of cereal, cartons of ice cream in a sitting. Then, disgusted, she forced herself to throw up." But neither *SI* nor *SI for Women* pursued the racial dimensions of eating disorders or discussed how Black women might encounter different messages about body image that obscured their struggles with anorexia and bulimia, further isolating them. Indeed, throughout the twentieth century

Black women's bodies were portrayed as problematic, not for being dangerously thin, but for being excessively fat.[41]

This was especially true for tennis player Taylor Townsend, who in 2012 was the top junior girls player. With her aggressive serve and volley game, Townsend had, by the age of sixteen, amassed an impressive resume: she had advanced to the second round of qualifying in the main draw of the U.S. Open in 2011, and then won the Australian Open junior title in both singles and doubles, repeating the latter title at Wimbledon. But the U.S. Tennis Association, concerned about her "long-term health," refused to fund the junior champion's expenses going forward until she focused on losing weight and improving her overall fitness. It was an unprecedented move by the organization, one that Serena Williams referred to as "a tragedy." Ultimately the USTA relented, but it had succeeded in focusing attention on Townsend's weight instead of her already impressive record. In her 2021 article "I Was Fat, and I Was Black, So They Took Away My Dream," Townsend, now twenty-five years old, insisted the USTA used her health as a distraction from the real issue, which was that she was fat, Black, and female. This was precisely Sabrina Strings's thesis of her book *Fearing the Black Body*, in which she asserted that concerns about a Black woman being overweight do not arise out of health concerns but instead are used to perpetuate racism and sexism.[42]

The numerous articles devoted to eating disorders in both *Sports Illustrated* and *Sports Illustrated for Women* underscored the ubiquity and the severity of the issue among female athletes. In doing so, however, they contributed to a racialized version of the frailty myth, overwhelmingly depicting disordered eating struggles as concerns for white sportswomen. While a more nuanced discussion was needed, authors did highlight that such behaviors were destructive but also especially seductive because they often produced positive results, sometimes for as a long as a year, before athletes' bodies became devastated. It was not unlike the use of performance-enhancing drugs, which offered extraordinary results, often for years, until athletes broke down under brutal training regimens that their bodies simply could not endure.

"Juiced-Up"

In the summer of 1969, *SI* addressed performance-enhancing drugs for the first time in a three-part series. The magazine acknowledged that the use of steroids by athletes was "far from new, but the increase in drug usage in the last 10 years [has been] startling." It predicted that athletes' use of drugs like anabolic steroids would "eventually explode into an epidemic." The article focused on male athletes, but in the years to come *Sports Illustrated* would feature both sportsmen and sportswomen in some of the most high-profile stories involving performance-enhancing drug abuse.[43]

For example, in 2000 the photogenic and talented Marion Jones had set her sights on five Olympic gold medals. While the track and field star did earn five medals—and became the first woman to do so in a single Olympics—she had to settle for three gold and two bronze. It was still an impressive haul, but by 2002 Jones was focusing on setting world records so she could be "considered one of the greatest ever." She was in a better place to do that than ever before, according to *Sports Illustrated Women*, having put a "difficult marriage behind her." Jones's marriage to shot-putter C. J. Hunter had become a source of public drama at the 2000 Games when "the day after Jones won her first gold in Sydney, the story broke that Hunter had tested positive for nandrolone—a performance-enhancing anabolic steroid." *SI Women* reported that "Jones herself has never been associated with steroids, growth hormones or stimulants, and she's clearly not interested in any gossip or innuendo."[44]

But rumors about Jones's steroid use persisted. Following the Sydney Games, *SI* went so far as to assert that "Jones and her crusade for five golds smelled rank. Now every starting-block TV closeup of her and the other competitors became a chance to study—no, not the determination etched upon their faces but the amount of acne or the length of jawline that might indicate drug use." By 2004, as the Athens Olympics approached, talk had only grown louder following the Bay Area Laboratory Co-Operative drug scandal, which had already implicated sprinter Kellie White and was threatening to ensnare Marion Jones as well. For her part, Jones, who had never failed a drug test, threatened legal action if the U.S. Anti-Doping Agency tried to prevent her from participating in the Athens games.[45] Three years later, Jones "pleaded guilty to lying to federal agents and admitted to using steroids before and during her Olympic run." It was really no surprise. As *SI* related, her "impassioned denials of steroid use over the years . . . rang hollow in the face of voluminous circumstantial evidence." Jones's admission of steroid use meant the forfeit of her Olympic medals and records. In addition, since she had lied about her steroid use to federal investigators, she was found guilty on two counts of perjury and given a sentence of six months in prison.[46]

Although Jones's case drew attention to a flawed testing process, the reality was that many athletes, women included, were choosing to dope. Such a circumstance served to complicate the frailty myth in significant and sometimes contradictory ways. As some women became stronger and faster than ever before owing to their use of performance-enhancing drugs, they seemed poised to dominate sport in ways that made them not just powerful but invincible. While no one could consider these women outwardly weak, fragile, or delicate, their immediate gains stemmed from banned practices that, for many, caused conditions that added an entirely new dimension to the frailty myth.

The East German *Wundermädchen*, who had dominated competitive swimming during the Cold War era, are a compelling case study in this regard. In 1991 *Sports Illustrated* reported that some twenty former GDR swim coaches admitted that they had given anabolic steroids to many of their swimmers throughout the 1970s and 1980s. Following the fall of the Berlin Wall in 1989, meticulous records—from the files of the East German secret police, no less—confirmed the claims, revealing the type and the amount of steroids that hundreds of women in a variety of sports had ingested as part of a state-sponsored initiative sustained by coaches, medical professionals, and government personnel. Although most of the swimmers had wondered neither about the amount or the type of "vitamins" they consumed, nor voiced any "suspicions" about their ability to train harder and recover faster at the time, plenty of others had raised questions. How had the East German female swimmers, who had not won any gold medals at the 1972 Olympics but a year later won multiple gold medals at the world championships, improved by so much and so quickly? By 1976, following an Olympic performance that included eleven gold medals (out of thirteen events), the American swimmer Shirley Babashoff accused the team of having doped, an allegation that was dismissed in 1976 as poor sportsmanship. But Babashoff was not alone in her conjecture. *Sports Illustrated*'s Jerry Kirshenbaum reported the remarks of a French doctor who had commented on the *Wundermädchen*'s "uncommon muscle development." By 1992 there was no question that East German coaches and officials had systematically administered massive doses of anabolic-androgenic steroids to their female swimmers without the athletes' knowledge so they would dominate their sport and secure glory for their homeland.[47]

The East German drug of choice was Oral Turanibol, a synthetic form of testosterone. Although both males and females have naturally occurring amounts of testosterone and estrogen in their bodies, females have, on average, considerably more estrogen and less testosterone than their male counterparts. Thus, although East Germany doped both male and female athletes, when females consumed anabolic-androgenic steroids, particularly at the high levels administered by East German officials, the effects in terms of increased speed, strength, and power—and athletic accolades—were profound. The head of East Germany's doping system, Dr. Manfred Höppner, confirmed as much in a 1977 internal report: "The positive value of anabolic steroids for the development of a top performance is undoubted. . . . From our experience made so far it can be concluded that women have the greatest advantage from treatments with anabolic hormones. . . . Especially high is the performance-supporting effect following the first administration of anabolic hormones, especially with junior athletes."[48]

In the simplest of terms, the GDR doped female athletes with massive amounts of anabolic-androgenic steroids and for long periods of time because they knew the resulting athletic achievements would be impressive. And they were. In 1976, East German sportswomen set records not just in swimming but in track and field and rowing, with East Germany winning nine of the fourteen events in track and field and four of the six rowing events. But those medals and records came at a price. *SI* acknowledged as much in 1991 when the magazine found it "hard not to feel sympathy for the generation of women athletes of other countries who had to swim in the shadow of their juiced-up East German counterparts."[49]

But it was not just East Germany's competitors who paid with their dashed hopes and lost medals. The East German women, a number of whom secured top honors, had been "guinea pigs for a three-decade-long sports-science experiment" and had encountered "massive health problems" as a result of being doped without their knowledge. *SI* noted that "at the Berlin doping trials, held from 1998 to 2000, victims vent[ed] their anger and describe[d] the steroid-induced medical problems they had suffered," which included cancer, liver disease, and birth defects in their children. In addition, athletes described bodies broken under the weight of a training regime that their skeletal structures were simply not designed to withstand. Of the hundreds of women who were doped, 167 testified and were each awarded $12,000, agreeing to suspend any further legal action.[50] It seemed paltry compensation for years of abuse and a multitude of chronic medical issues that would require life-long treatment.

Perhaps the biggest blow was that none of these complications came as a great surprise to the East German power structure. According to author Steven Ungerleider, "The GDR brain trust" realized "that women were more vulnerable when using anabolic steroids." And he also commented on how these women both upended and embraced the frailty myth: "On the one hand, their performances could be spectacular: greater, in fact, than that of the men, but the risks were a lot higher. Typical side effects resulting from administering these hormones to women include retarded growth, disturbances in fertility, and heart disease."[51] While performance-enhancing drugs could make many women athletically invincible for a short period of time, the long-term effects of ingesting them meant those same women would ultimately not upend the frailty myth but embrace it, with long-term health conditions that would in many cases plague them not just during their careers, but throughout their retirements as well.

The sports world condemned the coaches, medical personnel, and government officials who designed and perpetuated the system—only a few of whom were held accountable. But the East German focus on creating an extensive system to dope its athletes is notable. The belief that high doses of anabolic-androgenic steroids would yield bigger dividends among female athletes than males was a variation of the frailty myth, since it assumed that women, with just the right amount of synthetic testosterone, would be able to dominate their nondoping competition like never before.[52] *Sports Illustrated* duly reported the obsession with performance-enhancing drugs over the years and even acknowledged how sportswomen could enjoy "great[er] gains" than sportsmen, particularly from the use of anabolic-androgenic steroids.[53] But *SI* failed to grasp how the long-term effects of performance-enhancing drugs, which impacted women in unique and profoundly damaging ways, made female athletes perfect targets—and victims—of performing-enhancing drug schemes.

An additional cruelty of the East German doping program is that in trying to artificially enhance the capabilities of its female athletes, the authorities ultimately reinforced the image of sportswomen as fragile—and worse. The physical breakdown and mental trauma experienced by these athletes was precisely what the frailty myth held as true, but their fragility in this case was the result not of individual choice but of a state-sponsored initiative and imperative to win at any cost. And it was a system that exacted its greatest toll from women, not only in terms of physical and mental anguish associated with physical debilitation but also in having to testify in a courtroom years later against coaches and medical personnel who were supposed to have protected them. One East German athlete remarked, "My parents were not around. We did not have family; we were isolated. Our family were the athletes and the doctors, the pool our community. They were our mentors; we had to trust them."[54] Such unwavering trust, especially without oversight and accountability, was a recipe for abuse that was replicated in different sports in different ways and continued to victimize all athletes, but especially sportswomen.

"An Army of Survivors"

On December 17, 2012, *Sports Illustrated* honored the year's inspiring athletes, especially Cy Young winner R. A. Dickey and judo gold medalist Kayla Harrison "for their refusal" to be silent victims of sexual assault. The number of victims that *SI* reported was staggering: "one in four girls and one in six boys—with some experts convinced that the true number for all children was one in three."[55] Dickey and Harrison provided faces of an "epidemic" that proved sport was in many ways an environment well suited not only for allowing sexual abuse to happen but for promoting a silence that deterred athletes from speaking out about it once it had occurred.

Johnette Howard and Lester Munson had made this exact point in the spring 1997 inaugural issue of *Sports Illustrated Women/Sport*: "In many ways sports are an ideal setting for abusers. Experts say sexual predators typically seek the trust of both the parents and the child before beginning the abuse, so the child will be afraid to complain. . . . Toss in the fact that sports create an emotional bond between player and coach, and the fact that coaches often spend large chunks of time alone with their athletes and . . . 'you have all the makings for an at-risk situation.'" To prove their point, Howard and Munson shared the allegations of three female athletes who had accused their volleyball coach of sexual abuse when they were teenagers. While the coach acknowledged having sex with the three women, he "insist[ed] the relationships were consensual and took place when they were of age and out of his program." In addition, he "question[ed] why, if anything improper happened, the women waited so long to come forward. He argue[d] that their continued contact with him or the club after they left for college shatter[ed] their credibility." Such statements were often trotted out by those who questioned the honesty of alleged victims of sexual abuse, and the *SI* reporters used it as an opportunity to educate readers. Howard and Munson tapped Sharon Lamb, author of *The Trouble with Blame: Victims, Perpetrators, and Responsibility*, to comment on why "victims of sexual abuse are often slow to report such incidents, especially if an authority figure is involved or if they know their assailant." According to Lamb, "For young people, especially, there can be difficulty defining what an abuse experience is when the sexual abuse isn't, say, an attack on the street by a stranger. . . . With someone you know, small, exploitative things often happen first and the girl or woman may give the perpetrator the benefit of the doubt. By the time larger things happen, the victim feels complicit in it even though it's not her fault."[56]

Despite efforts like Howard and Munson's, discrediting victims because they waited to report the abuse or continued to play for an abusive coach continued to be recycled over the years to come. Such lines of reasoning mimicked other efforts to cast doubt on a victim's veracity by focusing on her past sexual relationships, what she was wearing, and how much she had to drink. Even as women embraced #MeToo (a term coined by the American activist Tarana Burke in 2006 only to go viral over social media in 2017), those affected by sexual violence continued to battle the same tropes that blamed them for their abuse or penalized them for when and how they reported it. Despite these obstacles, female athletes who endured sexual assault were coming forward and with a newfound fortitude; even in 1997, Howard and Munson noted that one of three accusers they had interviewed was becoming empowered: "When I started talking I was very scared. But by the end of my statement, I am *strong*. I am adamant. It was like I just got this power or strength, like, I can do this!"[57]

As sportswomen found their voices, accused their abusers, and initiated court proceedings, they upended the frailty myth. But obstacles remained, including overcoming societal tendencies that blamed victims, law enforcement that was often disinclined to investigate allegations of abuse, and a legal system that was reluctant to prosecute abusers. But with increasing exposure in social media and more traditional media sources like *Sports Illustrated,* more women were coming forward.

In 2018 *Sports Illustrated* invited those who had publicly testified during Larry Nassar's trial to take part in a photo shoot. *SI* encouraged readers: "Admire their strength. Remember their names."

In 2016, after the *Indianapolis Star* reported the failure of USA Gymnastics to inform authorities about allegations of sexual misconduct levied against more than fifty gymnastics coaches, the newspaper fielded an email from former gymnast Rachel Denhollander, who had allegations of her own—this time against a doctor with ties to USA Gymnastics and Michigan State University. Years earlier, a fifteen-year-old Denhollander, struck by the ease with which Larry Nassar had assaulted her, realized that she was not the first to be abused by him. But back in 2000, Denhollander was not confident that she would be believed. Reluctant to contact the police, she "began amassing a dossier documenting the abuse. That helped when, in 2016, she . . . [became] the first to attach her name to a complaint." Thanks to the statements of other athletes who came forward, the investigative journalism of *Star* reporters, the support of Michigan State Detective Lt. Andrea Munford, and the commitment of Assistant Attorney General Angela Povilaitis, Larry Nassar pled guilty to molesting seven girls and to possession of child pornography. While such charges were expedient—they were within the statute of limitations and represented cases that entailed the longest mandatory prison sentences—from the beginning the goal was expansive: to use the cases of just seven females, of the more than 500 individuals Nassar had sexually abused, to put him in jail, but to hear from all those who wished to make a victim statement. Povilaitis insisted on it as part of the plea agreement, and Judge

Rosemarie Aquilina allowed it, even when the original 88 females who wished to make victim impact statements ultimately became 156.[58]

In 2018 *Sports Illustrated* sought to honor those women, whose "strength was palpable, their words powerful—not just because of the courage it took for each woman to face her abuser and share horribly intimate details with the world, but also because they moved others to come forward." The magazine invited those who had publicly identified themselves during Nassar's prosecution to take part in a photo shoot; the forty-one who agreed displayed "their newfound sense of empowerment" in poses that were "defiant, confident, heroic." Among them was Amanda Thomashow, who had spoken powerfully to Nassar when it came time to give her statement in court: "You didn't realize you were building an army of survivors who see you for what you are—a sexual predator. We will rise as an army of female warriors who will never let you or another man drunk off of power get away with such evil again." *SI* encouraged readers to "admire their strength. Remember their names."[59]

But it was also important to remember that Larry Nassar was able to perpetuate his criminal behavior because of a culture that prized female sexual passivity and male sexual aggression—with or without consent—at any cost. It was an environment that produced thousands of victims and survivors and protected abusive coaches and trainers. Those who brought charges were often ignored by officials, discouraged by administrations to report, and targeted by rabid fans who prioritized athletic supremacy and collegiate reputation above anything else. Such disincentives for coming forward, in addition to the shame many women felt following a sexual assault, created a culture of silence that often allowed abusers to go unremarked for years.

In his 2015 article "A Hidden Epidemic," *Sports Illustrated*'s Ben Reiter reported on the instances of "high-profile" male athletes who had committed sexual assault, calling it a "too-frequent problem on college campuses." Reiter reviewed *The Hunting Ground,* a documentary that shed "light on the scourge" of sexual assault "and on those who suffer in the dark," noting that while "college athletes are not the film's central focus . . . it tells us that while less than 4% of college men are student-athletes, that group is responsible for 19% of reported assaults." Three decades earlier, in 1982, John Papanek had raised this issue, even if tangentially, when he reported that the University of San Francisco's star basketball guard had pled guilty to aggravated assault on a female student. The magazine focused more directly on the issue in 2004 when it reported on "lawsuits filed by three women who had alleged they were raped on a night they partied with Colorado football players and recruits." Although *SI*'s Kelli Anderson and George Dohrmann focused on the University of Colorado in their article, they asserted that the school was not alone in "selling sex to recruits," noting that other schools like Alabama, Oregon, Minnesota, and Brigham Young University had also offered such "perks."[60]

But referring to sexual access to women as "perks" ignores the coercion involved in such a "recruitment tool" and further objectifies the women involved, placing access to their bodies on a par with access to player lounges, juice bars, and mini movie theaters. Such an equation, according to Sharon Lamb, contributes to further victimization: "Victims are made victims not only by horrendous abuse but also by social forces, the oppression and abuse and sexism that give the message that their bodies are not whole but composed of parts, parts that are primarily valued as commodities over which they have little presiding rights. And when society supports sexual offenses against them and suppresses victims' speech about their humiliation and anger, they are truly marked from the outside, stigmatized, and seen as victims from without as well as from within."[61]

Lamb was addressing the experience of victim blaming—by the victims themselves, the perpetrators of sexual assault, and society more generally. The latter was particularly damaging for, with a boost from *Sports Illustrated,* female athletes were remembered not necessarily for impressive feats of skill but for misfortune. Thus, sportswomen remained victims of the frailty myth instead of survivors who were able to transcend it.

"From Champion to Tragedienne"

On October 8, 1956, *Sports Illustrated* bid "farewell to the Babe." Mildred "Babe" Didrikson (Zaharias) had succumbed to colon cancer just two weeks earlier at the age of 45, and the magazine tapped well-known novelist and sportswriter Paul Gallico to pen a tribute to "the greatest woman athlete of modern times." Gallico regaled *SI* readers with Didrikson's athletic triumphs, which included her success as an AAU basketball player in the late 1920s, her "private octathlon" at the Olympic trials in 1932, and her prowess on the golf course in the 1940s. For all of that (and more), she earned top honors in 1950 as "woman athlete of the half century."[62]

But Gallico sought an additional honor for Babe's performance at the All-American golf championship in 1953. By that time, she had been diagnosed with colon cancer and had undergone a colostomy; yet three months after the operation, she was in Niles, Illinois, playing in the Tam O'Shanter All-American Championship—colostomy bag and all. Although Babe failed to win, Gallico asserted that it was a "miracle" she had played at all: "Her presence on that first tee was an act of heroism that should have been rewarded with the Congressional Medal of Honor. The value of her example in inspiration to others, and the magnificence of the banner she waved aloft to those of less courage and steadfastness, cannot be overestimated." Gallico was given to hyperbole, but Didrikson's willingness to continue playing on the LPGA tour with a colostomy bag was a momentous paradigm shift in the fight against cancer in the 1950s. And yet it was one that *Sports Illustrated* had essentially ignored. Indeed, the first issue of *Sports Illustrated* hit the stands a week after the Babe returned to Tam O'Shanter in 1954, making it the fifth tournament she had won that year. Yet *SI* did not report those achievements at all. At a time when cancer was spoken about in furtive and hushed whispers, Didrikson changed the way people discussed the disease and how they looked at battling and living with it, but Didrikson was featured in *SI* only in 1956, once she was too ill to play and had finally succumbed to the disease.[63]

Almost four decades later, LPGA golfer Heather Farr used *Sports Illustrated* to draw attention to her own struggle with cancer. In the intervening years, cancer diagnoses had moved into the mainstream, but according to Farr, government funds remained woefully inadequate, especially for breast cancer research, even though one in nine women would contract it. Farr insisted that all women needed to be aware that it could happen to them. Farr herself had been diagnosed with breast cancer with "none of the ordinary risk factors": she was fit, young—just twenty-four years old—and not genetically predisposed. Nevertheless, Farr insisted that her condition "was not unique or special," but "frighteningly . . . common place." As she battled the disease, she exemplified the mantra that had sustained her through other hard times on the LPGA tour: "You just play through it."[64]

"Playing through" is a common sports phrase for overcoming adversity, and *Sports Illustrated Women's* Bill Finley used it in 2002, when he reported on eleven sportswomen who had survived breast cancer. He related how playing sports had "helped them endure the disease," highlighting both their pre- and post-diagnosis athletic accomplishments.[65] Finley's reference to the curative power of sport for women was a significant departure from the way the media had portrayed women's interests in athletics throughout the early part of the twentieth century. His reference to women athletes as survivors, not victims, was highly significant.

But how should one distinguish victimhood from survivorship, particularly in *Sports Illustrated*? Sharon Lamb's work on victimization, cited by *SI*'s Howard and Munson in 1997, is a useful starting point. But such a focus also represents only half of the story. Although *Sports Illustrated* made references to both victims and survivors, it did so without clearly defining the terminology for readers—often using both terms interchangeably and indiscriminately regardless of the traumas sportswomen endured. Such a failure is significant given what scholars Kaitlin M. Boyle and Kimberly B. Rogers regard as the tension between the two terms in cultural discourse; the authors note that "survivor" is often imbued with more "positive and powerful attributes" than "victim," and indeed the two terms appear "as diametrically opposed categories in a binary. While 'victims' are portrayed as having little responsibility, agency, or power . . . 'survivors' are characterized as strong, willful agents who cope positively and resist male violence."[66]

Finley's account was also important in highlighting the differences in the depictions of sportswomen in *SI* and *SI Women*. First, although *SI Women* featured sportswomen enduring trials and tribulations, there was also a commitment on behalf of the magazine to portray these same women as overcoming adversity, and thus exploding the frailty myth. *SI for Women* featured athletes like runner Marla Runyan, who, declared legally blind at the age of ten, had been "refusing, resisting in every way possible to live a compromised existence," and professional golfer Se Ri Pak, who, "once hounded by the expectations of her father and countrymen," had "achieved balance and happiness by playing and living on her own terms." Even as female athletes endured emotional and psychological hardship, their portrayal as athletes who were "playing through" gave the lie to any "frailty myth." Cindy Stefanko, who was depicted mid-battle in her fight against melanoma, rejected outright the twenty-first-century mental health struggle version of fainting couches and rest cures, refusing the "tendency" of coaches and family "to put me in a glass box" and dispelling the frailty myth's association of women with weakness and debility.[67]

But the frailty myth also described physical limitations that sportswomen simply could not overcome. And *Sports Illustrated for Women* was important in this regard as well, for it featured women in sports that challenged perceived notions of women's physical capabilities. The magazine featured "gravity-addicted" skydiving team Voodoo Booty, which included Christine DeFelice, who continued to skydive at five months pregnant, and Lottie Aston, one of the "most accomplished young female parachutists in the country." Cave diver Jill Heinerth was "involved in what's considered the world's most dangerous sport," while free diver Tanya Streeter routinely descended to depths of two hundred feet or more and insisted, "There's still room to test our limits. It's a basic human need, almost like breathing, to know what is at the bottom of things." Testing those boundaries was the subject of an article entitled "No Limits" about female athletes looking to avail themselves of "the science of sport," which was testing new frontiers in nutrition, training, and recovery and thus allowing female athletes to embrace "cutting-edge training methods."[68] But the impact of *SI for Women* (and its various iterations) was limited because of the short duration and infrequency of its publication schedule; over a five-year span, only twenty-five issues were published, the equivalent of a six-month *Sports Illustrated* subscription.

Historically, sportswomen's depictions in the media have been minimal, so when *Sports Illustrated* depicted them battling cancer—often losing their battles, courageous as they might have been—or being attacked, or suffering from depression, or succumbing to injury, it reinforced notions that female athletes were incapable of enduring the physical and mental rigors associated with sport. Sports historian Mary Jo Festle has written that it is these stories about women suffering tragedy and victimization—not the accounts of their victories—that remain in the popular mind and skew the public's view of the female athlete. Festle declared that while female athletes were "among the strongest and most capable of women," many sportswomen gained media coverage not because of their athletic triumphs but because of their personal tragedies.[69] There is no question that the stories *Sports Illustrated* chose to feature about female athletes contributed to this perception.

For example, the magazine depicted both men and women suffering ACL tears, but only women were in danger of having that injury used to restrict their participation in sports. Likewise, both male and female athletes confronted mental health challenges, but it was women's struggles that tended to dominate sports headlines. Although there was no question that more women battled eating disorders and negative body image than men, and experienced sexual assault at higher rates than men, the focus was on women's individual battles instead of on a toxic culture that made female bodies particularly vulnerable. Only women seemed to be the targets of bizarre attacks, and those singular moments came to define entire careers, regardless of how the targets of such violence responded to them.

And not only did female athletes garner media coverage because of such vulnerability, they were celebrated for it. For example, Monica Seles, who was "transformed from champion to tragedienne" because of the 1993 attack, "became far more popular than she was while winning all those titles." According to *SI*'s L. Jon Wertheim, "It became impossible to root against her, at first out of sympathy, then because she revealed herself to be so thoroughly thoughtful, graceful, dignified. When she quietly announced her retirement last week at age 34, she exited perhaps the most adored figure in the sport's history. As endings go, one could do worse."[70] Perhaps, but it calls for a conversation about why female athletes are more acceptable not at their dominant best but as they exit the scene, injured and traumatized. Moreover, additional discussions are needed to examine why such injuries defined entire careers and how they are used to cast doubt on women's general suitability for sport. Finally, a focus on the unique ways in which Black female athletes experience victimhood and survivorship is required. Overwhelmingly, the female victims depicted in *Sports Illustrated* have been white women—whether that is reflective of racist stereotypes portraying white women as vulnerable and Black women as strong, or of selective storytelling, more research is needed on this issue. Indeed, Boyle and Rogers acknowledged that "little is known about how race and gender shape access to, and the impact of, 'victim' and 'survivor' identities" and noted, "Discourses around sexual victimization have historically centered the experiences of white girls and women."[71] Positioning race as the main focus in a discussion about the ways in which female athletes of color experience and express trauma of all kinds is essential and long overdue.

In the end, regardless of whether sportswomen emerged from a *Sports Illustrated* story as a victim or a survivor of the frailty myth, their careers were defined in ways that diminished them as athletes and were often used to question the suitability of females in the sports world more generally. However, such treatment abated every four years when *SI* celebrated the feats of sportswomen, who advanced their countries' international agendas through their Olympic performances.

5

"The Olympic Ideal"

Two MONTHS after *Sports Illustrated* first appeared on newsstands in August 1954, sportswriter Don Canham made a dire prediction: "Russia will win the 1956 Olympics." This was a remarkable projection, especially since the Russians had only just returned to Olympic competition in 1952, after a forty-year hiatus. It was an ominous one as well, for it was clear that the Soviets had the Americans in their sights and were "waging a cold war in sports." There was more at stake than just Olympic medals: "Since 1948, the year the Soviets gave up mass-participation sports in favor of developing individual stars, the Russians have made a concerted effort to lead the world, in all athletics, but in particular track and field. As Adolf Hitler once strove mightily to win the Berlin Olympics and thus prove the superiority of the Master Race, the Russians today look upon supremacy on the playing fields as solid vindication of their system of government and way of life." It was quite a pronouncement, and for Americans who were not yet even a decade removed from the end of World War II, the comparison of Communist Russia with Nazi Germany was designed to elicit a sense of foreboding. What's more, the "Russian plan" left nothing to chance: "Vast sums of money are being spent on specialized sport training institutes and there is a system for conscription of top athletes. Those who have done well have won cash awards and stars have sometimes been given pensions and even property." And it was not just men who were part of the plan: "Red women were as good as [their] male counterparts," wrote Canham, citing the athletic contributions of "muscular" Nina Ponomaryeva, "gaunt (6ft., 2in.), mannish Aleksandra Chudina, . . . and chunky Nina Chernoschek."[1] Make no mistake, these were men and women—and a country—to be reckoned with.

The question was whether the Americans should go "all out" in building an Olympic team that could take on the burgeoning juggernaut. It was one that *SI* first posed in 1955, and the response was overwhelmingly in the affirmative, mostly because it mattered so much to the Russians. An American defeat "would give the Russians a big propaganda lift," while an American victory would "leave the impression that the American way of life is a good way to live." In another issue, *SI* asked eight former (male) Olympians what the United States should do to "win the Olympics in 1956." Responses included offering incentives, "fostering enthusiasm," and creating a mentoring program.[2] It was an American blueprint for success, but was it in line with the Olympic spirit?

Not according to Dr. Charles A. Bucher, an expert *SI* tapped to discuss "the concept of high sportsmanship." In 1955 Bucher concluded that "the Olympic ideal is dying," and lamented that "this great international festival is becoming cannon fodder in the cold war, with major stress on national pride, winning, scoring points and beating Russia at all costs." An Olympic revival grounded in "world sportsmanship and good will" had given way to nationalism, politics, and a laser-like focus on who was winning the overall medal count—all of which were "destroying the spirit of the games" and amounted to a cold war of sports.[3]

That cold war of sports was predicated on using the Olympic Games to win international hearts and minds. As *Sports Illustrated* noted in 2016, Olympic sport was an integral tool for countries in amassing "soft power" as they sought to persuade rather than coerce other countries to follow their lead. Sports became both a proving ground and a public relations opportunity, and the Olympics in particular were a valuable global platform. Mapped onto the Cold War era, the Olympic Games became a surrogate battleground where the United States and the Soviet Union—and ultimately China—could do battle without the threat of starting a third world war.[4]

And serving as soldiers, diplomats, and ambassadors in this conflict were female athletes. Although men's bodies and their athletic achievements had always performed such a role, the Cold War would draw attention to women's bodies and performances in unprecedented ways as they were used to promote their nation's athletic ambitions and international aspirations, making them synonymous with the successes—and failures—of their countries' social, political, and economic ideologies. But even as countries benefited from Olympic medal bragging rights secured in part—or sometimes on the whole—by their female athletes, not all sportswomen profited from such an arrangement. Indeed, in some cases, an Olympic platform, designed to showcase a country's strength and prestige, instead highlighted its shortcomings, especially in guaranteeing the rights and freedoms of all its citizens, regardless of gender or race.

Nevertheless, the Olympics not only acted as a backdrop for showcasing a country's soft power but served as proof that *Sports Illustrated,* when it chose to, could feature sportswomen prominently in its pages. Every four years—and starting in 1994, every two years—women would appear in the magazine's Olympic coverage as the subjects of multiple features. Still, their appearance was entirely episodic—they often faded from its pages once the closing ceremonies had concluded—and consistently sexualized, revealing *SI*'s continued emphasis on highlighting sportswomen's feminine attributes as prominently as their Olympic achievements.

A chronological approach reveals how Olympic sportswomen depicted in *Sports Illustrated* became visible and sometimes outspoken public defenders of their countries' ideological faiths during the Cold War, thereby shoring up soft power on a global scale. Such a role was evident by the mid-1950s, a time when the Soviet Union was asserting its dominance in Olympic competition and prevailing—at least for the time being—in the space race.

"First Sputnik, Now This!"

On October 5, 1957, at 7:28 p.m., the Soviet Union launched the world's first artificial Earth satellite. Seen from millions of American backyards across the nation, Sputnik circled the globe for three weeks and ignited a space race that the Americans would not "win" until they placed a man on the moon in 1969. Until that time, Sputnik haunted Americans as they peered into the night sky and spurred government efforts to close the space gap.

Writers in *Sports Illustrated* regularly referenced Sputnik either directly or obliquely in their coverage of American-Soviet athletic battles during the 1950s and early 1960s, particularly when the Americans were on the losing end of the competition. In 1959 *SI* compared the Soviet ice hockey team's dominance with "its epic reach into space," claiming that Moscow was, "as usual, practicing one-upmanship in sports as well as in cosmic matters." But while an American loss to the Soviets in ice hockey was disappointing, it was a 1959 defeat in basketball—a homegrown sport—that was catastrophic and had ramifications beyond the arena. As *SI* noted, "Victory in international basketball lifts the hearts and impresses the minds of millions. 'Look here,' Chileans were saying as they watched the game in Santiago's vast National Stadium or listened to it on a dozen radio stations, 'first sputnik and now this. The Yankees can't even win at their own game.'"[5] Clearly the Americans were having a crisis of confidence, and it was not lost on their allies to the south—countries that might be tempted to switch their allegiance to a Communist system that was taking the world's lead in both space and sport.

Throughout the 1950s, the United States and the Soviet Union engaged in frequent athletic skirmishes as they jockeyed for Olympic supremacy. In particular, success in track and field motivated the Soviets as they sought to end a dominance that the United States had enjoyed since the modern Olympics were revived in 1896. According to *Sports Illustrated*, "Next to putting a Soviet citizen in orbit, heads of the U.S.S.R. polity would probably rather drub the United States in the dual track meet in Philadelphia this week than achieve any other thing." Dual track meets were often regarded as previews of coming Olympic attractions, and the Soviets had a chance to win those matchups because "the Russian female, at least in track and field, is much deadlier than the male." Because the Soviets saw their female athletes as crucial contributors to the "Russian plan" of athletic dominance and devoted ten times the amount of support to its women than the United States did—particularly in track and field—American women often found themselves on the losing end of these dual track meets.[6] The response from American track and field officials was to insist on scoring the men and women separately—a demand the Soviets rejected, accurately claiming that such an approach was not the international norm. As a result, the Soviets often won these early dual track and field meets. While the American male could hold his own and best the Soviet male, the Soviet females throughout the 1950s dominated their American counterparts.

Their supremacy was evident across the board. According to *SI*, "Since 1946, Russian track and field women have been ripping off one astounding performance after another. They were the talk of the '52 Olympics and today hold world records in three of the nine events on the Olympic program, share the record in two others and are represented among the first four in the remaining events." In fact, the Russian women were so "highly trained and internationally experienced" that they "seem[ed] likely to thoroughly trounce the opposition and . . . have at least one woman placing in every one of the nine women's events" at the 1956 Olympics. That included shotputter and "solid blonde" Galina Zybina, who had already won gold in 1952, had broken her own world record eleven times, and was eyeing another gold in 1956. Such determination to excel was in stark contrast to American "javelinist" Karen Anderson, who was an "attractive blonde with light gray-blue eyes," and felt "sensibly about the Olympics: 'I'm not going to roll over and die if I don't win a medal. Life will go on for me.'" Such contrasting levels of dedication led *SI* to wonder, "Can the Soviet girls be stopped?" But the Americans had some outstanding talent of their own by 1956, including the "First Lady of U.S. Track," Mae Faggs, who at twenty-four was already "one of America's alltime greats who ha[d] represented the U.S. in every important national and international contest since the 1948 Olympics." Although Faggs was joined by other talented sprinters—including a sixteen-year-old Wilma Rudolph—the team was limited by the U.S. Olympic Board to ten "girls" for nine events.[7] It was not exactly a recipe for success, and the team won only three medals, all by women who had competed (or would compete) for coaches at a Historically Black College or University: Faggs and Rudolph were joined on the 4x100 meter relay team that won bronze by Isabelle Daniels and Margaret Matthews, Willye White earned a silver in the long jump, and Mildred McDaniel took gold in the high jump.

It was a tradition that predated the Olympic team of 1956. Olympic track and field events had showcased the potential of Black women as early as 1932 when hurdler Tidye Pickett and sprinter Louise Stokes had qualified for the Olympic team. Racist pranks by teammate Babe Didrikson and racist decisions by team coaches who refused to let the two women compete defined their experience in Los Angeles but did not deter them from trying to realize their Olympic dreams. Four years later, Pickett and Stokes qualified for the team once again, earning the right to travel to Berlin and compete in the 1936 Games. Pickett and Stokes were only two women of color on a thirteen-person American women's track and field team, but their presence would inspire succeeding generations of Black sportswomen; by the time the Olympics resumed after an eight-year hiatus due to World War II, Black females represented nine of the twelve American sportswomen on the 1948 track and field team, which included Audrey Patterson, the first Black woman to medal at the Olympics, winning bronze in the 200-meter sprint, and Alice Coachman, the first Black woman to win an Olympic event, earning gold in the high jump.

While *Sports Illustrated's* 1956 coverage of Black women in track and field is notable, it fails to place their performances in historical perspective, nor does it address the significance that Black sportswomen's Olympic success occurred *only* in track and field at this time because it was the one sport—Olympic or otherwise—in which Black women could compete against white women in a segregated America. It was also a sport, according to sports scholars Patricia Vertinsky and Gwendolyn Captain, "from which white women had largely withdrawn." Even as the magazine praised the efforts of Black women, it failed to address why it was "sensible" for a number of American white women not to worry about securing track and field honors.[8] *SI* simply ignored the racialized and classed connotations associated with the sport, as well as the implied concerns about the femininity—or lack thereof—of successful sprinters, throwers, and jumpers, be they "chunky" Russians or American women of color. Finally, although the United States was happy to count the medals of Black women and men toward an overall medal count, especially when it allowed them to defeat the Soviet Union, it was less interested in considering the barriers that kept them from participating fully in all Olympic sports and in American society. By the 1960s, as anxieties about Sputnik gave way to concerns about soft Americans and their inability to protect democracy at home and abroad, those oversights became even more pronounced.

"The Vigor We Need"

On December 26, 1960, *SI* featured an article by president-elect John F. Kennedy, who used the magazine—and its stature with the American people—to extol the glory of ancient Olympia as an object lesson for Americans who needed to be physically fit for themselves and for their nation. Kennedy noted that the winners of the ancient "Olympian Games" embodied "the prime foundations of a vigorous state," but JFK feared that modern Americans had forgotten "that the physical well-being of the citizen is an important foundation for the vigor and vitality of all the activities of the nation." And the timing could not have been worse: "We face in the Soviet Union a powerful and implacable adversary determined to show the world that only the Communist system possesses the vigor and determination necessary to satisfy awakening aspirations for progress and the elimination of poverty and want. To meet the challenge of this enemy will require determination and will and effort on the part of all Americans. Only if our citizens are physically fit will they be fully capable of such an effort."[9] Two years later, Kennedy once again used *Sports Illustrated* and references to the ancient Olympic Games to accentuate the connection between physically fit citizens and a strong nation state. In "The Vigor We Need," JFK continued to press his case with the American people to prioritize physical fitness as a means of national security. For the president, the pursuit of physical fitness was the price all Americans had to pay to defend their nation in a broader effort to secure world peace. JFK was not the first president to recognize the benefits of physical fitness, but he was the first to use *Sports Illustrated*—acknowledging its popularity with millions of subscribers and thus its status as a media influencer—to beseech Americans to take responsibility not only for their own health but for that of their country.[10]

Following JFK's assassination in 1963, his brother Robert F. Kennedy continued to use *Sports Illustrated* to emphasize the importance of America's dominance in Olympic sport. In 1964 RFK noted that "in this day of international stalemates nations use the scoreboard of sports as a visible measuring stick to prove their superiority over the 'soft and decadent' democratic way of life. It is thus in our national interest that we regain our Olympic superiority—that we once again give the world visible proof of our inner strength and vitality." Kennedy acknowledged that "part of a nation's prestige in the cold war is won in the Olympic games." And sport, in general, was important. RFK maintained that although "a nation's standing in international athletics is not the chief factor in its prestige, it does affect the reputation of its society and culture. During a military or nuclear stalemate such as the world is now experiencing athletics can become an increasingly important factor in international relations."[11] Kennedy had an eight-point plan for success that "urg[ed] and support[ed] greater participation by women in amateur athletics." Eight years before the passage of Title IX, RFK was calling for an investment in women's sport to advance America's Olympic prestige and to gain an edge in Cold War diplomacy. No longer an afterthought, women's athletic performances were crucial to securing soft power. Indeed, Kennedy believed that as women assumed "an increasingly important role in national life, our country should have more women athletes winning in

Wilma Rudolph's three gold medals at the 1960 Olympic Games in Rome made her popular with audiences throughout the world. But the unique challenges she faced as a Black athlete—and particularly as a Black female athlete—were not addressed in *Sports Illustrated*.

the Olympics," and he hoped more young women would follow the examples of Babe Didrikson, who had helped save Olympic track and field events for women in the 1930s, and Wilma Rudolph, whose three gold medals in 1960 captivated not just those who saw her race in Rome but a new made-for-TV audience as well.[12]

Wilma Rudolph's newfound stardom was clear during her post-Olympic tour through Europe following the summer games. *SI* found there were so many fans that "in Cologne it took mounted police to keep back her admirers; in Wuppertal, police dogs." It was a very different use of police dogs than what Black Americans would encounter three years later in Birmingham as they protested for their basic human rights. While Rudolph was not as active in civil rights protests as other athletes would be in the late 1960s, she did use her newfound Olympic fame to leverage a fully integrated homecoming ceremony in her hometown. Even as "Clarksville's mayor jovially claimed her for the television cameras," Rudolph's requests were met—albeit off camera and out of the public record.[13] Also missing from *SI*'s coverage was Rudolph's childhood battle with polio, which left her in leg braces, forced to travel an hour to Meharry Hospital two days a week because the local, all-white hospital in Clarksville refused to treat her. But race was simply not an issue that *Sports Illustrated* writers considered in the early 1960s, except perhaps to dismiss it as an issue at all.

In 1961, for example, *SI*'s Roy Terrell noted that "regimented Muscovites" were surprised by the interracial camaraderie of the American team, marveling at "the sight of Cliff Cushman and Wilma Rudolph sightseeing together in Red Square or John Thomas and Pat Daniels eating ice cream in front of the Metropole Hotel." This was particularly the case because "the Communist party line had been trumpeting that Negro athletes were a new kind of slave, competing unpaid for the prestige of the United States while fat whites sat back to reap the benefits." Terrell raised the issue only to set it aside: "The only visible benefits to white members of the U.S. team were friendship and ice cream cones."[14]

The Soviet hype that American Black athletes had been reduced to a veritable state of slavery was a popular tactic, as Terrell suggested, and an effective one, which he simply ignored. Clashes over the enforcement of school desegregation, lunch counter protests, and Freedom Rides all placed the lack of equality experienced by Black Americans and the brutal opposition to their battles for social justice on the front pages of national and international news media. The Soviets recognized the dependence of American medal counts on Black performances, a reliance that had been evident as early as 1936 when Black sprinter Jesse Owens won four gold medals as part of an eighteen-person Black contingent which won a total of fourteen medals—eight of them gold—to belie Nazi claims of Aryan superiority.[15] Like the Nazis, who had bemoaned an American dependence on "Black auxiliaries," the Soviets also recognized American reliance on its Black Olympians, even as they emphasized the hypocrisy of a nation celebrating its Black athletes once every four years while ignoring the structural economic, political, and social disadvantages that reduced them to second-class citizens, regardless of the Olympic cycle.[16]

The Soviet Union thus questioned the benefits of an American political and economic system that treated so many of its citizens so poorly, especially when they had performed so admirably for their country. The U.S. Olympic Committee had little recourse other than to celebrate decathlete Rafer Johnson, who became the first Black athlete to carry the American flag in the opening ceremonies at the 1960 Olympic Games. SI's depictions of race relations undoubtedly helped the USOC counter Soviet claims of African Americans' second-class citizenship. According to SI, the athletes themselves were more interested in enjoying a carefree ice cream cone with their teammates in a mixed-race setting than in engaging Russia's provocative claims. This framing of civil rights mirrored State Department efforts to ensure domestic tranquility at home and win hearts and minds abroad—particularly in African countries—and the State Department regularly used Black athletes for international tours that combined athletic exhibitions with political overtones.[17]

SI's reluctance to confront "the racial question" stemmed from both its disinclination to become a political player and its aversion to offending an overwhelmingly white readership. But by the mid-1960s Sports Illustrated was increasingly acknowledging the racism that existed in American society and thus in American sport. In 1965 one of the magazine's writers traveled with boxer Muhammad Ali and his entourage, chronicling the experience in "The World Champion Is Refused a Meal," which highlighted the prejudice and discrimination all Black Americans experienced no matter what they had achieved in sport or outside it.[18] It was an important moment for Sports Illustrated as the magazine began to engage race and sport in a serious way.

That commitment was particularly evident when SI published "The Black Athlete" in 1968. Conceived in 1967, the five-part, groundbreaking series by Jack Olsen represented the growing activism among Black athletes as well as a growing interest on the part of Sports Illustrated to explode misconceptions that American sport was enlightened in its race relations. For five straight weeks during the summer of 1968, Olsen bombarded the Sports Illustrated reader with evidence that sport was not the great equalizer that many athletic officials and Americans might have believed it to be: "Sport has long been comfortable in its pride at being one of the few areas of American society in which the Negro has found opportunity—and equality. But has sport in America deceived itself? Is its liberality a myth, its tolerance a deceit? Increasingly, Black athletes are saying that sport is doing a disservice to their race by setting up false goals, perpetuating prejudice and establishing an insidious bondage all its own."[19] This was exactly the argument proffered by sports sociologist and civil rights activist Harry Edwards, who, as the lead organizing force behind the Olympic Project for Human Rights, was encouraging African American athletes to consider a boycott of the 1968 Olympic Games in Mexico City: "For years we have participated in the Olympic Games, carrying the U.S. on our backs with our victories, and race relations are worse now than ever. Now they are even shooting people in the streets. We're not trying to lose the Olympics for the Americans. What happens to *them* is immaterial. If they finish first, that's beautiful. If they finish 14th, that's beautiful, too. But it's time for the Black people to stand up as men and women and refuse to be utilized as performing animals for a little extra dog food." *Sports Illustrated* noted that while there was initial widespread support for a boycott from a number of athletes, including sprinters Tommie Smith and Lee Evans, "no one is sure how effective the strike will be." But the proposal, which Olsen regarded as "no idle threat," had resonated with athletes and had prompted *Sports Illustrated* to explore "the roots and validity of the Black athlete's unrest," finding their criticisms "well founded."[20]

It was a startling revelation by the magazine, and Olsen's series would bring much needed attention to the plight of the Black male athlete, even as he completely ignored the experiences of Black sportswomen. And Olsen was not alone. While Harry Edwards had acknowledged the importance of Black men and women standing united, the Olympic Project for Human Rights did not actively involve Black sportswomen in its meetings or events. That left Wyomia Tyus, who won gold in the 100 meters at the 1968 Olympics, with no formal outlet to protest. Instead, she dedicated her gold medal to Tommie Smith and John Carlos, who had been dismissed from Mexico City by the IOC following their "black glove gesture." Having won the gold and bronze respectively in the 200-meter final, Smith and Carlos ascended the medal podium and threw their gloved fists in the air to protest the second-class status of Black Americans as the national anthem of the United States played; Smith and Carlos "were booed" by the crowd, censured by the IOC, and generally reviled by (white) Americans for their protest.[21]

Even as *SI* wrestled with whether the IOC had offered a measured response to Smith's and Carlos's actions, the magazine lamented the way in which the incident overshadowed other Olympians' achievements, like those of sixteen-year-old Debbie Meyer, whose Olympic performance was undoubtedly impressive—and unquestionably less threatening. Meyer "deserve[d] a ticker-tape parade" for becoming the first swimmer to win three individual gold medals in one Olympics and, no doubt, for offering *Sports Illustrated* readers a respite from the militant protests of (Black) America to focus instead on a (white) American swimmer whose biggest concerns seemed to be cosmetics and junk food.[22]

Although Mae Faggs, Wilma Rudolph, and Wyomia Tyus contributed the desired performances to prove American "vim and vigor" and to acquire the international prestige the Kennedy brothers had deemed essential, their efforts were ultimately on behalf of a country that did not prioritize or protect their individual freedoms. But if the American government was slow in addressing racial inequality, *SI* was equally unhurried in tackling pervasive racism in sport, choosing initially to focus on the easy camaraderie between Black and white athletes abroad rather than the realities of race relations at home, and ignoring the unique plight of Black women altogether. Nonetheless, the experiences and accomplishments of American Black sportswomen underscored the centrality of female athletes to an overall medal count and their value to national prestige.

"Assembly Line for Champions"

During the 1960s, American women made great strides in Olympic competition and were no longer startled by the aggressive play and "unladylike behavior" of their Russian opponents in basketball and track and field. As a result, *SI* noted that the United States was becoming downright "possessive about its women athletes and rightly: they shape up as a real Olympic threat." By 1964, then, American sportswomen seemed to have met the Olympic mark when *Sports Illustrated* announced: "At last, the girls are *ours.*"[23] It was a clear statement about the gains American women had made in closing the achievement gap with their Soviet counterparts and how important women had become in promoting American ideals on an Olympic stage during the Cold War.

Such an avowal also represented an investment in women's sports by an American government eager to secure the top spot in Olympic medal counts. Various initiatives to promote Olympic sports and women's participation in them were underway as early as the 1950s, when the Eisenhower administration promoted the founding of the U.S. Olympic Development Committee and created the President's Council on Youth Fitness. The Olympic committee, in particular, advanced women's sports by working with the Amateur Athletic Union to offer more women's track meets and lobbying the Division of Girls and Women's Sports to support increased competitive opportunities. Led by female physical education teachers, the Division of Girls and Women's Sports had long resisted women's competition in elite sports because it focused too much attention on the exceptional few and on winning—in short, it smacked too much of a male model of sports. But the female leaders of the DGWS reveled in the new-found attention and recognition of their professional expertise and thus tempered their anticompetitive stance, urging schools to adopt Olympic sports in their curricula and supporting women's participation in them.[24] In the succeeding decade, the DGWS would hold clinics for athletes and coaches alike, particularly encouraging women to avail themselves of opportunities in sports newly added to the Olympic docket.

By 1976 those sports included basketball, handball, and rowing. Yet throughout the 1970s, *Sports Illustrated* devoted most of its coverage, not to these "new" Olympic sports for women, but to swimming and gymnastics, in which women had contested since 1912 and 1936, respectively. This was not a surprise. Both sports represented "acceptable" options because sportswomen competed in them individually instead of on teams, and they incorporated qualities, like graceful movement, that were quintessentially female. Because of both the appropriateness and the resulting popularity of their sports, gymnasts and swimmers served throughout the 1970s as critical emissaries of their countries' desires to promote their political systems and press their advantages on a world stage.

By 1972 gymnasts had taken center stage at the Munich Olympics with their usual grace, but also with a newfound youth. The new darling of Olympic gymnastics, seventeen-year-old Olga Korbut, represented a paradigm shift as "women's gymnastics" became the province of younger girls whose thinner and shorter bodies allowed them to perform flips, twists, and other tricks never seen before. At Mexico City in 1968, twenty-six-year-old Vera Caslavska, who stood tall 5'3" and weighed 128 pounds, had successfully defended her Olympic gold from the 1964 all-around competition. Only four years later, the teenaged Korbut was eighty-four pounds and 4'10", and *SI* was simply giddy about the "elfin Russian girl" whose "biggest triumph was a brand-new move, never displayed before by anyone, anywhere. Its technical title is simply 'backflip,' but even the most casual observer knew down his spine that he had just seen something unique."[25]

But Korbut was not the only "diminutive" darling in Munich. According to *Sports Illustrated*, at 4'11", Cathy Rigby was "the typical little American girl. A nice, clean kid. The American ideal. Something like Shirley Temple." But a happy ending eluded the American "pixie." Although Korbut missed out on the big prize as well—teammate Ludmilla Turishcheva took home the gold in the all-around competition—it was Korbut who was the "star attraction of the Soviet women's gymnastic team" and heralded a new era in the sport.[26]

Four years later, Romanian Nadia Comăneci became a sensation in the Korbut mold, and then broke it, ushering in "the Comaneci era" by stunning fans and judges alike "not only with double backward somersaults and twists but also with an uncommon consistency and stability even in her most difficult moves." She displayed "an unflappable confidence and more stamina and strength than seemed possible for a body as apparently frail as hers. . . . everybody was talking about Comaneci," who was only fourteen. By the time she completed her Olympic debut in Montreal, the talk had turned to cheers, and nowhere was the acclaim greater than in *Sports Illustrated*. The importance of her Olympic performances enhanced the sport of gymnastics, even as it transcended it. According to *SI*, Comăneci's "precision and daring in gymnastics have never been seen before in an Olympics. And few heroines in any sport ever so captivated the Games. She was superbly cast for the moment, bursting upon the world with the first perfect Olympic gymnastic score, a 10.0, on the first day of competition, thereby dramatically ridding Montreal of much of the rancor and turmoil of international politics. Nadia Comaneci . . . was brilliant and beguiling, and because of her youth a great sense of hope and history was instantly attached to her." Even as Comăneci took center stage with her seven perfect 10.0s, a score no gymnast had ever earned, she shared with Korbut a lasting legacy that was similar in two important respects. First, Korbut's Olympic performance in 1972 sparked an American interest in gymnastics that Comăneci would augment after 1976. In addition, both of them revealed an image of Communism that was enchanting and hopeful. Korbut maintains that Soviet ambassador Anatoli Dobrynin told her that her brief repartee with Nixon during a White House visit in 1972 eased Cold War tensions between the countries and paved the way for Nixon's visit to Moscow in 1974. For its part, *SI* recounted that "once the Games began and Nadia Comaneci became the world's sweetheart," Olympic boycotts and international discord faded away—at least from the front page.[27]

Comăneci was not the only female and Communist star of the 1976 games. *Sports Illustrated* noted that she had some competition from the East German swimmer Kornelia Ender, who was "every bit as outstanding in her specialty." But there was a caveat. While "little" Nadia Comăneci was a "Carpathian princess," Ender was "a strapping *fräulein*"—one who was "a little too strapping for women viewers to identify with." Olympic competition was not new for Ender. She had earned silver in the 200-meter individual medley in 1972, but hers was the sole bright spot for a women's swim team that was lackluster at best. That all changed a year later at the world championships when "the Mighty Mädchen" from the German Democratic Republic smashed seven world records and won eleven of thirteen events. It was a stunning performance that left the American team reeling and *SI* questioning how "a nation of 17 million, a second-ranked power a few months ago, had so quickly moved to the top of women's swimming." The magazine attributed the change in part to "a broad-based fitness program in which 90% of GDR children learn to swim by age 4. This enables the coaches to identify promising swimmers early. They also pay more attention to fluid mechanics and sports medicine than most U.S. coaches, and the brawn and explosive power of their women in Belgrade suggested that they are more heavily into weight training, too." There were also rumors of steroid abuse, which East German coaches denied, insisting they had beaten the Americans at their own game, using what they had gleaned from watching them win for years.[28] A "budding rivalry" was on.

On the other side of that rivalry was Shirley Babashoff, the best chance the United States had for overcoming Ender and her crew. Like Ender, Babashoff had gained experience in Munich, and by 1976 she was "virtually a one-girl U.S. team holding back the East German flood."[29] But Babashoff would not be enough in Montreal to stem the tide, and the "East German women who had never before won an Olympic gold medal in swimming up until Montreal . . . made amends" when Ender single-handedly won four gold medals, becoming the first woman to win so many in a single Olympics.[30] *SI* attributed her dominance, and that of her team, to a system of sports clubs that represented a veritable "assembly line for champions." Club membership included some 12,000 athletes ranging in age from five to thirty-five, most of whom "live in dormitories on the club grounds, in an atmosphere of total sports immersion. Younger athletes usually attend special schools located on the premises, with classes arranged around their training schedules; older ones work at nearby jobs receiving whatever time off they need—at full pay—for practice and competition. Food is plentiful and sports doctors and coaches hover about." And the perks of being a state-supported athlete did not end there. Gold medalists and world record holders were "routinely awarded the Distinguished Service to the Fatherland medal, entitling recipients to generous extra pensions when they reach retirement age."[31]

Sport was part of the very fabric of the GDR, so much so that the country's constitution specifically referred to it as being "essential" to the "'development of a socialist personality,' thus inextricably tying up athletics with lofty notions of duty and discipline"—exactly the case JFK had tried to make to his fellow Americans in 1962. But sport in the GDR was about more than simply advancing health objectives and habits of self-control and restraint. *SI* informed American readers that "a related purpose is to go on supplying world-beaters who will perform 'for the glory of [their] socialist homeland,' as called for by Party Boss Erich Honecker in a recent speech extolling sport."[32] East Germany's decision to use female athletes to secure soft power underscored the important roles women had assumed in promoting their nation's prestige.

As Americans sought to keep up with their East European rivals in the pool and the gymnasium, they, like their athletic foes, assumed unprecedented visibility as the symbols of their respective systems' successes. Thus, using an Olympic platform to advance a country's own national interests had become a standard feature of soft power, and nations ran up medal counts to prove the power and legitimacy of their systems, an approach the Soviet Union and the United States had perfected and that other countries like East Germany sought to emulate. Essential to those medal counts and to a growing international profile were the athletic achievements and personas of sportswomen who had become not just national treasures but compelling diplomatic emissaries.

"A Sweat-Suit Diplomat"

At the 1984 Winter Olympics in Sarajevo, East German figure skater Katarina Witt seemed almost single-handedly to validate the GDR with her gold medal–winning performance, captivating *Sports Illustrated* reporters with her finesse and beauty. Four years later, Witt was poised to defend her title in Calgary, but by 1988 American Debi Thomas had emerged as a real threat to Witt's dominance. And with that a rivalry was born, one that was only enhanced when Witt, the "artistic beauty of the East," and Thomas, "the athletic fighter of the West," offered dueling versions of "Carmen" for their long program.[33] They also offered dueling visions of the political systems they represented.

In 1986 Witt touted the advantages of the East German system in the pages of *Sports Illustrated:* "Our system is good. Every child has a chance.

Audiences on both sides of the Iron Curtain were infatuated with East German figure skater Katarina Witt.

Parents don't have to have a lot of money. Our coaches don't have to be paid like in other countries." Years later, Witt continued to defend "the G.D.R.'s wunderkind system of Olympic success," which had covered all expenses associated with her training, asserting that without it she would never have become a figure skater—her family simply could not have afforded it. Witt was nothing if not an ambassador for her country and for Communism. Indeed, *SI* acknowledged in 1986 that Witt was "a sweatsuit diplomat for the East German way of sport," not only extolling the advantages of the Communist system but personifying it—in the best way possible. According to the magazine, Witt's beauty made her "a lousy enemy of capitalism." Forget "Raisa Gorbachev, here's Katarina, 5'5" and 114 pounds worth of peacekeeping missile." It seemed clear that should glasnost fail, Witt's status as a "socialist sex symbol" might be all it took to preserve cordial relations between East and West.[34] Like Olga Korbut and Nadia Comǎneci before her, Katarina Witt was a Communist everyone could love. Part of the adoration was certainly the winning athletic performances of these female athletes, but equally compelling was their physical packaging: diminutive and conventionally gorgeous, these were females who were persuasive and charming and thus delightfully nonthreatening. While they were just as ruthless as their male counterparts in terms of their Olympic performances, they seemed less likely to represent a way of life that was antagonistic and bellicose.

Although they represented the best of what Communism stood for, *SI* was careful to point out that their success and resulting stardom accrued certain privileges that allowed them to circumvent the more depressing aspects associated with a Communist way of life. In East Germany, for example, a citizen could "apply for a car" but "it takes 10 years to get it. You want an apartment? It can take nearly as long. You want to visit the West? No problem: When you're 65, you can visit the West." But if you were an athletic star on the magnitude of Katarina Witt, you enjoyed certain perks like having an apartment, a car, and the ability to travel—no application necessary. *SI* noted that "unless she applied for the apartment and the car at 10, she is getting the star treatment." But the magazine also acknowledged that "Witt is not just a star, she is a breathing, breathtaking billboard for the G.D.R."[35]

In sharp contrast to Witt and the "specialized sports high school" that allowed her to practice for hours every day, Debi Thomas "took a break from her late-hour studies" at Stanford University to win the U.S. figure skating championship in 1986. Although Thomas lived in the dorms, it was anything but "an atmosphere of total sports immersion." The American spent more time off the ice than on it owing to her premed studies; indeed, Thomas's insistence on maintaining her college course load at the same time she sought Olympic gold was, according to *SI*, even more remarkable than being "the first Black national champion in U.S. figure skating history." That was particularly true since so much about race relations in America had "changed in a generation." Thomas, herself, rarely thought about what she dubbed "The Black Question" ("How does it feel to be the first black champion in a lily-white sport?"); she had shared the rink with other Black skaters and was familiar with the pioneering achievements of Atoy Wilson, who was the men's national novice champion in 1966. Moreover, Thomas had never been made to feel she "was any different from anyone else," and her mother insisted that she didn't "even know the meaning of being discriminated against."[36]

It seemed that the civil rights battles of the 1960s had allowed Black Americans to enjoy a color-blind America by the mid-1980s. Proof of such a reality was not just a Black figure skating champion, but a presidential campaign launched by the Reverend Jesse Jackson in 1984, the same year that *The Cosby Show* premiered. These developments, among others, exploded stereotypes about Black Americans in the 1980s and their abilities to represent mainstream America. Thus, a Black figure skater competing for Olympic gold seemed illustrative of a country that had finally overcome racial prejudice. Indeed, Thomas's comments regarding her national title in 1986 had dispensed entirely with the need for any racial qualification: "Why on earth would I want to become the first black champion? I just wanted to be the champion."[37]

That *Sports Illustrated* pursued a similar tack was not surprising, given its history of ignoring painful racial realities. In the 1980s, those included a rise in racial violence, growing economic disparities, and a general "structural distance" between whites with privilege and the "Black underclass." But a focus on a prime-time media presence and political leadership, as well as antidiscrimination legislation, affirmative action, and the emergence of Black studies programs obfuscated ongoing and deeply ingrained racism, offering a vision of a country that had solved its race problem.[38] *SI* perpetuated this image with its features on Thomas, which focused on the stark contrast she offered as an American skater—not a Black American skater—in comparison with the East German Witt. And the comparisons were ubiquitous. Unlike the East German beauty, the studious American was "loath to devote all her time to skating because 'this sport is flaky' and because she harbors fears of 'frying my brain.'" Such an approach seemed quintessentially American, as did Thomas's ethic of individualism and merit-based advancement. But her split loyalties were driving her coach crazy, since he worried that "the East Germans are training up to eight hours a day."[39] Nevertheless, Thomas secured top honors at the 1986 World Championships, defeating Witt, the two-time defending champion. Thomas's performance had put the East German on notice.

And Witt responded. The following year, Witt regained the world championship title, impressing judges and fans alike and infuriating Thomas's coach who, according to *SI*, wanted the American crowd "to show some flag-waving nationalism to spur on Debi." But this was not the tense Cold War climate that had pervaded earlier East-West rivalries in the 1950s, nor was Katarina Witt your average East German foe. As dominant as Kornelia Ender and the "Mighty Mädchen," Witt had more in common with Olga Korbut and Nadia Comăneci in offering a graceful and friendly version of Communism. By the early 1990s, however, Witt's Olympic career and East Germany were both defunct; Witt had retired in 1988 after winning her second gold medal, and with the fall of the Berlin Wall in 1989, Germany reunified in 1990. In addition, the dissolution of the Soviet Union a year later not only ended an international Cold War that had divided the globe, but heralded an end to a Communist "sports machine" that had dominated Olympic events since 1952.[40] Female athletes were no longer symbolic foot soldiers whose Olympic performances provided an invaluable service in promoting democracy or Communism during the Cold War.

But even with the end of the Cold War and the resulting shifts in geopolitical rivalries, the importance of sportswomen's Olympic performances remained essential to elevating their country's global profile. As a result, although the players changed, soft power was no less potent. Looking to secure "comfortable legitimacy," China sought to fill the vacuum left by the reunification of Germany in 1990 and the Soviet Union's dissolution in 1991, using a dominance in Olympic sport to promote its own brand of Communism and become a player on the world stage. The United States had a new foe.

"The Birth of an Athletic Power"

In 1988 *Sports Illustrated* included a special report on sports in China. Heralding "the birth of an athletic power," the eight-article series included a feature that acknowledged that China was "fast becoming a world sports power" and that while "sport, of course, isn't the highest manifestation of civilization . . . it surely can be one of the more illusionary. If you can't outbomb everybody else, or outproduce them, or outdress them, or even outdream them, you can rather quickly outplay them." It evoked an earlier era of soft power in action: "What China is doing is no different from what East Germany and a lot of impoverished nations have done. Oh, to be sure, the Chinese pay lip service to the concept of universal exercise for the dear masses . . . but the fact is that the government's serious attention and most of its resources are devoted to the elite few who might bring Olympic glory to the People's Republic and thereby make it shine in the eyes of other countries and, more important, in those of its own citizens." The financial resources alone were impressive. *SI* noted that the Chinese government's budget for sport approached $300 million, "which may not sound like much, but it's a considerable sum . . . in a land that to a considerable degree lacks the most basic amenities like paved roads." Those funds went not only to "force-feeding" those "sports unfamiliar to China" but to "building facilities, training new coaches, [and] generally catching up, because a whole generation of sporting activity was lost to the Cultural Revolution."[41]

China's emergence as a serious athletic power on an international, Olympic stage was no surprise to *SI*'s William Johnson, who had traveled the country in 1973 with a basketball delegation of forty-six male and female players, "making it the largest of the American groups that had been allowed into China since Richard Nixon's historic visit there in the winter of 1972." During his visit, Johnson witnessed men and women engaged in "mass calisthenics in vacant factory lots and vast rooms full of absolutely savage Ping-Pong players scarcely as tall as the table." Those players' predecessors had changed the course of Sino-American relations; after years of diplomatic isolation, China had put out feelers to the United States in 1971 through an exchange of male and female ping-pong players that cleared a path for a formal visit by President Richard Nixon to China a year later. Johnson had commented on the exchange in *Sports Illustrated* in 1972, emphasizing the importance of sport as "the only bridge across the chasm of fear and vituperation that had separated Red China and the West." While the original visit seemed the stuff of fiction, Johnson noted that "the President of the U.S. had since trod where only table tennis addicts had gone before, and the world will never be quite the same again." Here was an example of sports directly paving the way for diplomatic relations between two previously hostile countries, and for star athletes like ping-pong player Chuang Tse-tung to become "a sort of statesman-sportsman." Tse-tung spoke about the power of such athletic exchanges: "We hope through our contests in this sport to build a growing understanding between China and Canada and the United States and Mexico. We are here to cultivate blooms of friendship." It was a stance that the legendary Mao Zedong had underscored when he "had chosen sports as his favored diplomatic vehicle."[42]

Fifteen years later, Johnson noted that while the importance of sports exchanges remained, the lip service the Chinese had given to their importance of promoting "friendship first, competition second" had given way to a singular emphasis on competition. In 1988 one Chinese sports official noted, "We believe that competition comes first, that losing is nothing, while winning is very, very important." With the country seeking to overcome the ravages wrought by the Cultural Revolution, Johnson had seen a huge change both in sports and society in the fifteen years since he had last visited China. And the next fifteen? Johnson predicted that "Beijing will be putting the finishing touches on a whole grand landscape of gleaming sports facilities as it gets ready to host the XXVIII Summer Olympics of 2004." Johnson missed the mark by only four years, but his second prediction, "that the Beijing Games will be a thundering success," was spot on. The Bird's Nest and the Water Cube dazzled spectators and athletes alike and served as sites for magnificent sporting performances—particularly Michael Phelps's record-setting eight gold medals in a single Olympics and a Jamaican sweep of the women's 100-meter finals.[43]

But perhaps most impressive was the Chinese athletes' performances at the 2008 Olympics. The home team netted a hundred medals in total, forty-eight of them gold. This was the culmination of an investment in sports facilities that *Sports Illustrated* writers had remarked upon in their 1988 special report and in the athletes themselves—particularly female athletes, who saw their participation in sports as a means to "defend the country and advance the socialist revolution." *SI* had highlighted the efforts of Chinese female athletes in 1988, particularly in gymnastics, noting that in China "no one is spared." As China looked to improve upon its "stunning performance" at the L.A. Games, where the team won thirty-two medals—fifteen of them gold—it "reaffirmed the official Chinese view that the Games give the developing country the biggest p.r. bang for its buck."[44]

By 1992 the stars of the Chinese sports machine were undoubtedly its women. Crucial to China's original vision of becoming an athletic power was its investment in female athletes, which was, according to scholar Fan Hong, "purposefully established and sustained." By the early 1990s its investment was yielding dividends. Of the fifty-four medals China won in Barcelona, women won thirty-four of them, including twelve golds. What factors contributed to their success? According to *SI*'s Alexander Wolff, Chinese sports officials believed "that the physiological differences between Asian and Western women were negligible compared with those between Asian and Western men, and were easier to overcome with rigorous training and diligent coaching." Chinese techniques were predicated on racist stereotypes, for, in truth, physiological differences between Asian and white women—particularly in height—were similar to those between Asian and white men. Of far more significance was how long Chinese women had participated in organized, international sport compared with Western women. Because the Olympics were slow to welcome *all* females, Western sportswomen had less of a head start on their Asian counterparts than Western sportsmen had on Asian men.[45]

But perhaps the biggest advantage for the Chinese women was cultural. Chinese women enjoyed a long history of acceptance as athletes, having participated in sport as far back as the Ming dynasty of the fifteenth and sixteenth centuries. But such toleration was not exactly progressive; according to Wolff, "male leaders of the time" avoided sport "because their creed exalted the cultivation of the mind over that of the body. Thus woman and sport were an ideal match: second-class citizen, frowned-upon pursuit." Furthermore, "Chinese women are born into a hard life" and were thus better suited to "*chi ku:* eat bitterness." And there was plenty of unpleasantness to be had, as an allegiance to Confucian principles girded a patriarchy that allowed male coaches and officials to abuse their female athletes verbally and physically without complaint and consequence. Wolff also surmised that with a 33 percent literacy rate among women and incidents of forced sterilization, "a Chinese woman might not find the task of winning an Olympic medal particularly daunting."

And its rewards were downright lucrative: "Women who excel in sports receive the same government support, bonuses (including up to $10,000 for an Olympic gold medal) and occasional endorsement opportunities as men—and more public approbation."[46] Chinese sports scholar and former athlete Dong Jinxia substantiated many of Wolff's points—from the expectation that Chinese sportswomen would "eat bitterness" to the harsh, brutal, and "authoritarian management style" that informed the attitudes of male coaches toward their female athletes. Those beliefs, Dong observed, were "deeply embedded in past patriarchal norms" and associated with the "Confucian theme" of obedience.[47]

The Chinese succeeded in becoming an athletic power, regardless of the controversial means by which they did so.[48] Their supremacy was particularly evident in women's diving, where they won the 10-meter platform diving event in four successive Olympic cycles, from 1984 through 1996, regaining top honors in 2008 and every Olympics since then. Accomplishments in the three-meter springboard have been even more impressive: after Gao Min won in 1988, a Chinese woman has been atop the medal podium at every Olympics thereafter. Much of the Chinese success—both in men's and women's diving—came at the expense of the Americans, who previously had dominated the events. *Sports Illustrated*'s reaction was one

Chinese female divers "revolutionized their sport," much like Russian gymnasts had theirs, with smaller bodies and increasingly challenging combinations.

of acceptance. The Chinese female divers had "revolutionized their sport," much like Russian gymnasts had for theirs, with smaller bodies and increasingly challenging combinations.[49]

As Americans ceded diving dominance to the Chinese throughout the 1990s, they held an edge over their global rival in a winter sports matchup. Fallout from the Cultural Revolution wreaked greater havoc with winter sports, but the Chinese had a plan in place to close the gap. *SI*'s Robert Sullivan noted that while "only murmurs may be heard from the Chinese at Calgary . . . there will certainly be louder sounds at future Winter Games." Sullivan was correct. China would secure its first medals at the 1992 Winter Olympics in Albertville with women winning three silvers, doing so in speed skating and short-track speed skating. Ten years later at Salt Lake City, Chinese women were dominating short-track speed skating in particular, winning the country's first two golds at the winter games. In 2010 the country had its best showing ever, eleven Olympic medals, five of them gold, and it was women who dominated every step of the podium, responsible for ten of China's eleven Olympic medals. If not exactly a Winter Olympic power, China had certainly made strides in sports like speed skating, figure skating, and aerial ski jumping, providing a foundation to build on for the future. Integral to this project was the country's investment in its women; of the fifty-nine winter Olympic medals China has secured at the Games since 1994, women have been solely responsible for thirty-eight of them, and partially responsible for four others. It was a trend that China has sustained. When Beijing hosted the Winter Games in 2022, China enjoyed its most successful winter Olympics performance to date, earning fifteen medals, nine of them gold. Women earned five of those medals (two of them gold) and were part of three other mixed teams that medaled. With such a performance, China was poised to make the most of the soft power that comes along with holding the Olympics.

In 1996 *SI*'s Alexander Wolff deemed China's female athletes its "greatest Olympic resource" and noted that "in centuries-old Chinese iconography the character for phoenix has been used to represent woman. As China makes like a firebird economically, the People's Republic is tracing a parallel ascent in international sports and doing so on the wings of the gender that Mao once said 'holds up half the sky.'"[50] Wolff's prediction underscores the importance of sportswomen's contributions to the athletic prowess of their countries and the concomitant soft power that accrues because of it. But even as nations used women's Olympic sporting success to "prove" their dominance on an international stage, other countries used the games and their female athletes to showcase the strides they were making at home in overcoming difficult colonial pasts which often included the cruel treatment of Indigenous peoples.

"Reconciliation"

In 2010 Vancouver became the first Olympic host city to include Native peoples as official partners, involving them in every aspect of the Games, from the bidding process to the logo to the actual events themselves—many of which were taking place on ancestral lands. Salt Lake City had given an important nod to Native influences in 2002 when it included a reference to Navajo weaving techniques in its logo, based all three mascots on animals that inspired Native American legends, and included references to Native American history in its opening ceremonies. But perhaps most important was the organizing committee's sanctioning of the Navajo Nation 2002 Pavilion, which had two distinct goals: to break down stereotypes and to promote tourism. With its official relationship to the Games, the Navajo Nation had access to public relations coordinators and was able to use the Olympic rings logo. In addition, its exhibits enjoyed "a prime location in The Gateway Project, next to the NBC media camp and the Medals Plaza." Also notable was that Navajo Nation president Kelsey Begay received honored guest status.[51] If not full reconciliation, this was an important start at recognizing and honoring peoples who had long been subjects of military incursions and cultural vendettas.

If nothing else, it was a far cry from Anthropology Days, a feature of the joint 1904 World's Fair and Olympic Games in St. Louis. The brainchild of James E. Sullivan, chief organizer of the 1904 Summer Olympics, Anthropology Days embraced early twentieth-century America's fascination with human zoos by including three thousand Indigenous peoples from Africa, Asia, and the Americas all arrayed in "mock ethnic villages." As throngs of tourists looked on, the "savage and uncivilized tribes" engaged in typical "primitive" pursuits while also participating, at Sullivan's behest, in sporting competitions that doubled as Olympic contests. IOC president Pierre de Coubertin, afraid that the Olympics would take a backseat to the World's Fair as it had done in Paris in 1900, "demanded that all sporting events at the Fair should be labeled as 'Olympic.'" As a result, "any and all competitive contests" were Olympian—including the telegraph pole–climbing event and the mud fight. In the end, the goal for Anthropology Days was to "prove" the superiority of imperialist (white) powers both in terms of military might and athletic dominance; in reality, it was, as de Coubertin described it, an "outrageous charade" that proved nothing about the white race's inherent, superior athletic abilities—only that they understood the rules of a game no one had bothered to explain to the Indigenous participants. De Coubertin predicted that "'when Black men, red men and yellow men learn to run, jump, and throw [they will] leave the white man far behind them.'"[52]

De Coubertin's racist statement missed the mark on at least two counts. First, he overlooked a rich sporting history that Indigenous peoples already enjoyed and that in fact had provided the basis for a number of modern games including basketball and lacrosse. Thus, for many Indigenous peoples, and especially Native Americans, it was not about "learning" the basics but about securing access to playing sports—and everything else that American society had to offer—on an equal basis. Second, de Coubertin's emphasis on "men" overlooked the athletic accomplishments of the Native American girls from the Fort Shaw Indian Boarding School in Montana who played basketball at the 1904 World's Fair. The girls were part of the Model Indian School, which was just one more human exhibit where tourists could view and applaud the assimilation efforts of a hundred federally funded government Indian schools across the nation. Sports were an important part of the so-called assimilation process at Indian schools for both males and females.[53]

Indeed, the Fort Shaw Indian School girls basketball team was undefeated during their regular season, playing a brand of five-on-five, full-court basketball that garnered lots of praise, lots of fans, and a free trip to St. Louis, where they secured the title of World Champions. But not Olympic champions. Even though basketball was a demonstration sport at the 1904 games, Sullivan refused to recognize the Native American female cagers as "Olympians," even though he recognized other demonstration sports as "Olympic" events. As a result, the history of Native Americans at the Olympic Games often overlooks the Fort Shaw Indian School girls basketball team in favor of Jim Thorpe's gold medal–winning efforts in the decathlon and pentathlon in 1912 and Billy Mills's astounding, come-from-behind victory in the 10,000-meter run in 1964.[54]

SI's coverage of Indigenous athletes included a 1964 acknowledgment that Mills was "seven-sixteenths Sioux Indian" when he became "the first

American ever" to win the 10,000-meter race. In 1982 *SI* recognized the recent reinstatement of Jim Thorpe's 1912 medals, which had been stripped in 1913, but noted that his surviving relatives had been rebuffed when they sued the town of Jim Thorpe, Pennsylvania, to have his body returned to ancestral ground. In 1996 E. M. Swift addressed the insensitivity associated with St. Louis's "Anthropological Days," resorting to some tactless language of his own when he described how Indigenous peoples "vied for supremacy in events such as mud fighting, which the Pygmies, who were no doubt the hardest to hit, won." None of the stories considered the struggles these athletes experienced inside and outside sport because of their Indigenous heritage, nor did *SI* consider ways in which the magazine perpetuated damaging stereotypes.[55]

That would change in 2000 when Cathy Freeman slung both the Australian and Aboriginal flags around her neck following her victory in the 400-meter run at the Sydney Olympics. *Sports Illustrated* reported that "while Freeman regularly voices and displays her pride for her indigenous heritage, she has never been stridently political. Nevertheless, through no

Cathy Freeman, the granddaughter of an Aboriginal who was a "Stolen Generations" survivor, slung both the Australian and Aboriginal flags around her neck and was heralded as a symbol of reconciliation.

design of her own, she has become an important figure, a positive role model in Australia's tentative, but inexorable, push for Aboriginal reconciliation." Cathy Freeman was "the granddaughter of an Aboriginal woman taken by authorities as a child and given to a white family, like tens of thousands of 'stolen generation' Aborigines." While *Sports Illustrated* made an important reference to crimes against Indigenous peoples, the magazine did little to detail "the grim side of Australia's colonial history." In contrast, *Sports Illustrated for Women* was unequivocal in its depiction of Freeman's combined flag demonstration at the 1994 Commonwealth Games, relating that when Freeman "draped [both the Aboriginal flag and] the Australian flag around her shoulders . . . she didn't feel she was making some big protest. She was celebrating her heritage, trying to give hope to a people who have been neglected, uprooted, treated often as no more than indigenous vermin since the colonization of Australia in 1788."[56]

Lambasted for such a move in 1994, Freeman was celebrated in 2000, particularly in *Sports Illustrated,* as everyone's favorite daughter who personified reconciliation. *SI* gushed that "Australia's Cathy Freeman, a world champion of Aboriginal descent who famously lit the cauldron during the opening ceremonies, won a gold medal that was beseeched by her nation. On the morning of the race, a front-page article in *The Sydney Morning Herald* read, 'There has been no single occasion when more has been expected of an Australian sports person. . . . Rightly or wrongly, Cathy carries with her not just the nation's sporting hopes . . . but its political aspirations.'" In addition to drawing attention to racism, the choice of Freeman to light the cauldron highlighted decades of entrenched sexism as well, for as "she waited as the torch passed through the last of 11,200 Australian hands, a couple of million tons of national baggage [was] about to go up in smoke. See, if all that cynicism could be incinerated by the flame, then why couldn't the white guys feed Aussie racism and sexism to it too? Why not have the last six torch bearers be sheilas—whoops, *women*—five of them former Olympians and the last of them a brown woman named Freeman?"[57] Utilizing some sexist language of its own (even as it offered an immediate self-correction), *SI* sought to portray Freeman as an athlete who single-handedly defied racist and sexist portrayals.

But while *Sports Illustrated* embraced Cathy Freeman as a symbol of reconciliation, there were others who vehemently resisted such a depiction. Authors Toni Bruce and Emma Wensing discovered strong opposition to such a view in the more than 1,000 letters sent to major Australian newspapers during the 2000 Olympic Games; one letter writer asserted, "I'm afraid the TV commentators and newsreaders have it wrong when they say all Australians are proud of Cathy Freeman." Another saw Freeman's lighting of the cauldron as "another great moment in Australia's history marred by political correctness." Still another could not have been clearer: "she's not one of us."[58] For an Olympic Games whose motto was "Celebrate Humanity," the Australian Olympic Committee was falling short of the mark in persuading the hometown crowd to embrace reconciliation, regardless of the commentary in *Sports Illustrated*. It was a failure of soft power, and a lesson to other nations that an Olympic spectacle—either hosting one or attending one—might not so easily resolve a troubling colonial past, nor be the best route for addressing long-entrenched habits of racism and sexism, regardless of how high a nation's Olympic medal counts and how much sportswomen had contributed to them.

"The Most Wonderful and the Most Wretched of Sporting Events"

In 1964 *SI*'s John Underwood recognized "that the Olympic Games are at once the most wonderful and the most wretched of sporting events. They reflect all that is right with man and all that he cannot make right. They represent more than they should and do less than they can. They are the resolution of many schisms and the solution to hardly anything." And lest anyone wonder whether the Games were—or ever could be—devoid of political overtones, Underwood assured *SI* readers that "it takes a heap of *naiveté* to be naïve enough to take the Olympics for the unencumbered sport they are supposed to be. A U.S. Senator tried to have the Russians banned from the Games in 1956. Russian victories in 1960 were not examples of individual excellence but of the viability of a new, all-encompassing athletic system." And the Americans were not alone in attaching importance to the Olympics:

> Recently Russian periodicals have been frantically reminding the 1964 Soviet team of the importance of "winning for the forces of socialism," that the Russian people "do not want tourists on our Olympic team" and that any falloff in performance "is difficult to explain to the population." There is some concern now, expressed by Sovyetski Sport, that the

apparent collapse of the Russian team in the July dual meet with the U.S. at Los Angeles was due to the growth of such "vices" as "individualism, conceit, self-seeking, greed and a passion for Western ways of life."[59]

That concern morphed into panic, when interest turned into action and Communist athletes embraced not just "Western ways of life," but an actual life in the West.

For example, in 1956 *Sports Illustrated* devoted coverage to the defection of "comely skater" Miroslava Náchodská, who "was the Czech national champion before she fled to the West." While *SI*'s James Poling acknowledged that Náchodská was Czech and not Russian, he believed that "the fact remains that political, economic and cultural ties between the Soviet-dominated countries are so strong that what is true of one is, with slight variations, generally true of the other." Here was "an Iron Curtain athlete" critical of a system that was undoubtedly "impressive" in churning out world-class athletes but offered a life in which an athlete was "treated like a prized pig."[60] Athlete defections like Náchodská's epitomized soft power—it was clear evidence that a democratic way of life had trumped a Communist one. And Náchodská was not a one-off.

Also in 1956, *Sports Illustrated* shared the story of thirty-five other athletes looking to flee a Hungary that had been brutally repressed by the Soviet regime for "a new life" in the United States. *SI* realized the sacrifices these athletes were making: "Olympic champions are important people in countries behind the Iron Curtain, relatively much more important than they are in free countries. They have assured, privileged positions involving little or no work outside their training which guarantees them a standard of living far above the average in Red-dominated lands." This was in stark contrast to the United States, where the athletes would "have to work hard for a living in strange surroundings and possibly at unfamiliar tasks." Even though the athletes "were ordered to return, begged to return, promised rewards and privileges if they would return," they chose to remain in the United States.[61]

This was a major public relations coup for the Americans, since such defections countered the praise heaped on the Communist system by its athletic ambassadors. The American State Department reveled in such disclosures, for it belied Soviet claims that the United States was "the epitome of selfishness and vicious exploitation." Those defections allowed the United States to emphasize the failings of the Communist system and the successes of the American system in comparison—even with a less-than-stellar record on civil rights and social justice.

The issue of civil rights was ignored or downplayed by *Sports Illustrated* until Olsen's groundbreaking series on Black athletes. Even then, the magazine continued to disregard the unique challenges Black sportswomen encountered in the United States as a result of both their race and their sex. Although *SI* celebrated the accomplishments of Mae Faggs, Wilma Rudolph, and other female track and field athletes in the 1950s and 1960s, it was not until the 1980s that the magazine regularly featured Black sportswomen in other sports, like figure skating and gymnastics, alongside the achievements of track stars like Florence Griffith Joyner and Jackie Joyner-Kersee. Even then, the magazine reported only part of the story. *Sports Illustrated* touted the achievements of Debi Thomas, but chose not to remember the discrimination endured by Mabel Fairbanks, who was barred from skating clubs, and thus the American Olympic team, during the 1930s. Dianne Durham appeared in *SI*'s 1983 preview of Olympic gymnastics, but in 1980 sixteen-year-old Luci Collins was the first Black woman to make an Olympic gymnastics team, although she did not get the chance to compete owing to the American boycott of the Moscow summer games.[62] For Black women, then, the historical context of their Olympic achievements was sorely lacking in a magazine that throughout the Cold War overwhelmingly depicted their Olympic participation in one sport, never questioning how such a singular focus on track and field was a product of racism, and how that type of coverage perpetuated debilitating stereotypes, even when the United States had supposedly transcended its racist past.[63]

But female athletes, regardless of their race, enjoyed more reporting in *Sports Illustrated* during an Olympic cycle than at any other time, often becoming the darlings of the sports world. This was true particularly of American sportswomen during the Cold War years when *SI*'s reporters regaled their readers with the accomplishments of homegrown heroines like swimmers Carin Cone and Donna de Varona in the 1960s, Janet Evans and Dara Torres in the 1980s, and ultimately Jenny Thompson, Simone Manuel, and Katie Ledecky in the twenty-first century. Figure skaters Peggy Fleming and Dorothy Hamill charmed American fans with their gold medal performances, inspiring a crop of American skaters like Kristi Yamaguchi, Tara Lipinski, and Sarah Hughes who would secure top Olympic honors throughout the 1990s. While coverage of gymnastics, swimming, sprinting, and figure skating has consistently dominated the magazine's Olympic coverage, *SI*'s writers also reported Joan Benoit's commanding performance in the first ever women's Olympic marathon in 1984, asserting that it provided "confirmation . . . of women's distance running's rightful place in the Games."[64] And the incomparable Bonnie Blair, who in 1994 became "the U.S.'s most gilded woman Olympian ever," was a winter Olympics mainstay for *SI* with her five gold medals in speed skating from three different Olympics.[65] By 1998, coverage of the winter games included not just the standard skiing, skating, and sliding events but snowboarding as well, setting the stage for well-known names like Lindsay Jacob-Ellis, Jamie Anderson, and Chloe Kim. By 2014, Olympic participation was more diverse for women than ever before after wrestling and boxing were included in the summer schedule, and ice hockey and ski jumping were added to the winter lineup.

American participation in sport reflected a culmination of investment in Olympic development that began in the 1950s when President Eisenhower promoted the U.S. Olympic Development Committee, which advanced women's sports by working with the Division of Girls and Women's Sports to encourage American women's participation in Olympic sports. As early as 1964, Robert Kennedy recognized the need to pump money and resources into women's sports so that the United States could remain competitive with the Soviet Union, which itself had already devoted large sums to the development of its sportswomen. For countries to realize their Olympic aspirations, if not "the Olympic ideal," women's accomplishments were vital both in shoring up national fitness and in attracting potential allies abroad. Korbut, Comăneci, and Witt were not just visible symbols but powerful motivators who inspired other countries to invest in sport for women as a means to amass soft power. In so doing, the Olympic Games also provided a platform to highlight not just the potential of female athletes but the unique oppressions they experienced as Black and Indigenous sportswomen. Yet these were issues *Sports Illustrated* routinely minimized or ignored altogether, even as sportswomen enjoyed greater visibility in the magazine than at any other time.

Thus greater prominence in *Sports Illustrated* did not necessarily convey greater understanding of the challenges female Olympians experienced, nor did it revolutionize the type of reporting they enjoyed. Indeed, although the amount of coverage the magazine devoted to sportswomen during the Olympics was different, *Sports Illustrated*'s focus on women's feminine attributes—or lack thereof—as opposed to their athletic achievements remained the same, regardless of the decade or the sport. From "elfin" gymnasts to "socialist sex symbols," and from "chunky" Soviets to American girls, *SI*—even as it previewed, relayed, and celebrated women's Olympian achievements—still communicated a status that they were not just Olympians. They were female Olympians.

For American women, the Olympics was a crucial platform for shoring up the prestige of their nation and drawing attention to their own athletic prowess. But even as some female athletes basked in an Olympic spotlight that featured and celebrated their achievements, such visibility—especially in *SI*—generally ended with the closing ceremonies. As sportswomen struggled to maintain a prominent media presence, nowhere was that struggle more pronounced than for those who sought to play for pay. Professional leagues offered the lucky few an opportunity to continue competing in the sports they loved, but professional sportswomen encountered major challenges in making the case that they deserved the same kind of respect, compensation, and opportunities their male counterparts enjoyed.

6

"A League of Their Own"

IN THE November 2001 edition of *Sports Illustrated for Women,* writer Katherine Cole announced the formation of a new professional sports league for women. In doing so, she placed the recently formed women's professional soccer association on notice: "Move over, WUSA. Here comes the new women's polo league."[1]

By the early twenty-first century, American female athletes had more opportunities to play professionally than ever before. In addition to golf, tennis, and basketball, professional leagues had either been suggested or created for a number of sports, including football, indoor volleyball, softball, soccer, and polo. But while some of these organizations enjoyed long histories—women have been playing professional golf on the LPGA tour since 1950—others were more fleeting. The U.S. Women's Polo League was defunct after a mere six months, having never contested a match. While the polo league had been "mired in mysterious woes" from the beginning, *SI for Women* highlighted the reality that "starting and sustaining a successful all-women's professional sports league is not an easy task. The American Basketball League lasted only two years; the Women's Professional Softball League will take this summer off to reorganize; and WUSA head Tony DiCicco had courted sponsors for nearly a decade before the women's league became a reality." It was clear that American female athletes, even in 2002, were "still far removed from the day when more than a handful of women can make sports a full-time job."[2] The question was why—what was the alchemy required to make women's professional sports leagues financially viable?

Sports Illustrated for Women had some ideas. In the fall of 1999, the WNBA had just completed its third season, and while there was much for the league to celebrate—the enhanced "quality of play," the new collective bargaining agreement that guaranteed year-round health insurance, and (slightly) higher salaries—there was still room for improvement given the league's slumps in attendance and television ratings. Even with the downturn, WNBA president Val Ackerman was "encouraged that we're holding onto our audience." But the magazine thought that was a low bar and offered suggestions for improvement, including "fixing" the "horrific inconsistency" of the officiating and creating "a larger pool of recognizable talent. The public knows approximately four players."[3] But *SI for Women* failed to mention one of the biggest challenges facing women in professional leagues: the assumption that women's sports were an inferior product in comparison to that offered by men. Such a belief hampered women at all levels of sport, but particularly those playing in leagues where profit was imperative to survival.

If *Sports Illustrated* believed that it had the power to influence their readers to watch certain sports and follow certain sports figures, then their coverage of efforts to establish and sustain women's professional leagues—where fan interest is paramount—is particularly significant. Not only has *Sports Illustrated* recorded the growth of those leagues, but its depictions have highlighted—and perpetuated—the challenges unique to women playing for pay: being both good enough and attractive enough to literally sell their sport. Even with those qualities, many women's professional leagues were, if not doomed to fail, fated to labor in obscurity, with the women who populated them depicted as little more than talented collaborators in publicity stunts as opposed to serious professionals plying their trade.

"This Is Not a Gimmick We're Trying to Pull"

Throughout the early 1900s, women played semiprofessional baseball on "Bloomer Teams," which took their name from a fashion made popular by Amelia Bloomer in the 1850s. Although the loose-fitting pants had failed the test of haute couture, they were well-suited to females interested in playing baseball. Numerous "Bloomer Girl" teams, which were independent clubs whose only connection to each other was their name, barnstormed America "playing a man's game by men's rules against men." They also often played *with* men, as the teams allowed one or two men, often in wigged "disguise," to compete as well. Bloomer teams never played each other, but generated interest nonetheless for their excellent performances on the field and their ribald antics off of it. As *Sports Illustrated* noted in a 1970 retrospective, such behavior "lent the Bloomer Girls a sideshow appeal that organized baseball could not provide. Perhaps it did not draw baseball fans so much as it drew the curious, but it did draw."[4]

Occasionally, women also competed on men's teams. During the 1920s, Lizzie Murphy earned a living as a first baseman on the American League All-Stars, a men's barnstorming baseball team. Her talent and skill were well known to teammates and fans alike, especially after she played in a charity game against the Boston Red Sox in 1922.[5] A decade later, Virne Beatrice "Jackie" Mitchell, former Bloomer Girl and then pitcher for the Double A Chattanooga Lookouts, took to the mound to meet both Babe Ruth and Lou Gehrig in what *Sports Illustrated* later recalled as "an epic confrontation." What happened next became the stuff of legend: on April 2, 1931, Mitchell took on the most feared members of the Yankees' famed "Murderer's Row," striking out Babe Ruth on four pitches before notching another K against Lou Gehrig. But *SI*'s 1988 query about the encounter—"Were the Yankees really trying or were they part of a stunt?"— became the enduring question, and thus effectively trivialized Mitchell's accomplishment.[6]

Regardless, both Lizzie Murphy and Jackie Mitchell had carved out an important niche for themselves. Yet they were, as *SI* observed, "defined by their status as the only ones" instead of being part of a decades-long history of women playing professional baseball.[7] *SI* celebrated Murphy and Mitchell as "exceptions," and their extraordinary status also marked them as "others." A path to baseball success, in terms of participation, remuneration, and ultimately media exposure in *SI* was possible for them but not for thousands of other women. In fact, their presence elicited a response that reinforced barriers to future participation. In 1931 Major League Baseball commissioner Kenesaw Mountain Landis voided Jackie Mitchell's contract with the Lookouts, deeming baseball too strenuous for women. Two decades later, Commissioner Ford Frick explicitly barred women from MLB—a rule that would hold until the league rescinded it forty years later.

Although women were excluded from MLB, they did enjoy an opportunity to play the sport professionally. In 1943 Cubs owner Philip Wrigley formed the All-American Girls Professional Baseball League as a patriotic gesture to bolster civilian spirits during World War II. The original host cities funded half the cost of the club while Wrigley matched their stakes and bankrolled the rest of the operation, paying player salaries and the costs of travel, uniforms, meals, and housing. Sixty years after the league folded, *Sports Illustrated* reminded readers that three hundred women had attended the first tryouts, competing for sixty spots on four teams: the Rockford Peaches, Kenosha Comets, Racine Belles, and South Bend Blue Sox. Hailing from midwestern towns, the teams were in driving distance of each other during a time of gas rationing, and they attracted large crowds from the beginning.[8]

Fan interest was due in part to their high level of play and to the league's insistence on an overt display of femininity. Those demonstrations required chaperones off the field, full-skirted uniforms on the field, and cosmetics at all times. According to *SI*, "league administrators believed—and rightly so, it appears—that the stringent dress and behavior codes, together with the chaperones' strict supervision, would lend a certain moral respectability to the players' reputations and thus help ensure the public's acceptance of the league." The ultimate goal was to "look like women and play like men." An inspiration for Penny Marshall's 1992 film *A League of Their Own*, the AAGPBL ultimately allowed over five hundred women to play a sport they loved while getting paid to do it. Popular throughout the war years, the league lasted from 1943 until 1954, meeting its demise, not with the end of WWII, but as a result of business decisions and changing American mores that no longer relied solely on local outlets for entertainment. In the end, *SI*'s retrospective featured two important facets of the AAGPBL that women's professional leagues still contend with: an emphasis on femininity and male control of women's sport. Indeed, "Women played, but men still pulled the strings. It was, for better or worse, anything but a league of their own."[9]

And not all women had the same opportunity to play. Like so many other leagues in the 1940s, the AAGPBL barred Black women's participation. It is impossible to know how many Black women would have tried out at Wrigley Field in 1943, but it seems clear that Marcenia "Toni" Stone would have found her way to Chicago. Stone had played baseball throughout her life, often as the sole woman on semiprofessional male teams. Barred from the AAGPL, Toni Stone found an opportunity to play in the Negro Leagues in 1953. By that time, an integrated MLB had ransacked the organization, cherry-picking its best talent (doing so without compensating the players' former franchises and their usually Black owners), leaving the Negro Leagues to find a way to stem the exodus not only of Black players on the field but of Black fans in the stadiums. In response, the Indianapolis Clowns decided to hire a female second baseman—Toni Stone.

Like with the AAGPBL, coverage of the Negro Leagues and its players rarely appeared in the pages of *Sports Illustrated*. An exception was a 1992 article that urged readers to remember a time when "there used to be two games of professional baseball, the Major Leagues and the Negro Leagues. They were separate and most definitely not equal." *SI* recognized that "the men of the Negro Leagues performed with skill, and passion, but for nickels and dimes." In order to help reclaim that history, the magazine shared the stories of eleven former players who related their memories of playing in the Negro Leagues.[10] It was a powerful addition to history but failed to acknowledge the existence of female players like Toni Stone, as well as Mamie "Peanut" Johnson and Connie Morgan, who had joined Stone on the Indianapolis Clowns by 1954. While female players did not join the league until well after its heyday and were often regarded as a gimmick, the players themselves took their participation seriously; when Toni Stone joined in 1953, she adamantly refused to wear the proposed uniform, a short dress that mimicked those worn by players in the AAGPBL. Management backed down, and Stone played in a traditional uniform until she retired from the league after the 1954 season.[11]

The silence about the history of Black women in baseball was particularly deafening when Mo'ne Davis stunned the baseball world with her brilliant play in the 2014 Little League World Series, throwing a complete game and making the cover of *Sports Illustrated*. Sports legends, analysts, and fans were enamored of the thirteen-year-old's 70 miles per hour fastball and her flawless mechanics. Equally compelling were the professional possibilities that might await her in MLB; sports commentator Keith Olbermann "had a serious debate on ESPN2 about whether she could play in the majors." Such a remark was a perfect opportunity to place her potential within a wider story of female Black talent in baseball. But *SI*'s cover story concentrated on the resurgence of urban baseball that Davis's team represented.[12] It was a focus that underscored the important issues of class and place, but it was also one that ignored the intersectional oppressions of race and gender.

As a result, Mo'ne Davis appeared as one more exception, much like Lizzie Murphy and Jackie Mitchell from a century before: a lone girl—and an exceptional one at that—in a boy's sport. But Davis's uniqueness had more to do with her race than her gender. In 1989 *Sports Illustrated* had reported that Julie Croteau, a walk-on "first baseperson" for St. Mary's College of Maryland, was "the first woman to play NCAA baseball"; five years later, *SI* introduced Ila Borders as the first woman recruited to play on a men's college baseball team.[13] A year after Davis's debut, *Sports Illustrated* featured French player Mélissa Mayeux, who in 2015 was a sixteen-year-old French shortstop who became the first female to be added to MLB's international registration list. While she had impressed two-time All-Star baseball player Steve Finley with her mechanics and "baseball I.Q.," it was simply "too early to tell" whether she would have a future in the pros. That assessment, according to Finley, had nothing to do with gender and everything to do with age. Regardless of her future, Mike McClellan, director of MLB International Game Development, praised her game, insisting that there was "no pandering involved. This is not a gimmick we're trying to pull."[14]

This was perhaps the most notable statement of all. McClellan's insisting that this was not a gimmick—unlike recruiting women to wear short-skirted dresses to launch a league or recruiting women to save a dying one. But because hyperfeminization and gimmicks—and the trivialization that often resulted—had long been the price of doing business, not all women enjoyed the same kind of treatment that Mélissa Mayeux received in being evaluated based on her skills alone. Nor did they receive coverage in *Sports Illustrated*. *SI* chose not to follow the admittedly brief professional careers of Croteau or Borders, even though they were the first women to play professional baseball since the 1950s. When *SI* did feature female sports professionals, the magazine tended to define them and their accomplishments in reference to men; it was a comparison that, despite their ability, almost always left women diminished, with their achievements devalued and their league regarded as an inferior product.

"If They Were Men, They Would Be Famous"

On May 6, 1974, *Sports Illustrated*'s William Johnson and Nancy Williamson featured the All American Red Heads, a traveling professional women's basketball team for whom red hair was as essential as a good defense. The authors asserted that the Red Heads were "the best women's basketball team in North America" even if readers did not know their names. Johnson and Williamson were using their article in part to remedy that oversight and to assert in no uncertain terms that had they been men, not only would they have had fame, "they would be rich. . . . They would have played before hundreds of thousands in the Garden, the Spectrum, the Forum, the Astrodome—tens of millions on television. However . . .”[15]

Johnson and Williamson did not complete that sentence. They did not have to, since everyone could do it for them. *However,* because they were women, they earned on average about $40,000 a season, traveling 60,000 miles and playing two hundred games before hundreds of fans (if they were lucky) in small-town high school gymnasiums across the nation. This was in contrast to the men in the NBA, who played an eighty-two-game season before hundreds of thousands of fans in dedicated arenas and earned an average of $90,000, while future Hall of Famers Kareem Abdul-Jabbar, John Havlicek, and Pete Maravich made as much as $400,000. In addition to their low salaries and mandatory red hair, the Red Heads possessed a pregame ritual that included “wandering through the crowd in their uniforms, selling programs for a dollar apiece”; after the game, they would split gate receipts with the local sponsor, often a high school student council, which had organized the opposing team—usually men who might have once been high school athletes but were “not basketball players anymore.”[16] Johnson and Williamson easily made their case that men’s and women’s professional basketball were simply so different as not to be the same sport.

And though the Red Heads were popular, they were not the only game in town. Other women’s teams, though not professional, were popular draws and cut into the Red Heads’ bottom line. One local organizer noted that a women’s basketball game that included “housewives, mothers—from P.T.A.’s all over the county . . . really drew ’em because people turn out to see their kinfolk perform. . . . The Red Heads themselves couldn’t have got that big a crowd.”[17] With that kind of competition, the Red Heads’ owner had to be cagey. He released the team’s playing schedule only a month in advance in an effort to prevent others from undercutting his team. The short window made an uncertain schedule even more difficult for the players, who already didn’t know how many games they would play a year; their season continued until they had earned enough to offset expenses. Regardless of such challenges, the *SI* reporters marveled at the players’ skill and talent: “Red Heads are slick ball handlers and their passes snap with precision. Many are thrown behind the back, perfectly. The women are wearing bright red lipstick and blue eyeshadow, as if they were going to the theater. But here they are, perspiring like mad and playing basketball like demons. They drive swiftly down the court. They shoot with deadly accuracy. . . . Their precision dazzles the crowd and, even though they are playing against butchers and insurance men and car salesmen, the All American Red Heads are plainly a splendid basketball machine." Twenty years after the All-American Girls Professional Baseball League had folded, the All American Red Heads still had to pair their impressive skills on the court with an overt show of femininity as well as a heavy reliance on "gags." For example, "The Pinch" featured a Red Head pretending that a man on the opposing team had pinched her on the behind and insisted that the referee call "a very personal foul" as hilarity ensued among the crowd.[18] These women were professional players, but with their dyed hair, cosmetics, and their "tricks," no one would ever confuse their team with an NBA franchise.

Gimmicks and a circus-like atmosphere surrounded the All American Red Heads, which often detracted from the players' talents and skill.

Offering innocuous sports entertainment was an approach made famous by another professional basketball team, one comprising Black men who had camouflaged their unmatched skill with the unthreatening appeal of a circus act. From 1927 to 1938, the Harlem Globetrotters played "regulation basketball, taking on all comers and generally dispatching them with ease." During one particular game in the 1939 season when their lead was 107 points, the players began "clowning around." The rest was history in an America where racism was de rigueur: "Over the years the Globies became known as court jesters, and the fact that they beat the Minneapolis Lakers in consecutive years ('48 and '49) and pounded a college all-star team in a series of well-publicized games throughout the '50s was secondary." Indeed, the Harlem Globetrotters became known for throwing buckets of confetti into a crowd and spinning balls on their fingers—harmless antics that disguised a skill level that would have made them the equals of white talent in the NBA had they been permitted to play in the segregated league.[19]

Like the Negro Leagues before them, the Harlem Globetrotters hired female talent in 1985 to bring "needed resuscitation after 59 years of playing the same game with the same jokes." According to SI, former Olympic star Lynette Woodard offered both "a feminine touch—and new vitality" to the struggling team. Once again, Black women served as a gimmick to save a failing Black sports league. By 2001, however, the Globetrotters were looking to get back to their origins: "We weren't clowns. We began as the best basketball team in the world. Champions. Warriors. We want to get back to that. We have to get back to that."[20] Both the Globetrotters and the Red Heads were compelled to mask their talent using gags and gimmicks in order to be accepted as paid professionals in their sport. And while they might have had the skills and the games commensurate with the best in the NBA, equality was sorely lacking, especially in terms of reputation and compensation, as well as opportunities to prove themselves against their peers.

The Red Heads had never matched their skill against the best women's teams, and players felt this privation particularly keenly as the 1976 Olympics approached. Women's basketball would be contested as an Olympic sport for the first time in Montreal, but given the Redheads' professional status, they were not eligible to compete. The players would have loved the opportunity to play the Chinese or Soviet national teams, or to play the AAU champions, or really "any women's team anywhere." One player insisted, "We could beat anyone in the world. I'm sure of it. But we'll never know. No one will ever know because we never play anyone but has-been men." *SI*'s Johnson and Williamson agreed, concluding that there was "really no way for the Red Heads to display their skill to the world, no way to prove they are one of the best women's basketball teams on earth."[21]

Instead, the Red Heads, like the Globetrotters, relied on a circus-like atmosphere that downplayed the players' abilities even as team owner Orwell Moore insisted that "furnishin' the folks a hee-haw is not our only objective. We also play a very classy game of basketball." Moore acknowledged that his business model mimicked that of the better-known Globetrotters, but it also imitated the All-American Girls Professional Baseball League, with a roster of white players and with rules against drinking and smoking. Moore's goal was to market the Red Heads as a "lovely wholesome crowd of girls," and that meant his players could not be tied to "any causes," particularly "Women's Lib."[22]

The Red Heads continued their barnstorming ways until finally folding in 1986. Their experience offered important lessons for other professional women's basketball leagues that would follow in its wake. Like the Harlem Globetrotters, the Red Heads had to camouflage their "classy basketball" with "hee-haws" in an effort to survive. Like players in the AAGPBL, the Red Heads were required to behave in a way that was overwhelmingly feminine, requiring women to devote time, energy, and money to maintain an image that was popular with potential fans. Professional possibilities and the chance of fulfillment for (white) female cagers seemed to be dependent on a combination of gimmicks and hyperfemininity which clearly differentiated their play from the serious competition that (white) men had enjoyed since 1946 with the founding of the NBA. As a result, it was easy to dismiss the Red Heads as more spectacle than serious sport.

In response, future women's professional basketball leagues like the short-lived Women's Basketball League and the even shorter-lived American Basketball League sought to ditch the gimmicks and an overt emphasis on feminine trappings. But they still struggled to be taken as seriously as their male counterparts. The Women's Basketball League suffered from a lack of media exposure and marketable talent and folded in 1981 after three years. As for the American Basketball League, its future, at first, seemed promising. Getting underway after the 1996 Olympics, the league had signed nine of twelve Olympians from the 1996 team, had attracted the best collegiate talent, and had secured "television and sponsorship deals." It looked like the ABL was poised to give women a professional experience akin to the men's. Even the name implied that the ABL was a singular opportunity for women; league cofounder Steve Hams refused to include "Women's" in the league name, adding that "if the NBA adds an M, we'll consider putting a W in ABL."[23] Bold as such a statement was in 1996, Hams's confidence in the league's ultimate success seemed justified.

By October 1996, the eight-team ABL was underway and was popular, and especially with sponsors. League cofounder Gary Cavalli sounded almost smug when he asserted, "Corporate sponsors aren't only returning our calls now, they're calling us first." However, despite the corporate support, player talent, and what seemed to be guaranteed media exposure, SI's Alexander Wolff sensed "a threat looming": NBA commissioner David Stern was "fine-tuning plans to launch his own women's league, the WNBA, in June." Wolff had some words of advice for the ABL on coexisting with what was bound to be not just a potential problem but a serious rival: "Remember that you're not a league, you're a movement." In addition, Wolff encouraged the ABL to anticipate how the NBA would leverage its advantages to promote the WNBA and secure future star talent. Wolff thought that if the ABL could keep those ideas in mind, its "future look[ed] promising." With the ABL and the WNBA "in different markets and seasons, with different philosophies and corporate backers," Wolff believed coexistence was possible.[24]

Possible, but not probable. While the ABL supposedly had the better talent and offered higher salaries on average, the WNBA simply drew more fans—hundreds more, even in the summer, basketball's traditional off-season. Playing in NBA arenas, with TV deals, sponsorship opportunities, and "an entertainment package that . . . included light shows, outdoor carnivals, indoor fireworks and celebrity sightings," the WNBA benefited from "the NBA's well-oiled marketing machine," which lined up multiyear TV contracts and commitments from corporate sponsors, promoted brisk sales of team and league merchandise, and came up with a signature catchphrase: "We Got Next." While sportswriters and analysts saw the ABL as "the better league," having secured the best talent in the draft for the following season, it was the WNBA's marketing power—all $15 million of it, in comparison to the ABL's $3 million (which was double the budget for its inaugural year)—which set it apart.[25]

The ABL sought to increase its profile by proposing an all-star game with the WNBA. League CEO Gary Cavalli appeared to be simply touting a good business venture that would benefit both leagues and be "good for professional women's basketball." But in truth, an interleague game would allow the struggling ABL to showcase its main advantage—its talent—and potentially allow it to defeat the WNBA, possibly during primetime, to gain some momentum. The WNBA was having none of it. League president Val Ackerman declined the offer, pleading an already overtaxed organization with expansion plans, an extended season, and a lengthened playoff format; the WNBA simply did not have the time or the resources to consider participation in such an event. Even when the ABL offered to make all the arrangements and cover the costs, the WNBA demurred. As *Sports Illustrated* pointed out, the proposed "game wouldn't be good for the losing team—which would likely be the WNBA."[26]

By May of 1998, the ABL was in serious trouble. According to *SI*'s Richard O'Brien, "The American Basketball League—outdrawn, outmarketed and outtelevised by the rival Women's National Basketball Association— has held one advantage over its rival league: better players. Last week's WNBA draft, however, revealed changes in the landscape of women's pro basketball that put the ABL in a defensive, even precarious, position." O'Brien noted that the WNBA had snagged the top players, doing it even when they paid their players $35,000 less than the ABL. But with thousands more fans per game and endorsement opportunities, the WNBA was too enticing for both new college talent and veteran players alike.[27] The ABL simply could not keep pace with such WNBA perks.

In December 1998, the ABL suddenly declared bankruptcy in the middle of the season. *SI* predicted that the "the demise of the ABL means a bigger, better WNBA will take the floor" with rosters that included a number of former ABL players. Although the players must certainly have appreciated the opportunity to keep playing professional basketball in the United States, they surely missed their old pay stubs. In April 1999 *SI*'s Kevin Cook noted that the minimum salary for the WNBA season was $15,000, which "forced many to play overseas or find part-time jobs in the off-season." The incongruity of a wealthy league and its poorly paid players was apparent to many, including Cook's fellow *SI* sportswriter Alexander Wolff, who had remarked when the WNBA kicked off its first season in 1997 that "the league best equipped to lavish huge salaries on players, the WNBA, is choosing not to do so."[28]

And there were other problems confronting the WNBA. Sports scholars and analysts debated the efficacy of the WNBA's decision to play in a traditional off-season, and the league wrestled with its reputation as the "little sister" of the NBA—and the diminution that such a moniker conveyed in skill, respect, and perks.[29] But it was the huge discrepancy in salaries— not only between the WNBA and the NBA but between the WNBA and international women's professional basketball leagues—which was the defining issue for the league in the twenty-first century.

Indeed, as the WNBA celebrated its tenth birthday, its biggest competitor came not from another league at home, but from abroad. American women had always played in international basketball leagues to more applause and far more money than their home courts allowed, but in 2008 that disparity seemed even greater than before. Alexander Wolff focused on Russian teams like Spartak Moscow, which featured the talents of WNBA stars Sue Bird and Diana Taurasi. Wolff noted that "free of WNBA payroll restrictions [players] earn up to 10 times more during a Russian season—around $500,000 for Taurasi, for example—than during a U.S. summer. After big Euroleague wins, Spartak players collect[ed] cash bonuses of $5,000 and diamond jewelry" and experienced a general standard that was "seven-star-hotel-chauffeur-style." And Spartak was not the exception: CSKA Moscow's owner "spen[t] lavishly on WNBA stalwarts" and the Yekaterinburg team was poised to pay Candace Parker $1.2 million for four months of play.[30] By 2015, Taurasi was earning almost fifteen times her WNBA salary with her Russian team, which also paid her an additional one million dollars to sit out the 2015 WNBA season so they could protect her physical health and their own investment. Taurasi took the money, and the WNBA was left without one of its most notable stars.

There was simply no way the WNBA could compete with Russian teams. For one, the teams operated at a loss; Russian billionaire owners invested millions of their own money annually, but with substantial player salaries, no paid admission, and owners having to pay for their games to be telecast, the teams lost money, and yet year after year owners made their investments in order to entertain a sports-crazed nation. Why? According to "sports sugar daddy" Shabtai von Kalmanovic, "There still isn't enough of a middle class in Russia for sport to pay for itself. And you cannot deduct expenses on sport [from your taxes]. So you need to have a very big heart and very big balls, and need to be something between a fanatic and a patriot. And a little bit crazy." And according to Wolff, more than a little aware that Russian billionaires operate at the pleasure of Vladimir Putin, when "Mother Russia tells men what to do with at least some of their money, sports is the great beneficiary."[31] This was particularly true for women's professional sports.

While the WNBA could not match the payrolls of Russian oligarchs, it could redress some of the pay inequities that had dogged the organization since its inception. Perhaps motivated by losing stars like Taurasi to the incentives provided by international leagues, in early 2020 "the WNBA and its union . . . announced a tentative eight-year labor deal . . . that will allow top players to earn more than $500,000 while the average annual compensation for players will surpass six figures for the first time." The collective bargaining agreement not only meant that players would earn an average of $130,000 per year—rookies would earn a minimum of $68,000—but allowed for 50–50 revenue sharing starting in 2021, as well as full compensation during maternity leave and a domestic violence policy. Perhaps most crucial to the WNBA was the "prioritization policy," which mandated that by 2024 players with three or more years in the WNBA had to commit to the season in its entirety. SI's legal analyst Michael McCann believed such a policy "could motivate foreign leagues to restructure their season and postseason schedules" to accommodate the WNBA's new rules. Most important, however, was "that the WNBA wants its players to prioritize the WNBA over other leagues." With increased player salaries, it was easier for WNBA players to do just that.[32]

Although WNBA executives and players alike eagerly endorsed and praised the policy, it did little to close the gap between WNBA salaries and those in the NBA. But pay equality had never been the goal—greater compensation was, and with a 30 percent rise in the WNBA salary cap, many viewed the new agreement as historic. And, as McCann noted, "At a time when the U.S. National Women's Soccer Team and U.S. Soccer are battling in court over pay disparities and questionable workplace conditions, WNBA players and their league have engaged in productive negotiations. Those negotiations produced a mutually beneficial workplace agreement and, most likely, a more marketable league to fans and consumers." Such a reality seemed more possible than ever. Even though attendance at WNBA games had declined by 13 percent to an average of 6,700 fans per game in 2018, ticket sales skyrocketed following the 2019 season, and TV viewership was up by 31 percent.[33] While arenas were not necessarily sold out, by 2020 the WNBA had seemed to achieve what had eluded many other professional women's leagues: stability and a measure of longevity. Yet the WNBA continued to wrestle with an image that branded it not as a professional basketball league but as the *women's* professional basketball league. This was an all-too-familiar experience for many professional female athletes—especially those who were part of the longest running professional women's sports league in the United States: the *Ladies* Professional Golf Association.

"Golf and the Women"

The LPGA was not the first professional golf association for females in the United States. The Women's Professional Golf Association emerged in 1944 in response to a growing number of women who were increasingly frustrated with the limited number of amateur competitions available to them. Spearheading the effort was Hope Seignious, who enjoyed three important advantages: she was an excellent amateur player herself, she had access to ample financial backing in the form of a supportive father, and she was joined in the endeavor by skilled golfers, including the charismatic Babe Didrikson. But from the beginning, the WPGA struggled; the women did not enjoy any backing or encouragement from their counterparts on the male tour, and it launched during a time when potential fans were consumed with winning World War II. This had not been a problem for the All-American Girls Professional Baseball League, but that league had been founded as a patriotic gesture to provide entertainment to baseball fans in midwestern towns and cities and also enjoyed corporate sponsorship from Philip Wrigley's company. The WPGA had neither of those advantages and folded after five years.[34]

The LPGA, which began in 1950, looked to avoid similar pitfalls. First, it enjoyed sponsorship from Wilson Sporting Goods, which regarded a professional women's tour as beneficial both to women's golf and to Wilson Sporting Goods. Second, the new league also benefited from the involvement of Fred Corcoran, who had begun his career in golf as a caddie but had more recently served as a tournament manager for the PGA. Corcoran possessed important contacts and experience organizing professional golf events, and he was interested in making a women's professional league viable. To that end, his first order of business was to see about using the WPGA's charter. When Hope Seignious refused, Corcoran simply swapped "Ladies" for "Women's" and the LPGA was in business.[35]

In 1956 *Sports Illustrated* featured the LPGA for the first time, and sportswriter Herbert Warren Wind assured readers that although the twenty-five "girls" of the LPGA did not have as many tournaments as the PGA, "they devote[d] the same long, wearying hours to their business that the men do." While Wind repeatedly referred to the women as "girls" and dubbed the LPGA "that ambulant sorority house," his coverage stands out for a focus on the excellence of the female players and his insistence that their games were just as impressive as the men's. Wind noted, "The fair sex has come so far on the fairway that there are dozens of women pros." He singled out Patty Berg, Betty Jameson, and Louise Suggs as "the best of the lady pros, [who] possess three of the finest swings golf has known." According to Wind, to watch them was "to get very close to the heart of the game." Repeatedly Wind talked about the fact that these women were excellent golfers, regardless of sex, and even when sex was introduced, they were just as good as, if not better than, the men, embodying the spirit of golf in a purer form than their male counterparts. From a twenty-first century perch, this was heady stuff indeed.[36]

Although the LPGA's top fan waxed rhapsodic about the games of "the Big 3," Wind remained concerned about the void left by Babe Didrikson (Zaharias), who had taken time away from the tour to battle colon cancer. Didrikson, according to Wind, was "the tour's primary attraction, what with her flair for showmanship and her zest for competition gilding her big and frequently brilliant game. The tour is certainly not the same without the Babe." And it never really would be. Almost twenty years after her death, *Sports Illustrated*'s William Oscar Johnson and Nancy Williamson credited her with having "created big-time women's golf. She launched it as a legitimate sport and brought gusts of freshness and fun to a game too often grim. She joked and clowned and had a rapport with fans that is rare. She had the ability to be cocky with charm, and the galleries loved her. Her booming power game lowered scores and forced others to imitate her." It was lightning in a bottle that the LPGA would try to recapture, and that sportswriters would diligently search for, in the years after Babe's death in 1956. In 1961, for example, *SI*'s Gwilym Brown entitled his article "Women's Golf Finds a New Zaharias," lauding the twenty-six-year-old Mickey Wright as the "finest golfer of this—and perhaps of any—era."

But even as she "rank[ed] ahead of the Babe in both long hitting and golf finesse," Wright's "personality lack[ed] the uninhibited color of the late Babe Zaharias." The search continued. In 1984 *SI*'s Barry McDermott was so impressed with Patty Sheehan's athleticism across a wide range of sports that he felt she "could be the second coming of Babe Zaharias." But it was Nancy Lopez, who in 1978 "burst on the scene with a record five wins in a row and as much charisma as anyone since Babe Didrikson Zaharias,"

Although the LPGA was the first women's professional sports organization, the tour has struggled to secure respect, purses, and galleries, always looking for at least one player who would resonate with fans and corporate sponsors. In 1978 Nancy Lopez emerged as "her sport's new heroine."

who seemed to be the savior of the LPGA in the mold of the incomparable Babe.[37]

But once found, the "new Babe" confronted a heavy burden. *SI's* Barry McDermott tagged Lopez in 1978 as "her sport's new heroine" who had "enough talent and charisma" not only to garner an *SI* cover but to make women's golf "take off." *SI's* Frank Deford agreed but pointed out that "the pressure upon [her] will be especially excruciating . . . because women's golf now depends on her. Golf is a sport that needs a popular champion for everyone to shoot at." And she was not just a benchmark of greatness on the course, she also had to singlehandedly rescue the tour from a sport that Deford had labeled in 1978 as "the very essence of male camaraderie, men in groups, the modern substitute for the hunt, that most masculine of all human endeavors." Such a characterization set up the women to fail in another regard: as *SI's* Dan Jenkins had noted in 1976, "One of the problems with women's golf is that nobody really believes a lady pro can do anything on the course as well as a man pro."[38] Wind had tried to put that matter to rest in 1956, but twenty years later women were still laboring in oblivion on a tour that struggled to get purses, fans, and respect. In addition, the LPGA was engaged in a Sisyphean task, one that *SI* helped to initiate and then certainly sustained, with its unrelenting search for a savior on the order of Babe Didrikson, who combined skill and showmanship in equal measure and would heighten the profile of the LPGA, but only for a time until she retired—when the search would begin anew.

Saviors would come and go—Nancy Lopez and Annika Sorenstam were particular *SI* favorites—but in times when the LPGA was rolling its boulder up the hill searching for a new redeemer, the tour relied on golfers with more sex appeal than talent. Though Laura Baugh did not dominate on the fairways—her best finish was in the top eight at the 1979 U.S. Women's Open—she brought "false eyelashes and dimples to a sport that can use a little makeup." In Jan Stephenson's case, "For years, [her] claim to fame was that she was the LPGA's designated pinup, but now her game is nearly a 10, too." Both women spun imitators like Laura Diaz, who in 2001 was "the media's go-to siren, much in the mold of Laura Baugh and Jan Stephenson before her." Even as Diaz welcomed the comparison, she insisted in a 2001 opinion piece for *SI* that everyone on the LPGA should also embrace the example set by Baugh and Stephenson decades earlier: "To attract new fans, the LPGA should take a lesson from our past and sell sex appeal."[39]

But even with sexy sirens and the periodic Babe-like personalities, the "shaky" LPGA "suffer[ed] from the criticism that its players lack luster." In the late 1980s, *Sports Illustrated* noted that the LPGA "is still struggling to find an image that will sell" and was risking total oblivion: "The LPGA tour has always played second fiddle to the PGA Tour, but now—and with the current resurgence in golf—the LPGA has sunk to third, behind the upstart Senior PGA Tour. Only dedicated golf fans can name the women's four majors . . . let alone the winners of them. After Nancy Lopez, the two words most commonly associated with the LPGA have become, Who cares?" Such comments were frustrating to LPGA Player of the Year Patty Sheehan, who told *SI* in 1989: "We never hear, 'You have a great game.' We hear, 'Your game is boring. It's not as good as the men's.' We are waiting for the time when being the greatest women players in the world will be enough." It would be a long wait. According to *Sports Illustrated*, the LPGA was "constantly struggl[ing] for recognition and credibility," battling "the perception, in what is still a male-oriented national sports consciousness, that women can't play excellent golf."[40] It was an assessment that would continue to haunt the LPGA into the next decade, even as the tour gained a new measure of interest thanks to the unparalleled dominance of Annika Sorenstam.

In the 1990s, Annika Sorenstam energized coverage of the LPGA partly because she had decided to try out her "excellent golf" at a PGA event—the first time a woman had "play[ed] with the men since Babe Zaharias in 1945." Once, again, coverage of women's golf in *SI* had circled back to the Babe and the need for a woman to test her mettle against the men to gain some recognition: "The world's best female golfer has labored in the obscurity of the LPGA but that's all changed now that she's preparing to tee it up with the big boys."[41] Players on the LPGA seemed stuck in the 1950s—still trying to measure individual personalities against the specter of Babe Didrikson Zaharias and still trying to prove that their games were just as good when compared with the men's. Sorenstam ultimately played the Colonial tournament in 2003 and missed the cut by four shots. She tied for ninety-sixth, ahead of eleven men, and the overall message that the public received was that the best of the best on the LPGA still fell considerably short when competing with the men. Sorenstam's chance to play with the guys was presented as a singular opportunity for an exceptional golfer.

It was clear that the LPGA had come a long way from its midcentury origins when the tour boasted fourteen events and a total of $50,000 in prize money and "consisted of a small band of impoverished players playing the back nines of America." However, as the LPGA celebrated its golden anniversary, it seemed clear that golf fans, sponsors, sportswriters, and even some of the female professionals themselves still seemed more interested in what the PGA had to offer. That was especially true for Michelle Wie, who arrived on the golf scene in 2004. It was, according to *SI*, "a moment when women's golf [was] more than ever in the shadow of the men's game, when despite the tremendous gifts of Annika Sorenstam and the wave of talented Korean golfers who have come on the scene in the past few years, the game seems increasingly an afterthought. Prize money has barely budged in five years. Total endorsement fees on the LPGA tour are estimated to be about equal to the $78 million per year that Tiger [Woods] commands." Wie, who possessed a powerful swing, had devised "an ambitious plan to dominate golf. Women's golf, men's golf, all of it." It was one that focused on becoming "a full-time PGA Tour player" as opposed to "another Annika Sorenstam on the LPGA Tour." According to her father, Wie had "been watching Tiger." As had everyone else. Tiger Woods represented "a near guarantee of higher viewership than usual" with "his rare power to move ratings" and uncanny ability to draw not only general sports fans but people who were not sports fans at all.[42] To play on a tour that headlined Tiger Woods meant increased visibility for those who joined him—especially for female players who were able to make the PGA cut.

While the Tiger effect was real, it was one that benefited from a long history of transformative players whose names—Bobby Jones, Ben Hogan, Arnold Palmer, and Jack Nicklaus—were as well known off the fairway as on it, and were supported by a cast of players who seemed to continually rewrite the record books. The LPGA had Annika Sorenstam, but with her imminent retirement in 2008, the tour was looking for its next heir apparent. Michelle Wie seemed to be it. A child prodigy and then a teen sensation, Wie at first spurned the LPGA for the more lucrative greens of the PGA. She garnered headlines and endorsements, but never made a cut on the men's tour, ultimately joining the LPGA full-time in 2009 where she enjoyed only modest success. Nevertheless, as Meg Mallon, a two-time U.S. Women's Open champion and mentor to Michelle Wie, asserted in 2014, "Whatever *it* is, Michelle has it. People are drawn in by her, they can't take their eyes off her. Every sport needs a person like that, and Michelle is it for women's golf." Wie was a "game changer," and a 2014 victory at the U.S. Women's Open didn't hurt. In fact, it was regarded as having "sweeping ramifications for the resurgent LPGA." Combining a new business plan with a charismatic star and solid talent, the LPGA was poised for "a stunning comeback."[43]

By 2019, however, the LPGA's momentum seemed to have stalled. Michelle Wie had disappeared from the leader board, and the LPGA had disappeared from *Sports Illustrated's* coverage. Even as the tour enjoyed millions of dollars in purses, it garnered only 20 percent of the prize money the PGA enjoyed in 2019. That meant fewer events for the women (33 compared with the men's 46) and smaller purses ($2.19 million on average per event compared with the men's $7.6 million) on a tour that throughout the 2000s just could not keep up—in compensation or in ratings—with the men. But the PGA was not the LPGA's only concern. The LPGA also had to contend with the more popular, and more profitable, women's tennis tour.[44] Once again, the LPGA would be on the losing end of an athletic match-up because of a pervasive homophobia and a perceived lack of athleticism.

As early as 1976, women players on the LPGA were "puzzled at how easily tennis did it. As [Judy] Rankin says, 'In tennis they were overnight darlings and we've been scrapping around here for years and years.'" In *SI*, there was a general consensus that "among women's athletics [golf] has been altogether eclipsed by tennis, not only because of Billie Jean King and Chris Evert, but also because tennis—and running and gymnastics and basketball—is properly strenuous, and thus in tune with the women's movement, its goals and propaganda alike."[45] But it wasn't just the visible exertion expended by these athletes that *SI* lauded in 1978 as being representative of second-wave feminism. It was also the athletes' visible heterosexuality—despite the outings of both Billie Jean King and Martina Navratilova in the early 1980s—which appealed both to *SI* and to a mainstream feminist movement eager to separate itself from what Betty Friedan described as the "lavender menace." It was women's golf that had to contend with "innuendoes about lesbianism" more often and more consistently than any other sport. Whether it was due to the sport's conservatism, or the tendency of the LPGA's early female pros to be unmarried, tour professionals suffered from a lesbian association in terms of fan support, sponsorship, and general acceptance. It offered a sharp contrast with women's tennis, whose popularity had in many ways equaled (and sometimes even exceeded) the men's professional tour by the twenty-first century.

"Tennis' Most Compelling Rivalry"

During the late 1960s, the U.S. Lawn Tennis Association dispensed with amateurism, ushering in a period of "open tennis" that allowed professionals to compete in major tournaments like Wimbledon and the U.S. Open and to win prize money for their play. Like the LPGA, it was not unusual for the male champion to earn from two and a half to eight times what a female winner got. When the women complained about the disparity and were rebuffed, Billie Jean King and eight other women started their own tour in 1970 with the help of Gladys Heldman, the founder and editor of *World Tennis* magazine, and Virginia Slims, a subsidiary of the Philip Morris Company. With top players like King and Margaret Court playing to large crowds that were only increasing, the USLTA was forced to respond. American tennis's governing body increased prize money for the women's tournaments and succeeded in landing two emerging talents, Evonne Goolagong and Chris Evert. Realizing that women's tennis could not sustain two separate professional tours, the USLTA and the Virginia Slims hammered out an agreement by which the "Slimsies" rejoined the USLTA in 1973, and the association would incorporate Slims tournaments—with their increased prize money—into its schedule. Despite the merger, King realized that the women needed to maintain their power as a group and spearheaded the formation of the Women's Tennis Association in 1973 to negotiate further improvements on the women's tour.[46]

In honor of Billie Jean King's leadership in the fight for equitable pay in tennis, *Sports Illustrated* named her Sportswoman of the Year in 1972. The first woman to win *SI*'s top honor, King took the opportunity to press the cause for equity in professional tennis. She asserted:

> [Women pros] do not want equal pay for equal work. We only want what we're worth. For two years we've outdrawn the men at Forest Hills [the site of the U.S. Open] by whatever criteria they've used, but this year the men's money is 2½ times the women's, and at Wimbledon it is twice as much even though I know we draw at least as many people there as the men

every year. We think our tournaments should be apart from the men's so we can be judged. If we don't draw as well, we shouldn't be paid as much.[47]

It was a bold statement by an incomparable advocate for women's tennis and women's sports. In arguing for female tennis players to be paid what they were worth, King was in fact making the case that they should receive *more* money than the men. *SI* recognized, correctly, that because of King's outspokenness, women's tennis champions were earning more prize money than ever before. In 1974 *SI*'s Joe Jares declared, "It was King who was chiefly responsible for the fat purse the women were pursuing and for the fatter purses that are sure to follow." He was right. Just a year later, Chris Evert won $40,000, "the highest first prize in the history of women's tennis."[48]

Because of King's activism, female champions were also earning prize money equal to that of the men at the U.S. Open, the first of the major tournaments to compensate them equitably. King's fight for pay equity mirrored the goals second wave feminists hoped to achieve with passage of the Equal Rights Amendment. In her autobiography, King regrets that she didn't lobby harder for the ERA, but also criticizes second wave feminists for not involving athletes more purposefully in their campaign. At the time, she called out Gloria Steinem for the lapse, but when Steinem disagreed, not seeing the obvious connection to politics, King remembers telling the legendary feminist that women tennis players, in particular, "*are* politics. You're not using us right! We can sell this movement! We're on TV, we sweat, we're real! We're out here doing and proving all these things that so many feminists are only talking about!" King notes that the Virginia Slims players personified "independence and empowerment. We challenged the male-dominated system to demand a living, and we were out there every day making it on our own."[49]

This newly empowered women's professional tennis tour, like the LPGA, had outstanding talents who graced the covers of *Sports Illustrated*, but they also had compelling matchups that kept them in the sports news, even when they weren't on the cover. Billie Jean King battled Margaret Court for the number one ranking, as Chris Evert and Evonne Goolagong went head-to-head. It was Evert who emerged as the leading force of "the Women's Big 4," and by 1976 she had won *Sports Illustrated* Sportswoman of the Year honors for having "dominated her game as no other man or

The rivalry between Martina Navratilova and Chris Evert is only one of the reasons the women's professional tennis tour has been just as compelling as the men's.

woman did in any sport." But Evert would become known less for her "overwhelming supremacy" in the 1970s than for being one half of a rivalry that transformed women's tennis.[50]

There are very few pure rivalries in sports, according to *Sports Illustrated*'s Frank Deford. Schools might play each other, but the participants always change; it was problematic to compare athletes across generations; and rivalries were often based on very few meetings. For Deford, then, Chris Evert (Lloyd) v. Martina Navratilova was a classic matchup. The participants remained the same, and by 1986 they had battled each other in fifty-seven matches over fourteen consecutive years. In addition, Evert and Navratilova had "competed for so long" they had "carved out somewhat different universes, so no one could fairly say for posterity, who might be the better. Chris the more consistent, casts the longer shadow, while Martina, the more sensational, shines the brighter light. Together, they form a complete whole. There has never been a rivalry like it in women's sports." In fact, Deford believed that one "could leave out the qualifying gender and [still] be correct."[51] It was the clearest statement about how sportswomen could offer as compelling a product as the men—if not more so. Evert and Navratilova really were "a pair beyond compare."

It all began in 1973 when Evert and Navratilova met and played for the first time in Akron, Ohio. Evert won that contest and most of their matches until the late 1970s. From 1978 to the end of 1982—what Deford considered their most evenly matched stage—the pair split victories. By 1982 the balance of power had shifted to Navratilova, who dominated throughout the mid-1980s, beating her rival consistently. Yet regardless of who won, the pair's matches were always must-see events. At the 1981 U.S. Open they "played one for the annals, a duel both brave and trenchant, highlighted by one remarkable point in the middle set that was as comprehensive an exercise in tennis as two women ever displayed." One year later, *SI* maintained that "without Borg-Connors and Borg-McEnroe, Evert Lloyd-Navratilova has become tennis' most compelling rivalry." The magazine was offering a backhanded compliment of sorts, but its coverage of Evert and Navratilova relayed just how important that rivalry was.[52]

By 1985 Evert and Navratilova were "the main story" at the French Open, where the two played, according to *SI*'s Deford, "the finest match of their long rivalry." Evert finally won the three-set battle, although Navratilova told *Sports Illustrated*, "It's too bad someone had to win. It was one of those matches that should go on forever." While that match had to end, the rivalry endured because of its unique circumstances. In addition to cultivating a real friendship, they developed a respect that drove them both to achieve greater feats. Particularly notable was Navratilova's training program in the early 1980s, which included longer practices, an improved diet, and a weight-lifting regimen. It was a routine that revolutionized the sport and forced those who wanted to compete, especially Chris Evert, to up their games as well.[53]

Even as the rivalry came to an end in 1989 with Evert's retirement, the players recognized how special their on-court relationship had been. As Evert prepared to leave the sport, Navratilova praised her rival's skill and dignity and spoke of their unique connection: "Not only did we bring out the best in each other . . . we brought it out for years longer than if either of us had been alone at the top. If she had never gotten there, I might have long since left the sport." In turn, Evert noted that she "could feel the rivalry emanating not only from us but from crowds around the world as well. The excitement and the tension were everywhere. When have No. 1 and No. 2 been so close for so long in any sport as Martina and I were?"[54]

The Evert-Navratilova rivalry stimulated further interest in a women's tour that, owing to Billie Jean King's efforts, had already gained financial solvency and fame. And succeeding rivalries, while perhaps not as long-lasting, came to define the women's game in ways that were both compelling and profitable. Steffi Graf was paired not only with Martina Navratilova following Evert's retirement, but with Gabriela Sabatini and then Monica Seles. In 2000 Martina Hingis and Venus Williams were the "game's most riveting rivalry," but it was one that was overshadowed by Venus's on-court battles with sister Serena, and then Serena's rivalry with essentially herself as she pursued Margaret Court's record of twenty-four Grand Slam tournament singles titles.[55]

Not only were women in the WTA earning more money than any of their professional playing female peers, they were receiving greater media coverage, especially in *Sports Illustrated*. Throughout the 1970s, *SI* featured female professional tennis players in dozens of articles and placed them on its cover eight times, two of which honored sportswomen of the year—Billie Jean King in 1972 and Chris Evert in 1976. Coverage continued into the late twentieth century, especially with the magazine's focus on Monica Seles. By the twenty-first century Venus and Serena Williams were "driving attendance, television ratings, general interest in tennis," and coverage in *Sports Illustrated*. As reporting of the LPGA declined in the magazine, even with its periodic starlets and saviors, *SI* continued to follow the story of the Williams sisters and their would-be challengers, who were growing increasingly younger even as the sisters stayed in the game, and Serena, in particular, became not only the "greatest female player of her generation" but of "all time."[56]

With its media coverage and captivating rivalries, the WTA did indeed seem to offer a blueprint for success that other professional leagues should follow. Although the WTA had its share of celebrity players and acknowledged concern about the retirement of both Williams sisters, especially Serena, the tour was not entirely dependent on either for continued success. Professional tennis players had managed to be appreciated for their own play, even when they were compared with the men. *SI* certainly contributed to that acceptance by consistently appreciating the women's play without qualification. In 1978 Deford maintained that when Chris Evert played Evonne Goolagong, it was on a different level than Bjorn Borg playing Connors, but still "the competition [was] absorbing for its own sake."[57] The women's tennis tour seemed to have it all: charismatic personalities, impressive talent, and compelling rivalries all packaged in short tennis skirts.

But such a winning combination did not always guarantee respect. In March 2016 SI.com reported that Indian Wells tournament director and CEO Raymond Moore had asserted that the women players had "rid[den] on the coattails of the men. They don't make any decisions, and they are lucky. They are very, very lucky. If I was a lady player, I would go down every night on my knees and thank God that Roger Federer and Rafa Nadal were born because they have carried this sport. They really have." Response was swift. Serena Williams retorted, "Obviously, I don't think any woman should be down on their knees thanking anybody like that." She added that Moore was simply wrong: "If I could tell you every day how many people say they don't watch tennis unless they're watching myself or my sister, I couldn't even bring up that number. . . . I think there is a lot of women out there who are more . . . are very exciting to watch. I think there are a lot of men out there who are exciting to watch. I think it definitely goes both ways." In response to a follow-up question, she admitted that she was surprised to hear such sexist remarks in 2016: "Yeah, I'm still surprised, especially with me and Venus and all the other women on the tour that's done well. Last year, the women's final at the US Open sold out well before the men. I'm sorry, did Roger play in that final or Rafa or any man play in that final that was sold out before the men's final? I think not." Moore had clearly blundered and apologized before resigning his leadership positions with the Indian Wells Tournament.[58]

Despite the success of the WTA and its clear position as the most successful of all professional women's sports leagues, in terms of both money and media coverage, sexist ideas about women's achievements in comparison with the men's—even when they were inaccurate—continued to circulate. Following the incident at Indian Wells in 2016, top men's player Novak Djokovic questioned whether women deserved equal pay with men because of the difference in the required number of sets. And when he took the lead on forming a new players association in 2020, he did not initially include the women.[59] Challenges remained for the most successful of the women's professional leagues, and they were even more numerous and more difficult for those female athletes looking to propose a new professional league in a team sport with plenty of physical contact.

"In Need of a Save"

The organizers of the 1999 Women's World Cup had modest expectations for spectator interest in the soccer matches that would be played throughout the United States. The American team had different plans. They held clinics, signed autographs, and by sheer force of will filled the stadiums with fans during the qualifying rounds. By the time the final rolled around, a number of the team's members were household names, having appeared in Nike commercials, graced the David Letterman show, and played gutsy soccer. It was a combination that secured a World Cup trophy, *Sports Illustrated* Sportswomen of the Year honors, and the first-ever professional soccer league for women in the United States, the Women's United Soccer Association.

As with women's basketball, American women soccer players had labored abroad as professionals before the founding of the WUSA in 2000. WUSA commissioner Tony DiCicco, the former coach of the 1999 champions, had envisioned American-based teams that rostered international talent, but in the end, the league became a platform for showcasing the talents of American women and especially what *Sports Illustrated* called its "one sure thing—Mia Hamm." But not even Mia Hamm could offset the "uphill struggles" that the WUSA faced. As DiCicco acknowledged, "We're launching a professional league, but it's a minor sport in America and it's women's athletics."[60] It was unclear which would be the more daunting task: selling soccer to an American audience crazy for American football, or convincing them that women's sports were worth watching.

And there were other problems. Most of the fans in the United States who had followed the "'99ers"—and it was an American audience the league targeted—were excited to see Mia Hamm and Brandi Chastain back in action, but not necessarily playing against each other. In addition, the league's eight teams had no more than three national team players per team, and of those, usually only one or two had seen World Cup play and thus enjoyed easy name recognition. Other challenges served to diminish its impact: the league did not release team names, schedules, and rosters until six months before play was slated to begin; it faced a possible challenge from Major League Soccer to start its own rival league; and it suffered from a general lack of support from U.S. Soccer. In addition to some early lackluster play and declining ticket sales, the WUSA was in serious trouble, failing to secure projected television ratings and attract additional sponsors, even as it spent its entire five-year budget in two years. Amid these economic concerns were reports that WUSA officials were looking to drum up interest in the league by "encouraging their players to pose nude for *Playboy*."[61] There was no clearer statement about how women could best sell their league—not on the basis of their athletic brilliance, but on their physical assets.

There were some positive developments. Players earned average salaries of $40,000, which was less than the WNBA but matched those of the men's in Major League Soccer. And the league showcased the future of women's soccer, providing a stage for future stars like Abby Wambach. But the positives were not enough to offset the negatives, particularly in what *SI* deemed a "saturated sports market." Following the conclusion of its third season, the WUSA folded, millions of dollars in debt and with the hopes of a lasting professional legacy in ashes.[62]

It was left to another generation to see if they could transform Olympic and World Cup success into sustained support for a professional women's league in the United States. By 2009 the Women's Professional Soccer league was ready to take the pitch, but it would do so without Mia Hamm (who had retired) and at a time when enthusiasm for women's soccer in the United States was waning.[63] From the beginning, fan interest and television ratings were disappointing, and by the third year, Women's Professional Soccer clubs were folding and others were barely surviving. *Sports Illustrated* did not cover the league until 2011, when it was already in trouble, acknowledging that the WPS, while rich in talent, was "in need of a save." It was too little too late. After just three seasons of play, the league suspended operations and officially folded in January 2012.[64]

Perhaps the third time was the charm, for in August 2012 *Sports Illustrated,* once again reported the formation of "a new, yet-to-be-named professional women's soccer league" with eight teams. The announcement followed the American women's gold medal–winning effort in that summer's Olympic Games and relied heavily on the marketability of national team star Alex Morgan. Given Morgan's dominance on the field and her model-like looks, comparisons with Mia Hamm were inevitable, from *Sports Illustrated* writers and fellow players alike. *SI* acknowledged that Morgan was "not a Hamm clone" but "in all of women's soccer, only Hamm has experienced the whirlwind of mainstream stardom that is now sweeping up Morgan, a fresh-faced scorer with limitless marketing potential." Abby Wambach remarked on the comparison, contrasting it with her own position on the team: "Alex is taking on a different role [from mine]. She'll have more of the mainstream popularity of being the pretty girl and being able to cross over to 15- and 25-year-old men—the Mia Hamm-like qualities that touch millions."[65] Once again women's sports—and the viability of a women's professional sports league—was predicated on the ability to showcase a pretty girl, who was almost always white and heterosexual, to attract the coveted male demographic.

Comparisons with one of the greatest soccer players aside, the big question, according to *SI*, was whether Morgan could achieve what even the legendary Mia Hamm had not: use her star power to make women's professional soccer "a viable business in the United States." As the National Women's Soccer League prepared to launch in 2013, questions about the new league's sustainability were more than fair given the ghosts of leagues past. But the real issue, according to Hamm's fellow "'99er" and former national team captain Julie Foudy, was figuring out "what the market will bear. So enough talk about 'you should do it' or 'it's a great cause.' It has to be about a business model that makes sense."[66]

Such a claim was in direct contrast to the advice *SI*'s Alexander Wolff had given the American Basketball League in 1996 when he had urged them to "*Remember that you're not a league, you're a movement.*" Two decades later, the counsel was completely the opposite. Given the precariousness of professional women's sports in general—including salaries that were mere fractions of men's in the same sports, insufficient media attention, and tours that were more afterthoughts than main draws—the focus, especially for women's professional soccer, on a business model and not just a good-looking savior was essential. And *Sports Illustrated* thought that this time around the plan "appears improved: The federations of the U.S., Canada and Mexico are paying the salaries of the national team players instead of the clubs having to do it." In addition, the NWSL benefited from a global audience smitten with women's soccer not just because of the 2012 Olympics but the 2011 World Cup as well; sold-out stadiums, impressive television ratings, and a record-long Twitter feed meant that more people than ever before were watching women's soccer, which had "reached new heights of competitiveness." The fact that "women's soccer may be more competitive than ever" meant that a future league would not see the disparity in skill between Americans and their international counterparts. In addition, colleges and universities as well as youth soccer programs provided important feeder systems for producing players whose talent could keep pace with the national team. Ten years out from the WUSA, this was probably the greatest change; teams were able to produce better soccer because everyone played at a higher level.[67]

But the feeling of déjà vu was one that SI's Grant Wahl acknowledged in 2015, after yet another American World Cup win and yet another women's professional soccer league had been organized in the United States. Wahl allowed that "the women's win was a great moment for their sport" but recognized that "we've been here before," asking, "Can this new energy propel a pro league forward?" It seemed to be the (multi-)million dollar question. New opportunities to grow the game occurred when the U.S. women won the 2015 World Cup and then embarked on a ten-game victory tour before focusing on winning probable Olympic gold in 2016. With a new television deal, online streaming, and national federations covering the cost of the salaries of their team members, media exposure was up, owners' costs were down, and there was faith among players that their "fans are going to buy into the NWSL."[68]

Sports Illustrated's Michael Rosenberg wasn't so sure. For Rosenberg, "Women's professional soccer feels like what it is: a start-up." And it was a start-up in a market that was inundated with "more than 100 major professional sports teams. Whatever we need in this country—nicer politicians, better funding for education, toilet-seat covers that stay on the toilet seat—we don't need more teams." Rosenberg seemed to think that it was less about gender and much more about supply and demand, especially for a professional league that was trying to sell itself with a business plan that "doesn't have enough money, reach and media exposure." But it was hard to believe that gender did not play a factor, especially when SI also covered the emergence of the men's Premier Lacrosse League, which had signed a deal with NBC to broadcast seventeen games on its Sports Network and stream twenty others, "prov[ing] it was possible to turn a niche sport into a lucrative business platform."[69]

But what did it say about American women's professional soccer when, after fifteen years of international dominance and millions of fans, prominent sportswriters still regarded it as a start-up and considered a niche men's sport like lacrosse a viable option for creating a professional league?[70] It was a clear indication that sports—especially professional sports—remained the purview of men. Regardless of how much talent women displayed or how many "pretty girls" their teams rostered, women's professional leagues continued to be seen as offering an inferior product to what men's professional leagues offered, regardless of the sport.

"Few Women Make a Living in Pro Sports"

In 2004 *Sports Illustrated*'s L. Jon Wertheim acknowledged that "female athletes make great role models and fierce competitors. But few women make a living in pro sports. How can they bolster their box-office appeal?" Wertheim had some ideas. First, he offered an important reminder: "It's a sport, not a cause. Successful women's pro leagues may be the ultimate manifestation of Girl Power, but selling the leagues as philanthropy and not athletics shortchanges the product." Most importantly, it meant that women's leagues had to compete for sponsorship opportunities not only with other professional sports but with charities as well. Second, stop focusing on selling women's professional sports to just women. "Most women's sports fans are likely to be girls and women. But men still make up the majority of the couch-potato demographic that drives TV ratings. And, positioned correctly, women's sports are the ideal antidote to the predominantly male grousing about the thugs, the poverty of fundamentals and the millionaire babies blighting the current men's sports landscape." Thus, if marketed correctly, women's professional leagues could offer fans a pure sports experience as it was meant to be—with a reliance on the basics and without the corruption of big money and even bigger egos. Third, "Sell sex appeal, not sex." Dispense with the nudity and the vulgarity, even as you sell female athletes as both strong and alluring. Next, "Think globally, act locally." Seek those corporate endorsements, but continue to reach out to local businesses that support the community. Finally, stop comparing women's professional leagues with the men's, "which have been accumulating fans and history for decades." Wertheim believed there was a market for women's professional sports but that it would "take some time and some savvier planning."[71]

While Wertheim offered sound advice, he didn't include any suggestions about securing media coverage—especially in *Sports Illustrated*. Without the clear and consistent reporting in *SI* that women's professional sports were just as compelling as the men's, women's opportunities to play for pay were doomed, if not to fail, then to suffer in comparison with the men. As early as 1973, Gilbert and Williamson had criticized "the amount of coverage given to women's athletics" as both "meager" and "atrocious." They noted that "rather than describing how well or badly the athlete performed or even how the contest turned out, writers tend to concentrate on the color of the hair and eyes, and the shape of the legs or busts of the women. The best-looking girls (by male standards) are singled out for attention, no matter how little their sporting talent may be." To prove how bad such reporting could be, they selected *Sports Illustrated*'s own Harold Peterson and his 1971 description of professional golfer Laura Baugh as "typical": "A cool, braided California blonde named Laura Baugh made quite a splash . . . her perfectly tanned, well-formed legs swinging jauntily. The hair on her tapered arms was bleached absolutely white against a milk-chocolate tan. Her platinum hair was pulled smartly back in a Viking-maiden braid." As Gilbert and Williamson made clear: "The difference in reporting men's and women's sporting events is obvious."[72] Obvious and Othering.

And the marginalization of female professionals in *Sports Illustrated* was a reality regardless of the sport. In baseball, women were the exceptions that proved the rule, whether it was Jackie Mitchell in 1931 or Ila Borders in 1991. Women experienced a measure of success in the AAGPBL, but short dresses and an abundance of cosmetics shored up their most important advantage—their white, heterosexual femininity. Similar kinds of priorities dogged the All American Red Heads, who relied on hair dye and on-court pranks to fund their tour. While the American Basketball League and the WNBA would dispense with such ploys and tout the skill and talent of its players, the WNBA played in NBA arenas during the men's off-season and struggled with an image of being a kid sister playing with her big brother's toys when he wasn't using them. The LPGA also labored in the shadow of the men's professional tour; even with its stars and its starlets, it could not make the case that its brand of golf was equal to that of the men's, nor was it equal to that of the Women's Tennis Association, which, while enjoying compelling rivalries, extensive media coverage, and a commitment to pay equity, still had to contend with comments that they were beholden to the men's tour for their success. By 2015, women's soccer had a sound business plan, but there was still doubt that the National Women's Soccer League would be regarded as anything but a start-up.

For decades, then, women's professional sports have struggled—for fan support, for media attention, and for simple respect. In 2021, on the

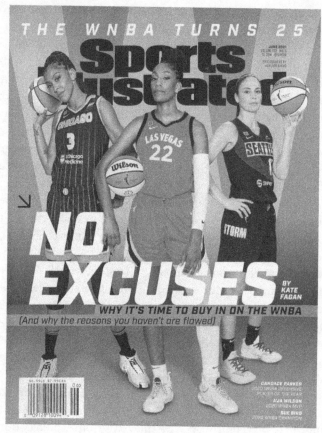

In June 2021 the WNBA celebrated its twenty-fifth anniversary with a *Sports Illustrated* cover turn. It was the first time professional female basketball players had appeared in such a capacity, underscoring the ways in which women's professional sports leagues had struggled for fan support and media attention.

twenty-fifth anniversary of the WNBA's inaugural season, *SI*'s Kate Fagan identified what she considered to be "the serial killer of women's professional leagues": the assumption that women simply don't run, jump, or throw at the level that men can. As a result, their performances, no matter the sport, are subpar. Such an explanation, Fagan asserted, was "pathological. It's chronic, and irrational." It was also an easy out for just about everyone: "This reasoning doesn't just absolve sports fans of any further introspection, but more important it absolves the marketers, the TV networks and the sports apparel companies." But, as Fagan argued, it shouldn't. According to business scholar Nefertiti Walker, "People in every other industry understand that demand is created by the marketers and the decision-makers. They know: People will watch what you tell them to watch, what you create bells and whistles around them watching." *Sports Illustrated* certainly embraced that approach, understanding that the magazine served as a guidebook for informing readers what sports were worth watching. At least for men's sports. Walker noted that when it came to women's sports, "sports people . . . throw up their hands and act like the consumers drive decisions." Dave Barry, professor of economics at Southern Utah, agreed; half of all NBA franchises lose money, but for NBA owners, "It's often a vanity project—just to be involved in the game. But suddenly when it's women's sports, you have to make a profit; now you're running a McDonald's? Now we have to pore over profit-and-loss statements? When did we decide that's how we evaluate things in sports?" And if we did, how many men's professional sports teams would suffer as a result? But the bottom line is that even as the sports world believes it is applying objective criteria to evaluate the "worth" of professional sports teams, the game is rigged in favor of men, regardless of the product they offer, because of continuing cultural misconceptions.[73]

To even the professional playing field, Fagan urged a more critical view of "the infrastructure of the sports world—i.e., the programming decisions by ESPN, the marketing dollars budgeted by Nike, the cover (and coverage) decisions by the magazine you're currently reading." When that happened, fans just might "wonder whether perhaps, maybe, women aren't invested in the same way men are."[74] It was the same argument Bil Gilbert and Nancy Williamson had made in their landmark series on women in sport in *Sports Illustrated* back in 1973.

But the WNBA experienced an additional liability that Gilbert and Williamson had not addressed and that its sister professional organizations did not encounter. According to Fagan, "No women's league has a higher percentage of Black athletes, meaning that for nearly a quarter century the WNBA has been rowing against the headwinds of racism, sexism and anti-LGBTQ sentiment."[75] It was a powerful statement, and one that placed racism in conversation with sexism and homophobia as continued sources of prejudice against women's professional sports and women's sports in general.

Such discrimination pervaded all of the women's professional leagues to such an extent that regardless of the sport, women—relying first on gimmicks and always on hyperfeminine displays—remained "the Other." While women had overcome some barriers in their quest to attain fulfillment in professional sport, the problem remained that sport echoed society. Thus sexism, racism, and homophobia continued to beleaguer women even at the highest levels of sport. Professional sportswomen found themselves on the losing end of continuous comparisons with men in a magazine that celebrated their successes only rarely. While *Sports Illustrated* featured female athletes and their various efforts to launch and cultivate professional leagues, its coverage was like that of other female athletes in the magazine: sporadic and sparse.

CONCLUSION

"A Pretty Girl on the Cover"

SHORTLY AFTER James Naismith invented the game of basketball in Springfield, Massachusetts, during the winter of 1891, Senda Berenson, a physical education teacher at nearby all-women's Smith College, introduced the game to her students. After three weeks of practice, Berenson hosted the first collegiate women's basketball game, which pitted Smith's sophomores against its freshmen. The sophomores eked out a 5–4 win in what the *New York Herald* described as "a close contest of two 15-minute halves." But that description failed to convey the intensity of the competition. As one onlooker reported, the girls were "running madly the entire length of the big floor, batting and snatching the ball." It was shocking behavior for the time, and Berenson immediately set to work adapting the guidelines of basketball to make them more acceptable for females. "Girls' rules" divided the court into thirds, required six players per team, and proscribed "batting," "snatching," and "running madly"—at least for the mostly white females at the Seven Sisters colleges.[1]

Those rules and restrictions had mostly disappeared by the 1960s, when American women starting playing—and losing—to their bitter Cold War rival the Soviet Union, which had adopted and perfected a five-on-five, full-court approach. By the mid-1970s, the modern women's game had been established through the efforts of UCLA cager Anne Meyers, Delta State center Lusia Harris, and Old Dominion point guard Nancy Lieberman; all three headlined the first American women's Olympic basketball team in 1976 and were stalwarts of their national championship–winning collegiate teams. Their pioneering efforts set the stage for Cheryl Miller, who led the University of Southern California to consecutive NCAA national championships in 1983 and 1984 and was part of the 1984 Olympic gold medal–winning team in Los Angeles.

As the 1985 season opened, Miller, then a senior at USC, shared a special issue *SI* cover previewing college basketball with Georgia Tech's Bruce Dalrymple and Mark Price. It was the first time a collegiate women's basketball player had ever graced the cover of *SI*—more than thirty years after the first male hoopster had done so, and almost one hundred years after females had first started playing the game. Yet Cheryl Miller, with all of her accolades, did not garner a cover of a regular issue all her own. While *SI* has published "special issues," "special commemorative issues," and "collector's editions" celebrating women's NCAA championships, the magazine has never once featured a collegiate woman basketball player by herself or with her team on the cover of a regular issue.[2]

Their absence is significant. Both American males and females started playing college basketball at approximately the same time, albeit with different rules. Men did have more opportunities than women to contest national titles, but among the hundreds of regular-issue covers *SI* has published since 1954, not one of them featured the exploits of female college basketball players.

Were they not compelling enough? The multiyear rivalry between the University of Connecticut and the University of Tennessee that headlined such talents as Sue Bird, Diana Taurasi, Chamique Holdsclaw, and Candace Parker belies such claims, as does UConn's 2008–10 win streak of ninety games, which surpassed UCLA's 1971–74 record of eighty-eight straight wins.[3] Not popular enough? Again, it was not unusual for UConn and the Lady Vols to draw tens of thousands of fans to a single game; in the case of Tennessee, the 1998 undefeated team outdrew some NBA teams.[4]

Not pretty enough? Perhaps. *SI*'s 1964 decision to put a "pretty girl on the cover" year after year is telling in this regard, as it casts into stark relief the magazine's commitment to promoting swimsuit models at the expense of offering similar exposure to female athletes.[5] In five separate years, a swimsuit model was the *only* female to appear on a *Sports Illustrated* cover. In fourteen other years, swimsuit models and female athletes enjoyed equal visibility with one cover each. It is a clear indication that the magazine prioritized swimsuit models and often valued their presence more than female athletes. And that was evident from the start. Just two weeks after *Sports Illustrated*'s inaugural issue on August 23, 1954, Pamela Nelson became the first female to grace an *SI* cover, doing so as the magazine's "girl in the surf." She was the first of ten swimsuit-clad females—both athletes and nonathletes—who preceded Babette March's official Swimsuit Issue debut in 1964. Since that time, *Sports Illustrated* has guaranteed that swimsuit models would enjoy not just a cover but ultimately an entire issue devoted to them. It was a commitment denied to sportswomen.

But female athletes were due for some special attention from *SI*. Following the retirement of Jule Campbell in 1996, the new Swimsuit Issue editor, Elaine Farley, "decided to make some changes," which included a stand-alone issue that "features swimsuit photos of professional athletes."[6] By 2002, both innovations were well established, and female athletes had become fixtures in the magazine's annual issue. In fact, *Sports Illustrated*'s visual representations of the female athlete and the swimsuit model had effectively become one and the same, highlighting a trajectory years in the making that successfully blurred the lines between swimsuit models and female athletes.

Thus, twenty-five years after sportswomen first appeared in the Swimsuit Issue, it serves as a valuable lens through which to recount the topics *Skimpy Coverage* explores and the lessons it imparts. Its use in this way reflects the reality that the Swimsuit Issue sportswoman has often enjoyed more exposure—both physical and editorial—than in the traditional magazine. From highlighting the challenges of sustaining professional leagues to serving as Olympic ambassadors to battles over equity, inclusion, and well-being, the Swimsuit Issue has referenced the issues that dominated *SI*'s reporting of female athletes. But whether those athletes appeared in *SI*, *SI for Women*, or in the Swimsuit Issue itself, it was *Sports Illustrated*'s commitment to showcasing a "pretty" girl who was overwhelmingly white, straight, cisgender, able-bodied, and unfailingly feminine that remained a constant.

"Also a Knockout"

In 1997 Steffi Graf, "the world's premier women's tennis player," became the first female athlete to appear in the *Sports Illustrated* Swimsuit Issue. "Fräulein February" was photographed by legendary Swimsuit Issue photographer Walter Iooss Jr. in five different bikinis, including a white one that, according to the magazine's Austin Murphy, "call[ed] attention to her terrific . . . assets." The photo spread highlighted the dissonance between Graf the "dazzling" swimsuit model and Graf the scowling tennis champion. Such a contrast was not lost on Murphy, who realized that "watching her dismember some hapless foe in 44 minutes, you don't reflect on how attractive she is. You reflect on what an efficient predator she is." But because of the *SI* swimsuit shoot, there was "no escaping the fact that Graf is also a knockout."[7]

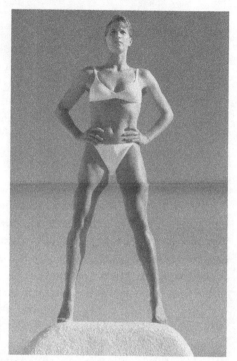

Photographed by legendary
swimsuit issue photographer Walter
Iooss Jr., Steffi Graf was the first
female athlete to appear in the
Swimsuit Issue, doing so in 1997.

An appearance in the Swimsuit Issue helped make the case that female athletes possessed both athleticism and femininity in abundance regardless of their musculature, race, or disability. For example, bodybuilder and six-time Ms. Olympia Lenda Murray's appearance in the Swimsuit Issue, also in 1997, showed how the bikini was particularly "well-suited to show off the hardest bodies," regardless of race. In 2018 Paralympian Brenda Huckaby, who became the first amputee to model in the Swimsuit Issue, was hoping "to help change the stigma behind disabilities." She "want[ed] other women, regardless of their body, to know they are powerful and sexy."[8] While Murray and Huckaby exploded stereotypes and upended narrow definitions associated with femininity, sportswomen in *SI* were nevertheless obliged to confirm their feminine credentials throughout the duration of their athletic careers. Only exceptional sportswomen like Chris Evert and Florence Griffith Joyner enjoyed a respite from constantly having to reaffirm their femininity.

Thus, irrespective of the physiques they honed, the elaborate hairdos they styled, the tears they shed, or the number of ruffles they donned, the *SI* sportswomen assiduously sought to prove that a feminine presentation and athleticism were not mutually exclusive. That was true whether female athletes adopted a dainty, "Big F" approach, or a new and "improved" version that embraced strength and sex appeal. Indeed, female athletes were so committed to the idea that they could make femininity and athleticism go together, they seldom questioned why they felt they should have to. Such a stance was informed by *Sports Illustrated* and the premium it placed on featuring sportswomen who could have been swimsuit model substitutes. Throughout its history, *SI* has become more inclusive of different bodies and races, but femininity is no less required of a *SI* sportswoman in 2022 than it was when the magazine first appeared in 1954. Thus it is no less a box that restricts female athletes who have to divert time, money, and energy to sustaining a feminine presentation that they could have devoted to their sport instead.

Given the premium on an acceptable and observable femininity, female athletes lacking clear feminine credentials—women who were neither mothers nor wives, or too strong and too fast—were vulnerable. They remained under suspicion not just for an unacceptable expression of femininity but for possessing an unfair advantage in sport.

"More Diverse and Inclusive a Community"

In 2019 the *Sports Illustrated* Swimsuit Issue website (https://swimsuit.si .com) celebrated a historic occasion: "Megan Rapinoe Proudly Poses as the First Openly Gay Woman in the *SI* Swimsuit Issue." The star soccer player, appearing alongside teammates Alex Morgan, Crystal Dunn, and Abby Dahlkemper, believed her inclusion in the magazine was "really quite a bold statement," in part because "there's such a narrow view of what it means to be gay and be athletic. So, to kind of just blow that up and do something totally different I think is really important." Rapinoe commented on the staying power of such damaging stereotypes, finding that they "still very much persist and they are just such incomplete views of who we really are as people, so I think for that reason it's really important to just continue to push those boundaries." While the Swimsuit Issue website explored the trailblazing development, the actual 2019 issue did not, opting instead to discuss the national team's "battle for equal pay" and the upcoming World Cup competition instead.[9] Thus although some barriers might have been broken online, they had yet to apply to the entirety of *SI*'s platforms. It was indicative of the magazine's treatment of the lesbian athlete throughout its history, as *SI* gradually abandoned innuendo and homophobia for an outright and unapologetic acceptance of lesbian sportswomen.

It was in stark contrast to the magazine's celebration of Jason Collins as "The Gay Athlete" on its May 6, 2013, cover. Such an appearance might have been possible in the 2010s, but not in the 1980s. For example, on September 19, 1983, tennis star Martina Navratilova won the U.S. Open and earned an *SI* cover, the first out lesbian athlete to do so, but the moment would go unremarked in the magazine—much like Rapinoe's Swimsuit Issue appearance in 2019. *Sports Illustrated* highlighted Navratilova's epic brilliance and dominance on the tennis tour, but not the seminal moment that it was for the magazine itself—and thus for the LGBTQ+ community at the time. It was typical of a magazine that had long regarded lesbianism in sport as problematic.

Although Rapinoe's identification as a member of the LGBTQ+ community might not have made it into the 2019 Swimsuit Issue, the 2022 edition celebrated five WNBA players who, according to veteran Sue Bird, were representative of the league as a whole: "This is who we are; this is the makeup of our league. We represent a variety of things: of course women, women of color, members of the LGBTQIA2+ community and much more. . . . The [Swimsuit] issue for so many years has been iconic and has represented a lot for women. Now you are seeing an evolution in what that can mean and what that can look like, and I think the WNBA players being a part of that is what makes it special. There is no better group of women to showcase that evolution."[10] That progress included a *SI* Swimsuit Issue that openly and proudly included out lesbians Sue Bird and Breanna Stewart, underscoring a wider acceptance of lesbians not just in professional women's basketball but in women's sport as a whole. It was a "coming out" party of sorts, but it was one that did not invite lesbian sportswomen of color, trans sportswomen, or female athletes with DSD. Nor did it make room for those who did not present as feminine. Indeed, former *SI* contributor Frankie de la Cretaz noted that it was "long past time to celebrate and uplift queer, masculine-of-center aesthetics as desirable." Thus, even as Rapinoe and Bird regarded the inclusion of lesbian sportswomen in the Swimsuit Issue as "bold" and "special," it was really more reflective of a decades-long approach in *Sports Illustrated* in which objectification of women and proscribed gender expressions were the norm.[11]

Nevertheless, the 2022 Swimsuit Issue was indicative of larger change where the LGBTQ+ community was concerned. In 2020 editor MJ Day celebrated the edition's first transgender model, Valentina Sampaio. A year later, Leyna Bloom became both the first trans person—and the first trans person of color—to cover the *SI* Swimsuit Issue, offering "further proof that the more diverse and inclusive a community is, the stronger it becomes."[12] That spirit had also informed *SI;* the magazine had educated its readers about the challenges facing both trans athletes and those sportswomen identified with Differences of Sex Development, offering compassionate portrayals in an effort to minimize stigma. By the twenty-first century the magazine had finally become an important advocate for the entire LGBTQ+ community. It was a tipping point, particularly as the magazine used its platform to draw attention to athletes who were being targeted and marginalized by both national and international sporting bodies.

As both *Sports Illustrated* and the Swimsuit Issue evolved, charting a more "diverse and inclusive" course, issues of social justice, equity, and equality became increasingly paramount. Those same issues were central to the 1972 passage of Title IX and remain essential to its goal of creating a sporting experience that is equal for all athletes, regardless of gender.

"Almost Identical"

In 2002 it seemed that real equality had been achieved at last. Title IX was thirty years old, but even without the anniversary celebration, there were indications in *Sports Illustrated* of gender equality. In that year's Swimsuit Issue, boxer Felix (Tito) Trinidad introduced model Molly Sims to "The Sweet Science." *Sports Illustrated* noted, "Having a three-time champ teach a supermodel to box seemed like a good idea—until she floored him with a wicked combination of beauty and brawn." *SI*'s Rick Reilly took the opportunity to ruminate about the similarities between supermodels and athletes, referencing their exceptional genetics and their unconventional work schedules. He concluded that "supermodels are amazingly similar to athletes."[13] That is to *male* athletes.

Reilly's cheeky commentary was designed to entertain, but his presumption that athletes were male and the ways in which he flippantly cataloged the similarities between sportsmen and supermodels is revealing, especially when "supermodels" are swapped with "sportswomen." Are female athletes "amazingly similar" to their male counterparts? Decades after Congress first passed Title IX, its impact in promoting women's equity in sports has been nothing short of transformational—especially given the status of women in sports before 1972. Because of the law, millions of American females have competed at the high school and collegiate levels, in more sports than ever before, and with increased access to equitable facilities, coaching, and travel schedules.

Sports Illustrated highlighted and ultimately celebrated those developments even as it ignored the ways in which inequities persisted, especially for Black sportswomen. In addition, the magazine tended to celebrate watershed moments popularly associated with the law, like Billie Jean King's triumph in the Battle of the Sexes, which had no legal ramifications that influenced the future of Title IX adherence; other incidents that *did* relate to Title IX were celebrated months or years after the fact, but not when the original events took place. Finally, while *SI* cited Title IX as the inspiration for a separate magazine for women, it was one that served to segregate female athletes; instead of simply adding pages to its weekly publication that would feature sportswomen, it opted for an approach that was inequitable and ultimately unsustainable. *Sports Illustrated* thus served as an important venue to educate and inform, but it continued to perpetuate inequalities and allow misperceptions to dominate the conversation, even as many federally funded institutions failed to comply fully with Title IX's most basic premise: the equitable treatment of female athletes. Supermodels might have achieved parity with sportsmen, but for sportswomen, equality remained elusive.

But Reilly found an additional point of commonality between sportsmen and supermodels: "Both suffer untold injuries and both must play with pain."[14] That was true for sportswomen as well, especially when, as a result of Title IX, so many more females were playing sports than ever before, and thus sustaining more injuries—both physical and psychological—than ever before.

"Well-Being of Athletes"

In many ways, 2021 was a tough year for Naomi Osaka. The tennis champion withdrew from both the French Open and Wimbledon to avoid the mandatory press briefings in an effort to protect her mental health. In response to Osaka's decision, the *SI* Swimsuit Issue celebrated her with a cover turn—the first Black female athlete and first biracial Black woman to

In 2021 Naomi Osaka withdrew from both the French Open and Wimbledon to avoid the mandatory press briefings in an effort to protect her mental health. In response to Osaka's decision, the *SI* Swimsuit Issue celebrated her with a cover turn—the first Black female athlete and first biracial Black woman to receive the distinction.

receive the distinction—praising the "naturally quiet" tennis player for "igniting a meaningful conversation about the mental well-being of athletes."[15] Osaka had transformed a personal challenge into an international discussion that had moved well beyond the tennis court, and into the pages of *Sports Illustrated.*

It was not the first time *Sports Illustrated* had addressed a health issue that had major ramifications inside and outside the field of play. As early as 1994, *SI* had highlighted the dangers associated with repeated concussions when it described "the terrible toll" they exacted, particularly in football.[16] The magazine repeatedly returned to the issue, devoting cover turns to concussions in 2001, 2012, and 2015, providing much-needed education on the injury's incidence and its effects. But the magazine's singular focus on football was problematic; although collegiate football saw the highest incidence of concussions, women's soccer ranked second among all collegiate sports, and women's ice hockey players also suffered higher rates of concussions than their male counterparts.[17] Nevertheless, when *Sports Illustrated* decided to tackle one of the biggest health issues related to sport, the magazine portrayed it overwhelmingly as a male concern.

The concussion discussion testifies not only to the invisibility of female athletes but to the presumed resilience of their male counterparts. Sportsmen were warriors, competing through concussions and recovering from ACL surgeries to emerge triumphant; they were lauded and indeed idolized for surmounting such obstacles. In contrast, sportswomen, especially in *Sports Illustrated,* were remembered for tragedies and trauma—victims of a frailty myth that appreciated them more for their mental and physical anguish than for their athletic brilliance and dominance. In sport, and in *Sports Illustrated,* female athletes continually battled a frailty myth that regarded them as being particularly susceptible to physical injury, mental health distress, eating disorders, performance-enhancing drug abuse, and sexual assault. Such portrayals, particularly in *Sports Illustrated,* prevented female athletes from becoming bona fide stars that the magazine acknowledged more for their athletic dominance than for their tragic circumstances. One twelve-month span of *SI*'s publication schedule clearly illuminates this phenomena: between Vendela appearing in a "monokini" in February 1993 and the Swimsuit Issue's thirtieth anniversary in February 1994, women appeared on the cover of *Sports Illustrated* four additional times: Seles's stabbing in May 1993 was followed in July by widows Laurie Crews and Patti Olin, whose husbands—both pitchers for the Cleveland

Indians—had died in a boating accident. In August, tennis player Mary Pierce was the subject of a special report that detailed the physical abuse she had endured at the hands of her father/coach, only to be followed in January by the clubbing of Nancy Kerrigan. *New York Times* contributor Lynda Truman Ryan noted at the time that if you were a woman, it seemed "all you have to do to get a [*SI*] cover is suffer."[18] The clear message was that *SI* sportswomen, in particular, were celebrated more for their tribulations than for their triumphs. Better by far to be a swimsuit model, enjoying sand, sun, and exotic locales than a female athlete, who appeared on the cover stabbed, threatened, and clubbed.

There were rare exceptions. Olympic gymnast Kerri Strug offered a "profile of courage" in 1996 when she guaranteed the United States its first Olympic team gold in women's gymnastics by performing her second vault even after having sustained a serious injury. Photos of Strug in agony following the vault and being carried to the medal podium by Coach Bela Karolyi—images of pain, vulnerability, and weakness—have endured, but are tempered by a bravery and heroism that are quintessentially Olympian. It was indicative of how the Olympics could showcase individual female greatness, even as it remained a powerful tool for nations to secure international glory and geopolitical advantage.

"Olympic Flames"

To celebrate the 2004 Olympic Games held six months previously, the 2005 Swimsuit Issue featured several "Olympic flames," including softball player Jennie Finch. And if there was any doubt about how the pitcher might have fared in Athens, *SI* offered some clues: Finch appeared in a gold bikini that happened to match the gold medal which she held triumphantly aloft. She shared the photo spread with fellow Olympians Lauren Jackson (silver medal in basketball) and Amanda Beard (a gold medal and two silver medals in swimming). Finch, Beard, and Jackson were not the only female athletes—or the only Olympians—in that issue. Venus Williams, who had won two gold medals in tennis at the 2000 Sydney games for women's singles and doubles, was, according to the Swimsuit Issue, "definitely ascending," even as she appeared in a section separate from her fellow Olympians. *SI* described her as "an interior designer, a pretty fair tennis player and a threat to win it all every time she steps into a swimsuit." It then asked, "Is there nothing Venus Williams can't do?"[19] Shimmering in a silver bikini, the answer seemed a no-brainer. More difficult was explaining why Venus Williams did not also qualify as an "Olympic flame."

Perhaps *SI* was focused on the most recent Olympiad, and thus featured only 2004 medal winners. But former Olympic rower and IOC vice president Anita DeFrantz's 1991 article in *SI* about the unique plight of the Black sportswoman offers an alternative explanation. Echoing Harry Edwards from the 1960s, DeFrantz proclaimed, "Sport doesn't lead society, it reflects it." And in 1991, as in 2004, American society was both racist and sexist. Indeed, DeFrantz asserted that even with all the obstacles faced by Black athletes, which had "scarcely diminished with time," it was "worse if you're female. And those who would deny all women their rights will oppose black women even more." DeFrantz's words reflected an intersectional analysis and represented a seminal moment in *SI* as the challenges faced by Black sportswomen—as expressed by a Black sportswoman—gained the spotlight. Nevertheless, *SI* failed to use De-Frantz's statement as a starting point to examine how issues important to women in sports—Title IX, eating disorders, homophobia, femininity, and even Olympic recognition—might be experienced differently because of race. It was a missed opportunity for *Sports Illustrated,* as was highlighting Venus Williams's Olympic accolades in tennis, especially when *SI,* historically, had focused so much attention on Black women's Olympic success in track and field.

Nevertheless, the medals Williams, Finch, and other women won boosted their country's medal counts, their country's international profiles, and their own depictions in *SI.* Indeed, the magazine devoted hundreds of pages and numerous covers to the Olympics and elevated the stature of sportswomen whose visibility was enhanced by their Olympic feats. Such athletic brilliance reflected the growing attention, as well as the increased investment in women's sports during the Cold War era. This development was evident not just in Communist countries, which created institutions to discover and nurture Olympic talent, but also in the United States, which began to devote more resources to women's sports even before Title IX's passage in 1972. Olympic success allowed women to serve as ambassadors for their countries, as public relations specialists for their governments, and as role models for their fans and fellow citizens.

It was the rare case where sportswomen commandeered the spotlight—at least every four years (and then every two)—in the sports world, and especially in *Sports Illustrated*. Crucially, it underscored the magazine's ability to feature sportswomen when it elected to do so. But how much choice was actually involved? Given the importance of women's Olympic exploits to national prestige, *SI* had few alternatives but to feature the prowess of female Olympians, particularly if it wanted to continue justifying itself as the arbiter of sports media coverage. In the end, *SI*'s Olympic coverage was less a benevolent exception and more reflective of the general rule in *SI*'s reporting of sportswomen. In the case of the Olympics, nationalism trumped sexism in the magazine's decision to prominently depict sportswomen on its covers and in its pages.

Regardless of the motivation, women's prominence on the Olympic stage certainly elevated their public profiles, especially in *Sports Illustrated*. However, their visibility during the games underscored the dearth of coverage female athletes enjoyed in the magazine when the Olympic spotlight had dimmed. This was a concern for all sportswomen, but it was particularly troublesome for those female athletes who sought to make a living from playing their sport.

"Women Don't Get Paid the Same as Guys Do"

The layout of the 2012 Swimsuit issue mimicked those of past years. One lucky model earned the cover turn, and as usual the magazine introduced its comely "rookies" and devoted space to athletes. There was also a section devoted to models with their swimsuits painted on—a feature *SI* had introduced to much acclaim in 1999. But there was one new wrinkle. Instead of supermodels appearing in body paint, it was sportswomen: "For the first time, *SI*'s canvases were athletes—in fact, three of the world's best." Golfer Natalie Gulbis, swimmer Natalie Coughlin, and soccer star Alex Morgan underwent the hours-long process that had *SI* announcing: "Watching paint dry has never been so riveting." The sports analyst Dan Patrick used the occasion to interview Morgan about her initial reaction to "wearing body paint" (there were "mixed emotions") and which teammate she might choose to join her in a future Swimsuit Issue (Heather Mitts and Shannon Box made the shortlist). He then asked: "As a woman, how much do looks play into your success? Do you have to use them to capitalize since there's not that big payday as with male athletes?" Morgan's reply was indicative of the challenges professional sportswomen encountered regardless of their sport: "It's difficult because women don't get paid the same as guys do. So we do need to branch out and look at different avenues to make more for ourselves."[20] That lower salary was reflective of a widespread belief that the best women playing their sports were not regarded as capable enough or interesting enough—or worthy enough—as the best men playing those same sports.

The marginalization of women's professional sports in the media, and especially in *Sports Illustrated,* was particularly damaging. For instance, *SI* depicted women playing professional baseball as more novelty and gimmick than serious business, choosing to disregard the long history of women who had played the sport since the 1920s. Likewise, the WNBA was often portrayed as the NBA's kid sister, competing in NBA arenas and earning a fraction of NBA salaries. *SI* depicted the LPGA as constantly searching for, and failing to find, a personality in the mold of a Babe Didrikson who could attract fans, sponsors, and the media in equal measure. The Women's Tennis Association—the most successful of the women's professional leagues in terms of financial compensation and media coverage—encountered an environment where, despite its advantages, sexism continued to prevail. And the National Women's Soccer League, despite being staffed with marquee talent from World Cup–winning teams, was described in *SI,* when it appeared at all, as a start-up.

Although there were those *SI* writers who emphasized the talent of the women pros, the usual focus was on sex appeal and the leagues that had it and benefited from it—women's tennis, for instance—and the leagues that did not and suffered mightily because of it, like women's golf. In 2004 *SI*'s L. Jon Wertheim's five-point plan to elevate women's professional sports included number three: "Sell sex appeal, not sex." Even as he encouraged the female professionals to ditch "nude pictorials," he noted that "plenty of today's women are comfortable being both strong athletes and alluring celebrities." He cited Serena Williams in particular, challenging anyone to consider her "less of a tour de force because she's as at home on the catwalk, or in a bikini, as she is ripping off a forehand winner."[21] Even as Wertheim exploded stereotypical assumptions about Black sportswomen's lack of femininity, he underscored how being good at one's sport *and* looking good in a swimsuit was imperative for professional sportswomen—even those considered the greatest of all time. Females playing for pay needed to be exceptional athletes, but unlike their male counterparts, they needed more than just physical dominance to sell their league, their sport, and their brand. A spread in the Swimsuit Issue thus became a valuable confirmation of feminine credentials before an audience of millions of fans who consumed the Swimsuit Issue year after year after year, and who might just be compelled to watch the athletes when they had swapped their swimsuits for uniforms.

ON THE fiftieth anniversary of the Swimsuit Issue, editor Christian Stone found that "one in four American adults will see this print issue before the first day of spring," and "it will reach more 18- to 34-year-olds than the Super Bowl." That is considerable influence for an issue that was created simply to provide "readers something to look forward to" but ultimately served "as a wonderful platform for the women who appear in its pages."[22] This was particularly the case for "the legends," who, according to Stone, "are the embodiment of the possibilities that come with appearing in the SPORTS ILLUSTRATED Swimsuit Issue, women who have gone on to become successful captains of industry, media moguls, social advocates and Emmy winners. Like elite athletes who need only a single name to be recognized (Magic, Michael, LeBron), these women are similarly identifiable (Kathy, Christie, Tyra)."[23] Each of the three had been a "pretty girl on the cover" and clearly was empowered as a result.

By 2016, the "pretty girl on the cover" was now a female athlete, after Ronda Rousey became the first sportswoman to appear on one of the three Swimsuit Issue covers released that year.[24] It is unsurprising that sportswomen, when given the chance to appear in the Swimsuit Issue, agreed to participate. According to authors Kayoung Kim and Michael Sagas, a Swimsuit Issue appearance served as a survival strategy for female athletes who gained a tacit acknowledgement and confirmation of their feminine credentials, thereby allowing them to "benefit from media attention, endorsements, fan approval, and reduced heterosexist discrimination." Rousey personified that dynamic. Combining, according to SI, "beauty, brains, brawn and humility," Rousey embodied what scholars Pam R. Sailors and Charlene Weaving have called the "Glamazon" ideal, one also exemplified by Swimsuit Issue icon Heidi Klum. Taller and perhaps more muscular than the average woman, "Glamazons" were "different" from other women, but they "also fit societal ideals and gender norms. They are feminine and heterosexual." Rousey, like Klum, embraced SI's well-known beauty formula: "healthy, curvy, vivacious and bold."[25] It was a formula that informed the magazine's choices for its swimsuit models and also for its female athletes.

And it was one with a long history. In 1973 SI's Bil Gilbert and Nancy Williamson had noted that "the best-looking girls (by male standards) are singled out for attention, no matter how little their sporting talent may be." They further cataloged the ways in which "sport is unfair to women," acknowledging a "campaign . . . directed against her appearance and sexuality." The authors noted that not only were pre-Title IX athletic budgets for girls unequal, they were practically nonexistent—in some cases less than 1 percent of what their male counterparts enjoyed. Similar inequities faced those women interested in playing for pay. And in the Olympic arena? A response to female discus thrower Olga Connolly being selected in 1972 as the flag bearer during the opening ceremonies is telling; a male teammate openly opposed the choice by insisting that "a woman's place is in the home." Gilbert and Williamson had used their series to make the successful case that "the role of girls in sport is determined by society, and until now that role has been an inferior one."[26]

Such a status was not unique to sport and was being challenged by a vibrant (and predominantly white) second-wave feminist movement that was looking to expand that "place" into boardrooms, lecture halls, and, ultimately, playing fields. There was a fair amount of work to be done, and resistance to the inequities women experienced came from multiple fronts. Those airline hostesses whom SI had depicted as cavorting about in their winter playground in 1971 (see chap. 3) had, by 1977, sparked a movement to form their own union to address longtime concerns that were familiar to sportswomen: inequitable compensation, sexist advertising, skimpy uniforms, and a mandated femininity. Stewardesses had gained tactical strategies from Gloria Steinem (an early supporter) and had been inspired by Billie Jean King's performance in the Battle of the Sexes and her advocacy for equal prize money.[27]

Other examples of feminist activism targeted Sports Illustrated and the Swimsuit Issue. In 1989, Ann Simonton, SI's 1974 cover model and founder of Media Watch, requested that Sports Illustrated "discontinue" the issue "and replace it with a magazine devoted solely to women athletes." She believed that "the Swimsuit Issue encourages violence and hatred toward women. It dehumanizes women, turns them into objects." Simonton's campaign, which the magazine detailed in its twenty-fifth anniversary of the Swimsuit Issue, further illustrated the close connection between swimsuit models and sportswomen, since Simonton urged a transformation in "the fundamental attitudes we have toward women, including women in sports." Such change required a shift in society's attitudes, which devoted "too much airtime and too many printed words" to men's sports, particularly football. Simonton asserted that if the media focused as much attention on sports in which women excelled, like long-distance swimming, "then our whole concept of sports might change, because we'd see women outdoing men left and right." She also questioned why a female athlete like Flo Jo felt she had "to dress in a way that proves her sexuality."[28] In 1989, Simonton's critiques fell on deaf ears, given the popularity of the Swimsuit Issue and of *Sports Illustrated*.

As of 2022, however, the halcyon days of *Sports Illustrated*'s market dominance in sports reporting has largely disappeared. *SI*'s print schedule has been reduced to a monthly run, down from an original schedule of fifty-two issues per year; the magazine also relies more heavily on an online presence in which it competes with ESPN.com (and numerous other sites) for viewer interest. As such, this is a perfect time to consider the magazine's historical treatment of women in sport.

Throughout the 1950s, *SI* featured horses, dogs, and water fowl on its cover in equal numbers to sportswomen. That trend had disappeared by the 1960s, but even if sportswomen no longer had to vie for space with elephant seals and lions, they had clearly been displaced by swimsuit models, if not in frequency, than in recognition. As *Sports Illustrated* extolled its bathing beauties and their obvious femininity—and increased its investment in the Swimsuit Issue—sportswomen were held to the same kind of narrow definition of femininity, just without the same kind of financial or editorial support. *SI* marginalized all kinds of women who did not embrace the Swimsuit Issue's winning formula, especially those who expressed not only differences in sexual orientation but, by 2018, differences in sex development as well. By the 1970s, more females than ever before—tens of thousands of them—were playing sports thanks to Title IX, but opposition to the law was immediate and long lasting. Although the magazine celebrated Title IX anniversaries, its reporting often referred to Title IX gains for women as losses for sportsmen, ignoring how true equity eluded all sportswomen, especially female athletes of color. Throughout the 1980s, *SI* reveled in the accomplishments of female Olympians, but often ignored how sexism and racism affected their careers when the Olympic spotlight had dimmed. In the 1990s, *SI* detailed the attempts to launch new professional leagues for women, even as it encouraged aspiring pros to emphasize their sex appeal. By the 2000s, *SI* had devoted important attention to health issues and sexual abuse allegations, but because female athletes appeared so infrequently in the magazine, they were often remembered more as tragic victims than triumphant survivors.

As the magazine celebrated yet another anniversary of Title IX in June 2022, it noted the "new battlegrounds and issues that will define the future of the fight for equality and dominate conversations for years to come." From mainstream acceptance and transgender athletes to televised media coverage, equal pay, and sports merchandise, the female athlete had work to do to continue "leveling the playing field."[29] But absent from that list was compulsory femininity. It was a notable omission, especially given the ways in which *Skimpy Coverage* has detailed how a sportswoman's femininity helped determine her success as a professional athlete, enhanced her Olympic profile, contributed to an ongoing frailty myth, hampered equitable treatment, and protected her against a lesbian stigma. A sportswoman's proof of femininity was not just an advantage in *Sports Illustrated,* it was a requirement, one that changed over time, becoming more inclusive, yet remaining remarkably similar to that embraced by Swimsuit Issue models.

As such, it is helpful to return to Ann Simonton and her critique of the Swimsuit Issue and its lessons for sportswomen in *Sports Illustrated.* Her queries and suggestions, though dismissed by many in 1989 as radical feminist gibberish, offer some interesting what-ifs in 2023: What if *Sports Illustrated* had dedicated at least one issue every year to women's sports—much like they would dedicate an annual issue to swimsuit models? What if *SI* had eliminated the need for female athletes to prove their femininity and had focused on their athleticism instead? What if, in general, the magazine also covered sportswomen consistently, and not just during an Olympic cycle? Possibly, Christian Stone might have compared the women in the Swimsuit Issue not with the male athletes whom we know on a first-name basis but with female athletes like Billie Jean, Serena, and Megan instead. Perhaps even more importantly, we would be more familiar with the names of sportswomen than with those of swimsuit models. Such treatment in *Sports Illustrated* might have indeed contributed to a wholesale change in the "concept of sports," in which sportswomen were regarded first and foremost as athletes worthy of more than just skimpy coverage.

NOTES

INTRODUCTION

1. Frank Deford, "How It All Began," *Sports Illustrated* 70, no. 6 (February 1989): 41; "1964 College Basketball," *Sports Illustrated* 19, no. 24 (9 December 1963): 34. The first Super Bowl was still three years off in 1964.

2. Although women in swimsuits had appeared on the cover of *Sports Illustrated* previously, 1964 marks the first official Swimsuit Issue.

3. Deford, "How It All Began," 39, 41; Laurel Davis, *The Swimsuit Issue and Sport*, 16, 17.

4. Frank Deford, "The Bare Facts," 18, 24, 26, 28.

5. Leigh Montville, "Letters and More Letters," *Sports Illustrated* 70, no. 6 (February 1989): 278; Michael MacCambridge, *The Franchise*, 356.

6. Deford, "How It All Began," 47.

7. MacCambridge, *The Franchise*, 13–16, 31.

8. Ibid., 4, 23–24.

9. Jack W. Berryman, "The Tenuous Attempts of Americans," 49; Pamela Creedon, *Women, Media and Sport*, 109–10, 111, 115; MacCambridge, *The Franchise*, 22, 24, 36.

10. MacCambridge, *The Franchise*, 21, 18–19, 42; Donald J. Barr, "From the Publisher," *Sports Illustrated* 71, no. 21 (15 November 1989): 1.

11. MacCambridge, *The Franchise*, 42.

12. Ibid., 27, 45, 44; H. H. S. Phillips Jr., "Memo," *Sports Illustrated* 1, no. 1 (16 August 1954): 11.

13. MacCambridge, *The Franchise*, 356–57. As late as 2017, MacCambridge found that "there's not a great deal of diversity on the staff—'It's a lot of white dudes,' admitted one writer." See Michael MacCambridge, "Who Can Explain the Athletic Heart?," https://www.theringer.com/2018/4/11/17220176/sports -illustrated-future-meredith-sale-history, retrieved August 30, 2021.

14. MacCambridge, *The Franchise*, 6, 8; Echo Media: Print Media Experts, "Sports Illustrated," 2009, https://echo-media.com/medias/details/4489 /sports+illustrated, retrieved March 4, 2022; Rebecca Bredholt, "Most-Read Magazines in America," https://www.cision.com/2012/07/most-read -magazines-in-america-change-little-from-last-year/, retrieved March 4, 2022; Mandie Brandt and Adelia Carstens, "The Discourse of the Male Gaze," 235. The feminist film scholar Laura Mulvey discussed the male gaze in her well-known 1975 essay "Visual Pleasure and Narrative Cinema."

15. Bil Gilbert and Nancy Williamson, "Sport Is Unfair to Women," *Sports Illustrated* 38, no. 21 (28 May 1973): 95.

16. Mary Jo Kane, "Media Coverage of the Female Athlete"; Angela Lumpkin and Linda D. Williams, "An Analysis of *Sports Illustrated* Feature Articles, 1954–1987"; Gina Daddario, "Swimming Against the Tide"; Janet S. Fink and Linda Jean Kensicki, "An Imperceptible Difference"; Kayoung Kim, Michael Sagas, and Nefertiti A. Walker, "Athletic or Sexy?"

17. As early as 1979, scholars Leonard N. Reid and Lawrence C. Soley found that between 1956 and 1976, *SI* had not increased its coverage of sportswomen, concluding that for *SI*, "sports is still a man's domain." This was in contrast to Donna Mae Miller and Kathryn R. E. Russell's survey of women in *SI* from 1954 to 1967, which, according to Ellen Gerber et al., was "about the best coverage of women available." Almost twenty-five years later, Ronald Bishop found that coverage to be not just minimal but essentially nonexistent, noting, "The almost complete absence of women from the feature pages of *SI*." That was true both for feature articles and cover photos. In 1983 Mary A Boutilier and Lucinda SanGiovanni examined *Sports Illustrated* covers and found that the lack of female athletes in cover photos sent a clear message: "women do not belong in sports." See Reid and Soley, "*Sports Illustrated*'s Coverage of Women in Sports," 863; Ellen W. Gerber, Jan Felshin, Pearl Berlin, and Waneen Wyrick, *The American Woman in Sport*, 252–53; Bishop, "Missing in Action," 192; Boutilier and SanGiovanni, *The Sporting Woman*, 209; and Adam Martin and Mary G. McDonald, "Covering Women's Sport?"

18. Bil Gilbert and Nancy Williamson, "Programmed to Be Losers," *Sports Illustrated* 38, no. 23 (11 June 1973): 65.

19. Statista, "Most Popular Sports Magazines in the United States as of August 2016, by Circulation." Cision, 10 August 2016; Statista, "Number of *Sports Illustrated* Readers in March 2015, by Platform." Cision, March 2015.

20. Aditi Kinkhabwala, "Players," *Sports Illustrated* 106, no. 17 (23 April 2007): 18; Kelli Anderson, "Standing Pat," *Sports Illustrated* 106, no. 16 (16 April 2007): 24; Richard Deitsch, "Women's Top 10," *Sports Illustrated* 107, no. 20 (19 November 2007): 72.

21. Kinkhabwala, "Players," 17, 18; Kelli Anderson, "A Pillar of Strength," *Sports Illustrated* 107, no. 20 (19 November 2007): 70.

22. Kinkhabwala, "Players," 18.

23. Because the term LGBTQ+ was not widely used until recently, I restrict usage of the term to the late twentieth and early twenty-first century to represent a community with diverse sexual identities and gender expressions.

24. Deford, "How It All Began," 39.

1. "The Big F"

1. Kenny Moore, "The Latest in a Long Line," *Sports Illustrated* 61, no. 4 (18 July 1984): 317, 314.

2. Susan Brownmiller, *Femininity*, 18, 15, 317, 320.

3. Michael Messner, "Sports and Male Domination," 200, 203; Jennifer Hargreaves, *Sporting Females*, 145.

4. Brownmiller, *Femininity*, 35, 46.

5. *Sports Illustrated* 1, no. 3 (30 August 1954): cover, 5; *Sports Illustrated* 2, no. 8 (21 February 1955): cover, 7; *Sports Illustrated* 7, no. 9 (26 August 1957): cover, 3; *Sports Illustrated* 9, no. 3 (21 July 1958): cover, 3; *Sports Illustrated* 11, no. 2 (13 July 1959): cover, 3; *Sports Illustrated* 16, no. 15 (16 April 1962): cover; *Sports Illustrated* 20, no. 3 (20 January 1964): cover, 32; "The Story of Swim: In the Words of Those Who Lived It," Sports Illustrated *Swimsuit* (New York: Time Home Entertainment, 2013), 19.

6. *Sports Illustrated* 96 (Winter 2002): cover; *Sports Illustrated* 98 (Winter 2003): cover; *Sports Illustrated* 102 (Winter 2005): cover; *Sports Illustrated* 112 (Winter 2010): cover.

7. Jack McCallum, "Unflagging," *Sports Illustrated* 93, no. 6 (14 August 2000): 52.

8. "The World's Loveliest Sportswomen," *Sports Illustrated* 15, no. 26 (25 December 1961): 62; Dan Jenkins, "Last Week They Held the Masters," *Sports Illustrated* 44, no. 15 (12 April 1976): 32.

9. Kenny Moore, "Making a Hole in the Sky," *Sports Illustrated* 50, no. 13 (26 March 1979): 32, 34–35; Bob Ottum, "Dolls on the Move to Mexico," *Sports Illustrated* 29, no. 10 (2 September 1968): 16, 18, emphasis in the original.

10. Dan Levin, "Here She Is, Miss, Well, What?," *Sports Illustrated* 52, no. 12 (17 March 1980): 66, 72, 75.

11. Jaime Schultz, *Qualifying Times*, 147. For more on the aerobics movement, see Danielle Friedman's *Let's Get Physical*, especially chap. 4.

12. Richard Hoffer, "Ready, Willing and Able," *Sports Illustrated* 83, no. 7 (14 August 1995): 66; Jennifer Hargreaves, *Heroines of Sport*, 187; Hélène Joncheray and Rémi Richard, "Disabled Sportswomen and Gender Construction," 5.

13. Carmen Renee Thompson, "Iron Maidens," *Sports Illustrated for Women* 3, no. 4 (July/August 2001): 81; Ruth Silverman, "Choosing Your Class: Female," https://www.bodybuilding.com/content/class-confusion-how-to -find-your-fit-in-physique-competition.html, retrieved March 6, 2022. Currently, six competitive divisions exist for women with varying levels of musculature: bikini, fitness, figure, wellness, women's physique, and women's bodybuilding. Men have three divisions: bodybuilding, class physique,

and men's physique. Schwarzenegger maintained that a woman's muscles should account for more than her sex appeal; see Levin, "Here She Is, Miss Well, What?" 66.

14. Patricia Vertinsky and Gwendolyn Captain, "More Myth than History," 541; Maya A. Jones, "New Study Examines History of Black Women Fighting to be Respected as Athletes," https://andscape.com/features/morgan -state-university-study-examines-history-of-black-women-fighting-to-be -respected-as-athletes/, retrieved March 6, 2022. For more on how such stereotypes contributed to the oppression of Black sportswomen, see Jenny Lind Withycombe, "Intersecting Selves."

15. Elizabeth Newman, "No Room for Body Image Criticism in Serena Williams' Grand Slam Chase," SI.com, July 14, 2015, https://www.si.com/tennis /2015/07/14/serena-williams-body-image-wta-tennis, retrieved July 30, 2021.

16. Helen Lenskyj, *Out of Bounds*, 133; Rick Reilly, "The Goal-Goal Girls!" *Sports Illustrated* 91, no. 1 (5 July 1999): 100.

17. Reilly, "The Goal-Goal Girls!" 100; Jere Longman, *The Girls of Summer*, 34, 37, 98.

18. Erika Rasmusson, "Strong Signals," *Sports Illustrated for Women* 1, no. 4 (Winter 1999/2000): 31; Rick Reilly, "Bare in Mind," *Sports Illustrated* 93, no. 9 (4 September 2000): 112; Kelli Anderson, "The Other Side of Jenny," *Sports Illustrated Women* 2, no. 5 (November/December 2000): 120, emphasis in the original. At the time, sports sociologist Mary Jo Kane maintained that Chastain's nude pose in *Gear* "set [women] back a million years." See Longman, *Girls of Summer*, 40.

19. Longman, *Girls of Summer*, 40, 39; Robert Sullivan, "Goodbye to Heroin Chic," http://content.time.com/time/subscriber/article/0,33009,991541,00 .html, retrieved July 29, 2021.

20. Michael Silver, "Beauty and the Beach," *Sports Illustrated* 86, no. 7 (21 February 1997): 217, 222, 224, 228.

21. Frank Deford, "Anna Kournikova," *Sports Illustrated* 92, no. 23 (5 June 2000): 95; "New Stars of Money: Anna Kournikova Attacks the Net," https://www.forbes.com/forbes/2000/0320/6507171a.html?sh=18818b48578e, retrieved December 28, 2021.

22. L. Jon Wertheim, "Who's That Girl?," *Sports Illustrated* 97, no. 9 (2 September 2002): 65, 60, 63, 60. Hundreds of readers fell for the hoax, as did various media outlets, which in turn deluged the Women's Tennis Association with requests to interview the new tennis sensation. The WTA was not amused by the ruse and denounced *SI* for the stunt, asserting that it would have been better to devote the five pages the magazine gave to the fictional Popova to a real-life player on the tour. See Marc Berman, "Tennis Hoax

Is 'Stunning,'" https://nypost.com/2002/09/03/tennis-hoax-is-stunning-mags-spoof-over-the-line-officials-cry/, retrieved September 25, 2022.

23. Silver, "Beauty and the Beach," 231.

24. "The Girls from the Mountain Next Door," *Sports Illustrated* 32, no. 11 (16 March 1970): 36.

25. William Oscar Johnson, "Opening Up Those Golden Gates," *Sports Illustrated* 44, no. 8 (23 February 1976): 15.

26. Brownmiller, *Femininity*, 208, 209.

27. Michele Wallace, *Black Macho and the Myth of the Superwoman*, 107.

28. S. L. Price, "It's a Mad, Mad, Mad, Mad Game," *Sports Illustrated* 111, no. 11 (21 September 2009): 61, 62.

29. S. L. Price, "The Seven Year Itch," *Sports Illustrated* 96, no. 23 (3 June 2002): 75; Price, "It's a Mad, Mad, Mad, Mad Game," 61, 62; Price, "The Outrage Open," *Sports Illustrated* 115, no. 11 (19 September 2011): 72.

30. Brownmiller, *Femininity*, 210.

31. S. L. Price, "A Different Kind of Competitor," *Sports Illustrated* 129, no. 7 (24 September–1 October 2018): 55, 55, 57. Such a contrast was evident in early March 2022 when tennis player Alexander Zverev hit the chair umpire's stand. Zverev was eliminated from the tournament and fined $40,000. Serena Williams quipped, "I would probably be in jail if I did that." Riley Morgan, Yahoo!sports, March 10, 2022, https://au.sports.yahoo.com/tennis-2022-serena-williams-backed-alexander-zverev-callout-225717902.html, retrieved March 11, 2022.

32. Brittney Cooper, *Eloquent Rage*, 6–7.

33. Kimberly Seals Allers, "Black Women Have Never Had the Privilege of Rage," https://www.huffpost.com/entry/opinion-angry-black-women_n_5bbf7652e4b040bb4e800249, retrieved July 23, 2021. See also Audre Lorde's 1981 essay, "The Uses of Anger: Women Responding to Racism," in *Sister Outsider*, which is a call to arms for women of color to use anger to their benefit.

34. Brownmiller, *Femininity*, 216, 215.

35. Coles Phinizy, "Fencing," *Sports Illustrated* 3, no. 23 (5 December 1955): 47.

36. Shannon Brownlee, "Moms in the Fast Lane," *Sports Illustrated* 68, no. 2 (30 May 1988): 57, 60. Twenty years later, David Epstein touted the physiological benefits of pregnancy in *SI*, particularly as a performance enhancer akin to blood doping. The findings seemed to engender debate about "abortion doping"—that sportswomen would get pregnant simply to benefit from hormonal changes due to pregnancy to aid their competition, and then end the pregnancy. However, Epstein found no proof of abortion doping to have occurred in 2008. See "Baby Boost," *Sports Illustrated* 109, no. 6 (18 August 2008): 62.

37. Emily Wughalter, "Ruffles and Flounces"; "Chasing Equity," https://www
.womenssportsfoundation.org/wp-content/uploads/2020/01/Chasing
-Equity-Full-Report-Web.pdf, 33, retrieved July 23, 2021.

38. Gussie Moran and Deirdre Budge, "Something for the Girls . . . ," *Sports
Illustrated* 1, no. 7 (27 September 1954): 35; Gwilym S. Brown, "A Little Lace
Goes a Long, Long Way," *Sports Illustrated* 31, no. 1 (7 July 1969): 46, 45. For
a history of women's tennis togs and how they changed over time, see Jaime
Schultz, "What Shall We Wear for Tennis?," in *Qualifying Times*, 15–46. For
more on Ted Tinling, see Frank Deford, "A Head to Heed," *Sports Illustrated* 61, no. 2 (9 July 1984): 72–76+.

39. Brownmiller, *Femininity*, 96; Curry Kirkpatrick, "Wow!," *Sports Illustrated*
63, no. 2 (8 July 1985): 23.

40. "Champions in Fine Plumage," *Sports Illustrated* 9, no. 25 (22 December 1958): 36; Frank Deford, "Love and Love," *Sports Illustrated* 54, no. 18
(27 April 1981): 70; Chris Evert with Sally Jenkins, "I've Lived a Charmed
Life," *Sports Illustrated* 76, no. 20 (25 May 1992): 63. By the early 1990s, haute
couture and women's sport had come full circle as sportswomen once again
wore designer confections, this time for competition. Vera Wang famously
designed skating costumes for Nancy Kerrigan, and, more recently, Stella
McCartney has teamed with Adidas to create a tennis collection worn by
Caroline Wozniacki, Angelique Kerber, and Garbiñe Muguruza.

41. Curry Kirkpatrick, "Say Hello to the Girl Next Door," *Sports Illustrated* 45,
no. 9 (30 August 1976): 78; Joe Jares, "Battle of the Ages," *Sports Illustrated*
41, no. 12 (16 September 1974): 22; Dora Jane Hamblin, ". . . And Cloudy
Days for Chris," *Sports Illustrated* 39, no. 1 (2 July 1973): 26; L. Jon Wertheim, "My Three Sons," *Sports Illustrated* 105, no. 1 (3–10 July 2006): 112;
Deford, "Love and Love," 72.

42. Laurel Wamsley, "'One Must Respect the Game,'" https://www.npr.org/2018
/08/24/641549735/one-must-respect-the-game-french-open-bans-serena
-williams-catsuit, retrieved July 23, 2021. For more on the racial meanings
associated with Serena Williams's 2002 catsuit, see Jaime Schultz, "Reading
the Catsuit."

43. Schultz, *Qualifying Times*, 16; Israel Shenker, "Curls and Cold Steel," *Sports
Illustrated* 20, no. 4 (27 January 1964): 40; "Battle of the Surfside Sixes,"
Sports Illustrated 29, no. 11 (9 September 1968): 27.

44. Richard Hoffer, "Dig This!" *Sports Illustrated* 97, no. 7 (19 August 2002):
48; Luke Winn, "Bangers and Mash," *Sports Illustrated* 117, no. 5 (6 August
2012): 14.

45. Alexis Morgan, "There's More to Beach Volleyball than Just the Bikini,"
SI.com, September 19, 2014, https://www.si.com/extra-mustard/2014/09/19/
theres-more-beach-volleyball-just-bikini; retrieved January 12, 2023;

International Handball Federation, "IX. Rules of the Game: Beach Handball," 91, https://www.ihf.info/sites/default/files/2019-05/0_09%20-%20 Rules%20of%20the%20Game%20%28Beach%20Handball%29_GB.pdf, retrieved July 27, 2021; George Ramsay, "International Handball Federation Changes 'Sexist' Uniform Regulations Following Criticism," CNN, November 1, 2021, https://www.cnn.com/2021/11/01/sport/handball-uniform -regulations-spt-intl/index.html; retrieved January 12, 2023.

46. Gwilym S. Brown, "Good Looks and Good Golf on the Ladies' Tour," *Sports Illustrated* 18, no. 22 (3 June 1963): 37; "All-American Girls Professional Baseball League Rules of Conduct," https://www.aagpbl.org/history/rules-of -conduct, retrieved July 25, 2021; Ryan Hatch, "A Style of Their Own," *Sports Illustrated* 120, special issue (20 March 2014): 28–29, emphasis in the original. For context, talking back to an umpire resulted in a ten-dollar fine.

47. Curry Kirkpatrick, "Relax, Girls, It's a Mann's World," *Sports Illustrated* 28, no. 18 (6 May 1968): 22, 23.

48. Jaime Diaz, "Belles of the Ball," *Sports Illustrated* 65, no. 22 (19 November 1986): 110, 109, 108; Alexander Wolff, "Oh La La, Steffi!" *Sports Illustrated* 72, no. 17 (23 April 1990): 45. The Golden Slam included winning all four major tennis tournaments—Australian Open, French Open, Wimbledon, and U.S. Open in a calendar year—in addition to winning the gold medal at the Olympic Games.

49. Anne Fulenwider, "Downhill Diva," *Sports Illustrated Women* 4, no. 8 (December 2002/January 2003), 29; Kristina Grish, "Behind the Seams," *Sports Illustrated for Women* 2, no. 4 (September/October 2000): 45.

50. Tim Layden, "Bare Naked Lady," *Sports Illustrated for Women* no. 3 (Fall 1999): 110–11.

51. Gilbert Rogin, "Flamin' Mamie's Bouffant Belles," *Sports Illustrated* 20, no. 16 (20 April 1964): 30, 31.

52. Ibid., 30, 31, 35.

53. Gwilym S. Brown, "Teen-Ager on a Comeback Trail," *Sports Illustrated* 26, no. 8 (20 February 1967): 23.

54. Brownmiller, *Femininity*, 65–66; Charlotte Perkins Gilman, *Herland*, 30; Karen Stevenson, "Hair Today, Shorn Tomorrow?," 219, 220, 229, 230.

55. Brownmiller, *Femininity*, 66; Dorothy Hamill, "Why I love my hair short," Clairol beauty advertisement, 1977, https://www.google.com/search?q= hamill+%22why+I+love+my+hair+short%22&client=firefox-b-1-d&sxsrf =ALeKk03wRKhDwsbxAgX_xFSRMXDJtc4abw:1627231401566&tbm= isch&source=iu&ictx=1&fir=GGKEM8KDkSDO8M%252C29CkjJH3U _q8UM%252C_&vet=1&usg=AI4_-kRSoTeuiRaBEwlAnQAL4hecoWiepw &sa=X&ved=2ahUKEwjF-KCt1f7xAhX5MlkFHXXeBpoQ9QF6BAgKEAE #imgrc=GGKEM8KDkSDO8M, retrieved July 25, 2021.

56. Lisa Altobelli, "The Beat," *Sports Illustrated* 101, no. 24 (20 December 2004): 26; Alexander Wolff, "The Ponytail Express," *Sports Illustrated* 123, no. 23 (14 December 2015): 60–61; Schultz, *Qualifying Times*, 1–8; Mechelle Voepel, "WNBA Announces 'Refresh' of Brand, New Logo," https://www .espn.com/wnba/story/_/id/26469391/wnba-announces-refresh-brand -new-logo, retrieved July 25, 2021. Many of the NCAA sports also use a pony-tailed figure in their logos to denote a woman's team.

57. S. L. Price, "Dateline: Wimbledon, England, June 28, 1997," *Sports Illustrated* 87, no. 1 (7 July 1997): 26.

58. Brownmiller, *Femininity*, 72.

59. "French Cut," *Sports Illustrated* 86, no. 23 (9 June 1997): 3; S. L. Price, "Over the Top," *Sports Illustrated* 86, no. 14 (7 April 1997): 65–66.

60. Michael Silver, "Serena's at Peace with Herself," *Sports Illustrated* 90, no. 12 (22 March 1999): 46; L. Jon Wertheim, "We Told You So," *Sports Illustrated* 90, no. 14 (5 April 1999): 68; L. Jon Wertheim, "The Two and Only," *Sports Illustrated* 96, no. 25 (17 June 2002): 62; Lonnae O'Neal, "The Struggle Is Real," https://andscape.com/features/the-struggle-is-real -the-unrelenting-weight-of-being-a-black-female-athlete/, retrieved April 2, 2022.

61. Brownmiller, *Femininity*, 76.

62. William Talbert, "The New Gibson Girl," *Sports Illustrated* 5, no. 1 (2 July 1956): 19–20.

63. Sarah Palfrey, "Althea," *Sports Illustrated* 7, no. 10 (2 September 1957): 30, 28; "Bioperse: Althea Gibson," *Sports Illustrated* 5, no. 1 (July 2, 1956): 60; "Althea Accommodates History," *Sports Illustrated* 7, no. 12 (16 September 1957): 45; Michael Bamberger, "Inside the White Lines," *Sports Illustrated* 91, no. 21 (29 November 1999): 115.

64. Jennifer H. Lansbury, *A Spectacular Leap*, 132–33; Wilma Rudolph, *Wilma*, 43–44; "Moments to Remember: 1960," *Sports Illustrated* 13, no. 26 (26 December 1960): 38; James Murray, "A Big Night for Wilma," *Sports Illustrated* 14, no. 4 (30 January 1961): 48; Rita Liberti and Maureen M. Smith, *(Re)Presenting Wilma Rudolph*, 52–53.

65. Liberti and Smith, *(Re)Presenting Wilma Rudolph*, 70.

66. Pat Jordan, "From the Land of Cotton," *Sports Illustrated* 43, no. 23 (8 December 1975): 98, 92; Kimberlé Crenshaw, "Mapping the Margins." The civil rights and women's rights activist Pauli Murray described the twin issues of racism and sexism as Jane Crow. See her groundbreaking 1965 article, "Jane Crow and the Law."

67. Kenny Moore, "Give the Girl a Great Big Hand," *Sports Illustrated* 51, no. 10 (3 September 1979): 23; Moore, "The Spoils of Victory," *Sports Illustrated* 70, no. 16 (10 April 1989): 50, 52; Moore, "On Top of the Worlds," *Sports Illustrated*

67, no. 12 (14 September 1987): 21; Moore, "Getup and Go," *Sports Illustrated* 69, no. 4 (25 July 1988): 14. In 2021 Serena Williams wore a one-legged tennis outfit during the Australian Open in a nod toward the track great.

68. Moore, "The Spoils of Victory," 52.

69. Tim Layden, "Leading Off: Florence Griffith Joyner (1959–1998)," *Sports Illustrated* 89, no. 13 (28 September 1998): 6; Amira Rose Davis, "Olympic Icon Flo Jo Raced to the Top and Took Us with Her," https://zora.medium.com/remembering-flo-jo-the-olympic-icon-who-raced-to-the-top-and-took-us-with-her-969c4f27e764, retrieved March 4, 2022.

70. S. L. Price, "Serena Williams Is *Sports Illustrated's* Sportsperson of the Year," *Sports Illustrated* 123, no. 24 (21 December 2015): 68; Christian Stone, "More than a Champion," *Sports Illustrated* 123, no. 24 (21 December 2015): 8; Juliet Spies-Gans, "What Serena's *SI* Cover Reveals."

71. Jimmy Jemail, "Hotbox: Do Competitive Sports Tend to Make Women Less Feminine?," *Sports Illustrated* 1, no. 9 (11 October 1954): 4.

72. Ibid.

73. Ibid., 4, 5. Charlotte Perkins Gilman had addressed "old-fashioned notions of women as clinging vines" as early as 1915 in *Herland,* 21.

74. Jemail, "Hotbox," 4; Brownmiller, *Femininity,* 237.

75. Rick Reilly, "This Girl Gets Her Kicks," *Sports Illustrated* 89, no. 16 (19 October 1998): 100, emphasis in the original.

76. Gary Smith, "The Secret Life of Mia Hamm," *Sports Illustrated* 99, no. 11 (22 September 2003): 68; Reilly, "The Goal-Goal Girls!" 100; Rasmusson, "Strong Signals," 33.

77. Jill Filipovic, "Elite Male Athletes Play in Shorts," https://www.cnn.com/2021/07/27/opinions/sexualized-uniforms-women-olympics-filipovic/index.html, retrieved July 30, 2021; Vanessa Friedman, "Who Decides What a Champion Should Wear?," https://www.nytimes.com/2021/07/29/fashion/olympics-dress-codes-sports.html?action=click&module=Top%20Stories&pgtype=Homepage, retrieved July 30, 2021.

78. Shane Peacock, "Beauty and the Biathlon," *Sports Illustrated* 92, no. 7 (21 February 2000): 26.

79. Deford, "Anna Kournikova," 104; Dimity McDowell, "Wonder Women," *Sports Illustrated for Women,* no. 4 (Winter1999/2000): 96.

80. Spies-Gans, "What Serena's *SI* Cover Reveals"; Davis, "Olympic Icon Flo Jo."

81. Brownmiller, *Femininity,* 235, 17.

2. "Girls Like That"

1. Frank Deford, "Mrs. Billie Jean King!" *Sports Illustrated* 42, no. 20 (19 May 1975): 80.

2. Jerry Kirshenbaum, "Facing Up to Billie Jean's Revelations," *Sports Illustrated* 54, no. 20 (11 May 1981): 13.

3. Jaime Diaz, "Find the Golf Here?," *Sports Illustrated* 70, no. 7 (13 February 1989): 63.

4. Bil Gilbert and Nancy Williamson, "Are You Being Two-Faced?," *Sports Illustrated* 38, no. 22 (4 June 1973): 46.

5. Bil Gilbert and Nancy Williamson, "Programmed to Be Losers," *Sports Illustrated* 38, no. 23 (11 June 1973): 98.

6. Susan Cahn, *Coming On Strong*; Cahn, "Crushes, Competition, and Closets," 330–31; Susan Birrell and Nancy Theberge, "Ideological Control of Women in Sport," 353.

7. Cahn, *Coming On Strong*, 165; William Oscar Johnson and Nancy Williamson, "Babe: Part 2," *Sports Illustrated* 43, no. 15 (13 October 1975): 51.

8. Paul Gallico, "Farewell to The Babe," *Sports Illustrated* 5, no. 15 (8 October 1956): 66, 67.

9. Joan Flynn Dreyspool, "Conversation Piece: Subject: Babe and George Zaharias," *Sports Illustrated* 4, no. 20 (14 May 1956): 31, 83; Cahn, *Coming On Strong*, 200, 178.

10. Cahn, *Coming On Strong*, 180–81.

11. Ashley Brown, "'Uncomplimentary Things,'" 251.

12. Pat Jordan, "From the Land of Cotton," *Sports Illustrated* 43, no. 23 (8 December 1975): 98.

13. Dorothy Stull, "Be Happy, Go Healthy with Bonnie," *Sports Illustrated* 5, no. 3 (16 July 1956): 38; "Some Play for Fun," *Sports Illustrated* 16, no. 14 (9 April 1962): 26.

14. Dan Jenkins, "Out There with Slow-Play Flo," *Sports Illustrated* 35, no. 6 (9 August 1971): 52; Pat Putnam, "She Never Played with Dolls," *Sports Illustrated* 36, no. 12 (20 March 1972): 33.

15. Harold Peterson, "Don't Go Near the Water? Phooey!" *Sports Illustrated* 40, no. 19 (13 May 1974): 57; Mary Jo Festle, *Playing Nice*, 230–31. In addition to Festle, Susan Cahn and Helen Lenskyj also note that the use of terms such as "mannish" and "masculine" to describe female athletes are often coded references to lesbianism. See Cahn, *Coming On Strong*, 162; and Lenskyj, *Out of Bounds*, 95.

16. Frank Deford, "Nancy with the Laughing Face," *Sports Illustrated* 49, no. 2 (10 July 1978): 31. For more on the continued association of the LPGA with lesbianism, see Mariah Burton Nelson, *Are We Winning Yet?*, 132–41.

17. For more on the history of gay and lesbian communities and early activism, see George Chauncey, *Gay New York*; Lillian Faderman, *Odd Girls and Twilight Lovers*; and Eric Marcus, *Making Gay History*. For more on the Gay Games and its significance, see Caroline Symons, *The Gay Games*.

18. Mary A. Boutilier and Lucinda SanGiovanni, *The Sporting Woman*, 119; Roberta S. Bennett, K. Gail Whitaker, Nina Jo Woolley Smith, and Anne Sablove, "Changing the Rules of the Game," 373.

19. Helen Lenskyj, "Female Sexuality and Women's Sport," 386.

20. Sarah Pileggi, "Martina's Garden Party," *Sports Illustrated* 54, no. 15 (6 April 1981): 63; Pileggi, "Merrily She Rolls Along," *Sports Illustrated* 56, no. 21 (24 May 1982): 110.

21. Although Billie Jean King would admit to a "homosexual liaison" in 1981, she would not identify openly as a lesbian until the mid-1990s. See Billie Jean King, *All In*, 371–75. Several months following King's outing, Navratilova was outed as well. Initially identifying as a bisexual, Navratilova would ultimately identify as a lesbian. *Sports Illustrated* ignored the trauma associated with Navratilova's outing, and likewise failed to discuss the difference between bisexuality and homosexuality, essentially treating Navratilova as a lesbian because of her relationships with other women. In her 1985 autobiography, *Martina*, Navratilova admitted to being "suspicious of all the sexual labels" and regarded herself as "not a one-sex person." See *Martina*, 193, 194.

22. Frank Deford, "Talk about Strokes of Genius," *Sports Illustrated* 61, no. 3 (16 July 1984): 16.

23. Frank Deford, "Love and Love," *Sports Illustrated* 54, no. 18 (27 April 1981): 70; Martina Navratilova with George Vecsey, *Martina*, 214–15; Chris Evert with Sally Jenkins, "I've Lived a Charmed Life," *Sports Illustrated* 76, no. 20 (25 May 1992): 63.

24. Susan Cahn, "'So Far Back in the Closet,'" 220.

25. Bil Gilbert and Nancy Williamson, "Are You Being Two-Faced?," *Sports Illustrated* 38, no. 22 (4 June 1973): 47; Frank Deford, "Now Georgy-Porgy Runs Away," *Sports Illustrated* 40, no. 16 (22 April 1974): 30.

26. Pam Shriver with Frank Deford, "To Wimbledon and Beyond," *Sports Illustrated* 63, no. 12 (9 September 1985): 40.

27. Jill Lieber and Jerry Kirshenbaum, "Stormy Weather at South Carolina," *Sports Illustrated* 56, no. 5 (8 February 1982): 33, emphasis in the original.

28. Grant Wahl, L. Jon Wertheim, and George Dohrmann, "Passion Plays," *Sports Illustrated* 95, no. 10 (10 September 2001): 61, 63. Mariah Burton Nelson devoted an entire chapter to this issue in her book *The Stronger Women Get, the More Men Love Football*, 159–94.

29. Pat Griffin, *Strong Women, Deep Closets*, 201. Studies show that anywhere between 76 to 96 percent of those who perpetrated sexual violence against athletes were male. See Ingunn Bjørnseth and Attila Szabo, "Sexual Violence Against Children."

30. Pat Griffin, "Homophobia in Women's Sports," 193.

31. Griffin, *Strong Women, Deep Closets*, 208–12.

32. Gary Smith, "The Nude Olympics," *Sports Illustrated* 91, no. 23 (13 December 1999): 30.

33. Dot Richardson, "Sex, Lies and Softball," *Sports Illustrated Women/Sport* (Spring 1997): 44; Dot Richardson, *Living the Dream*, 46; Griffin, *Strong Women, Deep Closets*, 54.

34. Michael Bamberger, "Living with a Lie: When CBS Decided to Defend Announcer Ben Wright, It Attacked the Truth," *Sports Illustrated* 83, no. 24 (4 December 1995): G36; Richard Sandomir, "Golf: CBS Pulls Wright Off the Air"; Larry Gross, *Up from Invisibility*, 205.

35. "She Said, He Said," *Sports Illustrated* 82, no. 20 (22 May 1995): 16; "Two Wrongs Do in a Wright," *Sports Illustrated* 84, no. 3 (22 January 1996): 21.

36. Tim Layden, "No More Disguises," *Sports Illustrated* 84, no. 11 (18 March 1996): 71, 72, 77.

37. Tim Layden, "Coming Out Party," *Sports Illustrated* 90, no. 5 (8 February 1999): 59, 60.

38. Ibid., 60.

39. Tim Layden, "Out in the Open," *Sports Illustrated for Women*, no.1 (Spring 1999): 22; Layden, "Coming Out Party," 60.

40. Michael Silver, "Ladies and Gentlemen, Your Philadelphia Liberty Belles!" *Sports Illustrated Women* 3, no. 8 (December/January 2002): 80, 81, 82; Jessica Dulong, "Out in the Field," https://www.thefreelibrary.com/Out+in+the+field%3A+pro+footballer+Alissa+Wykes+talks+about+breaking...-a083375448, retrieved September 15, 2021, emphasis in the original.

41. L. Jon Wertheim, "Fast Times in the WNBA," *Sports Illustrated* 97, no. 5 (5 August 2002): 63, 61, 62; Sarah Banet-Weiser, "Hoop Dreams," 404. As early as 2001, the Los Angeles Sparks had acknowledged Pride Month, and as of 2019 the WNBA was celebrated for being "the biggest trailblazer for LGBTQ inclusion in all of American sports." See Ken Schultz, "WNBA Continues to Lead the Way," https://www.outsports.com/2019/7/22/20701939/wnba-lgbtq-inclusion-pride-night-los-angeles-sparks-womens-basketball, retrieved March 7, 2022.

42. Jennifer Hargreaves, *Heroines of Sport*, 145–46.

43. "Outed," *Sports Illustrated* 103, no. 18 (7 November 2005): 23; LZ Granderson, "Three-time MVP," https://www.espn.com/wnba/news/story?id=2203853, retrieved September 8, 2021.

44. Richard Deitsch, "Q&A: Sheryl Swoopes," *Sports Illustrated* 104, no. (26 June 2006): 39. Griner came out in an exclusive interview with ESPN, which *SI* addressed only on its online platform. See Brian Kotloff, "Brittney Griner Says Baylor Told Her to Keep Her Homosexuality Private," SI.com,

May 18, 2013, https://www.si.com/si-wire/2013/05/18/brittney-griner-gay
-baylor; retrieved July 27, 2019. In 2011 Swoopes announced her engagement to a man. At the time, founder of Outsports.com, Cyd Zeigler, surmised that Swoopes might be bisexual (she did not comment) but found
labels to be irrelevant, seeing Swoopes as a "great role model for everyone
struggling with their sexuality." See Zeigler, "Sheryl Swoopes Is Not a Lesbian," https://www.outsports.com/2011/7/14/4051542/sheryl-swoopes-is
-not-a-lesbian-now-engaged-to-marry-a-man, retrieved February 6, 2022.

45. Griffin, *Strong Women, Deep Closets*, 164.
46. Jack Dickey, "Express Yourself. Or Not," *Sports Illustrated* 119, no. 6 (12 August 2013): 20; Alexander Wolff, "Host-ilities," *Sports Illustrated* 120, no. 4
(3 February 2014): 13.
47. Brian Burke, "To Russia, with Love," *Sports Illustrated* 119, no. 9 (2 September 2013): 166.
48. Ray Kennedy, "She'd Rather Switch—and Fight," *Sports Illustrated* 45,
no. 10 (6 September 1976): 17. Assigned male at birth, Richards captained
the men's tennis team at Yale and played competitive tennis in the male,
over-35 division, earning a career-high sixth-place ranking.
49. Ibid., 17, 18.
50. Ibid.
51. Kennedy, "She'd Rather Switch," 17.
52. Austin Murphy, "Gender Flap," *Sports Illustrated* 97, no. 12 (23 September
2002): A24.
53. Pablo Torre and David Epstein, "The Transgender Athlete," *Sports Illustrated* 116, no. 22 (28 May 2012): 66, 68, 70.
54. Ibid., 69.
55. Sheila L. Cavanagh and Heather Sykes, "Transsexual Bodies at the
Olympics," 77–78, 88.
56. Pat Griffin and Helen Carroll, "NCAA Inclusion of Transgender Student-
Athletes," 2011, https://ncaaorg.s3.amazonaws.com/inclusion/lgbtq/INC
_TransgenderHandbook.pdf, retrieved September 22, 2021; Griffin and
Carroll, "On the Team: Equal Opportunity for Transgender Student Athletes," 2010, http://www.nclrights.org/wp-content/uploads/2013/07/Trans
genderStudentAthleteReport.pdf, retrieved September 22, 2021.
57. Torre and Epstein, "The Transgender Athlete," 72. Size alone cannot predict athletic superiority. See Paul Lazdowski, "7-footers"; and Eli Horowitz,
"Welcome to the WNBA."
58. David Epstein, "Come Out Fighting," *Sports Illustrated* 118 (18 March
2013): 18; "Ronda Rousey to Fight Transgender Fallon Fox?," http://www
.latinospost.com/articles/61653/20150518/ronda-rousey-fight-transgender
-fallon-fox-news-details-here.htm, retrieved June 28, 2021.

59. "The Mail," *Sports Illustrated* 116 (June 18, 2012): 15.

60. Martina Navratilova, "The Rules on Trans Athletes Reward Cheats," https://www.thetimes.co.uk/article/the-rules-on-trans-athletes-reward-cheats-and-punish-the-innocent-klsrq6h3x, retrieved September 22, 2021; Dawn Ennis, "Martina Navratilova on Trans Athletes," https://www.outsports.com/2019/2/17/18227992/martina-navratilova-trans-athletes-are-men-competing-as-women-is-unfair, retrieved June 28, 2021. On December 4, 2019, Rachel McKinnon announced she had officially changed her name to Veronica Ivy.

61. David Crary, "Trans Athletes Make Great Gains," https://www.apnews.com/e927df7bf03344258791300d474fe778, retrieved June 28, 2021. Studies have shown that children as young as four or five are aware of their identity not matching what they were assigned at birth. See Ed Yong, "Young Trans Children Know Who They Are."

62. Robert Sanchez, "'I Am Lia: The Trans Swimmer Dividing America Tells Her Story," SI.com, March 3, 2022, https://www.si.com/college/2022/03/03/lia-thomas-penn-swimmer-transgender-woman-daily-cover, retrieved March 3, 2022; Sanchez, "To Swim as Herself," *Sports Illustrated* 133, no. 3 (April 2022): 61.

63. Ariel Levy, "Either/Or: Sports, Sex, and the Case of Caster Semenya," https://www.newyorker.com/magazine/2009/11/30/eitheror, retrieved September 22, 2021.

64. David Epstein, "Well, Is She Or Isn't She?," *Sports Illustrated* 111, no. 9 (7 September 2009): 24–25. In particular, Epstein discussed the case of Maria José Martínez-Patiño, whose buccal smear revealed XY chromosomes. The first woman to challenge the IAAF's testing, Martínez-Patiño's efforts led to an exception for those women whose bodies did not read any testosterone, a condition called Androgen Insensitivity Syndrome. For more on the history of sex testing in sport, see Lindsay Parks Pieper, *Sex Testing*.

65. Epstein, "Well, Is She?," 25.

66. In 2017 the IOC awarded Semenya the gold medal following evidence that first-place finisher Russian Mariya Savinova-Farnosova had been doping.

67. Tim Layden, "Engendering Debate," *Sports Illustrated* 125, no. 4 (15 August 2016): 33–34.

68. Ibid., 34, 37.

69. Tim Layden, "Cast Aside," *Sports Illustrated* 128, no. 10 (7 May 2018): 23. Layden is not alone in believing that such a ruling is targeted. See particularly Katrina Karkazis and Rebecca Jordan-Young, "The Treatment of Caster Semenya."

70. Chris Chavez, "Caster Semenya Loses Landmark Case against IAAF, Must Lower Testosterone to Compete vs. Women," SI.com, May 1, 2019,

https://www.si.com/olympics/2019/05/01/caster-semenya-appeal-iaaf -rule-testosterone-levels-female-athletes-court-of-arbitration-for-sport, retrieved June 28, 2021; Chavez, "Caster Semenya to Race Doha Diamond League 800m after Losing Case to IAAF," SI.com, May 2, 2019, https://www .si.com/olympics/2019/05/02/caster-semenya-doha-diamond-league-cas -ruling, retrieved June 28, 2021; Chavez, "Caster Semenya Will Not Retire or Take Medication after IAAF Rule Change," SI.com, May 3, 2019, https:// www.si.com/olympics/2019/05/03/caster-semenya-retirement-rumor -iaaf-world-championships-medication-hell-no, retrieved June 28, 2021; Chavez, "Caster Semenya Files Appeal: 'IAAF Will Not Drug Me or Stop Me From Being Who I Am,'" SI.com, May 29, 2019, https://www.si.com /olympics/2019/05/29/caster-semenya-appeals-iaaf-testosterone-rules -statement-track-and-field, retrieved June 28, 2021.

71. Chris Chavez, "Swiss Court Suspends IAAF Rules Barring Caster Seme- nya from Competing vs. Women," SI.com, June 3, 2019, https://www.si .com/olympics/2019/06/03/caster-semenya-iaaf-testosterone regulations -appeal-switzerland-supreme-court, retrieved June 28, 2021.

72. *Sports Illustrated* 118, no. 19 (6 May 2013): cover; S. L. Price, "So Here We Are, at Last," *Sports Illustrated* 118, no. 19 (6 May 2013): 45, 43.

73. Gary Smith, "Forty for the Ages," *Sports Illustrated* 81, no. 12 (19 Septem- ber 1994): 46; Alexander Wolff, "Martina Navratilova," *Sports Illustrated* 81, no. 12 (19 September 1994): 80.

74. Kirshenbaum, "Facing Up to Billie Jean's Revelations," 13.

75. *Time Magazine,* June 9, 2014, cover.

76. Grant Wahl, "Unquiet American," *Sports Illustrated* 117, no. 5 (6 August 2012): 58, 59, 60; Jenny Vrentas, "2019 Sportsperson of the Year: Megan Rapinoe," *Sports Illustrated* 130, nos. 35/36 (16–23 December 2019): 45, 52; Brownmiller, *Femininity,* 235; Grant Wahl, "Unflappable. Unapologetic. Unequaled." *Sports Illustrated* 130, no. 19 (15 July 2019): 28.

77. Pat Griffin, *Pat Griffin's LGBT Sport Blog,* July 3, 2012, http://ittakesateam .blogspot.com/2012/07/us-soccer-star-megan-rapinoe-to-world.html, re- trieved June 29, 2021.

78. As of January 2022, those barriers include new laws adopted by the IOC and the NCAA that effectively grant individual sporting bodies complete control over policies for their own sport. While both the IOC and the NCAA have touted the change as one that will bring about greater inclusion, LGBTQ+ watchdog agencies like Athlete Ally see it as a harbinger of retrenchment, especially with the NCAA's decision to remove nondiscrimination language from its constitution. See Wyatt Ronan, "Human Rights Campaign."

3. "An Odd Way to Even Things Up"

1. Curry Kirkpatrick, "There She Is, Ms. America," *Sports Illustrated* 39, no. 14 (1 October 1973): 31, 32.
2. Curry Kirkpatrick, "Mother's Day Ms. Match," *Sports Illustrated* 38, no. 20 (21 May 1973): 36.
3. Andrew Crichton, "Fair's Fair," *Sports Illustrated* 40, no. 20 (20 May 1974): 17.
4. Andrew Crichton, "Counting Down," *Sports Illustrated* 41, no. 1 (1 July 1974): 11. Walter Byers was an avowed opponent of Title IX, and the NCAA actually waged a lawsuit against the law before it was dismissed by a judge who deemed that the organization had no standing.
5. Crichton, "Fair's Fair"; Bil Gilbert and Nancy Williamson, "Women in Sport: A Progress Report," *Sports Illustrated* 41, no. 5 (29 July 1974): 31.
6. Kent Hannon, "Too Far, Too Fast," *Sports Illustrated* 48, no. 13 (20 March 1978): 34–36+.
7. "Women: One," *Sports Illustrated* 43, no. 25 (22–29 December 1975): 18.
8. John Underwood, "Look Who's Up and About," *Sports Illustrated* 43, no. 10 (8 September 1975): 24, 25, 28. The Association for Intercollegiate Athletics for Women (AIAW) did provide some support, but the organization had little funding and was of short duration (1971–1982). See particularly Mary Jo Festle, *Playing Nice,* chap. 7.
9. John Underwood, "An Odd Way to Even Things Up," *Sports Illustrated* 50, no. 6 (5 February 1979): 18.
10. Bil Gilbert and Nancy Williamson, "Sport Is Unfair to Women," *Sports Illustrated* 38, no. 21 (28 May 1973): 88–89.
11. Bil Gilbert and Nancy Williamson, "Are You Being Two-Faced?," *Sports Illustrated* 38, no. 22 (4 June 1973): 47, 48.
12. Ibid., 68; "Play Now . . . Fly Later," *Sports Illustrated* 34, no. 3 (18 January 1971): 16.
13. Gilbert and Williamson, "Women in Sport: A Progress Report," 28–30, 31.
14. Michael Bamberger, "Naked Power," *Sports Illustrated* 116, no. 19 (7 May 2012): 53–54; Mary Mazzio, *A Hero for Daisy.* For the article that ran in the *New York Times,* see "Yale Women Strip to Protest," https://timesmachine.nytimes.com/timesmachine/1976/03/04/75577448.html?pageNumber=47, retrieved July 21, 2021.
15. Jerry Kirshenbaum, "Spartan No Longer," *Sports Illustrated* 50, no. 8 (19 February 1979): 7; Jamie Lisanti, "Carol Hutchins," *Sports Illustrated* 133, no. 5 (June 2022): 37.
16. Gilbert and Williamson, "Women and Sport: A Progress Report," 28, 31.
17. Ibid., 31; Robert Sullivan, "A Law That Needs New Muscle," *Sports Illustrated* 62, no. 9 (4 March 1985): 9.

18. For more on the growing opposition to the achievements of second wave feminism, see Susan Faludi, *Backlash*.
19. Craig Neff, "Equality at Last, Part II," *Sports Illustrated* 68, no. 12 (21 March 1988): 70; Sullivan, "A Law That Needs New Muscle," 9.
20. Neff, "Equality at Last, Part II," 70, 71.
21. Phil Taylor, "William and . . . ," *Sports Illustrated* 74, no. 7 (25 February 1991): 57; Alison Muscatine, "William and Mary Restores 4 Sports," https://www.washingtonpost.com/archive/sports/1991/02/23/william-and-mary-restores-4-sports/dabc060c-a6dd-49da-9cf1-28ed21256138/, retrieved March 12, 2022. *Sports Illustrated* reported multiple examples in which colleges and universities cut women's sports and found themselves as defendants in Title IX lawsuits. See, for example, Robert Sullivan, "Toughening Title IX," *Sports Illustrated* 76, no. 11 (23 March 1992): 10; Kelly Whiteside, "A State of Enlightenment," *Sports Illustrated* 77, no. 13 (28 September 1992) 56; Kelli Anderson, "The Unkindest Cut," *Sports Illustrated* 77, no. 13 (28 September 1992): 58.
22. Sullivan, "Toughening Title IX," 10. Sullivan was referring to the Supreme Court's 1992 ruling in *Franklin v. Gwinnett County Public Schools*. The decision allowed the victim to sue for damages.
23. Alexander Wolff, "The Slow Track," *Sports Illustrated* 77, no. 13 (28 September 1992): 53, 54–55.
24. Craig Neff, "Not O.K., Oklahoma," *Sports Illustrated* 72, no. 15 (9 April 1990): 19; Wolff, "The Slow Track," 58.
25. Maureen H. Maroney, "The Numbers Don't Add Up," *Sports Illustrated* 86, no. 18 (5 May 1997): 78.
26. "Letters," *Sports Illustrated* 86, no. 23 (9 June 1997): 15.
27. Maroney, "The Numbers," 78.
28. "Sports and Title IX, No Providence for Three Teams," *Sports Illustrated* 89, no. 16 (19 October 1998): 28.
29. Ivan Maisel, "Use a Scalpel, Not an Ax," *Sports Illustrated* 92, no. 16 (17 April 2000): 23; Susan Casey, "The Games Women Play," *Sports Illustrated* 96, no. 26 (24 June 2002): 21.
30. Rick Reilly, "Under Covered," *Sports Illustrated* 98, no. 3 (27 January 2003): 94; "Letters," *Sports Illustrated* 98, no. 6 (17 February 2003): 12.
31. Reilly, "Under Covered," 94; "NCAA Sports Sponsorship and Participation Rates Report, 1981–82—2004–05," (May 2007), https://www.ncaapublications.com/productdownloads/PSR07.pdf, retrieved, July 2, 2021; Rick Reilly, "Taking One for the Team," *Sports Illustrated* 98, no. 23 (9 June 2003): 80.
32. Wolff, "The Slow Track," 56, 57, 58, emphasis in the original.
33. Casey, "Games Women Play," 21.

34. Ibid.; R. Vivian Acosta and Linda Jean Carpenter, "Women in Intercollegiate Sport," http://www.acostacarpenter.org/2014%20Status%20of%20Women %20in%20Intercollegiate%20Sport%20-37%20Year%20Update%20 -%201977-2014%20.pdf, retrieved July 2, 2021.

35. Douglas Looney, "Major Minors," *Sports Illustrated* 72, no. 12 (26 March 1990): 42–49; Kelly Whiteside, "World Beater," *Sports Illustrated* 82, no. 22 (5 June 1995): 73; Grant Wahl, "America's Host," *Sports Illustrated* 90, no. 25 (21 June 1999): 66.

36. Michael Farber, "Score One for Women," *Sports Illustrated* 85, no. 7 (12 August 1996): 72, 74–76; Grant Wahl, "Kicking Butt," *Sports Illustrated* 91, no. 1 (5 July 1999): 58, 59; Wahl, "Out of This World," *Sports Illustrated* 91, no. 3 (19 July 1999): 39, 40–42 (also see cover); Steve Rushin, "Quick! Cover That Woman!" *Sports Illustrated* 91, no. 6 (16 August 1999): 24.

37. Richard Hoffer, "Our Favorite Teams," *Sports Illustrated* 91, no. 9 (6 September 1999): 73; Michael Bamberger, "Dream Come True," *Sports Illustrated* 91, no. 24 (20 December 1999): 49–51, 60; "Letters," *Sports Illustrated* 91, no. 9 (6 September 1999): 12.

38. "Letters," *Sports Illustrated* 91, no. 9 (6 September 1999): 12; Bamberger, "Dream Come True," 48.

39. "Hear the Roar," *Sports Illustrated* 116, no. 19 (7 May 2012): 44; "Letters," *Sports Illustrated* 91, no. 9 (6 September 1999): 12; Susan Ware, *Game, Set, Match,* 44; E. M. Swift, "Bring on the Dancing Bears," *Sports Illustrated* 77, no. 13 (28 September 1992): 71.

40. Donald M. Elliman Jr., "To Our Readers," *Sports Illustrated* 86, no. 15 (14 April 1997): 5.

41. Ibid.; Sandra Bailey, "Editor's Letter," *Sports Illustrated Women/Sport* (Spring 1997): 8; Robert Lipsyte, "Magazine Explores Its Feminine Side," https://timesmachine.nytimes.com/timesmachine/1997/04/13/590010 .html?pageNumber=344, retrieved July 2, 2021. For more on *womenSports,* see Britni de la Cretaz, "An Audience of Athletes: The Rise and Fall of Feminist Sports," https://longreads.com/2019/05/22/an-audience-of-athletes -the-rise-and-fall-of-feminist-sports/, retrieved May 10, 2022.

42. Marketing brochure featuring letter from editor Sandra Bailey found in *Sports Illustrated for Women,* no. 1 (Spring 1999): between 16 and 17; Lipsyte, "Magazine Explores Its Feminine Side," 2; Michael Messner, *Taking the Field,* 92–93.

43. Messner also drew attention to the fact that *SI* was not referred to as "*Sports Illustrated for Men.*" See Messner, *Taking the Field,* 93.

44. David Carr, "Time Inc. Is Closing *Sports Illustrated Women*"; Reilly, "Under Covered," 94. Marie Hardin, Susan Lynn, and Kristie Walsdorf discuss the

failure of *Sports Illustrated Women* and question whether the decision to shutter *SI Women* was purely an economic one, and if its demise was necessarily a bad thing. See their "Challenge and Conformity on 'Contested Terrain,'" 114.

45. Gilbert and Williamson, "Sport Is Unfair to Women," 91; Alexander Wolff, "Sportsman/Sportswoman of the Year," *Sports Illustrated* 115, no. 23 (12 December 2011): 54; Crichton, "Fair's Fair," 17.

46. Neff, "Equality at Last, Part II," 71; Craig Neff, "Equality and Horseshoes," *Sports Illustrated* 70, no. 8 (20 February 1989): 11; Kelli Anderson, "No Room at the Top," *Sports Illustrated* 77, no. 13 (28 September 1992): 62; Kelli Anderson, "The Power of Play," *Sports Illustrated* 116, no. 19 (7 May 2012): 49.

47. Jenna Ashendouek, "Title IX: A Milestone for Women in Sports," https://msmagazine.com/2020/07/14/title-ix-a-milestone-for-women-in-sports-but-unfulfilled-promise-for-black-women/, retrieved March 6, 2022; "Her Life Depends On It," https://www.womenssportsfoundation.org/wp-content/uploads/2016/08/her-life-depends-on-it-women-of-color-brief-full-citations-final.pdf, retrieved March 7, 2022.

48. Jennifer E. Bruening, "Gender and Racial Analysis in Sport," 336; William C. Rhoden, "Black and White Women Far from Equal under Title IX," https://www.nytimes.com/2012/06/11/sports/title-ix-has-not-given-black-female-athletes-equal-opportunity.html, retrieved July 2, 2021.

49. Rhoden, "Black and White Women."

50. Ibid.; Jenny Lind Withycombe, "Intersecting Selves: African American Female Athletes' Experiences of Sport," *Sociology of Sport Journal* 28 (2011): 490.

51. Rhoden, "Black and White Women"; Brianna Scurry, *My Greatest Save*, 6; Grant Wahl, "As Good As Dunn," *Sports Illustrated* 125, no. 2 (25 July 2016): 73. Bruening had made that connection in 2005, finding that Black sportswomen participated in those sports that were familiar and to which they had access. See her "Gender and Racial Analysis in Sport," 334.

52. Rhoden, "Black and White Women"; Combahee River Collective, *The Combahee River Collective Statement*; Alice Walker, *In Search of Our Mothers' Gardens*; Kimberlé Crenshaw, "Demarginalizing the Intersection of Race and Sex."

53. "The New Gibson Girl," *Sports Illustrated* 5, no. 1 (2 July 1956): 19–20, 60–61. The insidious policy of "separate but equal" limited the accomplishments of Black Americans in all arenas, including athletics. In the late nineteenth century, Black Americans created sporting structures that allowed them the ability to play in a segregated society. Even as color barriers to sports participation began to fall during the 1940s, tennis symbolized one of the last bastions of segregation in sports. The Black American Tennis

Association sought to desegregate the world of tennis, and the incredibly talented Althea Gibson represented the ATA's best bet to accomplish that goal.

54. L. Jon Wertheim, "When Billie Beat Bobby," *Sports Illustrated* 116, no. 19 (7 May 2012): 60, 61.
55. Ware, *Game, Set, Match,* 43–44.
56. George Gerbner and Larry Gross, "Living with Television"; Gaye Tuchman, "The Symbolic Annihilation of Women by the Mass Media"; Gilbert and Williamson, "Sport Is Unfair to Women," 95.
57. Gilbert and Williamson, "Sport Is Unfair to Women," 96; Reilly, "Under Covered," 94; Ware, *Game, Set, Match,* 44; Trisha Blackmar and Mark Bechtel, "First and Fearless," *Sports Illustrated* 97, no. 3 (15–22 July 2002): 116–17.
58. Steve Wulf, "Title Waves," https://www.espn.com/espnw/title-ix/story/_/id/7985418/espn-magazine-1976-protest-helped-define-title-ix-movement, retrieved October 1, 2021.
59. Phil Taylor, "Spirits of '72," *Sports Illustrated* 116, no. 19 (7 May 2012): 58–59; Alexander Wolff, "Father Figures," *Sports Illustrated* 116, no. 19 (7 May 2012): 65–66. For the photo spread, see Anderson, "The Power of Play," 46–47, 50–51, 56–57, 62–63.
60. Michael Farber and Richard Deutsch, "Endangered Species Save the Wails—At Least Until You've Read This Guide to the Spotted Owls of the Sports World," *Sports Illustrated* 87, no. 13 (29 September 1997): 93. There are numerous articles that make such a connection: Martin Dugard, "Hell on Wheels," *Sports Illustrated* 85, no. 24 (9 December 1996): 17; Paul Gutierrez, "Guess Who Came to Dinner," *Sports Illustrated* 86, no. 10 (10 March 1997): 74; Kevin Cook and Mark Mavric, "Title IX's Toll: Red Ink Kills Redhawks," *Sports Illustrated* 90, no. 17 (26 April 1999): 22; "Letters: Nein to IX," *Sports Illustrated* 97, no. 3 (15–22 July 2002): 16; Bill Syken, "All-around Thriller," *Sports Illustrated,* SI.com, April 12, 2004, https://vault.si.com/vault/2004/04/12/allaround-thriller-a-depleted-ncaa-field-put-on-an-electrifying-show, retrieved July 2, 2021; "Letters: The Power of IX," *Sports Illustrated* 116, no. 22 (28 May 2012): 13.
61. Alexander Wolff, "The Third Sex," *Sports Illustrated* 82, no. 5 (6 February 1995): 15.
62. Maggie Mertens, "Then and Now," *Sports Illustrated* 133, no. 5 (June 2022): 30, 31.
63. Allie Bidwell, "U. of Southern California Settles Title IX Complaint," https://www.chronicle.com/article/u-of-southern-california-settles-title-ix-complaint-over-womens-crew/, retrieved July 2, 2021; Wesley Jenkins, "Hundreds of Colleges May Be Out of Compliance," https://www

.chronicle.com/article/hundreds-of-colleges-may-be-out-of-compliance -with-title-ix-heres-why/, retrieved April 4, 2021.

64. Taylor, "Spirits of '72," 59, 58.

4. "The Frailty Myth"

1. Meesha Diaz Haddad, "Required Reading," *Sports Illustrated for Women* 2, no. 4 (September/October 2000): 30.
2. Charles Hirshberg, "Books," *Sports Illustrated* 93, no. 13 (2 October 2000): 34.
3. Haddad, "Required Reading," 30; Colette Dowling, *The Frailty Myth*, 6; Bil Gilbert and Nancy Williamson, "Are You Being Two-Faced?," *Sports Illustrated* 38, no. 22 (4 June 1973): 45, 47.
4. Patricia Vertinsky, "Body Shapes"; Dowling, *The Frailty Myth*, 3–41; Gwendolyn Captain, "Enter Ladies and Gentlemen of Color," 87; Carroll Smith-Rosenberg and Charles Rosenberg, "The Female Animal," 14.
5. Dowling, *The Frailty Myth*, 186–87, 199, 6; MacCambridge, *The Franchise*, 356.
6. Mark Graham, "Monica Seles," https://www.tennis365.com/tennis-tales /monica-seles-one-of-the-darkest-and-saddest-tales-tennis-has-to-offer/, retrieved July 5, 2021.
7. Sally Jenkins, "Savage Assault," *Sports Illustrated* 78, no. 18 (10 May 1993): 18, 19, 21.
8. *Sports Illustrated* 83, no. 3 (17 July 1995): cover; Johnette Howard, "Home Alone," *Sports Illustrated* 82, no. (10 April 1995) 45, 46; S. L. Price, "The Return," *Sports Illustrated* 83, no. 3 (17 July 1995): 26.
9. Sally Jenkins, "Back in Full Swing," *Sports Illustrated* 83, no. 6 (7 August 1995): 44; Jenkins, "Still the One," *Sports Illustrated* 83, no. 9 (28 August 1995): 36; S. L. Price, "There's Something about Monica," *Sports Illustrated* 89, no. 10 (7 September 1998): 56; L. Jon Wertheim, "Girl Interrupted," *Sports Illustrated* 108, no. 8 (25 February 2008): 22.
10. Price, "The Return," 24; *Sports Illustrated* 80, no. 2 (17 January 1994): cover; E. M. Swift, "Violence," *Sports Illustrated* 80, no. 2 (17 January 1994): 16, 17, 19.
11. E. M. Swift, "On Thin Ice," *Sports Illustrated* 80, no. 3 (24 January 1994): 16, 20; Swift, "Not Your Average Ice Queen," *Sports Illustrated* 76, no. 1 (13 January 1992): 54–56+.
12. E. M. Swift, "Stars and Scars," *Sports Illustrated* 80, no. 4 (7 February 1994): 74; Steve Rushin, "As the World Turns," *Sports Illustrated* 80, no. 7 (28 February 1994): 33, 37. For more on the contrast between the two skaters, see Sandy Flitterman-Lewis, "Tales of the Ice Princess and the Trash Queen."
13. Susan J. Douglas, *Where the Girls Are*, 224.

14. Swift, "Stars and Scars," 74, 76.

15. E. M. Swift, "Silver Belle," *Sports Illustrated* 80, no. 8 (7 March 1994): 25; Swift, "Violence," 21, 18.

16. "Hot Spots," *Sports Illustrated* 108, no. 9 (3 March 2008): 56.

17. Melissa Segura, "Ronda Rousey Lays the Smack Down," *Sports Illustrated* 117, no. 18 (5 November 2012): 67, 70; *Sports Illustrated* 122, no. 20 (18 May 2015): cover; L. Jon Wertheim, "The Unbreakable Ronda Rousey," *Sports Illustrated* 122, no. 20 (18 May 2015): 53.

18. L. Jon Wertheim, "Fading Fast," *Sports Illustrated* 127, no. 1 (3–10 July 2017): 15, 14.

19. L. Jon Wertheim, "Prisoners of Depression," *Sports Illustrated* 99, no. 9 (8 September 2003): 71, 72.

20. Ibid., 72; Kelli Anderson, "Happy in Her World," *Sports Illustrated* 110, no. 23 (8 June 2009): 49, 50.

21. Ruth White, "Why Mental Health Is Stigmatized in Black Communities," https://dworakpeck.usc.edu/news/why-mental-health-care-stigmatized -black-communities, retrieved February 5, 2022; Wertheim, "Prisoners of Depression," 73–74; Pablo Torre, "Dangerous Minds," *Sports Illustrated* 15, no. 6 (15 August 2011): 12; Michael Bamberger, "Emotional Rescue," *Sports Illustrated* 117, no. 21 (26 November 2012): 15–16.

22. Wertheim, "Prisoners of Depression," 76; Torre, "Dangerous Minds," 12; Bamberger, "Emotional Rescue," 15; Andrew Lawrence, "Where Are They Now: Catching Up with Chamique Holdsclaw," July 10, 2014, https:// www.si.com/college/2014/07/10/catching-former-wnba-star-chamique -holdsclaw, retrieved February 5, 2022.

23. *Sports Illustrated* 123, no. 19 (16 November 2015): cover.

24. Tim Layden, "A New Man," *Sports Illustrated* 123, no. 19 (16 November 2015): 54, 60, 58, 62, 63.

25. Jon Wertheim, "Naomi Osaka's French Open Withdrawal Puts the Spotlight on Mental Health," May 31, 2021, https://www.si.com/tennis/2021/05 /31/naomi-osaka-withdraws-french-open-press-boycott, retrieved July 3, 2021; Robin Lundberg, "Simone Biles Doesn't Owe the Olympics Everything: Unchecked," July 27, 2021, https://www.si.com/olympics/2021/07/27 /simone-biles-olympics-2021-tokyo-withdraws-team-gymnastics-mental -health, retrieved March 7, 2022.

26. Tim Layden, "Scarred, Yes, But Never Scared," *Sports Illustrated* 128, no. 1 (15 January 2018): 56, 58, 57; Layden, "Ready to Rock," *Sports Illustrated* 112, no. 5 (8 February 2010): 54.

27. Richard Demak, "One False Move," *Sports Illustrated* 74, no. 16 (29 April 1991): 52, 55, 58, 57.

28. Jack McCallum, "Out of Joint," *Sports Illustrated* 82, no. 6 (13 February 1995): 44, 46, 45.
29. Ibid., 47, 53; Demak, "One False Move," 54, 55.
30. Gilbert and Williamson, "Are You Being Two-Faced?," 46; Frank Deford, "Now Georgy-Porgy Runs Away," *Sports Illustrated* 40, no. 16 (22 April 1974): 30. Such beliefs had staying power; in 2014 there were concerns that women's bodies simply were not suited for ski jumping, because of potential injury. See Nick Zaccardi, "Russian Men's Ski Jump Coach."
31. McCallum, "Out of Joint," 48.
32. Dana Sullivan, "On Mended Knee," *Sports Illustrated for Women* 3 (January/February 2001): 64, 65, 62, 66–67.
33. "Repair and Replace," *Sports Illustrated* 127, no. 3 (24 July 2017): 20; "Treatment as Usual," *Sports Illustrated* 127, no. 3 (24 July 2017): 18.
34. J. D. Reed, "They Hunger for Success," *Sports Illustrated* 46, no. 10 (28 February 1977): 65, 66, 67, 71.
35. Merrell Noden, "Dying to Win," *Sports Illustrated* 81, no. 6 (8 August 1994): 54, 56. "Appearance" or "aesthetic" sports like gymnastics, figure skating, and long-distance running reward "performance thinness," favoring athletes with leaner bodies. The growing prominence of eating disorders in sport mirrored that in society more generally. Throughout the late 1970s, popular magazines increasingly began to cover anorexia nervosa, and in 1978 the psychiatrist Hilde Bruch published *The Golden Cage*, in which she aimed to educate the general public about the disease. See Joan Jacobs Brumberg, *Fasting Girls*, 11–13.
36. Noden, "Dying to Win," 56, 58.
37. Ibid., 58, 54, 60.
38. Kelli Anderson, "Losing to Win," *Sports Illustrated for Women* 3, no. 3 (May/June 2001): 89, 90, 94, 90–91.
39. Kenny Moore and J. E. Vader, "Living a Dream," *Sports Illustrated* 71, no. 22 (27 November 1989): 70, 74, 76; Kelli Anderson, "'It Can Happen to Anyone,'" *Sports Illustrated for Women*, no. 2 (Summer 1999): 82, 83 85; Anderson, "Hero of the Huskies," *Sports Illustrated for Women* 2, no. 1 (March/April 2000): 122, 124, 125; Brian Cazenueve, "Salad Days," *Sports Illustrated* 93, no. 14 (9 October 2000): 64, 65; Noden, "Dying to Win," 59; Anderson, "Losing to Win," 92, 90.
40. L. Jon Wertheim, "Slam-Bang Return," *Sports Illustrated* 106, no. 5 (5 February 2007): 50, 51, 52.
41. Susan Bordo, *Unbearable Weight*, 63; https://www.nationaleatingdisorders.org/people-color-and-eating-disorders; Anderson, "Losing to Win," 92; Moore and Vader, "Living a Dream," 74; Sabrina Strings, *Fearing the Black Body*, 4.

42. Courtney Nguyen, "Taylor Townsend Dispute: USTA Cuts Funding until No.1 Junior Loses Weight," September 7, 2012, https://www.si.com/tennis /2012/09/07/taylor-townsend-usta-controversy, retrieved July 3, 2021. Alexander Abad-Santos, "Serena Williams Defends Taylor Townsend," https://www.theatlantic.com/national/archive/2012/09/taylor-townsends -tennis-should-be-more-important-her-weight/323747/, retrieved July 3, 2021; Atahabih Germain, "'I Was Fat, and I Was Black," https://atlantablackstar .com/2021/06/09/i-was-fat-and-i-was-black-so-they-took-away-my -dream-taylor-townsend-claims-u-s-tennis-association-nearly-ended-her -career-because-of-her-weight/, retrieved July 3, 2021; Strings, *Fearing the Black Body*, 4.

43. Bil Gilbert, "Drugs in Sport: Part 1: Problems in a Turned-On World," *Sports Illustrated* 30, no. 25 (23 June 1969): 64, 72; "How We Got Here," March 11, 2008, https://www.si.com/more-sports/2008/03/11/steroid -timeline, retrieved March 7, 2022. Those features included a 1988 cover story and special report devoted to Olympian Ben Johnson's positive drug test following his gold medal–winning performance in the 100 meters; a 1991 cover story featuring Lyle Alzado, who admitted to years-long use of performance-enhancing drugs that he believed resulted in his inoperable brain cancer; a 2002 special report (and cover story) that addressed ste- roids in baseball; and several stories that addressed the growing scandal associated with BALCO (Bay Area Laboratory Co-operative).

44. Susan Reifer, "'There Is Nothing Stopping Me . . . Except Me," *Sports Illus- trated Women* 4, no. 5 (September 2002): 92–95.

45. Gary Smith, "Wonder Down Under," *Sports Illustrated* 93, no. 14 (9 Octo- ber 2000): 38.

46. Tim Layden, "Disgrace Jones," *Sports Illustrated* 107, no. 15 (15 October 2007): 20; "Sentenced," *Sports Illustrated* 108, no. (21 January 2008): 18.

47. Merrell Noden, "Setting the Records Straight," *Sports Illustrated* 75, no. 26 (16 December 1991): 138; Jerry Kirshenbaum, "Stemming a Red Tide," *Sports Illustrated* 41, no. 11 (9 September 1974): 23; Kenny Moore, "Babashoff and Ender," *Sports Illustrated* 77, no. 2 (13 July 1992): 60, 56, 58. By 1992, many of those East German coaches had found new jobs in Communist China, where their techniques were welcomed, causing concern about the doping of Chinese athletes, particularly women. See Christine Brennan, "Critics Take Chinese Swimmers to Task."

48. Thomas M. Hunt, *Drug Games*, 53–54.

49. Noden, "Setting the Records Straight," 138. That was especially true for Shirley Babashoff, who wanted the IOC "to do the right thing," which in- cluded correcting the Olympic record book and offering duplicate gold medals. See Paul Newberry, "Time for IOC to Make Right a 40-Year-Old

Wrong," July 1, 2016, https://www.si.com/olympics/2016/07/02/ap-oly
-swm-paul-newberry-last-gold, retrieved July 8, 2021.

50. Craig Neff, "East Germany Made Lab Animals of Its Finest Athletes—and Got Away with It," *Sports Illustrated* 94, no. 26 (25 June 2001): 46.

51. Steven Ungerleider, *Faust's Gold*, 40.

52. Ibid., 96, 109. In 2022 sportswomen continued to grab doping headlines when fifteen-year-old Russian figure skater, Kamila Valieva, tested positive for the banned substance trimetazidine, exposing Russia once again to allegations of an abusive, state-sponsored doping system. See Stephanie Apstein, "Kamila Valieva's Collapse Was a Fitting End to a Controversial Olympics," SI.com, February 17, 2022, https://www.si.com/olympics/2022/02/17/kamila-valieva-collapse-fitting-end-to-controversial-olympics, retrieved March 1, 2022. In 2016, *Sports Illustrated* reported findings from the World Anti-Doping Agency of an "institutional conspiracy" in Russia that "corrupted the drug-testing system," particularly at the 2014 Sochi Olympics. See "WADA Doping Report Details 'Institutional Conspiracy' in Russia," December 9, 2016, https://www.si.com/olympics/2016/12/09/wada-report-russian-doping, retrieved January 4, 2023.

53. Michael Bamberger and Don Yaeger, "Over the Edge," *Sports Illustrated* 86, no. 15 (14 April 1997): 67.

54. Ungerleider, *Faust's Gold*, 72, 101.

55. Gary Smith, "Stand Up & Speak Out," *Sports Illustrated* 117, no. 24 (17 December 2012): 66, 68.

56. Johnette Howard and Lester Munson, "Betrayal of Trust," *Sports Illustrated Women/Sport* (Spring 1997): 70, 76, 77.

57. Ibid., 76, 77.

58. Stephanie Apstein, "Rachel Denhollander," *Sports Illustrated* 129, no. 13 (17–24 December 2018): 88–90; Bonni Cohen and Jon Shenk, directors, *Athlete A.*

59. "Standing Strong," *Sports Illustrated* 128, no. 5 (26 February 2018): 60, 61.

60. Ben Reiter, "A Hidden Epidemic," *Sports Illustrated* 122, no. 10 (9 March 2015): 46, 47; John Papanek, "More Tremors in San Francisco," *Sports Illustrated* 57, no. 4 (26 July 1982): 9; Kelli Anderson and George Dohrmann, "Out of Control?," *Sports Illustrated* 100, no. 8 (23 February 2004): 64, 67.

61. Sharon Lamb, *The Trouble with Blame*, 158.

62. Paul Gallico, "Farewell to the Babe," *Sports Illustrated* 5, no. 15 (8 October 1956): 66, 68.

63. Ibid., 68; Joan Flynn Dreyspool, "Subject: Babe and George Zaharias," *Sports Illustrated* 4, no. 20 (14 May 1956): 30–31+.

64. Richard Hoffer, "'You Just Play Through It,'" *Sports Illustrated* 77, no. 8 (24 August 1992): 56, 54. Farr would lose her battle in 1993. See Richard

Hoffer, "A Battler to the End," *Sports Illustrated* 79, no. 2 (29 November 1993): 30–31.

65. Bill Finley, "Playing Through," *Sports Illustrated Women* 4, no. 6 (October 2002): 65–67.

66. Kaitlin M. Boyle and Kimberly B. Rogers, "Beyond the Rape 'Victim'-'Survivor' Binary."

67. Kelli Anderson, "A Cycling Star's Tragic Ride," *Sports Illustrated for Women* 3, no. 4 (July/August 2001): 101, 103; Kate Meyers, "A Hard-Won Peace," *Sports Illustrated Women* 4, no. 3 (May/June 2002): 100; Kelli Anderson, "The Race of Her Life," *Sports Illustrated for Women* 1 (Spring 1999): 99, 100.

68. Gretchen Reynolds, "My Name Is Lottie. I'm a Gravity Addict." *Sports Illustrated Women* 4, no. 5 (September 2002): 106–12; Bucky McMahon, "The Underneath," *Sports Illustrated Women* 3, no. 5 (September 2001): 3, 115; Gretchen Reynolds, "The Curiosity," *Sports Illustrated Women* 3, no. 6 (October 2001): 100, 105; "No Limits," *Sports Illustrated Women* 4, no. 7 (November 2002): 5, 69.

69. Mary Jo Festle, *Playing Nice*, xxiii.

70. Wertheim, "Girl Interrupted," 22.

71. Boyle and Rogers, "Beyond the Rape Binary," 324.

5. "The Olympic Ideal"

1. Don Canham, "Russia Will Win the 1956 Olympics," *Sports Illustrated* 1, no. 11 (25 October 1954): 10, 11, 61, 62. See also "Stars of Track and Field," *Sports Illustrated* 5, no. 21 (19 November 1956): 51 and "The Women," *Sports Illustrated* 5, no. 21 (19 November 1956): 59.

2. Jimmy Jemail, "Hotbox: Should the U.S. Go All Out to Build an Olympic Team That Can Beat Russia in 1956?," *Sports Illustrated* 2, no. 24 (13 June 1955): 6, 7; Jemail, "Hotbox: As a Former Olympian, What Should the United States Do to Win the Olympics in 1956?," *Sports Illustrated* 2, no. 7 (14 February 1955): 4; Canham, "Russian Will Win," 65.

3. Charles A. Bucher, "Are We Losing the Olympic Ideal?," *Sports Illustrated* 3, no. 6 (8 August 1955): 52, 57.

4. Alexander Wolff, "The Powers That Be," *Sports Illustrated* 124, no. 20 (30 May 2016): 14. See also Joseph S. Nye Jr., "Soft Power."

5. Robert Boyle, "Red Icemen Come, See and Conquer," *Sports Illustrated* 10, no. 2 (12 January 1959): 8; Jeremiah Tax, "First Sputnik, Now This!" *Sports Illustrated* 10, no. 6 (9 February 1959): 11.

6. Tex Maule, "Here They Come!" *Sports Illustrated* 11, no. 3 (20 July 1959): 10; "Distaff Diplomats on the Mark," *Sports Illustrated* 8, no. 14 (7 April 1958): 31; Mary Snow, "Can the Soviet Girls Be Stopped?," *Sports Illustrated*

5, no. 9 (27 August 1956): 11, 10. For more on sports exchanges between the two countries, see Jennifer Parks, *The Olympic Games*.

7. "The Women," *Sports Illustrated* 5, no. 21 (19 November 1956): 59; Snow, "Can the Soviet Girls Be Stopped?," 9–10, 6–7, 8.

8. Patricia Vertinsky and Gwendolyn Captain, "More Myth than History," 533. For more on the acceptability of track and field for Black women, see Cat M. Ariail, *Passing the Baton*.

9. John F. Kennedy, "Sport on the New Frontier: The Soft American," *Sports Illustrated* 13, no. 26 (26 December 1960): 15–16, 17.

10. John F. Kennedy, "The Vigor We Need," *Sports Illustrated* 17, no. 3 (16 July 1962): 12–14; Robert H. Boyle, "The Report That Shocked the President," *Sports Illustrated* 3, no. 7 (15 August 1955): 30.

11. For more on the relationship between sport and the Cold War, see Erin Elizabeth Redihan, *The Olympics and the Cold War*; and Toby C. Rider and Kevin B. Witherspoon, eds., *Defending the American Way of Life*.

12. Robert F. Kennedy, "A Bold Proposal for American Sport," *Sports Illustrated* 21, no. 4 (27 July 1964): 13, 14, 15.

13. Barbara Heilman, "Like Nothing Else in Tennessee," *Sports Illustrated* 13, no. 20 (14 November 1960): 48, 49; Jennifer H. Lansbury, "Foxes Not Oxes," in *A Spectacular Leap*, 118, 139–40. For more on Wilma Rudolph and the civil rights movement, see Cat Ariail, "'One of the Greatest Ambassadors'"; and Liberti and Smith, *(Re)Presenting Wilma Rudolph*, particularly chap. 1, "'Wilma's Home Town Win'? Race on Parade in Clarksville."

14. Roy Terrell, "Very Good, Very Tired and Winners All the Way," *Sports Illustrated* 15, no. 5 (31 July 1961): 12.

15. Hansi Lo Wang, "Black U.S. Olympians Won in Nazi Germany," https://www.npr.org/sections/thetorch/2016/08/13/489773389/black-u-s-olympians-won-in-nazi-germany-only-to-be-overlooked-at-home, retrieved March 8, 2022. Those fourteen medals represented a quarter of the fifty-six medals won by the entire American team.

16. For more on the Soviet press's coverage of race relations in the United States, see particularly Mary L. Dudziak, *Cold War Civil Rights*.

17. See particularly Damion L. Thomas, *Globetrotting*.

18. MacCambridge, *The Franchise*, 158, 159; Frank Deford, "The Negro Athlete Is Invited Home," *Sports Illustrated* 22, no. 20 (14 June 1965): 26–27; George Plimpton, "The World Champion Is Refused a Meal," *Sports Illustrated* 22, no. (17 May 1965): 24–27.

19. Jack Olsen, "The Black Athlete—A Shameful Story: Cruel Deception," *Sports Illustrated* 29, no. 1 (1 July 1968): 12.

20. Johnathan Rodgers, "A Step to an Olympic Boycott," *Sports Illustrated* 27, no. 23 (4 December 1967): 30, 31; Olsen, "The Black Athlete," 12, emphasis in

the original. For more on the Black athlete and activism, see Louis Moore, *We Will Win the Day,* especially chap. 7. See also Harry Edwards, *The Revolt of the Black Athlete,* for his explanation for organizing the boycott.

21. John Underwood, "A High Time for Sprinters—and Kenyans," *Sports Illustrated* 29, no. 18 (28 October 1968): 22; Wyomia Tyus and Elizabeth Terzakis, *Tigerbelle,* 173. See especially chaps. 7 and 8, for Tyus's comments about the boycott, Smith and Carlos, and the involvement of Black women in the Olympic Project for Human Rights. Tyus would win a second gold medal in the 4x100-meter relay in 1968.

22. Underwood, "A High Time for Sprinters—and Kenyans," 22; Bob Ottum, "Fresh, Fair and Golden," *Sports Illustrated* 29, no. 19 (4 November 1968): 20, 23.

23. "Oh, Those Russian Gals!" *Sports Illustrated* 11, no. 23 (7 December 1959): 21; Tom C. Brody, "At Last the Girls Are *Ours,*" *Sports Illustrated* 21, no. 7 (17 August 1964): 68, emphasis in the original.

24. Mary Jo Festle, *Playing Nice,* 79–90.

25. Martha Duffy, "Hello to a Russian Pixie," *Sports Illustrated* 38, no. 11 (19 March 1973): 25.

26. Anita Verschoth, "Sugar and Spice—and Iron," *Sports Illustrated* 37, no. 8 (21 August 1972): 27, 22, 23; Pat Putnam, "Saved by a Very Fast Wottle," *Sports Illustrated* 37, no. 11 (11 September 1972): 22.

27. Anita Verschoth, "A Great Leap Backward," *Sports Illustrated* 44, no. 15 (12 April 1976): 94; Frank Deford, "Nadia Awed Ya," *Sports Illustrated* 45, no. 5 (2 August 1976): 28, 29–30; Frank Deford, "High, Wide and Handsome," *Sports Illustrated* 45, no. 5 (2 August 1976): 16; Georgia Cervin, *Degrees of Difficulty,* 69.

28. Deford, "High, Wide and Handsome," 17; Deford, "Nadia Awed Ya," 28; Jerry Kirshenbaum, "A Big Splash by the Mighty Mädchen," *Sports Illustrated* 39, no. 12 (17 September 1973): 44, 49.

29. Sarah Pileggi, "Up from Plop, Plop," *Sports Illustrated* 44, no. 25 (21 June 1976): 31, 32; Jerry Kirshenbaum, "Guaranteed to Make Waves," *Sports Illustrated* 45, no. 3 (19 July 1976): 48.

30. Jerry Kirshenbaum, "Theirs Was a Midas Stroke," *Sports Illustrated* 45, no. 5 (2 August 1976): 19.

31. Jerry Kirshenbaum, "Assembly Line for Champions," *Sports Illustrated* 45, no. 2 (12 July 1976): 63.

32. Ibid., 62.

33. Kenny Moore, "All Out for Glory," *Sports Illustrated* 69, no. 12 (14 September 1988): 10; E. M. Swift, "To Witt, the Victory," *Sports Illustrated* 68, no. 10 (7 March 1988): 38.

34. Rick Reilly, "Behold the Shining Star of the G.D.R.," *Sports Illustrated* 64, no. 3 (20 January 1986): 46, 40, 39, 41; Jennifer Arnold and Senain Kheshgi, directors, *The Diplomat.*
35. Reilly, "Behold the Shining Star," 46.
36. E. M. Swift, "Books or Blades, There's No Doubting Thomas," *Sports Illustrated* 64, no. 7 (17 February 1986): 22; Swift, "Another Miracle on Ice?," *Sports Illustrated* 64, no. 11 (17 March 1986): 54, 55–56.
37. Reilly, "Behold the Shining Star," 41; Swift, "Books or Blades," 22.
38. Richard Lowy, "Yuppie Racism: Race Relations in the 1980s."
39. Swift, "Another Miracle on Ice?," 56.
40. E. M. Swift, "All That Glittered Was Gold," *Sports Illustrated* 66, no. 7 (16 February 1987): 64; Swift, "Thou Swell, Thou Witt-y," *Sports Illustrated* 66, no. 12 (23 March 1987): 22; Swift, "Soviet Disunion," *Sports Illustrated* 77, no. 2 (13 July 1992): 46. Witt made a comeback in 1994 and qualified for the Lillehammer Olympics, where she finished seventh.
41. Frank Deford, "An Old Dragon Limbers Up," *Sports Illustrated* 69, no. 7 (15 August 1988): 36, 38, 39. The Cultural Revolution was initiated by Mao Zedong in an effort to establish a pure version of Chinese Communism. Lasting from 1966 until Mao's death in 1976, it upended the country's economic, religious, educational, and cultural traditions. With an enmity for anything that smacked of capitalism or privilege, elite sport was a target as China withdrew from Olympic competition, reclaimed or razed athletic facilities, and arrested athletes, coaches, and sports officials. See Lu Zhouxiang, "Sport and Politics."
42. William Johnson, "Faces on a New China Scroll," *Sports Illustrated* 39, no. 13 (24 September 1973): 84; William Johnson, "Gentle Tigers of the Tables," *Sports Illustrated* 36, no. 15 (10 April 1972): 24, 25. For more on the importance of table tennis in Sino-American relations, see Nicholas Griffin, *Ping-Pong Diplomacy.*
43. Johnson, "Faces on a New China Scroll," 86; William Oscar Johnson, "The Image Has Altered," *Sports Illustrated* 69, no. 7 (15 August 1988): 88.
44. Johnson, "Faces on a New China Scroll," 84; Rick Reilly, "Here No One Is Spared," *Sports Illustrated* 69, no. 7 (15 August 1988): 70–71, 73.
45. Fan Hong, *Footbinding, Feminism and Freedom,* 11; Alexander Wolff, "On the Move from Shanghai to Tianjin," *Sports Illustrated* 85 (22–29 July 1996): 152.
46. Wolff, "On the Move," 152.
47. Dong Jinxia, *Women, Sport and Society in Modern China,* 203, 204. In November 2021, tennis player Peng Shuai's revelations drew attention to the sexual abuse that Chinese sportswomen also endured under such a

system. See Eva Dou and Alicia Chen, "Chinese Tennis Star's Sexual Assault Allegation."

48. Those means became even more questionable following rumors of performance-enhancing drug abuse during the 1990s.

49. Robert Sullivan, "Orient Express," *Sports Illustrated* 68, no. 21 (23 May 1988): 45.

50. Wolff, "On the Move," 152.

51. Becky Pallack, "Navajo Using Olympics as Tourism Showcase," https://azdailysun.com/navajo-using-olympics-as-tourism-showcase/article _fc5983b4-a177-5cc7-acf0-b5854b7c303d.html.

52. William Johnson, "The Taking Part," *Sports Illustrated* 37, no. 2 (10 July 1972): 41; Shoshi Parks, "Scientists Staged a Racist Olympics," https://timeline.com /anthropology-days-scientists-racist-olympics-prove-white-superiority -7a45289071cf; Sean Edgecomb, "Inharmonious Pursuits," 48, 50.

53. For more on the American Indian School experience, see David Wallace Adams, *Education for Extinction*.

54. Linda Peavy and Ursula Smith, *Full Court Quest*.

55. John Underwood, "We Win the Five and Ten," *Sports Illustrated* 21, no. 17 (26 October 1964): 22; Jack McCallum, "The Regilding of a Legend," *Sports Illustrated* 57, no. 18 (25 October 1982): 48–49+; E. M. Swift, "Made in the U.S.A.," *Sports Illustrated* 85, special issue (22 July 1996): 21.

56. Paul Connolly, "Great Expectations," *Sports Illustrated*, special issue (1 October 2000): 62–68; Gary Smith, "Torch Song," *Sports Illustrated* 93, no. 12 (25 September 2000): 42, 43; Leigh Montville, "Fast Company," *Sports Illustrated for Women* 2, no. 4 (September/October 2000): 120.

57. Tim Layden, "The Start of Something Big," *Sports Illustrated* 93, no. 13 (2 October 2000): 47; Smith, "Torch Song," 43, emphasis in the original.

58. Toni Bruce and Emma Wensing, "'She's Not One of Us,'" 94, 95.

59. John Underwood, "The Tokyo Games," *Sports Illustrated* 21, no. 14 (5 October 1964): 34–35.

60. James Poling, "How the Reds Pay a Champion," *Sports Illustrated* 4, no. 13 (26 March 1956): 36, 42.

61. "Hungary's Heroes in Their Hour of Staggering Strain," *Sports Illustrated* 5, no. 23 (3 December 1956): 22–23; Andre Laguerre, "Down a Road Called Liberty," *Sports Illustrated* 5, no. 25 (17 December 1956): 14, 15–16; Richard L. Neale, "Across a Free Land," *Sports Illustrated* 6, no. 14 (8 April 1957): 37. *SI* not only reported the story but facilitated the Hungarian athletes' defections. See Toby C. Rider, *Cold War Games*.

62. Bob Ottum, "The Double Romanian Twist," *Sports Illustrated* 58, no. 24 (13 June 1983): 68, 70; Bonnie D. Ford and Alyssa Roenig, "How Dianne Durham . . . Paved the Way," https://www.espn.com/olympics/story/_

/id/29469312/how-dianne-durham-bela-karolyi-first-national-champion
-paved-way-black-gymnasts. Dianne Durham missed the 1984 Olympics owing to injury, making way for Mary Lou Retton's spectacular
performance.

63. Notable exceptions who pursued sports other than track and field include
Flo Hyman (volleyball) and Anita DeFrantz (crew), both of whom were
vocal opponents of President Jimmy Carter's decision to boycott the 1980
Summer Olympic Games in Moscow. Indeed, lawyer and antiboycott
leader DeFrantz concluded the athletes' argument by pressing for attendance. See in particular Kenny Moore, "The Decision: No Go on Moscow,"
Sports Illustrated 52, no. 17 (21 April 1980): 33; Moore, "Stating 'Iron Realities,'" *Sports Illustrated* 52, no. 14 (31 March 1980): 17.

64. Kenny Moore, "They Got Off on the Right Track," *Sports Illustrated* 61,
no. 8 (13 August 1984): 79, 68; Moore, "Triumph and Tragedy in Los Angeles," *Sports Illustrated* 61, no. 9 (20 August 1984): 26.

65. Alexander Wolff, "Bonnie's Bounty," *Sports Illustrated* 80, no. 9 (7 March
1994): 43–44.

6. "A League of Their Own"

1. Katherine Cole, "Pony Tale," *Sports Illustrated for Women* 3, no. 7 (November 2001): 28.

2. Ellen Zavian, "Strings Attached," *Sports Illustrated for Women* 2, no. 3
(July/August 2000): 26; Saj Kuriakos, "Polo a No-Go," *Sports Illustrated
for Women* 4, no. 3 (May/June 2002): 28; L. Jon Wertheim, "Ladies' Day,"
Sports Illustrated 101, no. 19 (15 November 2004): 18.

3. Kelli Anderson, "5 Easy Pieces," *Sports Illustrated for Women*, no. 3 (Fall
1999): 85.

4. Larry Keith, "Not Every Bloomer Held a Girl," *Sports Illustrated* 33, no. 19
(9 November 1970): M3.

5. John Hanlon, "Queen Lizzie Plays First Base," *Sports Illustrated* 22, no. 25
(21 June 1965): E3–E4.

6. William Jeanes, "High Jinks or High Skill?," *Sports Illustrated* 68, no. 14
(4 April 1988): 134. While Engel might have regarded it as a stunt, Jackie
Mitchell, who died in 1987, was unwavering in her belief that both the contest and the outcome were on the up-and-up. See Talya Minsberg, "Overlooked No More: Jackie Mitchell, Who Fanned Two of Baseball's Greats,"
New York Times, 7 November 2018.

7. Emma Baccellieri, "Ball for All," *Sports Illustrated* 129, no. 6 (10 September
2018): 15–16. For more on the history of women in baseball, see Gai Ingham Berlage, *Women in Baseball*.

8. Ryan Hatch, "A Style of Their Own," *Sports Illustrated* 120, special issue (20 March 2014): 28. For more on the history of the AAGPBL, see Lois Browne, *Girls of Summer*; Susan E. Johnson, *When Women Played Hardball*; and Merrie A. Fidler, *The Origins and History of the All-American Girls Professional Baseball League*.

9. Hatch, "A Style of Their Own," 28; Jay Feldman, "All But Forgotten Now, A Women's Baseball League Once Flourished," *Sports Illustrated* 62, no. 23 (10 June 1985): 85, 87, 90.

10. Shelley Smith, "Remembering Their Game," *Sports Illustrated* 76, no. 26 (July 6, 1992): 80–92.

11. Martha Ackmann, *Curveball*, 123.

12. Albert Chen, "The Ace of the Place," *Sports Illustrated* 121, no. 7 (25 August 2014): 5, 8, 9. Little League amended its charter to permit girls to play baseball in 1974.

13. "Diamond Pioneer," *Sports Illustrated* 70, no. 13 (27 March 1989): 17; "Resigned," *Sports Illustrated* 74, no. 23 (17 June 1991): 98; Shelley Smith, "Ila Borders," *Sports Illustrated* 80, no. 9 (7 March 1994): 66.

14. "Pioneering 16-Year-Old Breaking Baseball Barriers for Women," SI.com, July 1, 2015, https://www.si.com/mlb/2015/07/01/ap-bbo-female-french -prospect, retrieved July 14, 2021; "All-Star Likes What He Sees of Pioneering Girl at MLB Camp," SI.com, July 3, 2015, https://www.si.com/mlb/2015/07/03 /ap-bbo-french-female-prospect, retrieved July 14, 2021. As of 2022, Mélissa Mayeux is playing softball for the University of Louisiana at Lafayette.

15. William Johnson and Nancy Williamson, "All Red, So Help Them Henna," *Sports Illustrated* 40, no. 18 (6 May 1974): 76.

16. Ibid., 88, 78.

17. Ibid., 78.

18. Ibid., 80, 78.

19. Jack McCallum, "Surely They Jest," *Sports Illustrated* 94, no. 12 (19 March 2001), https://vault.si.com/vault/2001/03/19/surely-they-jest-the-globetrotters-want -to-be-the-best-at-a-lot-more-than-clowning-around, retrieved July 12, 2021.

20. Franz Lidz, "Is This Georgia Brown?," *Sports Illustrated* 64, no. 1 (6 January 1986): 45.

21. Johnson and Williamson, "All Red, So Help Them Henna," 86.

22. Ibid., 79, 87–88.

23. Jack McCallum, "Another Try for Women's Hoops," *Sports Illustrated* 83, no. 16 (9 October 1995): 24.

24. Alexander Wolff, "A Survival Guide," *Sports Illustrated* 85, no. 26 (23 December 1996): 126, emphasis in the original.

25. Steve Lopez, "They Got Next," *Sports Illustrated* 86, no. 26 (30 June 1997): 45, 46; Michael Farber, "Dateline," *Sports Illustrated* 87, no. 16 (20 October

1997): 28; Hank Hersch and Kostya Kennedy, "They Got Less," *Sports Illustrated* 87, no. 5 (4 August 1997): 22; David Fleming, "Still the One," *Sports Illustrated* 88, no. 12 (23 March 1998): 38; Alexander Wolff, "Won for All," *Sports Illustrated* 87, no. 10 (8 September 1997): 58.

26. Richard Hoffer and Phil Taylor, "A Plucky Proposition," *Sports Illustrated* 88, no. 6 (16 February 1998): 28, 30.

27. Richard O'Brien, "WNBA Wins Star Wars," *Sports Illustrated* 88, no. 19 (11 May 1998): 22; Jeff Pearlman, "Big Time, Big Bucks," *Sports Illustrated* 89, no. 4 (27 July 1998): 38.

28. John Walters, "The Only Game in Town," *Sports Illustrated* 90, no. 24 (14 June 1999): 20; Kevin Cook, "DisABLed List," *Sports Illustrated* 90, no. 16 (19 April 1999): 26; Wolff, "Won for All," 58.

29. L. Jon Wertheim, "Fast Times in the WNBA," *Sports Illustrated* 97, no. 5 (5 August 2002): 62.

30. Alexander Wolff, "To Russia with Love," *Sports Illustrated* 109, no. 24 (15 December 2008): 60. Brittney Griner played for Yekaterinburg—also romanized as Ekaterinburg—for ten years to supplement her WNBA salary and enjoy the perks that Wolff referenced in his article. In February 2022 Griner was returning to the United States for the upcoming WNBA season when she was detained by Russian officials for attempting to smuggle illegal narcotics into the country. She has since been convicted of that charge and sentenced to nine years in a penal colony. As of September 2022, Griner is appealing her sentence.

31. Ibid., 60, 67.

32. "WNBA, Players Reach Tentative Eight-Year Labor Deal," SI.com, January 14, 2020, https://www.si.com/wnba/2020/01/14/wnba-cba-deal-salary-raise, retrieved July 12, 2021; Michael McCann, "Analyzing the WNBA's New CBA Deal and What It Means for the Future of the League," SI.com, January 14, 2020, https://www.si.com/wnba/2020/01/14/wnba-cba-labor-salary-raise-players-association, retrieved July 12, 2021.

33. McCann, "Analyzing the WNBA's New CBA Deal"; Trisha Blackmar, "How WNBA Players Are Fighting for Greater Share of League Revenue," SI.com, September 19, 2018, https://www.si.com/wnba/2018/09/19/how-wnba-players-are-fighting-more-compensation-share-league-revenue, retrieved July 12, 2021. The USWNT settled its dispute in February 2022. See Zach Koons, "USWNT, U.S. Soccer Agree to $24 Million Settlement in Equal Pay Lawsuit," February 22, 2022, https://www.si.com/soccer/2022/02/22/us-soccer-uswnt-equal-pay-lawsuit-settlement, retrieved March 13, 2022.

34. Roger Vaughan, *Golf,* 81–82.

35. Ibid., 82–83.

36. Herbert Warren Wind, "Golf and the Women," *Sports Illustrated* 5, no. 4 (23 July 1956): 29; Herbert Warren Wind, "The Big Three," *Sports Illustrated* 4, no. 9 (27 February 1956): 38–40; "Champions in Fine Plumage," *Sports Illustrated* 9, no. 25 (22 December 1958): 36–40.

37. Wind, "The Big Three," 39; William Oscar Johnson and Nancy Williamson, "Babe: Part 3," *Sports Illustrated* 43, no. 16 (20 October 1975): 48; Gwilym Brown, "Women's Golf Finds a New Zaharias," *Sports Illustrated* 15, no. 2 (10 July 1961): 18–19; Barry McDermott, "Nothing Pitty-Pat about Patty," *Sports Illustrated* 60, no. 12 (19 March 1984): 38; Jaime Diaz, "Time for the Pat and Nancy Show," *Sports Illustrated* 66, no. 6 (9 February 1987): 84.

38. Barry McDermott, "All Smiles While She Tears Up the Tour," *Sports Illustrated* 48, no. 26 (19 June 1978): 22; Frank Deford, "Nancy with the Laughing Face," *Sports Illustrated* 49, no. 2 (10 July 1978): 31, 26; Dan Jenkins, "Last Week They Held the Masters," *Sports Illustrated* 44, no. 15 (12 April 1976): 32.

39. Barry McDermott, "Birthday Present for Herself," *Sports Illustrated* 39, no. 5 (30 July 1973): 18; McDermott, "More than a Pretty Face," *Sports Illustrated* 56, no. 2 (18 January 1982): 30; Cameron Morfit, "Flirting with Success," *Sports Illustrated Women* 3, no. 7 (November 2001): 24; Laura Diaz, "My Shot," *Sports Illustrated* 95, no. 9 (3 September 2001): G14. In 1981 the LPGA had players pose as legendary Hollywood pinups. For example, Jan Stephenson reenacted Marilyn Monroe's famous scene from *The Seven Year Itch*.

40. Jaime Diaz, "Find the Golf Here?," *Sports Illustrated* 70, no. 7 (13 February 1989): 58, 59.

41. Michael Bamberger, "A Woman among Men," *Sports Illustrated* 98, no. 8 (24 February 2003): 62, 66–67.

42. Karl Taro Greenfeld, "Miss Wie It's Your Tee Time," *Sports Illustrated* 100, no. 18 (3 May 2004): 64, 68; Alexandra Fenwick, "Louise Suggs: 1923–2015," *Sports Illustrated* 123, no. 6 (17 August 2015): 16; Richard Sandomir, "Ratings Star: Tiger Woods," https://www.nytimes.com/2000/03/04/sports/networks-enthusiastically-share-ratings-star-tiger-woods.html, retrieved July 12, 2021.

43. Alan Shipnuck, "Look At Me Now," *Sports Illustrated* 120, no. 26 (30 June 2014): 48; Shipnuck, "The Case for . . . the LPGA," *Sports Illustrated* 118, no. 8 (25 February 2013): 32, emphasis in the original.

44. "2019 LPGA Schedule and Results," https://golfweek.usatoday.com/2019/08/11/golf-2019-lpga-schedule-results/, retrieved July 12, 2021; "PGA Tournament Schedule, 2018–2019," https://www.pgatour.com, retrieved, July 12, 2021; Cameron Morfit, "Flirting with Success," *Sports Illustrated Women* 3, no. 7 (November 2001): 24.

45. Jenkins, "Last Week They Held the Masters," 32; Deford, "Nancy with the Laughing Face," 26.
46. Festle, *Playing Nice*, 147–49.
47. Curry Kirkpatrick, "The Ball in Two Different Courts," *Sports Illustrated* 37, no. 26 (25 December 1972): 30, 33. King shared honors with legendary UCLA men's basketball coach John Wooden.
48. Joe Jares, "A Bell Ringer for Goolagong," *Sports Illustrated* 41, no. 18 (28 October 1974): 31; Joe Jares, "Love Conquers All," *Sports Illustrated* 42, no. 15 (14 April 1975): 24, 26, 27; Walter Bingham, "An Ambush on the Comeback Trail," *Sports Illustrated* 47, no. 20 (14 November 1977): 34. By 1977, because of additional corporate sponsorships, players earned up to $100,000 in bonuses.
49. Billie Jean King, *All In*, 209–10. Wimbledon would be the last of the major tournaments to grant equal prize money, doing so in 2007, thanks in part to Venus Williams picking up King's baton. See particularly Ava DuVernay's documentary *Venus Vs.* Although King and her fellow Slimsies challenged the male establishment, they were not necessarily successful in replacing the men in charge at most levels of sport. Over a decade later, Sarah Ballard acknowledged this issue in *Sports Illustrated*: thousands of females were playing sports, thanks to Title IX, but when it came down to those with the power in sport, men continued to "determine the athletic destinies of women." Ballard singled out the IOC, the USOC, and the NCAA, and in 2022 those organizations are still largely controlled by men. See Ballard, "The Most Powerful Woman in Sports," *Sports Illustrated* 65, no. 14 (29 September 1986): 56–57.
50. Joe Jares, "A Bloomin' Winner," *Sports Illustrated* 39, no. 3 (16 July 1973): 14; Sarah Pileggi, "The Court Belongs to Chris," *Sports Illustrated* 45, no. 25 (20–27 December 1976): 42; Joe Jares, "Extra! Chrissie Loses First Set!" *Sports Illustrated* 46, no. 15 (4 April 1977): 24. Evert was the first woman to win Sportsperson of the Year without having to share the award with a male athlete.
51. Frank Deford, "A Pair Beyond Compare," *Sports Illustrated* 64, no. 21 (26 May 1986): 72. Chris Evert married John Lloyd in 1979 and played the next seven years as Chris Evert Lloyd. After her divorce in 1986, she returned to playing under the name Chris Evert.
52. Deford, "A Pair Beyond Compare," 76; Pileggi, "Merrily She Rolls Along," *Sports Illustrated* 56, no. 21 (24 May 1982): 105; Frank Deford, "Another Big Mac Attack," *Sports Illustrated* 55, no. 13 (21 September 1981): 21; Barry McDermott, "Chrissie Got the Back of Martina's Hand," *Sports Illustrated* 57, no. 27 (27 December 1982–3 January 1983): 30–31.

53. Frank Deford, "The Day Chrissie Reclaimed Paris," *Sports Illustrated* 62, no. 24 (17 June 1985): 28, 33, 37; Deford, "A Pair Beyond Compare," 80, 82, 84. For more on the Evert/Navratilova rivalry, see Johnette Howard, *The Rivals*.

54. Martina Navratilova, "A Great Friend and Foe," *Sports Illustrated* 71, no. 9 (28 August 1989): 88; Chris Evert and Curry Kirkpatrick, "'Tennis Was My Showcase,'" *Sports Illustrated* 71, no. 9 (28 August 1989): 78.

55. Bruce Newman, "Talk about Net Gains," *Sports Illustrated* 68, no. 18 (2 May 1988): 54; S. L. Price, "Strokes of Genius," *Sports Illustrated* 93, no. 11 (18 September 2000): 53. As of September 2022, Serena Williams had retired with twenty-three Grand Slam tournament singles titles.

56. L. Jon Wertheim, "The Two and Only," *Sports Illustrated* 96, no. 25 (17 June 2002): 62; Wertheim, "Serena Supreme," *Sports Illustrated* 113, no. 1 (12 July 2010): 37.

57. Deford, "Nancy with the Laughing Face," 31.

58. "Indian Wells CEO: Women's Tennis Players Ride the Coattails of Men," SI .com, March 20, 2016, https://www.si.com/tennis/2016/03/20/indian-wells -ceo-raymond-moore-wta-comments, retrieved July 14, 2021.

59. "Novak Djokovic Questions Whether Women Deserve Equal Pay in Tennis," https://www.espn.com/tennis/story/_/id/15031425/novak-djokovic -questions-whether-women-deserve-equal-pay-tennis, retrieved July 14, 2021; Ben Rothenberg, "Djokovic and Other Top Men Are Creating a Players' Association," https://www.nytimes.com/2020/08/28/sports/tennis /tennis-union-men-djokovic.html, retrieved July 14, 2021. At the four Grand Slam tournaments, women play best-of-three sets while the men play best-of-five sets; the format for most other tournaments is best-of-three sets for both men and women.

60. Adam Zagoria, "Summer Job, with Benefits," *Sports Illustrated Women* 4, no. 3 (May/June 2002): 27–28; Grant Wahl, "Mia's Excellent Adventure," *Sports Illustrated for Women* 3, no. 2 (March/April 2001): 65–68; Wahl, "This Sun Shines Bright," *Sports Illustrated for Women* 3, no. 2 (March/ April 2001): 69. International leagues in Denmark and France have existed since the early 1970s.

61. Wahl, "Mia's Excellent Adventure," 66; "The Pioneers," *Sports Illustrated for Women* 3, no. 2 (March/April 2001): 67–68; Grant Wahl, "Battle of the Sexes," *Sports Illustrated* 92, no. 18 (1 May 2000): 38; "WUSA Report," *Sports Illustrated for Women* 4, no. 7 (November 2002): 32; Grant Wahl, "Strong Finishing Kick," *Sports Illustrated* 95, no. 9 (3 September 2001): 50, 52; Caitlin Murray, *The National Team*, 82–83.

62. Kesa Dillon, "Scoring the Freshman League," *Sports Illustrated for Women* 3, no. 5 (September 2001): 25; Michael Silver, "Playing for Keeps," *Sports*

Illustrated for Women 3, no. 4 (July/August 2001): 86; "Folded," *Sports Illustrated* 99, no. 11 (22 September 2003): 20.

63. Murray, *The National Team,* 146.

64. Grant Wahl, "In Need of a Save," *Sports Illustrated* 115, no. 9 (5 September 2011): 38; Wahl, "Flash Drive," *Sports Illustrated* 114, no. 19 (9 May 2011): 32; "Suspended," *Sports Illustrated* 116, no. 5 (6 February 2012): 15.

65. "Announced," *Sports Illustrated* 117, no. 7 (20 August 2012): 24; Grant Wahl, "Alex in Wonderland," *Sports Illustrated* 118, no. 26 (24 June 2013): 54, 53.

66. Wahl, "Alex in Wonderland," 54.

67. Wolff, "A Survival Guide," 126; Wahl, "Alex in Wonderland," 54, 56; Grant Wahl, "Guts and Glory," *Sports Illustrated* 115, no. 3 (25 July 2011): 36, 41, emphasis in the original. At the end of U.S.-Japan final in the 2011 women's World Cup, Twitter was logging 7,196 posts per second, an all-time high and a figure that dwarfed the Super Bowl's feed.

68. Grant Wahl, "Here We Grow," *Sports Illustrated* 123, no. 2 (20 July 2015): 46.

69. Michael Rosenberg, "Uniformly Bounded," *Sports Illustrated* 123, no. 2 (20 July 2015): 72.

70. In 2022 the NWSL consisted of three divisions, each with four teams.

71. Wertheim, "Ladies' Day," 18–19.

72. Bil Gilbert and Nancy Williamson, "Sport Is Unfair to Women," *Sports Illustrated* 38, no. 21 (28 May 1973): 95–96.

73. Kate Fagan, "Don't Look Away," *Sports Illustrated* 132, no. 5 (June 2021): 37, 36, 40, 44.

74. Ibid., 39, 38.

75. Ibid., 37.

CONCLUSION

1. Amy Nutt, "Hullabaloo over Hoops," *Sports Illustrated* 78, no. 12 (22 March 1993): 6; Senda Berenson, ed., *Line Basket Ball or Basket Ball for Women.* While Berenson's "Girls' rules" dominated East Coast women's basketball, females out west played full-court, five-on-five basketball.

2. *Sports Illustrated* 63, no. 23 (20 November 1985): cover. *SI* featured Santa Clara's Ken Sears on its December 20, 1954, cover. Female basketball coaches had also appeared on the cover of *Sports Illustrated.* Pat Summit, legendary coach of the University of Tennessee women's program, appeared on the March 2, 1998, issue as "The Wizard of Knoxville," and then shared sportsperson of the year honors with coach of the Duke men's basketball team, Mike Krzyzewski, on November 20, 2011.

3. Coached by the legendary John Wooden, UCLA's winning streak netted seven covers. UConn's 2008–10 record was to be outdone only by itself

when it won 111 games from 2014 to 2016. In both cases the UConn women set historic winning streaks and won back-to-back national titles.

4. Jere Longman, "1998 N.C.A.A. Tournament," https://www.nytimes.com /1998/03/26/sports/1998-ncaa-tournament-tennessee-redefining-the -women-s-game.html, retrieved July 15, 2021.

5. On *Sports Illustrated*'s fiftieth anniversary, the magazine devoted an entire section to the "'The Beauties," a retrospective in which swimsuit model Marissa Miller re-created ten of the most iconic Swimsuit Issue poses "from *SI*'s most illustrious—and sometimes notorious—spin-off." See "Looking Back," *Sports Illustrated* 101, no. 12 (27 September 2004): 11, 176.

6. Bill Colson, "To Our Readers," *Sports Illustrated* 86, no. 7 (21 February 1997): 8.

7. Austin Murphy, "Steffi," *Sports Illustrated* 86, no. 7 (21 February 1997): 179, 181, 186, 190.

8. "Bikini Mania," *Sports Illustrated* 86, no. 7 (21 February 1997): 245; "Brenna Huckaby on Becoming the First Paralympian to Appear in SI Swimsuit," SI.com, February 13, 2018, https://swimsuit.si.com/swimnews/brenna -huckaby-para-snowboarder-si-swimsuit-2018, retrieved, May 15, 2022. Beach volleyball players Gabrielle Reece, Karri Poppinga, Holly McPeak, Linda Hanley, and Patty Dodd also appeared in the February 1997 issue in bikinis for a story on "what role sex appeal will play in expanding the popularity of their sport." See Michael Silver, "Beauty and the Beach," *Sports Illustrated* 86, no. 7 (21 February 1997): 216–22+.

9. Xandria James, "Megan Rapinoe Proudly Poses as the First Openly Gay Woman in the *SI* Swimsuit Issue," May 8, 2019, https://swimsuit.si.com /swimnews/megan-rapinoe-first-openly-gay-woman-si-swimsuit-issue -us-womens-soccer, retrieved March 9, 2022; "Squad Goals," *Sports Illustrated* 130, nos. 11/12 (13 May 2019): 107.

10. Dorothy J. Gentry, "A League of Its Own," *Sports Illustrated* (Swimsuit 2022): 86. Bird's use of the acronym LGBTQIA2+ is inclusive of those who identify as lesbian, gay, bisexual, trans, queer/questioning, intersex, asexual, two-spirited, with the plus sign indicating additional identities not specifically included in the acronym.

11. Frankie de la Cretaz, "Opinion," https://www.cnn.com/2022/05/19/opinions /women-basketball-wnba-sports-illustrated-swimsuit-cretaz/index.html, retrieved May 19, 2022.

12. MJ Day, "Beauty Knows No Boundaries," *Sports Illustrated* 131, nos. 8/9 (1–2 August 2020): 7; Day, "Editor's Letter," *Sports Illustrated* 132, no. 8 (August 2021): 4.

13. Franz Lidz, "A Punch Judy Show," *Sports Illustrated* 96, no. 9 (26 February 2002): 176; Rick Reilly, "Model Athletes," *Sports Illustrated* 96, no. 9 (26 February 2002): 228.

14. Reilly, "Model Athletes," 228.

15. "Naomi Fierce," *Sports Illustrated* 132, no. 8 (August 2021): 42.

16. Peter King, "Concussions: The Hits That Are Changing Football," *Sports Illustrated* 113, no. 16 (1 November 2010): 34–38; Farrell Evans, "Early Warning," *Sports Illustrated* 113, no. 16 (1 November 2010): 47; Terry McDonell, "Staggered by the Impact," *Sports Illustrated* 113, no. 16 (1 November 2010): 14–15; David Epstein, "The Damage Done," *Sports Illustrated* 113, no. 16 (1 November 2010): 42; Ben Reiter, "Brain Trust," *Sports Illustrated* 123, no. 25 (28 December 2015): 29–31; Michael Farber, "The Worst Case," *Sports Illustrated* 81, no. 25 (19 December 1994): 39, 40.

17. Luke M. Gessel, Sarah K. Fields, Christy L. Collins, Randall W. Dick, and R. Dawn Comstock, "Concussions among United States High School and Collegiate Athletes."

18. Lynda Truman Ryan, "Swimsuit Models or Victim Stories."

19. "Olympic Flames," *Sports Illustrated* 102, no. 7 (18 February 2005): 9, 163, 169; "Venus," *Sports Illustrated* 102, no. 7 (18 February 2005): 13, 208.

20. "Brush with Stardom," *Sports Illustrated* 116, no. 7 (17 February 2012): 111; Dan Patrick, "Dan Patrick . . . Kicks It with Alex Morgan," *Sports Illustrated* 116, no. 7 (17 February 2012): 32.

21. L. Jon Wertheim, "Ladies' Day," *Sports Illustrated* 101, no. 19 (15 November 2004): 19.

22. "All That Glitters Is Gold," *Sports Illustrated* 120, no. 6 (21 February 2014): 17.

23. Christian Stone, "Editor's Letter," *Sports Illustrated* 120, no. 6 (21 February 2014): 57.

24. Steffi Graf was the first athlete to appear in the Swimsuit Issue in 1997, but she did not earn a cover turn.

25. MJ Day, "Editor's Letter," *Sports Illustrated* (Winter 2016): 19; Kim and Sagas, "Athletic or Sexy?," 127; Pam R. Sailors and Charlene Weaving, "Foucault and the Glamazon," 432.

26. Bil Gilbert and Nancy Williamson, "Sport Is Unfair to Women," *Sports Illustrated* 38, no. 21 (28 May 1973): 95, 97, 90, 92, 94.

27. Nell McShane Wulfhart, *The Great Stewardess Rebellion*, 170, 160.

28. Jill Lieber, "The Woman Warrior," *Sports Illustrated* 70, no. 6 (February 1989): 133, 132, 134.

29. "The Next Frontiers," *Sports Illustrated* 133, no. 5 (June 2022): 56–63.

BIBLIOGRAPHY

PRIMARY SOURCES

SI.com, 2001–present
Sports Illustrated, August 1954–June 2022
Sports Illustrated for Women, Spring 1999–July/August 2001
Sports Illustrated Swimsuit Issue, 1964–2022
Sports Illustrated Women, September 2001–December/January 2003
Sports Illustrated Women/Sport, Spring–Fall 1997

SECONDARY SOURCES

"2019 LPGA Schedule and Results." usatoday.com.

Abad-Santos, Alexander. "Serena Williams Defends Taylor Townsend: 'Everyone Deserves to Play.'" *Atlantic,* 11 September 2012, theatlantic.com.

Ackmann, Martha. *Curveball: The Remarkable Story of Toni Stone, the First Woman to Play Professional Baseball in the Negro League.* Chicago: Lawrence Hill Books, 2010.

Acosta, R. Vivian, and Linda Jean Carpenter. "Women in Intercollegiate Sport: A Longitudinal, National Study. Thirty Seven year Update, 1977–2014." acostacarpenter.org, 2014.

Adams, David Wallace. *Education for Extinction: American Indians and the Boarding School Experience, 1875–1928,* 2nd ed. Lawrence: University of Kansas Press, 2020.

"All-American Girls Professional Baseball League Rules of Conduct." aagpbl.org.

Allers, Kimberly Seals. "Black Women Have Never Had the Privilege of Rage." *HuffPost,* 14 October 2018, huffpost.com.

Ariail, Cat M. "'One of the Greatest Ambassadors That the United States Has Ever Sent Abroad': Wilma Rudolph, American Athletic Icon for the Cold War and the Civil Rights Movement." In *Defending the American Way of Life: Sport, Culture, and the Cold War,* edited by Toby C. Rider and Kevin B. Witherspoon, 141–54. Fayetteville: University of Arkansas Press, 2018.

———. *Passing the Baton: Black Women Track Stars and American Identity.* Urbana: University of Illinois Press, 2020.

Arnold, Jennifer, and Senain Kheshigi, directors. *The Diplomat.* In the series *Nine for IX.* ESPN Films, 2013.

Ashendouek, Jenna. "Title IX: A Milestone for Women in Sports, but Unfulfilled Promise for Black Women." msmagazine.com, 14 July 2020.

Banet-Weiser, Sarah. "Hoop Dreams: Professional Basketball and the Politics of Race and Gender." *Journal of Sport and Social Issues* 23 (November 1999): 403–20.

Baughman, Cynthia, ed. *Women on Ice: Feminist Responses to the Tonya Harding/Nancy Kerrigan Spectacle.* New York: Routledge, 1995.

Beauvoir, Simone de. *The Second Sex.* New York: Vintage Books, 1952.

Belkin, Lisa. "A Mother and a Champion." *New York Times,* 14 September 2009, nytimes.com.

Bennett, Roberta S., K. Gail Whitaker, Nina Jo Woolley Smith, and Anne Sablove. "Changing the Rules of the Game: Reflections Toward a Feminist of Sport." *Women's Studies International Forum* 10 (1987): 369–79.

Berenson, Senda, ed. *Line Basket Ball or Basket Ball for Women.* New York: American Sports Publishing Company, 1901.

Berlage, Gai Ingham. *Women In Baseball: The Forgotten History.* Westport, CT: Praeger, 1994.

Berman, Marc. "Tennis Hoax Is 'Stunning—Mag's Spoof over the Line, Officials Cry." *NY Post* 3 September 2002.

Berryman, Jack W. "Preface." *Journal of Sport History* 10 (Spring 1983): 5–6.

———. "The Tenuous Attempts of Americans to 'Catch-up with John Bull': Specialty Magazines and Sporting Journalism, 1800–1835." *Canadian Journal of History of Sport and Physical Education* 10 (May 1979): 33–61.

Berryman, Jack W., and Joann Brislin. "The Ladies' Department of the *American Farmer,* 1824–1830: A Locus for the Advocacy of Family Health and Exercise." In *Her Story in Sport: A Historical Anthology of Women in Sports,* edited by Reet Howell, 57–59. West Point, NY: Leisure Press, 1982.

Bidwell, Allie. "U. of Southern California Settles Title IX Complaint over Women's Crew." *Chronicle of Higher Education* 10 (18 January 2013), chronicle.com.

Biggs, Mary. Review of *Femininity,* by Susan Brownmiller. *Library Journal,* 1 February 1984, 189.

Birrell, Susan, and Nancy Theberge. "Ideological Control of Women in Sport." In *Women and Sport: Interdisciplinary Perspectives,* edited by D. Margaret Costa and Sharon R. Guthrie, 350–60. Champaign, IL: Human Kinetics, 1994.

Bishop, Ronald. "Missing in Action: Feature Coverage of Women's Sport in *Sports Illustrated.*" *Journal of Sport and Social Issues* 27 (May 2003): 184–94.

Bjørnseth, Ingunn, and Attila Szabo. "Sexual Violence Against Children in Sports and Exercise: A Systematic Literature Review." *Journal of Child Sexual Abuse* 27 (2018): 365–85.

"The Body Issue." ESPN.com.

Bordo, Susan. *Unbearable Weight: Feminism, Western Culture, and the Body.* Berkeley: University of California Press, 1993, 2003.

Boutilier, Mary A., and Lucinda SanGiovanni. *The Sporting Woman.* Champaign, IL: Human Kinetics, 1983.

Boyle, Kaitlin M., and Kimberly B. Rogers. "Beyond the Rape 'Victim'-'Survivor' Binary: How Race, Gender, and Identity Processes Interact to Shape Distress." *Sociological Forum* 35 (June 2020): 323–24.

Boyle, Lex. "Flexing the Tensions of Female Muscularity: How Female Bodybuilders Negotiate Normative Femininity in Competitive Bodybuilding." *Women's Studies Quarterly* 33 (Spring/Summer 2005): 134–49.

Brandt, Mandie, and Adelia Carstens. "The Discourse of the Male Gaze: A Critical Analysis of the Feature Section 'The Beauty of Sport' in *SA Sports Illustrated.*" *South African Linguistics and Applied Language Studies* 23, no. 3 (2005): 233–43.

Bredholt, Rebecca. "Most-Read Magazines in America Change Little from Last Year." *Cision,* 25 July 2012.

Brennan, Christine. "Critics Take Chinese Swimmers to Task." *Washington Post,* 13 September 1994.

Brown, Ashley. "'Uncomplimentary Things': Tennis Player Althea Gibson, Sexism, Homophobia, and Anti-Queerness in the Black Media." *Journal of African American History* 106, no. 2 (Spring 2021): 249–77.

Browne, Lois. *Girls of Summer: The Real Story of the All-American Girls Professional Baseball League.* Toronto: HarperCollins, 1992.

Brownmiller, Susan. *Femininity.* New York: Fawcett Columbine, 1984.

Bruce, Toni, and Emma Wensing. "'She's Not One of Us': Cathy Freeman and the Place of Aboriginal People in Australian National Culture." *Australian Aboriginal Studies* 2 (2009): 90–100.

Bruening, Jennifer E. "Gender and Racial Analysis in Sport: Are All the Women White and All the Blacks Men?" *Quest* 57 (2005): 330–49.

Brumberg, Joan Jacobs. *Fasting Girls: The History of Anorexia Nervosa.* New York: Vintage Books, 1988.

Cahn, Susan. *Coming On Strong: Gender and Sexuality in Women's Sport.* Toronto: Free Press, 1994, 2015.

———. "Crushes, Competition, and Closets: The Emergence of Homophobia in Women's Physical Education." In *Women, Sport and Culture,* edited by Susan Birrell and Cheryl L. Cole, 327–39. Champaign, IL: Human Kinetics, 1994.

———. "'So Far Back in the Closet We Can't Even See the Keyhole': Lesbianism, Homophobia, and Sexual Politics in Collegiate Women's Athletics." In *The New Lesbian Studies: Into the Twenty-First Century,* edited by Bonnie Zimmerman and Toni A. H. Morrison, 215–22. New York: Feminist Press, 1996.

Captain, Gwendolyn. "Enter Ladies and Gentlemen of Color: Gender, Sport, and the Ideal of African American Manhood and Womanhood During the Late Nineteenth and Early Twentieth Centuries." *Journal of Sport History* 18, no. 1 (Spring 1991): 81–102.

Carr, David. "Time Inc. Is Closing *Sports Illustrated Women*," *New York Times*, 17 October 2022, C7.

Cavanagh, Sheila L., and Heather Sykes. "Transsexual Bodies at the Olympics: The International Olympic Committee's Policy on Transsexual Athletes at the 2004 Athens Summer Games." *Body & Society* 12, no. 3 (2006): 75–103.

Cayleff, Susan E. *Babe: The Life and Legend of Babe Didrikson Zaharias.* Urbana: University of Illinois Press, 1995.

Cervin, Georgia. *Degrees of Difficulty: How Women's Gymnastics Rose to Prominence and Fell from Grace.* Urbana: University of Illinois Press, 2021.

Chauncey, George. *Gay New York: Gender, Urban Culture, and the Making of the Gay Male World, 1890–1940.* New York: Basic Books, 1994.

"Chasing Equity: The Triumphs, Challenges, and Opportunities in Sports for Girls and Women." *Women's Sports Foundation* (2020): 33.

Coakley, Jay. *Sports in Society: Issues and Controversies.* New York: McGraw Hill, 2009.

Cohen, Bonni, and John Shenk, directors. *Athlete A.* Actual Films, 2020.

Cohen, Greta L., ed. *Women in Sport: Issues and Controversies.* Newbury Park: Sage Publications, 1993.

Combahee River Collective. *The Combahee River Collective Statement.* Albany: Kitchen Table, 1986.

Cooper, Brittney. *Eloquent Rage: A Black Feminist Discovers Her Superpower.* New York: St. Martin's Press, 2018.

Costa, D. Margaret, and Sharon R. Guthrie, eds. *Women and Sport: Interdisciplinary Perspectives.* Champaign, IL: Human Kinetics, 1994.

Crary, David. "Trans Athletes Make Great Gains, Yet Resentment Still Flares." *AP News,* 23 February 2019.

Creedon, Pamela. *Women, Media and Sport: Challenging Gender Values.* Thousand Oaks: Sage Publications, 1994.

Crenshaw, Kimberlé. "Demarginalizing the Intersection of Race and Sex: A Black Feminist Critique of Antidiscrimination Doctrine, Feminist Theory and Antiracist Politics." *University of Chicago Legal Forum*, volume 1989, issue 1, article 8, 139–67.

———. "Mapping the Margins: Intersectionality, Identity Politics, and Violence Against Women of Color." *Stanford Law Review* 43, no. 6 (July 1991): 1241–99.

Daddario, Gina. "Swimming Against the Tide: *Sports Illustrated*'s Imagery of Female Athletes in a Swimsuit World." *Women's Studies in Communication* 15 (1992): 49–64.

Davis, Amira Rose. "Olympic Icon Flo Jo Raced to the Top and Took Us with Her." *Zora*, 26 February 2020.

Davis, Laurel, R. *The Swimsuit Issue and Sport: Hegemonic Masculinity in* Sports Illustrated. New York: State University of New York Press, 1997.

De la Cretaz, Britni. "An Audience of Athletes: The Rise and Fall of Feminist Sports." *Longreads,* May 2019.

De la Cretaz, Frankie. "Opinion: Sports Illustrated's Swimsuit Issue Is a Step Back in Time. And Not in a Good Way." CNN.com, 19 May 2022.

Deford, Frank. "The Bare Facts." In *Sports Illustrated Knockouts: Five Decades of Swimsuit Photography,* edited by Steve Hoffman and Rick Reilly, 16–28. New York: Time, Inc., 2001.

Dichter, Heather L., and Andrew L. Johns, eds. *Diplomatic Games: Sport, State-craft, and International Relations since 1945.* Lexington: University Press of Kentucky, 2014.

Donegan, Lawrence. "Revealed: The Curse of the Front Page." *Guardian,* 19 January 2002.

Dou, Eva, and Alicia Chen. "Chinese Tennis Star's Sexual Assault Allegation Against Former Top Leader Prompts Online Blackout." *Washington Post,* 2 November 2021.

Douglas, Susan J. *The Rise of Enlightened Sexism: How Pop Culture Took Us from Girl Power to Girls Gone Wild.* New York: St. Martin's Griffin, 2010.

———. *Where the Girls Are: Growing Up Female with the Mass Media.* New York: Three Rivers Press, 1994.

Dowling, Colette. *The Frailty Myth: Women Approaching Physical Equality.* New York: Random House, 2000.

Dudziak, Mary L. *Cold War Civil Rights: Race and the Image of American Democracy.* Princeton: Princeton University Press, 2011.

Duggan, Lisa. "Making It Perfectly Queer," *Socialist Review* 22, no. 1 (March 1992).

Dulong, Jessica. "Out in the Field." *The Advocate,* 19 February 2002.

Duncan, Margaret Carlisle. "Sports Photographs and Sexual Difference: Images of Women and Men in the 1984 and 1988 Olympic Games." *Sociology of Sport Journal* 7 (1990): 22–43.

DuVernay, Ava, director. *Venus Vs.* In the series *Nine for IX.* ESPN Films, 2013.

Echo Media: Print Media Experts. "Sports Illustrated." echo-media.com, 2009.

Edgecomb, Sean. "Inharmonious Pursuits: Performing Racism at the Olympic Games." *Popular Entertainment Studies* 2 (September 2011): 43–58.

Edwards, Harry. *The Revolt of the Black Athlete.* New York: Free Press, 1969.

Ennis, Dawn. "Martina Navratilova on Trans Athletes: 'Letting Men Compete as Women Is Unfair.'" outsports.com, 17 February 2019.

Faderman, Lillian. *Odd Girls and Twilight Lovers: A History of Lesbian Life in Twentieth-Century America.* New York: Columbia University Press, 1991.

Fagan, Kate, and Luke Cyphers. "Five Myths about Title IX." *ESPNW,* 23 March 2012.

Faludi, Susan. *Backlash: The Undeclared War Against American Women.* New York: Crown, 1991.

Festle, Mary Jo. *Playing Nice: Politics and Apologies in Women's Sports.* New York: Columbia University Press, 1996.

Fidler, Merrie A. *The Origins and History of the All-American Girls Professional Baseball League.* Jefferson, NC: McFarland, 2006.

Filipovic, Jill. "Elite Male Athletes Play in Shorts and Tank Tops, Women Basically in Bikinis." CNN.com, 17 July 2021.

Fink, Janet S., and Linda Jean Kensicki. "An Imperceptible Difference: Visual and Textual Constructions of Femininity in *Sports Illustrated* and *Sports Illustrated for Women.*" *Mass Communication and Society* 5 (2002): 317–39.

Flitterman-Lewis, Sandy. "Tales of the Ice Princess and the Trash Queen: Cultural Fictions and the Production of 'Women.'" In *Women on Ice: Feminist Responses to the Tonya Harding/Nancy Kerrigan Spectacle,* edited by Cynthia Baughman, 165–81. New York: Routledge, 1995.

Ford, Bonnie D., and Alyssa Roenig. "How Dianne Durham, Bela Karolyi's First National Champion, Paved the Way for Black Gymnasts." ESPN.com, 18 July 2020.

Friedman, Danielle. *Let's Get Physical: How Women Discovered Exercise and Reshaped the World.* New York: G. P. Putnam's Sons, 2022.

Friedman, Vanessa. "Who Decides What a Champion Should Wear?" *New York Times,* 29 July 2021.

Galst, Liz. "The Sports Closet." *Ms.,* September/October 1998, 74–78.

Gerber, Ellen, Jan Felshin, Pearl Berlin, and Waneen Wyrick. *The American Woman in Sport.* Reading, MA: Addison Wesley, 1974.

Gerbner, George, and Larry Gross. "Living with Television: The Violence Profile." *Journal of Communications* 26 (Spring 1976): 172–99.

Germain, Atahabih. "'I Was Fat, and I Was Black, So They Took Away My Dream': Taylor Townsend Claims U.S. Tennis Association Nearly Ended Her Career Because of Her Weight." *Atlanta Black Star,* 9 June 2021.

Gessel, Luke M., Sarah K. Fields, Christy L. Collins, Randall W. Dick, and R. Dawn Comstock. "Concussions among United States High School and Collegiate Athletes." *Journal of Athletic Training* 42 (October–December 2007): 495–503.

Gilman, Charlotte Perkins. *Herland.* New York: Pantheon Books, 1979.

Graham, Mark. "Monica Seles." *Tennis365,* 14 February 2018.

Granderson, LZ. "Three-Time MVP 'Tired of Having to Hide My Feelings.'" *ESPN The Magazine*, 25 October 2005.

Griffin, Nicholas. *Ping-Pong Diplomacy: The Secret History Behind the Game That Changed the World*. New York: Skyhorse, 2014.

Griffin, Pat. "Homophobia in Women's Sports: The Fear That Divides Us." In *Women in Sport: Issues and Controversies*, edited by Greta L. Cohen, 193–203. Newbury Park: Sage, 1993.

———. *Pat Griffin's LGBT Sport Blog*. 3 July 2012.

———. *Strong Women, Deep Closets: Lesbians and Homophobia in Sport*. Champaign, IL: Human Kinetics, 1998.

Griffin, Pat, and Helen Carroll. "On the Team: Equal Opportunity for Transgender Student Athletes." nclrights.org, 2010.

———. "NCAA Inclusion of Transgender Student-Athletes." ncaa.org, 2011.

Gross, Larry. *Up from Invisibility: Lesbians, Gay Men, and the Media in America*. New York: Columbia University Press, 2001.

Grundy, Pamela, and Susan Shackelford. *Shattering the Glass: The Remarkable History of Women's Basketball*. Chapel Hill: University of North Carolina Press, 2005.

Guthrie, Sharon. "Homophobia: Its Impact on Women in Sport and Physical Education." MA thesis, California State University at Long Beach, 1982.

Hardin, Marie, Susan Lynn, and Kristie Walsdorf. "Challenge and Conformity on 'Contested Terrain': Images of Women in Four Women's Sport/Fitness Magazines." *Sex Roles* 53, nos. 1/2 (July 2005): 105–17.

Harding, Kate. "Victim." In *Pretty Bitches*, edited by Lizzie Skurnick, 91–102. New York: Seal, 2020.

Hargreaves, Jennifer. *Heroines of Sport: The Politics of Difference and Identity*. New York: Routledge, 2000.

———. *Sporting Females: Critical Issues in the History and Sociology of Women's Sport*. New York: Routledge, 1994.

Harold, Zack. "Jackie Mitchell Couldn't Win." *Lapham's Quarterly*, 28 March 2018.

Harris, John, and Barbara Humberstone. "Sport, Gender and International Relations." In *Sport and International Relations: An Emerging Relationship*, edited by Roger Levermore and Adrian Budd, 48–61. New York: Routledge, 2004.

"Her Life Depends On It III & Girls and Women of Color." *Women's Sports Foundation*, 21 January 2016.

Hill Collins, Patricia. *Black Sexual Politics: African Americans, Gender and the New Racism*. New York: Routledge, 2005.

Hoffman, Steve, and Rick Reilly, eds. *Sports Illustrated Knockouts: Five Decades of Swimsuit Photography*. New York: Time Inc., 2001.

Hong, Fan. *Footbinding, Feminism and Freedom: The Liberation of Women's Bodies in Modern China*. London: Frank Cass, 1997.

Horowitz, Eli. "Welcome to the WNBA: Good Luck Finding a Job." *New York Times*, 5 May 2018.

Howard, Johnette. *The Rivals: Chris Evert vs. Martina Navratilova: Their Epic Duels and Extraordinary Friendship*. New York; Crown, 2005.

Howell, Reet, ed. *Her Story in Sport: A Historical Anthology of Women in Sports*. West Point, NY: Leisure Press, 1982.

Hunt, Thomas C. *Drug Games: The International Olympic Committee and the Politics of Doping, 1960–2008*. Austin: University of Texas Press, 2011.

International Handball Federation. "IX. Rules of the Game: Beach Handball." www.ihf.info, 8 July 2014.

International Olympic Committee. "IOC Approves Consensus with Regard to Athletes Who Have Changed Sex." olympics.com, 17 May 2004.

Jenkins, Wesley. "Hundreds of Colleges May Be Out of Compliance with Title IX. Here's Why." *Chronicle of Higher Education* 66 (1 November 2019).

Jinxia, Dong. *Women, Sport and Society in Modern China: Holding Up More than Half the Sky*. London: Frank Cass, 2003.

Johnson, Susan E. *When Women Played Hardball*. Seattle: Seal Press, 1994.

Joncheray, Hélène, and Rémi Richard. "Disabled Sportswomen and Gender Construction in Powerchair Football." *International Review for the Sociology of Sport*, 2015, 1–21.

Jones, Maya. "New Study Examines History of Black Women Fighting to be Respected as Athletes." *Andscape*, 25 June 2018.

Kane, Mary Jo. "Media Coverage of the Female Athlete before, during, and after Title IX: *Sports Illustrated* Revisited." *Journal of Sport Management* 2 (July 1988): 87–99.

Karkazis, Katrina, and Rebecca Jordan-Young. "The Treatment of Caster Semenya Shows Athletics' Bias Against Women of Colour." *Guardian*, 26 April 2018.

Kim, Kayoung, and Michael Sagas. "Athletic or Sexy? A Comparison of Female Athletes and Fashion Models in *Sports Illustrated* Swimsuit Issues." *Gender Issues* 31, no. 2 (June 2014): 123–41.

Kim, Kayoung, Michael Sagas, and Nerfertiti A. Walker. "Replacing Athleticism with Sexuality: Athlete Models in *Sports Illustrated* Swimsuit Issues." *International Journal of Sport Communication* 4, no. 2 (June 2011): 148–62.

King, Billie Jean. *All In: An Autobiography*. New York: Alfred A. Knopf, 2021.

Lamb, Sharon. *The Trouble with Blame: Victims, Perpetrators, and Responsibility*. Cambridge, MA: Harvard University Press, 1996.

Lansbury, Jennifer H. *A Spectacular Leap: Black Women Athletes in Twentieth-Century America*. Fayetteville: University of Arkansas Press, 2014.

Lazdowski, Paul. "7-footers: 17-percent Chance of Playing in NBA." *Boston Globe,* 9 March 2014.

Lehmann-Haupt, Christopher. "Book of the Times." *New York Times,* 12 January 1984.

Lenskyj, Helen. "Female Sexuality and Women's Sport." *Women's Studies International Forum* 10 (1987): 381–86.

———. *Out of Bounds: Women, Sport and Sexuality.* Toronto: Women's Press, 1986.

Levermore, Roger, and Adrian Budd, eds. *Sport and International Relations: An Emerging Relationship.* New York: Routledge, 2004.

Levy, Ariel. "Either/Or: Sports, Sex, and the Case of Caster Semenya." *New Yorker,* 19 November 2009.

Liberti, Rita, and Maureen M. Smith. *(Re)Presenting Wilma Rudolph.* Syracuse, NY: Syracuse University Press, 2015.

Lichtenstein, Grace. "Net Profits." In *Nike Is a Goddess: The History of Women in Sports,* edited by Lissa Smith, 57–77. New York: Atlantic Monthly Press, 1998.

Lipsyte, Robert. "Magazine Explores Its Feminine Side." *New York Times,* 13 April 1997, sec. 8.

Longman, Jere. "1998 N.C.A.A. Tournament; Tennessee Redefining the Women's Game." *New York Times,* 26 March 1998.

———. *The Girls of Summer.* New York: HarperCollins, 2000.

Lorde, Audre. *Sister Outsider: Essays and Speeches.* New York: Crossing Press, 2007.

Lowy, Richard. "Yuppie Racism: Race Relations in the 1980s." *Journal of Black Studies* 21, no. 4 (June 1991): 445–46.

Lumpkin, Angela, and Linda D. Williams. "An Analysis of *Sports Illustrated* Feature Articles, 1954–1987." *Sociology of Sport Journal* 8 (March 1991): 16–32.

MacCambridge, Michael. *The Franchise: A History of* Sports *Illustrated.* New York: Hyperion, 1997.

———. "Who Can Explain the Athletic Heart?" *The Ringer,* 13 April 2018.

Marcus, Eric. *Making Gay History: The Half-Century Fight for Lesbian and Gay Equal Rights.* New York: Perennial, 2002.

Marshall, Megan. "Our Bodies, Our Burdens." *New Republic,* 13 February 1984.

Martin, Adam, and Mary G. McDonald. "Covering Women's Sport? An Analysis of *Sports Illustrated* Covers from 1987–2009 and *ESPN The Magazine* Covers from 1998–2009." *Graduate Journal of Sport, Exercise & Physical Education Research* 1 (2012): 81–97.

Mazzio, Mary, director. *A Hero for Daisy.* 50 Eggs Films, 1999.

Messner, Michael. "Sports and Male Domination: The Female Athlete as Contested Ideological Terrain," *Sociology of Sport Journal* 5 (1988): 197–211.

———. *Taking the Field: Women, Men and Sports.* Minneapolis: University of Minnesota Press, 2002.

Minsberg, Talya. "Overlooked No More: Jackie Mitchell, Who Fanned Two of Baseball's Greats." *New York Times,* 7 November 2018.

Moore, Louis. *We Will Win the Day: The Civil Rights Movement, the Black Athlete, and the Quest for Equality.* Lexington: University Press of Kentucky, 2017, 2021.

Moore, Orwell, and Tammy Moore Harrison, with Howard Rankin. *Breaking the Press: The Incredible Story of the All American Red Heads.* Self-published, 2016.

Moston, Stephen, Brendan Hutchinson, and Terry Engelberg. "Dying to Win? The Goldman Dilemma in Legend and Fact." *International Journal of Sport Communication* 10 (2017): 429–43.

Mulvey, Laura. "Visual Pleasure and Narrative Cinema." In *Film Theory and Criticism: Introductory Readings,* edited by Leo Braudy and Marshall Cohen, 833–44. New York: Oxford University Press, 1999.

Murray, Caitlin. *The National Team: The Inside Story of the Women Who Changed Soccer.* New York: Abrams Press, 2019.

Murray, Pauli. "Jane Crow and the Law: Sex Discrimination and Title VII." *George Washington Law Review* 34 (2): 232–56.

Muscatine, Alison. "Men and Women in Sports: The Playing Field Is Far from Level." *USA Today,* 1 November 1996, 33–34.

———. "The Rules on Trans-athletes Reward Cheats and Punish the Innocent." *Sunday Times* (London), 17 February 2019.

———. "William and Mary Restores 4 Sports." *Washington Post,* 23 February 1991.

Navratilova, Martina, with George Vecsey. *Martina.* New York: Alfred A. Knopf, 1985.

"NCAA Sports Sponsorship and Participation Rates Report, 1981–82—2004–05." ncaapublications.com, May 2007.

Nelson, Mariah Burton. *Are We Winning Yet? How Women Are Changing Sports and Sports Are Changing Women.* New York: Random House, 1991.

———. *Embracing Victory: Life Lessons in Competition and Compassion—New Choices for Women.* New York: William Morrow, 1998.

———. *The Stronger Women Get, the More Men Love Football: Sexism and the American Culture of Sports.* New York, Avon Books, 1994.

"New Stars of Money: Anna Kournikova Attacks the Net." *Forbes,* 20 March 2000.

"Novak Djokovic Questions Whether Women Deserve Equal Pay in Tennis." ESPN.com, 21 March 2016.

Nye, Joseph S., Jr. "Soft Power." *Foreign Policy,* no. 80 (Autumn 1990): 153–71.

O'Neal, Lonnae. "The Struggle Is Real: The Unrelenting Weight of Being a Black, Female Athlete." *Andscape,* 25 June 25 2018.

Pallack, Becky. "Navajo Using Olympics as Tourism Showcase." *Arizona Daily Sun,* 11 July 2001.

Parks, Jenifer. *The Olympic Games, the Soviet Bureaucracy, and the Cold War: Red Sport, Red Tape.* New York: Lexington Books, 2017.

Parks, Shoshi, "Scientists Staged a Racist Olympics in 1904 to 'Prove' White Superiority." *Timeline,* 2 March 2018.

Peavy, Linda, and Urusal Smith. *Full Court Quest: The Girls from Fort Shaw Indian School, Basketball Champions of the World.* Norman: University of Oklahoma Press, 2014.

"PGA Tournament Schedule, 2018–2019." pgatour.com.

Pieper, Lindsay Parks. *Sex Testing: Gender Policing in Women's Sports.* Urbana: University of Illinois Press, 2016.

Plymire, Darcy C., and Pamela J. Forman. "Breaking the Silence: Lesbian Fans, the Internet, and the Sexual Politics of Women's Sport." *International Journal of Sexuality and Gender Studies* 5 (2000): 141–53.

Reardon, Claudia L., and Shane Creado. "Drug Abuse in Athletes." *Substance Abuse and Rehabilitation* 5 (2014): 95–105.

Redihan, Erin Elizabeth. *The Olympics and the Cold War, 1948–1968: Sport as Battleground in the U.S.-Soviet Rivalry.* Jefferson, NC: McFarland, 2017.

Reid, Leonard N., and Lawrence C. Soley. "*Sports Illustrated*'s Coverage of Women in Sports." *Journalism Quarterly* 56, no. 4 (1 December 1979): 863.

Rhoden, William C. "Black and White Women Far from Equal under Title IX." *New York Times,* 10 June 2012.

Richardson, Dot. *Living the Dream.* New York: Kensington Books, 1997.

Rider, Toby C. *Cold War Games: Propaganda, the Olympics, and U.S. Foreign Policy.* Urbana: University of Illinois Press, 2016.

Rider, Toby C., and Kevin B. Witherspoon. *Defending the American Way of Life: Sport, Culture, and the Cold War.* Fayetteville: University of Arkansas Press, 2018.

Ronan, Wyatt. "Human Rights Campaign, Athlete Ally and Other Advocacy Groups Urge NCAA to Include Non-Discrimination Language in New Constitution." *Human Rights Campaign,* 20 January 2022.

"Ronda Rousey to Fight Transgender Fallon Fox?" *Latinos Post,* 18 May 2015.

Rothenberg, Ben. "Djokovic and Other Top Men Are Creating a Players' Association." *New York Times,* 28 August 2020.

Rudolph, Wilma. *Wilma: The Story of Wilma Rudolph.* New York: Signet, 1977.

Ryan, Lynda Truman. "Swimsuit Models or Victim Stories, Who Will Cover for Me?" *New York Times,* 20 February 1994, S11.

Sachs, Adam. "Ice Maiden." *GQ,* August 2000, 119–21.

Sailors, Pam R., and Charlene Weaving. "Foucault and the Glamazon: The Autonomy of Ronda Rousey." *Sport, Ethics and Philosophy* 11, no. 4 (2017): 428–39.

Sandomir, Richard. "Golf: CBS Pulls Wright Off the Air." *New York Times,* 10 January 1996, B9.

———. "Ratings Star: Tiger Woods." nytimes.com, 4 March 2000.

Schoenfeld, Bruce. *The Match: Althea Gibson & Angela Buxton: How Two Outsiders—One Black, the Other Jewish Forged a Friendship and Made Sports History.* New York: Amistad, 2004.

Schultz, Jaime. "Reading the Catsuit: Serena Williams and the Production of Blackness at the 2002 U.S. Open." *Journal of Sport and Social Issues* 29, no. 3 (August 2005): 338–57.

———. *Qualifying Times: Points of Change in United States Women's Sports.* Urbana: University of Illinois Press, 2014.

Schultz, Ken. "WNBA Continues to Lead the Way for Other Leagues in LGBTQ Inclusion." outsports.com, July 22, 2019.

Scurry, Brianna. *My Greatest Save: The Brave, Barrier-Breaking Journey of a World-Champion Goalkeeper.* New York: Abrams Press, 2022.

Silverman, Ruth. "Choosing Your Class: Female." bodybuilding.com.

Smith, Lissa, ed. *Nike Is a Goddess: The History of Women in Sports.* New York: Atlantic Monthly Press, 1998.

Smith-Rosenberg, Carroll, and Charles Rosenberg. "The Female Animal: Medical and Biological Views of Women and Their Role in Nineteenth Century America." In *From "Fair Sex" to Feminism: Sport and the Socialization of Women in the Industrial and Post-Industrial Eras,* edited by J. A. Mangan and Roberta J. Park, 13–37. London: Frank Cass, 1987.

Spies-Gans, Juliet. "What Serena's *SI* Cover Reveals about How We See Female Athletes in 2015." huffpost.com, 14 December 2015.

Sports Illustrated: The 50th Anniversary Book, 1954–2004. New York: Time Inc., 2004.

Stevenson, Karen. "Hair Today, Shorn Tomorrow? Hair Symbolism, Gender, and the Agency of Self." In *Charlotte Perkins Gilman: Optimist Reformer,* edited by Jill Rudd and Val Gough, 219–42. Iowa City: University of Iowa Press, 1999.

"The Story of Swim: In the Words of Those Who Lived It." In *Sports Illustrated Swimsuit: 50 Years of Beautiful,* 15–29. New York: Time Home Entertainment, 2013.

Strings, Sabrina. *Fearing the Black Body: The Racial Origins of Fat Phobia.* New York: New York University Press, 2019.

Sullivan, Robert. "Goodbye to Heroin Chic. Now It's Sexy to Be Strong." time.com, 19 July 1999.

Symons, Caroline. *The Gay Games: A History.* New York: Routledge, 2010.

Tebbel, John, and Mary Ellen Zuckerman. *The Magazine in America, 1741–1990*. New York: Oxford University Press, 1991.

Thomas, Damion L. *Globetrotting: African American Athletes and Cold War Politics*. Urbana: University of Illinois Press, 2012.

Tuchman, Gaye. "The Symbolic Annihilation of Women by the Mass Media." In *Culture and Politics*, edited by Lane Crothers and Charles Lockhart, 150–74. New York: Palgrave Macmillan, 1978.

Tyus, Wyomia, and Elizabeth Terzakis. *Tigerbelle: The Wyomia Tyus Story*. Brooklyn: Edge of Sports, 2018.

Ungerleider, Steven. *Faust's Gold: Inside the East German Doping Machine*. New York: Thomas Dunne Books, 2001.

Van Natta, Don. *Wonder Girl: The Magnificent Sporting Life of Babe Didrikson Zaharias*. New York: Little, Brown, 2011.

Vaughan, Roger. *Golf: The Women's Game*. New York: Stewart, Tabori & Change, 2000.

Vertinsky, Patricia. "Body Shapes: The Role of the Medical Establishment in Informing Female Exercise and Physical Education in Nineteenth-Century North America." In *From "Fair Sex" to Feminism: Sport and the Socialization of Women in the Industrial and Post-Industrial Eras*, edited by J. A. Mangan and Roberta J. Park, 256–81. London: Frank Cass, 1987.

Vertinsky, Patricia, and Gwendolyn Captain. "More Myth than History: American Culture and Representations of Black Female's Athletic Ability." *Journal of Sport History* 25, no. 3 (Fall 1998): 532–61.

"Victim or Survivor: Terminology from Investigation Through Prosecution." *SAKI: Sexual Assault Kit Initiative*, 1–2. 2015.

Voepel, Mechelle. "WNBA Announces 'Refresh' of Brand, New Logo." ESPN .com, 8 April 2019.

Walker, Alice. *In Search of Our Mothers' Gardens*. New York: Harcourt, 1983.

Wallace, Michele. *Black Macho and the Myth of the Superwoman*. London: Verso, 2015.

Wamsley, Laurel. "'One Must Respect the Game': French Open Bans Serena Williams' Catsuit." npr.org, 24 April 2018.

Wang, Hansi Lo. "Black U.S. Olympians Won in Nazi Germany Only to Be Overlooked at Home." npr.org, 13 August 2016.

Ware, Susan. *Game, Set, Match: Billie Jean King and the Revolution in Women's Sports*. Chapel Hill: University of North Carolina Press, 2011.

Warner, Patricia Campbell. *When the Girls Came Out to Play: The Birth of American Sportswear*. Amherst: University of Massachusetts Press, 2006.

Weaving, Charlene. "Examining 50 Years of 'Beautiful' in *Sports Illustrated* Swimsuit Issue." *Journal of the Philosophy of Sport* 43, no. 3 (2016): 380–93.

Weaving, Charlene, and Jessica Samson. "The Naked Truth: Disability, Sexual Objectification, and the *ESPN Body Issue*." *Journal of the Philosophy of Sport* 45, no. 1 (2018): 83–100.

White, Ruth. "Why Mental Health Is Stigmatized in Black Communities." usc .edu, 12 February 2019.

Wiggins, David K. *More than a Game: A History of the African American Experience in Sport*. New York: Rowman & Littlefield, 2018.

Willard, Frances. *A Wheel within a Wheel: A Woman's Quest for Freedom*. Bedford, MA: Applewood Books, 1997.

Withycombe, Jenny Lind. "Intersecting Selves: African American Female Athletes' Experiences of Sport." *Sociology of Sport Journal* 28 (2011): 478–93.

Wollstonecraft, Mary. *A Vindication of the Rights of Woman: With Strictures on Political and Moral Subjects*. London: Printed for J. Johnson, 1792.

Wughalter, Emily. "Ruffles and Flounces: The Apologetic in Women's Sports." *Frontiers: A Journal of Women's Studies* 3 (Spring 1978): 11–13.

Wulf, Steve. "Title Waves." ESPN.com, 9 May 2012.

Wulfhart, Nell McShane. *The Great Stewardess Rebellion: How Women Launched a Workplace Revolution at 30,000 Feet*. New York: Doubleday, 2022.

"Yale Women Strip to Protest a Lack of Crew's Showers." *New York Times*, 4 March 1976.

Yong, Ed. "Young Trans Children Know Who They Are." theatlantic.com, 15 January 2019.

Young, Iris Marion. "Throwing Like a Girl: A Phenomenology of Feminine Body Comportment Motility and Spatiality." *Human Studies* 3 (April 1980): 137–56.

Zaccardi, Nick. "Russian Men's Ski Jump Coach Against Women Ski Jumping." nbcsports.com, 20 January 2014.

Zeigler, Cyd. "Sheryl Swoopes Is Not a Lesbian, Now Engaged to a Man." outsports.com, 14 July 2011.

Zhouxiang, Lu. "Sport and Politics: The Cultural Revolution in the Chinese Sports Ministry, 1966–1976," *International Journal of the History of Sport* 33, no. 5 (2016): 569–85.

INDEX

Italicized page numbers refer to illustrations.

Acuff, Amy, 38
Akers, Michelle, 108–9
Ali, Muhammand, 168
All-American Girls Professional Baseball League, 35, 36–37, 51, 195–96
All-American Red Heads, 198–202, *202*, 225
Allers, Seals, 30–31
American Basketball League (ABL), 193, 202–4, 222, 225
American Turf Register and Sporting Magazine (Skinner), 5
American Woman in Sport, The (Berlin, Felshin, Gerber, and Wyrick), 8
Anderson, Kelli, 142–43, 154
anterior cruciate ligament (ACL) injuries, 138–40, 157, 238

Babashoff, Shirley, 147, 173–74, 270n49
Bailey, Sandra, 112–13, 114
Bamberger, Michael, 99–100, 109–11
baseball: and All-American Girls Professional Baseball League, 35, 36–37, 51, 195–96, 197, 199–200, 202, 207, 225; and Babe Ruth, 195; and Black female athletes, 196–97; and "Bloomer Girl" teams, 194; and dress codes, 196, 197; fans of, 196, 206; and Frenchwoman player Mayeux, 197–98; history of, 242; and Ila Borders, 225; and Kathryn Massar, 122; and Little League baseball, 64, 122, 139, 197; and Lou Gehrig, 195; and Major League Baseball (MLB), 1, 5, 195, 196, 197, 198; and Marcenia "Toni" Stone, 196, 197; and men's American League All-Stars, 195; and Mo'ne Davis, 197; and Philip Wrigley's company, 206; and spring training, 1; and St. Louis Cardinals, 5; and umpire Pan Postema, 122; and Virne Beatrice "Jackie" Mitchell, 195, 197, 225, 277n6; women players of, 194–98; and women's outfits, 35, 194; women's participation in, 194–95
basketball: and All-American Red Heads, 198–202, *200;* and American Basketball League, 193, 202–4, 222, 225; and Chamique Holdsclaw, 126–27; and coaches, 11, 12, 40, 65, 116, 283n2; and college rivalries, 230; fans of, 70, 199, 200, 203, 227; and female athletes, 170–71, 200, 227, 229–30, 234; and female Olympians, 229; and Fort Shaw Indian Boarding School, 188; and gay athletes, 86–87, 234; and the Harlem Globetrotters, 200–202; and high school and college levels, 229; and international basketball, 161–61, 205–6; and inventor James Naismith, 229; and John Havlicek, 199; and Kareem Abdul-Jabbar, 199; and Kye Allums, 75–76; and Lindsey Walker, 77, 78; and Louisiana Tech's women's basketball team, 37; and Mildred "Babe" Didrikson Zaharias, 154; and National Basketball Association (NBA), 5, 71, 136, 138, 199, 200, 201–5, 225, 227, 230, 242; and Native peoples, 185; and Negro Leagues, 196–97, 201; and Nike sponsorship, 72; as an Olympic sport, 171; and Pam Parsons, 65;

basketball (*continued*)
   and players, 45, 65, 71–72, 76, 86,
   124, 135, 198–202, 205, 229, 230, 234;
   and professional sports organizations, 14, 193, 201; and Rebecca
   Lobo, 140; revenue from, 123; and
   Ron Arteset's mental health, 136; and
   the Scarlet Knights of Rutgers, 10,
   11–12; Senda Berenson's role in, 229;
   and sexual assault, 153; and Shelley
   Garcia, 143; and Sheryl Swoopes,
   71; and Smith College, 229; and
   Tennessee Lady Vols, 10–11, 116, 230;
   and U.S. Women's basketball team,
   77, 229; and women's basketball,
   114, 116, 117, 126–27, 135, 198–202,
   220, 229, 234, 283n1; and Women's
   Basketball League, 202; and women's
   college basketball, 10–12, 95, 102–3,
   126–27, 138–39, 229–30; and women's
   movement, 213; and Women's
   National Basketball Association
   (WNBA), 40–41, 70, 71, 124, 126,
   135, 140, 193–94, 203–7, 221, 225–26,
   227, 234, 242, 258n41, 279n30; and
   women's salaries, 242
Battle of the Sexes, 90, 91–93, 92, 121,
   122, 236, 244
Baugh, Laura, 210, 225
Beauvoir, Simone de, 9
Beckham, David, 26
Berenson, Senda, 229
Berlin, Pearl, 8
Biles, Simone, 137
Bird, Sue, 205, 230, 234–35
*Black Macho and the Myth of the
   Superwoman* (Wallace), 29
Black Panther (film), 35
Blair, Bonnie, 191
Blankers-Koen, Fannie, 31
Bloomer Girl Baseball, 194–95
Brinkley, Christie, 3
Brown, Ashley, 58
Brown, Rita Mae, 61

Brownmiller, Susan, 13, 17, 18, 20, 28–29,
   31. *See also* femininity; *Femininity*
   (Brownmiller)
Bruening, Jennifer E., 117
Bucher, Dr. Charles A., 160
Burke, Tarana, 151

Campbell, Jule, 14, 231
Carlos, John, 169–70
Carroll, Helen J., 77
Carter, Jimmy, 277n63
Chand, Dutee, 83
Chastain, Brandi, 24–25, 25, 26, 50, 112,
   220
Chavez, Chris, 85
China: Communism in, 179–80, 275n41;
   and the Cultural Revolution, 179, 180,
   183, 275n41; and doping, 270n47; and
   East German coaches, 270n47; and
   female athletes, 180–83, 182; Gao Min
   of, 182; and gymnasts, 180–81; and
   investment in sport's facilities, 180;
   and Mao Zedong, 180, 183, 275n41;
   mass calisthenics in, 179; Ming
   Dynasty in, 181; and Olympic sports,
   160, 179–84; patriarchy in, 181–82;
   and ping-pong players, 179; sports
   budget of, 179; and women's diving,
   182–83; and women's participation in
   sports, 181–82
Coachman, Alice, 163
Cohen v. Brown, 104–6, 124
Collins, Jason, 86–87
Collins, Patricia Hill, 118
Comăneci, Nadia, 172–73, 176, 178, 191
Coming On Strong (Cahn), 8
Connors, Jimmy, 62, 217, 218
Cooper, Brittney, 30
Coughlin, Natalie, 241
Court, Margaret, 32, 91, 214, 215, 218
Court of Arbitration for Sport (CAS),
   83–85
Crenshaw, Kimberlé, 45, 119, 122

Daddario, Gina, 8
Daniels, Isabelle, 163
Davis, Amira Rose, 47–48, 52–53
Deford, Frank, 27, 34, 52; and Chris Evert, 216; and "How It All Began," 3; and lesbianism, 59–60, 62; and Martina Navratilova, 62, 216; and women's golf, 210; and women's tennis, 216–17, 218
DeFrantz, Anita, 240, 270n63
de la Cretaz, Frankie, 234
Denhollander, Rachel, 152
Derek, Bo, 41
de Varona, Donna, 19, 26, 52, 190
Diaz, Laura, 210
Differences of Sex Development (DSD), 56, 80–86, 89, 235
DiMaggio, Joe, 49
Division of Girls and Women's Sports (DGWS), 171, 191
doping, 146–50, 251n36, 260n66, 270n43, 270n47, 271n52
Dowling, Colette, 126–27, 128
Dumaresq, Michelle, 74–75, 76

East Germany: and Communism, 175–76, 178; Erich Honecker of, 174; as a nation, 175, 178; pensions for athletes of, 174; and performance-enhancing drugs, 147–50, 173; physical education in, 174; skater Katarina Witt of, 175–76, 177; and soft power, 178; sports clubs in, 174; swimmer Kornelia Ender of, 173–74, 178; and the *Wundermädchen*, 147–48
eating disorders, 140–45, 157, 238, 240, 269n35
Edwards, Harry, 169
Ellis, Havelock, 56
Ellison, Margaret, 38, 39
Ender, Kornelia, 173–74
Epstein, David, 75, 77, 81–83, 87, 251n36, 260n64

equal pay, 88, 94, 116, 121, 192, 194–95, 204–7, 214–15, 219, 225, 241–43
Ernst, Chris, 99
ESPN, 10, 42, 71
Evans, Lee, 169
Evert, Chris, 34, 46, 52, 62, 64, 129, 215–18, 216. *See also* tennis

Fagan, Kate, 226–27
Faggs, Mae, 163, 170, 190
Fearing the Black Body (Strings), 145
Felshin, Jan, 8
femininity: and aerobics, 45; and American society, 40, 43, 45–46, 56, 57–59, 137; and American women, 17, 21–22, 49, 50–51, 57–58; and anger, 29–30; and athleticism, 45–48, 50, 51–53, 57–58, 64, 231–32, 246; and attractiveness to men, 31; and basketball, 70; and beauty, 17, 18, 20–21, 24, 38, 39, 44, 45; and Black female athletes, 23–24, 29–30, 41–44, 45, 46–48, 51, 52–53, 58, 242; and Black women, 29, 43–44, 51; and bodybuilding, 21–22, 23; and Chris Evert, 34, 52; and Chris von Saltza, 44; and disabled female athletes, 22–23; and Donna de Varona, 26, 52; and emotions, 51, 53; and eroticism, 19, 21, 24; and Felicia Zimmerman, 37–38; and female athletes, 4, 8, 12, 13, 15, 18, 20–28, 32, 33–40, 48–53, 56, 62, 70, 161, 164, 202, 232, 240, 242, 246; and figure skaters' competition, 131; and Florence Griffith Joyner, 45, 46, 46–47, 52–53; and the frailty myth, 244; and freedom of movement, 33–34; and Gilman's ideals, 39–40; and hairstyles, 38–42; and heterosexuality, 225; and June Byers, 49; and Katie Hnida, 50; and Katie Ledecky, 84; and lesbian stigmas, 244; and Martina Navratilova, 62–63, 64; and Mia Hamm, 50; and motherhood,

femininity (*continued*)
32, 50, 51; and Myriam Bedard's suit, 51–52; overt displays of, 32, 51, 64, 200, 228; and Paula Sperber, 59; and players' appearances, 36–37, 48, 51, 62–63; and "Rules of Conduct" for baseball, 36; and Serena Williams, 47, 48, 52; and sexuality, 57; and shot-putter Maren Seidler, 21; and Simonya Popova (fictional), 27, 50; and skin, 20, 53; and Soccer Barbie, 24; and sports, 20–28, 53, 61, 89, 164; *Sports Illustrated* feature on, 49; and Susan Brownmiller, 33, 41, 42, 49, 53, 89; and swimsuit models, 19; and Tiina Lillak, 17; and track and field, 164; and U.S. Women's Soccer Team, 24–25; valorization of, 43; and white female athletes, 44; and white femininity, 12, 18, 19, 225; and Williams sisters, 27, 34–35, 42, 44; and Wilma Rudolph, 44, 47, 52; and women's baseball, 196; and women's muscles, 21–22, 23, 24–25, 28, 48, 49, 51, 52; and women's sports uniforms, 35–37, 52. See also *Femininity* (Brownmiller); women's sports outfits
Femininity (Brownmiller), 13, 17, 18–19, 53
feminism: and Billie Jean King, 54, 214; and Black women, 118–19; and Equal Rights Amendment, 215; and female athletes, 4, 9–10, 21–22, 39, 46, 54, 202; and Gloria Steinem, 215, 244; and intersectionality, 119; and lesbianism, 60, 61; and National Organization for Women, 60; and patriarchal order, 61; and physical freedom, 9, 10; and second-wave feminism, 21–22, 118–19, 213, 215, 245; and sports, 9–10, 101, 118–19, 213; and third-wave feminism, 119; and "Throwing Like a Girl" (Young), 9; and women and girls of color,

118; and women as weaker sex, 126, 127–28; and women's athletic competition, 9; and women's equality, 9, 10, 118–19, 126; and women's liberation, 37, 119; and women's short hair, 39–40. See also Kane, Mary Jo; Morgan, Robin
Festle, Mary Jo, 157
Fink, Janet S., 8
Fitzgerald Mosley, Benita, 117, 118
Fleming, Peggy, 190
football: and Allisa Wykes, 69–70; and American Football Coaches Association, 123; and American Football League (AFL), 5; and college game, 1, 95, 96, 103, 106, 107, 123; concussions from, 238; and Dave Kopay, 54; donations to, 103; fans of, 220; and Katie Hnida, 50; and National Football League (NFL), 5, 21, 106, 136; and National Women's Football League (NWFL), 70; and professional sports organizations, 193; revenue from, 123; and Ricky William's struggles, 136; and sexual assault, 153–54; Super Bowl, 84; and Title IX, 94, 106, 107, 123
Frailty Myth, The (Dowling), 126
Freeman, Cathy, 186–88, *186*
Freidan, Betty, 213
Freud, Sigmund, 56

Garnett, Kevin, 71
Gay Games, 60
gender: and American society, 12, 17, 34, 52–53, 55–58, 74, 80, 103, 112, 114, 126–28, 139–40, 228, 235, 240; and Babe Didrikson Zaharias, 57; and baseball, 195–98; and Battle of the Sexes, 112, 120–21; and body weight and/or fat, 142; and case of Dutee Chand, 83, 86; in China, 181–82, 183, 275–76n47; and cisgender people, 74, 76, 78, 79; and Court of Arbitration

for Sport (CAS), 83, 85, 86; and debate about unfair advantages, 74, 75, 76–80, 84, 88; and Differences of Sex Development, 56, 86, 235; and disabled female athletes, 22–23; and discrimination, 120, 228; and Emily Wughalter's "Apologetic" theory, 32, 34; and emotions, 28–31, 76, 84, 135; and equality, 235; and equal pay, 35, 54; and female athletes, 21, 28–31, 32, 34, 39, 43–44, 49, 51, 52, 56–58, 71–74, 76, 81–90, 93–101, 119, 126, 127, 128, 137; and femaleness at birth, 73, 76; and the frailty myth, 135, 137; and gender-affirming surgery, 75, 76, 77, 79; and gender equity, 120; and gender identity, 80, 81, 82–83, 86; and gender stereotypes, 32, 51; and Gerbner's symbolic annihilation, 121; and golf, 208; and history, 4, 10, 81, 92; and homosexuality, 58; and hormone levels, 81–82, 83, 84, 148; and hormone treatments, 74–79, 83, 85; and human rights, 73; and hyperandrogenism, 83, 84, 85; and inequality in sports, 118; and intersexed athletes, 77, 88; and Laverne Cox, 72, 88; and lesbianism, 56, 57, 58, 256n15; and LGBTQ+ people, 248n23, 261n78; and Lia Thomas, 80; and maleness at birth, 79; and masculinity, 17–18, 21, 22, 23, 34, 39, 43, 45, 48, 49, 51, 52, 53, 55, 56, 58, 64, 137, 210; and mental health, 134–35, 137; and NCAA's Inclusion of Transgender Student Athletes, 77; and Olympics, 160; and "On the Team: Equal Opportunity for Transgender Athletes" (Carroll and Griffin), 77; and physical empowerment, 9–10; and professional sports leagues, 228; and sex chromosome tests, 73–74, 81; and sexism, 12, 13, 52, 98, 145, 187, 210, 218, 219, 226–27, 240, 241, 245, 254n66; and sexual abuse, 153–54; and sports-related injuries, 138–40; and tennis, 48, 73–74, 216; and "The Transgender Athlete" (Epstein and Torre), 75; and Title IX, 117; and transgender athletes, 60, 73–81, 87–88; and transgender children, 260n61; and trans men, 76, 78; and trans people, 73–81, 235; and trans women, 13, 75–76, 77, 78, 79, 80; and treatment of Chris Chavez, 85; and uniforms of sports, 36, 91; and Veronica Ivy, 79; and victimization, 158; and women as weaker sex, 12, 14, 17, 135, 137; and women of color, 235; and women's muscles, 55, 84; and women's soccer, 223–24. *See also* Brownmiller, Susan; femininity; Gilman, Charlotte Perkins; Title IX

Gerber, Ellen, 8

Gerbner, George, 121

Germany, 81, 159, 163, 165, 178. *See also* East Germany

Gibson, Althea, 42–43, 44, 119, 265–66n53

Gilbert, Bil, 7, 9, 12–13, 55–56, 64, 88, 96–99, 101, 121, 127, 244. *See also* sports; *Sports Illustrated*

Gilman, Charlotte Perkins, 9, 39

golf: and Annika Sorenstam, 210, 211, 212; and Bauer sisters, 60; and Carol Mann, 37; and Charlie Belijan's accomplishments, 136; and commentator Ben Wright, 67; and corporate sponsorships, 207, 209, 212; and Estelle Hoagland, 49; excellent players of, 208–10, 212; fans of, 208, 210, 212, 213; and female athletes, 59, 154–55, 156, 207–14; and Heather Farr's cancer, 155; and Helen Alfredsson, 68; and Hope Seignious, 207; and Jan Stephenson, 20–21, 60; and Ladies Professional Golf Association (LPGA), 14, 36, 55, 57, 59–60, 67, 68, 76, 154, 193, 207–14, 215, 218,

golf (*continued*)
225, 242; and Lana Lawless, 76; and Laura Baugh, 225; and Lennie Wirtz, 36; and lesbians, 67–68, 213, 256n16; major championships of, 5, 212–13; and Meg Mallon, 212; and men's events, 212, 227; and Mildred "Babe" Didrikson Zaharias, 154–55, 207, 208–10; and Muffin Spencer-Devlin, 67–68, 70; and Nancy Lopez, 32, 60, 209–10; and Patty Sheehan, 209, 211; and PGA Tour, 210–12; and professional sports organizations, 14, 37, 67–68, 193, 207–14; and Se Ri Pak, 156; and sportswomen's attractiveness, 20–21, 36, 37, 60; and Tam O'Shanter All-American Championship, 155; and Title IX, 108; and U.S. Women's Open, 213
Goolagong, Evonne, 32, 214, 215, 218
Graf, Steffi, 27, 37, 129, 130, 218, 231, 232. See also *Sports Illustrated*
Green, Tina Sloan, 117–18
Griffin, Pat, 55, 65, 66–67, 77, 89
Griner, Brittney, 71, 279n30
Grove City College v. Bell, 101–2
Gulbis, Natalie, 241

Hamill, Dorothy, 40, 190
Hamm, Mia, 24, 50, 110, 123, 220, 221. See also soccer
Harding, Tonya, 131–32
Harlem Globetrotters, 201
Henrich, Christy, 142–43
Herland (Gilman), 9, 39
Heywood, Leslie, 23
Hingis, Martina, 27, 29, 41, 68–69, 218
Hnida, Katie, 50
Holdsclaw, Chamique, 126–27, 128, 135, 136–37, 230
homophobia, 54–70, 87–90, 213, 227–28, 234, 240
homosexuality, 55–66, 71, 72. See also homophobia; sexuality

Howard, Johnette, 150–51, 156
hyperandrogenism, 82–85

ice hockey, 5, 72, 108, 122, 238
Imus, Don, 11, 12
International Amateur Athletic Federation (IAAF), 80–86, 260n64
International Handball Federation, 36
International Olympic Committee (IOC), 72, 76, 79, 80, 81, 84, 169–70, 184–85, 260n66, 261n78, 270n49, 281n49
intersexuality, 83–84. See also sexuality
Ireland, Kathy, 3
Ivy, Veronica, 78–79, 260n60

Jackson, Jesse, 177
Johnson, Ben, 270n43
Johnson, Rafer, 168
Johnson, William, 179–80, 198–99, 202, 208
Joncheray, Helene, 22
Jones, Marion, 146–47
Jordan, Michael, 26
Joyner, Florence Griffith, 45–47, 52–53, 232

Kane, Mary Jo, 8, 65, 70
Kayoung, Kim, 8
Kennedy, Florynce, 119
Kennedy, President John F., 164–65
Kennedy, Ray, 73, 74, 87
Kennedy, Robert F., 165, 191
Kensicki, Linda Jean, 8
Kerrigan, Nancy, 128, 131, 132–33, 239
King, Billie Jean: and American society, 121, 213; and Battle of the Sexes, 90, 91–92, 92, 110, 112, 120–21, 122, 236, 244; and founding of women's tennis tour, 214, 217; and gay and lesbian movement, 86–87; and lesbianism, 13, 67, 87, 88, 90, 257n21; magazine of, 114; and pay equity, 214–15, 244, 281n49; political acuity of, 27, 214–15; as Sportswoman of the Year for

SI, 214, 218; as a tennis player, 54,
91–93, 111, 112, 120, 213, 215, 244; and
women's rights, 3, 4, 10, 54, 214, 215
Kirkpatrick, Curry, 33, 37, 91
Kirshenbaum, Jerry, 54–55, 65, 87,
100–101, 147
Korbut, Olga, 142, 172–73, 176, 178, 191
Kournikova, Anna, 27

Ladies Professional Golf Associa-
tion (LPGA), 207–14, 218, 225, 242,
280n39
Laguerre, Andre, 7, 14
Lamb, Sharon, 151, 154, 156
Lawless, Lana, 76
Layden, Tim, 46–47, 68–69, 83–85,
137–38
League of Their Own, A (film), 196
Ledecky, Katie, 84, 190
Lenskyj, Helen, 24, 61
lesbianism, 53, 54–72, 86–90, 213,
234–35, 256n15, 257n21. *See also* ho-
mophobia; homosexuality; sexuality
Leslie, Lisa, 123, 124–25
Letterman, David, 24
LGBTQ+ (Lesbian, Gay, Bisexual,
Transgender, Queer/Questioning and
Other Identities). *See* sexuality
Liberti, Rita, 44
Lillak, Tiina, 17, *18*
Lopez, Nancy, 209–10, *209*
Luce, Henry, 5–6
Lumpkin, Angela, 8

MacCambridge, Michael, 3, 128
Manuel, Simone, 190
March, Babette, 1, 19, 230
Martina (Navratilova), 62–63
Matthews, Margaret, 163
Mauresmo, Amélie, 68–70
McDaniel, Millie, 163
McEnroe, John, 29, 217
media: and American society, 10,
11–12, 35, 66, 67–68, 86–88, 109, 112,

203, 223, 225–27; and Ann Simonton, 244–45, 246; and attention to
women's outfits, 35; and Battle of the
Sexes, 112; and Black Americans,
177; and Black press, 58; and Black
sportswomen, 23, 197; and business
plans for leagues, 223; and CBS's
Ben Wright, 67; and Chris Evert,
34; and civil rights in America, 167;
and coach-athlete relationships,
66; and commentary, 45; *ESPN The
Magazine*, 10, 71; and ESPN's Lonnae
O'Neal, 42; and ESPN's programming, 227; and ESPN.com, 243;
and female athletes, 11–12, 23–24,
50–51, 52, 53, 61, 62, 98, 99–100,
108–9, 121–24, 126, 131–33, 156, 157,
158, 202; and figure skaters, 131–32;
Gear magazine, 24, 25; and Gerbner's symbolic annihilation, 121;
and harassment of Navratilova, 62;
and heterosexuality, 114; *Imus in the
Morning*, 11; and Keith Olbermann's
commentary, 197; and lack of coverage, 222; and lesbian athletes, 61, 62,
67–71, 87–90; and Megan Rapinoe,
88–89; newspapers, 152; *Newsweek*,
109; *New Yorker*, 80; *New York
Herald*, 229; *New York Times*, 23, 99,
100, 114, 117, 239; and Paul Gallico,
57, 154–55; *People* magazine, 24, 109;
and posing nude for *Playboy*, 221; and
professional sports leagues, 223–24;
and the Scarlet Knights of Rutgers,
10–12; SI.com, 4; social media, 151,
222; sports magazines, 5–7, 10, 12, 15,
87, 105, 109, 112–15, 133, 151–52, 165,
195, 227–28, 240–42; sports print
media, 1, 3, 4, 5–7, 10, 115, 242; *Sunday
Times* (London), 78; and team media
guides, 70; television networks, 12,
36, 91, 110, 165, 166, 184, 193, 203,
205, 218, 220–21, 223–24, 227,
246; and tennis players, 216, 218;

media (*continued*)
Time magazine, 72, 88, 109; and Title IX, 115; and transgender athletes, 74, 78, 79–80, 87–88; and victimization, 157–58; and women's professional sports, 241–42; and women's soccer, 108–9; and women's sports leagues, 225; and Women's Tennis Association, 219, 225; and women's tennis tour, 14, 222; and women's World Cup, 283n67; *World Tennis* (magazine), 214. See also *Sports Illustrated; Sports Illustrated for Women;* Time Inc.
Mertens, Maggie, 123–24
Messner, Michael, 114
Meyer, Debbie, 170
Miller, Cheryl, 229–30
Mills, Billy, 185–86
Mitchell, Virne Beatrice "Jackie," 195, 277n6
mixed martial arts, 77, 133–34
models: and Amy Acuff, 38; and Babette March, 1, 19; and Becky Collins, 2; and Betty di Bugnano, 19; Black models, 41; and Brooklyn Decker, 19; and Cheryl Tiegs, 2, 19; and Christie Brinkley, 3; and Chris von Saltza, 2; and Countess Consuelo Crespi, 19; and Donna de Varona, 2; and Elle MacPherson, 3; and Elsa Benitez, 115; and Gabrielle Reece, 26; and Heidi Klum, 243; and Karol Fageros, 43; and Kathy Ireland, 3; and Molly Sims, 235; and Pamela Nelson, 19; and *SI*'s Swimsuit Issue, 244; and supermodels, 235–36, 241; swimsuit models, 239, 243, 244, 245, 246; and Tyra Banks, 19; and Valentina Sampaio, 235; and Valeria Mazza, 19; and Yamila Diaz-Rahi, 19. See also *Sports Illustrated*
Monroe, Marilyn, 49
Moore, Kenny, 17, 18, 19, 21, 28, 45–47. See also *Sports Illustrated*

Moran, Gussie, 33
Morgan, Alex, 221–22, 233, 241–42
Morgan, Robin, 9–10
Mosley, Benita Fitzgerald, 117–18
Munson, Lester, 150–51, 156
Murphy, Lizzie, 195
Murray, Lenda, 232
Murray, Pauli, 119

Namath, Joe, 26
Nassar, Larry, 152, 153
National Collegiate Athletic Association (NCAA), 76, 77, 80, 94, 95, 117, 123, 254n56, 261n78, 262n4, 281n49
National Women's Football League (NWFL), 69, 70
National Women's Soccer League (NWSL), 40, 222–24, 242, 283n70
Navratilova, Martina, 63; autobiography of, 62–63; and corporate sponsorships, 63, 68; and lesbianism, 61, 62, 64, 67, 68, 69, 234, 257n21; and rivalry with Chris Evert, 216–17; sports outfits of, 63; as a tennis player, 61, 63, 64, 79, 87, 129, 216–18, 234; and U.S. gay rights movement, 86–87; views on transgender athletes of, 78–80. See also tennis
Negro Leagues, 196–97
Nelson, Mariah Burton, 26
Nicklaus, Jack, 212
Nike Is a Goddess (Smith), 8
Nixon, President Richard, 173, 179

Olsen, Jack, 87, 168–69
Olympic Games: in Albertville (1992), 183; and America, 159–60, 162, 163, 164–74, 189–91, 221, 273n15; ancient Olympics, 164; and Anthropology Days in St. Louis, 185, 186; in Athens (2004), 146, 180; in Atlanta (1996), 108–9; and Australia's relationship with Aboriginal peoples, 186–88; and Babe Didrikson, 57; in Barcelona

(1992), 181; and beach volleyball, 35–36; in Beijing (2008), 133, 136, 180, 183; in Berlin (1936), 159, 163; and Black athletes, 167–69, 273n15; and Black women, 163–64, 190, 191, 240; and Brenda Huckaby, 232; and Caster Semenya, 83; and Cathy Rigby, 172; and China, 160, 179–84; and Chloe Kim, 191; and the Cold War, 160, 165, 171, 173, 178, 190, 240; and countries' investments in athletes, 84–85, 159–60, 170–71, 191, 240; coverage of, 7, 161, 190, 191; and Debbie Meyer, 170; and Debi Thomas, 175, 176; and democracy, 178; and discus, 244; and Dot Richardson, 66–67; and East Germany, 148, 178; and Evelyn Ashford, 45; and Fallon Fox's eligibility, 77–78; and Fannie Blankers-Koen, 31–32; and female athletes, 12, 45, 46, 51, 77, 83–84, 158, 160–64, 170–76, 178, 181–83, 190–92, 239–41; and female Olympians, 14, 25–26, 37, 45, 131–32, 137, 159, 190–92, 239, 240; and Florence Griffith Joyner, 45, 46, 46; and Fort Shaw Indian Boarding School, 185; and gymnastics, 172–73, 183, 239; and hyperandrogenism, 83; and ice hockey, 191; in Innsbruck (1976), 100; and International Olympic Committee (IOC), 72, 76–77, 79, 80, 81, 83, 84, 169–70, 184, 240, 261n78; and Jamie Anderson, 190; and Jim Thorpe, 186; and Joan Benoit, 191; and Kerri Strug, 239; and Kornelia Ender, 173; in L.A. (1984), 181; and Lindsay Jacob-Ellis, 190; and Lindsey Vonn, 137–38; and Lindsey Walker, 77, 78; and Lisa Leslie, 124; in London (2012), 88, 136; and Maren Seidler, 21; and Marion Jones, 146–47; and medals, 160, 162, 163, 164, 165, 166, 167, 169, 170, 173, 174, 180, 182–83, 185, 186, 190, 191, 229, 239, 240, 273n15; in Melbourne (1956), 159, 160, 162, 163; in Mexico City (1968), 169, 172; and Michael Phelps, 136–37; and modern Olympics, 162; in Montreal (1976), 173; in Moscow (1980), 277n63; in Munich (1972), 171, 173; and Nancy Kerrigan, 131–33; and Native peoples, 184–88, 191; and Olympic ideal, 14, 160, 191; and Olympic teams, 142, 163, 167, 169, 189–90; and Olympic trials, 45, 46, 57, 131, 154; proposed boycott of, 169; in Rio (2016), 83–84, 136; in Rome (1960), 44, 165, 166, 167; and Rosi Mittermaier, 28; in Salt Lake City (2002), 183, 184; in Sarajevo (1984), 175; in Seoul (1988), 45; and Shannon Bahrke, 37; and ski jumping, 190; in Sochi, Russia (2014), 72; soft power of, 14, 160, 161, 174, 178, 183, 188, 191; and Soviet Union, 160, 170–71, 178, 188–89; and speed skating, 183, 190; sports of, 171, 190; and the Stockholm Consensus, 76–77; in Sydney (2000), 146, 186; and tennis, 240; and Tom Wadell, 54, 60; and track and field, 162–63, 165–66, 167, 185, 240; trans athletes in, 80; uniforms of, 35–36; and U.S. men's ice hockey team, 72; and U.S. women's basketball team, 77; and U.S. women's soccer team, 221–22; and U.S. women's track and field team, 43, 163; in Vancouver (2010), 183; and Willye White, 58; and Wilma Rudolf, 44, 170; and women's basketball, 201, 202, 229; and women's diving, 182–83; and wrestling, 190; and Wyomia Tyus, 169, 170. See also *Sports Illustrated*; United States

Olympic Project for Human Rights, 169, 274n21

O'Neal, Shaquille, 71

Osaka, Naomi, 31, 32, 137, 237–38, *237*

Owens, Jesse, 167

Palmer, Arnold, 212
Palmer, Jim, 26
Patterson, Audrey, 163
Phelps, Michael, 136–37, 180
Pickett, Tidye, 163
Playing Nice (Festle), 8
Popova, Simonya (fictional tennis player), 27, 50, 250n22
professional leagues: All-American Red Heads, 198–202, 225; business plans for, 222–27; challenges of, 231; and competition for sponsorships, 223; and international basketball leagues, 205–6; Ladies Professional Golf Association (LPGA), 207–14, 225; National Basketball Association (NBA), 225; National Hockey League (NHL), 5; National Women's Soccer League, 222, 225; Negro Leagues, 196–97, 201; and Olympics, 241; and players' salaries, 221; and tennis, 242; U.S. Women's Polo League, 193; and Virne Beatrice "Jackie" Mitchell, 195; Women's Basketball League, 202; and women's sports leagues, 35–37, 51, 191–92, 193, 195, 224, 225–26; Women's Tennis Association, 218, 219, 225; Women's United Soccer Association (WUSA), 220–21. *See also* baseball; basketball; *League of Their Own, A* (film); soccer; tennis
Putin, Vladimir, 72, 206

Qualifying Times (Schultz), 8

race: and activism, 168–69; and American society, 118–19, 135–36, 164, 165–69, 177, 240; and Anthropology Days contests, 184; and Black athletes, 135–36, 145, 163–64, 166–69, 176–77, 196–97, 227; and Black female athletes, 7, 13, 23–24, 30, 31, 41–48, 51, 52–53, 71–72, 84, 86, 117, 119, 143–44, 145, 158, 163–64, 166–67, 169, 197; and Black male athletes, 169–70; and Black studies programs, 177; and Black women, 30–31, 44–45, 51, 117–18, 119, 144–45, 163–64, 237–38; and civil rights protests, 166, 167; and claims of Aryan superiority, 167; and coaches of color, 116–17; and discrimination, 119, 168–69, 176–77, 190; and Don Imus's commentary, 11–12; and eating disorders, 143–45; and Elizabeth Newman's reporting, 23–24; and emotions, 29–31, 51, 71; and equality, 167, 168–69, 170, 201; and female athletes, 7, 10, 23–24, 30, 31, 40–45, 51, 71–72, 116–19, 158, 232, 233, 240; and female athletes of color, 158; and femininity, 20, 23–24, 29, 51; and Florence Griffith Joyner, 45, 46–47; and Gerbner's symbolic annihilation, 121; and Grand Slam tournaments, 43; and hairstyles, 40–41, 42; and International Amateur Athletic Federation (IAAF)'s policies, 86; and intersectional analysis, 45, 47, 122, 240; and the Master Race, 159; and mental health, 135–36; and Nazis, 167; and Olsen's series on Black athletes, 88, 168–69; and Olympics, 160, 163, 167–68, 169–70; and professional sports leagues, 227; and racial stereotypes, 31, 43, 177, 190; and racial violence, 177; and racism, 11–12, 13, 30, 31, 42–43, 47, 71–72, 122, 135–36, 145, 163, 166, 168–69, 177, 184–85, 188, 190–91, 201, 227, 243, 254n66; and segregation, 201, 265n53; and Serena Williams, 252n42; and skin color, 20, 41, 42, 45, 51, 52; and slavery, 167; and *Sports Illustrated*, 122; and stereotypes in China, 181; and tennis, 41–43, 47, 119, 145; and Title IX, 117–18; and United States Lawn Tennis Association (USLTA), 42; and white females, 7, 29, 30, 31, 43, 116–17,

118, 119, 127–28, 144, 145, 158, 163, 164; and whiteness, 18, 19, 20, 86; and white privilege, 177; and Williams sisters, 23–24, 30, 41–42; and women in sports, 96, 117–19, 163–64, 240; and women's soccer, 118

Rapinoe, Megan: activism of, 4, 13, 88–89; coverage of, 244; as a lesbian, 13, 88–89, 233, 234; as Sportsperson of the Year for *SI*, 13, 88–89, *89*; Swimsuit Issue appearance of, 233, 234

Reece, Gabrielle, 26, 27, 28

Reilly, Rick, 24, 26, 50, 106–7, 115–16, 121–22, 235–36

Richard, Remi, 22

Richards, Renée, 73–74, 76, 77, 78, 79, 87

Rigby, Cathy, 142, 172

Riggs, Bobby, 91, 92, 93, 110, 112, 120. *See also* tennis

Robinson, Jackie, 119

Rousey, Ronda, 77–78, 133–34, 136–37, 243

Rudolph, Wilma, 43–44, 47, 52, 163, 165–67, *166*. *See also* Olympic Games; *Sports Illustrated*

Russia: and Aleksandra Chudina, 159; and athlete defections, 189; and basketball teams, 205–6, 229; and Brittney Griner, 279n30; and the Cold War, 178; and Communism, 159, 164, 167, 178, 189–90; and competition with United States, 159–62, 164, 174, 229; dissolution of, 178; and doping, 270n47; and female athletes, 159, 162–63, 164, 191; Moscow, 173, 277n63; and Nina Chernoschek, 159; and Nina Ponomaryeva, 159; and Olympic competition, 159, 162–63, 188–89; and payment for basketballers, 205–6; and pensions and property for athletes, 159; and the space race, 161–62; and speed skaters' "costumes," 35; support for athletes in, 162; and "To Russia With Love"

(Burke), 72; and track and field women, 162–63; and "Western ways of life," 189; and Winter Olympics in Sochi, 72

Rutgers Scarlet Knights, 10–12

Ryan, Joan, 3

Sagas, Michael, 8

Scheftel, Stuart, 6

Schultz, Jaime, 22, 35, 40

Schwarzenegger, Arnold, 21

Scurry, Brianna, 118

Second Sex, The (de Beauvoir), 9

Seidler, Maren, 21

Seles, Monica, 128–31, *129*, 133, 158, 218. See also *Sports Illustrated*

Semenya, Caster, 80–86, *82*, 260n66

sex testing, 81, 260n64

sexuality: and American society, 55, 57–62, 64, 65–67, 72–73, 92, 154; and athlete models, 8, 19; and Billie Jean King, 54, 92; and Black women, 58, 86; and coach-athlete relationships, 65–66; and Differences of Sex Development, 13, 56, 86, 89–90; and emotional support, 71; and female athletes, 10, 13, 23, 26, 26–27, 28, 54–56, 57, 58, 59–62, 64–66, 71–72, 233–35; and femininity, 26, 55–56; and Florence Griffith Joyner, 245; and the frailty myth, 154; and gay and lesbian movement, 60, 66, 72–73, 86–90; and hate crimes, 72; and heterosexuality, 65, 71, 213, 243; and HIV and AIDS, 60; and homophobia, 12, 55, 56, 58, 60, 61–62, 63, 64, 65, 69, 71, 72, 87, 90, 227, 234, 240; homosexuality, 55–66, 71, 72; and intersexuality, 83–84; and lesbianism, 13, 53, 54, 55–60, 61, 62, 64, 65, 66–71, 72, 213, 233–34; and LGBTQ+ people, 13, 60, 66, 79, 87, 89, 227, 233, 234–35, 248n23, 256n17, 258n41; and Martina Navratilova, 61–64, 67, 69, 78–80, 234;

sexuality (*continued*)
  and masculinity, 55, 56–57, 64; and
  Megan Rapinoe, 233, 234; and oppression, 119; and professional beach
  volleyball, 26–27; and protection
  against discrimination, 66–67; and
  right to same-sex marriage, 72; and
  role blurring, 64; and sex appeal,
  225; and sexism, 154; and sexual
  abuse, 243; and sexual identity, 17, 56,
  60; and sexual orientation, 118, 121,
  243; and *SI*'s Swimsuit Issue, 19; and
  Stonewall resistance, 60; and trans
  identity, 69; and transphobia, 69, 78,
  80; and transsexual athletes, 79, 80;
  and victim blaming, 154; and women
  of color, 234; and women's bodies, 50–51, 57, 61, 154; and women's
  coming out, 66, 67–72, 86–87, 88,
  90, 234; and women's muscles, 57,
  61; and women's outfits, 244. *See
  also* femininity; gender; transgender
  athletes
Shepard, Matthew, 71
Shriver, Pam, 64–65, 69
Simonton, Ann, 244–45, 246
skiing, 28, 37, 137–38
Skinner, John Stuart, 5
Sloan Green, Tina, 117, 118
Smith, Maureen M., 44
Smith, Tommie, 169–70
soccer: and Abby Wambach, 221; and
  Alex Morgan, 221, 233, 241–42; and
  Australian women's national team,
  67; and Black female athletes, 117,
  118; and captain Julie Foudy, 222; and
  college soccer, 114; and concussions,
  238; and coverage of U.S. Women's
  World Cup soccer team, 24–25, 50,
  52, 108–12, 220, 222–23, 234; and
  equal pay for women, 89, 233; fans of,
  109, 110, 220, 223; and Julie Foudy, 24;
  and Major League Soccer, 220; and
  Mia Hamm, 220, 221; and National

Women's Soccer League, 40, 222, 223,
  225, 242; and players' salaries, 221;
  and professional sports organizations, 14, 40, 193, 219–23; and Rose
  Bowl venue, 110; and Title IX, 108,
  110–12; and U.S. Women's Soccer
  Team, 10, 24, 52, 88, 108–12, 118, 122,
  206; and women's soccer, 108–12,
  206, 219–24, 238; and Women's
  United Soccer Association (WUSA),
  220–21; and Women's World Cup, 88,
  89, 108, 109–10, 122, 220, 222–23. *See
  also* Chastain, Brandi; Hamm, Mia;
  Rapinoe, Megan
Sorenstam, Annika, 210, 211–12
Soviet Union. *See* Russia
Spencer-Devlin, Muffin, 67–68, 70, 71
Spies-Gans, Juliet, 47, 52
Sporting Woman, The (Boutilier and
  SanGiovanni), 60–61
sports: aerobics, 22, 45; and American
  public, 5, 58, 61–62, 64, 70–71, 84, 91,
  108; and American society, 240; and
  Amy Acuff, 38; and Angela Rock,
  26, 27, 35–36; and Anne-Caroline
  Chausson, 75; and athletes' eating
  disorders, 140–45; and athletic directors, 116–17; and baseball, 242; and
  basketball players, 70–71; and Battle
  of the Sexes, 120–21; beach handball,
  51; and Black female athletes, 45–47,
  51, 58, 116–19, 169–70, 176–77, 265n51;
  and Black Women in Sport Foundation, 117; boating, 5; bodybuilding,
  21–22, 23, 232, 249n13; and body
  weight and/or fat, 142, 145; bowling,
  5, 59; boxing, 5, 54–55, 168, 190, 235;
  and breast cancer, 154–55; cave and
  free diving, 157; and Christy Henrich's death, 142; and Cindy Stefanko,
  156; and C. J. Hunter, 146; and coach-
  athlete relationships, 65–66; and
  coaches, 38, 39, 40, 43, 65–66, 90, 94,
  95, 96, 106, 115, 116–17, 122, 123, 124,

125, 131, 139, 142, 143, 144, 147–48, 149, 150–53, 163, 171, 173, 174, 176, 178, 182, 236, 239, 270n47; cold war of, 159–60, 161; and commodification of women, 28; and Communism, 162; and corporate sponsorships, 203, 207, 214–15, 281n48; and corrective surgery, 85; cricket, 40; and culture of silence for victims, 153; cycling, 74–75, 143; as a diplomatic vehicle, 180; and disabled athletes, 22–23; discrimination in, 90, 93–108; diving, 182–83; and doping, 84, 146–50, 251n36; and Earlene Brown, 44; and endorsements, 24, 45, 53, 60, 63, 64, 67, 68, 69, 71, 72, 78, 90, 110, 127, 131, 211, 212, 224; and equal pay, 89, 94, 205–6, 245–46; fans of, 90, 91, 121, 153, 172, 185, 190, 206, 223, 224, 226–27, 242; and fashion of women's outfits, 33–38, 39, 45, 91, 132, 138, 194, 198, 245, 252n40; and female athletes, 4, 9–10, 13–14, 15, 43–47, 49, 53, 54, 58–71, 80–81, 87, 88–90, 91, 92, 93–99, 106–25, 138, 148–50, 151, 153–56, 159, 162–63, 170–73, 174; and femininity, 57–58, 62–63, 131, 225, 228, 244; figure skaters, 45, 52, 54–55, 128, 131–33, 174–76, 183, 189, 190; football, 245; and the frailty myth, 147, 149–50, 151; and gay athletes, 86–87; and the "Gay Games," 60; and gender equality, 93–99, 117–19; girls participation in, 117; golf, 5, 20, 55, 57, 59, 59–60, 207–14, 242; gymnastics, 45, 52, 103, 141–42, 152, 152–53, 171–73, 180–81, 183, 190; and hair styles, 38–42; handball, 171; and harmful health effects of steroids, 148–49; and high school and college levels, 12, 50, 59, 77, 78, 80, 92–96, 99–100, 101–8, 111, 112, 114–17, 123, 126–27, 138–39, 151, 152, 153–54, 222–23, 229–30, 236, 238, 283–84n3; history of, 4, 15, 112, 121, 158; and Holly McPeak, 26, 27; and

homophobia, 65, 66; homosexuality in, 54–56, 58–66; horse racing, 5; ice hockey, 108, 161, 190, 238; and ideal of beauty, 26; and International Amateur Athletic Federation (IAAF), 80, 81, 82, 83, 84, 85, 86; and international relations, 165; judo, 150; and lack of girls' programs, 97–98; lacrosse, 117, 185, 223; and Lamar University, 57; and Leontien Sijlaard-van Moorsel, 143; and lesbianism, 56–73, 86–87, 90; and LGBTQ+ athletes, 90; and Linda Hanley, 27; and male athletes, 148, 149, 150, 153–54, 159, 162, 164, 244; and Manon Rheaume, 122; and Margaret Ellison, 43; martial arts, 77–78, 133–34; and Mary Decker Slaney, 32; and masculinity, 18; and men's sports, 93, 94, 95, 96, 98, 102, 103–7, 115, 123, 136–37, 224, 225; and mental health issues, 134–37, 149–50; and Michael Messner, 18; and Native peoples, 183–87; and Nike sponsorship, 227; and Norwegian women's beach handball team, 36; and Pat McCormick, 32; and performance-enhancing drugs, 238, 270n43; and Phoebe Wright, 84; and physical fitness education, 171; polo, 193; and popularity of women's football, 70; powerchair football, 22; professional beach volleyball, 26, 28, 35–36; and professional opportunities, 12, 14, 191; and professional sports organizations, 5, 10, 14, 40, 67–68, 70, 73–74, 75, 191; and Radcliffe crew team, 59; recreational sports, 5; riflery, 20; and Roberta Gibb, 122; rowing, 99–100, 108, 117, 122, 124, 148, 171, 277n63; rugby, 40; running, 114, 122, 156, 190, 213; in Russia, 159; and segregation, 265–66n53; and series on women and sport (Gilbert and Williamson), 7, 9, 88, 116, 121; sexual abuse in, 150–54;

sports (*continued*)
and sexual assault, 238; skiing, 28, 190; ski jumping, 269n30; skydiving, 157; softball, 5, 67, 117, 193, 239; speed skating, 100; and sports magazines, 5–6, 7, 112–15; and sports-related injuries, 236, 238, 239; swimming, 3, 59, 80, 117, 147–48, 244; table tennis, 5; and television, 6; and Title IX, 92–93, 116, 117, 236; track and field, 17, 18, 32, 38–39, 43, 44, 45, 49, 57, 80–81, 82–84, 85, 117, 141, 146, 148, 159, 162, 163–64, 190, 277n63; and transgender athletes, 73–81, 243–44; and U.S. Women's World Cup team (1999), 40; and Valerie Brisco, 32; volleyball, 40, 150, 277n63; and volleyball league, 103, 193; water skiing, 20; and women as weaker sex, 125; and women's athletic programs, 93–97, 99–100, 102, 103–5, 108, 111, 116–17, 141; and women's bodies, 83–84, 122, 138, 139, 140, 142, 143–45, 159, 160, 171–72, 183, 192, 221, 225, 231–33, 269n30; and women's earnings, 14, 127, 192, 193, 194, 198–99, 203–4, 206, 211–14, 215, 219, 221–24, 241, 244; and women's movement, 101, 118–19, 124–25, 213; and women's muscles, 147; women's participation in, 98, 104, 105, 106, 107–8, 112–13, 116–18, 122, 123–25, 126, 127, 139, 158, 165, 170–71; and women's strength, 126, 127–28; wrestling, 106, 108, 190; and youth baseball leagues, 64, 122. *See also* anterior cruciate ligament (ACL) injuries; baseball; basketball; football; golf; ice hockey; Olympic Games; soccer; *Sports Illustrated;* swimming; tennis

Sports Illustrated: and Alex Morgan, 241; and Althea Gibson, 42, 43; and American society, 243; and American sports agenda, 7, 15, 93, 159–60, 194, 213; and Anita DeFrantz article, 240; and Anna Kournikova, 27; and athlete defections, 189; and athletes' eating disorders, 140–41, 143, 144, 145, 157; and athletes with differences of sex development, 90; and athletic budgets, 244; and beach volleyball, 36; and Billie Jean King, 54, 67, 86–87, 91, 93, 120–21, 122, 214–15, 218, 236; and Black athletes, 240; and Black female athletes, 42–47, 51, 52–53, 119, 122–23, 158, 163–64, 169, 170, 176–77, 190, 191, 232, 236, 237–38, 240; and body image controversy, 23–24; and Bonnie Pruden, 58; and the "Bouffant Belles," 38–39; and Brian Burke's "To Russia With Love," 72; and cancer, 155, 157; and Cathy Freeman, 186–87; and Chris Evert, 64, 216, 218, 232; and College of William and Mary, 102–3; and Dara Torres, 190; and disabled athletes, 22, 232; and discrimination against women, 96–108; and editor Christian Stone, 243, 246; and equity for women, 101, 231, 244; and female baseball players, 198; and female basketball players, 198–202; and female Olympians, 191, 240–41, 245–46; female readers of, 3; and femininity, 19–24, 26–27, 28, 51, 52–53, 55, 56, 161, 191, 210, 231–33, 234, 242, 243, 245, 246; and figure skaters' competition, 131–32; first issue of, 4, 6–7; and Florence Griffith Joyner, 45, 46, 46, 190, 232; and football, 238; and the frailty myth, 128, 133, 138–39, 140, 142, 145, 158, 238; and Frankie de la Cretaz, 234; and gay athletes, 90, 234; and gender equality, 235; and Gussie Moran, 33; and gymnastics, 171–73, 213; history of, 128; and Holly Holm, 134; and ideal of beauty, 15, 17, 20–21, 45, 50, 231, 243; and Indigenous people, 185–87; and intersex athletes, 88; and

Jackie Joyner-Kersee, 190; and Jack Olsen's "The Black Athlete," 168–69, 190; and Janet Evans, 190; and Jason Collins, 86; and Jenny Thompson, 26; and Jimmy Jemail's "Hotbox," 48–49; and John F. Kennedy articles, 164–65; and Jule Campbell, 14–15; and Katarina Witt, 175–76; and Kayla Harrison, 150; and lack of coverage for women's sports, 224–25, 227–28, 246, 248n17; and Ladies Professional Golf Association (LPGA), 207–10, 242; and lesbianism in sport, 58–62, 64, 65, 66, 67–68, 70–72, 233–34; and Leyna Bloom, 235; and LGBTQ+ community, 234–35; and Lia Thomas, 80; and L. Jon Wertheim, 27, 34, 42, 65, 70, 120–21, 134–35, 136, 137, 158, 224, 242, 250n22; and Louise Dyer, 31; and Louisiana Tech's women's basketball team, 37; and Lynette Woodard, 201; and male athletes, 15, 105–7, 136, 141, 146, 157, 160, 235–36; male readers of, 7, 110; and Marian McKibben, 58; and Marie Mulder, 39; and Martina Navratilova, 61, 62, 67, 80, 86–87; and Mélissa Mayeux, 197–98; and men's sports, 93, 227; and mental health of athletes, 136–37, 157, 237–38, 245; and Mia Hamm, 50, 123; and Michael MacCambridge, 7; and Michelle Akers, 108–9; and Mildred "Babe" Didrikson Zaharias, 57, 154–55, 207, 208–10; and mixed martial arts, 133–34; and Monica Seles, 130–31, 238; and motherhood, 31–32; name of, 6; and Naomi Osaka, 137, 237–38; and nationalism, 241; and National Women's Soccer League, 242; and Negro Leagues, 196–97; and objectification of women, 235, 244; Olympic coverage of, 240–41, 246; online presence of, 245; and Pam Parsons, 65; and Paula Sperber, 59;

and performance-enhancing drugs, 146, 147, 148, 149; and players' appearances, 225, 239–40; and president Donald M. Elliman Jr., 112–13; and professional prospects for women, 4, 14, 42; and professional sports leagues, 193–94, 223–24, 245–46; and publisher H. H. S. Phillips Jr., 7; and Putin's antigay law, 72; and race, 167, 168–70, 177; and R. A. Dickey, 150; rankings of, 11; and Rapinoe as Sportsperson of the Year (2019), 13, 88–89, *89*; readership of, 1–3, 6–7, 8, 10, 20, 59, 74, 78, 87, 88, 93, 96, 110, 121, 128, 134, 165, 168, 235; and Renée Richards, 73; and Serena Williams, 30, *47*, 52; and series on women and sport (Gilbert and Williamson), 7, 9, 12–13, 55–56, 64, 96–99, 121, 127, 227, 244; and sexism, 122, 210; and sexual abuse, 150–52, 153, 157–58; sexuality in, 19, 20, 284n8; and SI.com, 4, 23, 85, 136, 137, 219; and Simonya Popova (fictional), 27, 50; and skiing, 28; and sports history, 4, 12, 56, 81–86; and *Sports Illustrated Women*, 11; and *Sports Illustrated Women/Sport*, 67; and sports in China, 179–83; and sports-related injuries, 138–40, 157; and Sportswomen of the Year, 109, 110–11; and the Sputnik satellite, 161; and Steffi Graf, 231; subscriptions to, 2, 10, 128, 157; and Sue Wicks, 70–71; and Summer Sanders, 123; and survivorship, 156, 158, 243; and swimming, 171, 191; Swimsuit Issue of, 1–3, 2, 4, 8, 14–15, 19, 20, 24, 26, 115, 133, 230–35, 237, 238, 241, 242–43, 244, 245, 246, 247n2, 284n5; and swimsuit models, 3–4, 8, 10, 15, 19, 20, 115, 230, 231, 233, 284n5; and Title IX, 13–14, 90, 93–94, 95, 96, 99–108, 110, 116, 120–24, 236, 245; and "The Transgender Athlete" (Epstein and Torre), 75,

Sports Illustrated (*continued*)
77, 87; and transgender athletes, 75–78, 80–81, 87, 89–90, 235; and twenty-fifth anniversary issue, 2, 3; and U.S. Department of Health, Education, and Welfare, 96; and U.S. Women's Soccer Team, 24, 52, 108–9, 110–12, *111*, 122, 218; and Venus Williams, 240; and victimhood, 130, 131, 132, 133, 156, 157, 158, 243; and Virne Beatrice "Jackie" Mitchell, 195; and white women's accomplishments, 122; and Williams sisters, 41, 42, 218–19; and Wilma Rudolf, 44, 165–67, 190; and women of color, 243; women on covers of, 80, 115, 128, 129, 131, 133, 197, 209, 215, 218, 226, 229–30, 234, 237–39, 241, 243, 248n17; and women's bodies, 158, 233; and women's clothing, 34; and women's coming out, 66, 68, 70–73; and women's equality, 127; and women's muscles, 21, 22, 23–24, 126; and Women's National Basketball Association (WNBA), 225; and Women's Professional Soccer League, 221; and women's professional sports, 241–42; and women's sports leagues, 14, 203–4, 206, 221; yearly revenues of, 1; and Zina Garrison, 144
Sports Illustrated writers: Aditi Kinkhabwala, 11–12; Alexander Wolff, 40, 72, 103, 106, 107–8, 181–82, 183, 203, 204, 205, 206, 222, 279n30; Andrew Crichton, 94, 96; Andrew Lawrence, 136; Austin Murphy, 74–75; Barry McDermott, 209; Ben Reiter, 153; Bil Gilbert, 7, 9, 12–13, 55–56, 64, 88, 96–99, 101, 121, 127, 244; Charles Hirshberg, 126, 127, 128; Chris Chavez, 85; Christian Stone, 47; Craig Neff, 101, 102; Curry Kirkpatrick, 33, 37, 91; Dan Jenkins, 7, 59, 210; David Epstein, 75, 77, 81–83, 87, 251n36,

260n64; Don Canham, 159; E. M. Swift, 132, 186; Erika Rasmusson, 50; George Dohrmann, 65, 154; Grant Wahl, 65, 88, 223; Gwilym S. Brown, 33; Herbert Warren Wind, 208, 210; Ivan Maisel, 106; Jack Dickey, 72; Jack MacCallum, 138–40; Jack Olsen, 87, 168–69; Jaime Diaz, 55; Jerry Kirshenbaum, 54–55, 65, 87, 100–101, 147; Jill Lieber, 65; John Underwood, 188; Kate Fagan, 226–27; Kelli Anderson, 142–43, 154; Maggie Mertens, 123–24; Maureen H. Maroney, 104–5; Merrell Noden, 141, 142; Michael Bamberger, 99–100, 109–11; Michael Rosenberg, 223; Michael Silver, 26; Nancy Williamson, 7, 9, 12–13, 55–56, 64, 88, 96–99, 101, 121, 127, 208, 244; Pablo Torre, 75, 77, 87; Paul Gallico, 154–55; Ray Kennedy, 73, 74, 87; Richard Demak, 138, 139; Richard O'Brien, 203; Rick Reilly, 24, 26, 50, 106–7, 115–16, 121–22, 235–36; Robert Sullivan, 183; Roy Terrell, 166; Sarah Pileggi, 61; Shane Peacock, 51; Shannon Brownlee, 32; Susan Casey, 108; Tim Layden, 46–47, 68–69, 83–85, 137–38; William Johnson, 179–80, 198–99, 202, 208; Bill (William) Leggett, 7
Sports Illustrated for Women: and Allisa Wykes, 69–70; Carmen Renee Thompson's article in, 23; and Cathy Freeman, 186; and Chamique Holdsclaw, 126; Dana Sullivan of, 140; duration of, 157; and eating disorders, 142–43, 144, 145; and Felicia Zimmerman, 37–38; and female athletes, 114, 140, 142–43, 144, 145, 156–57, 231, 236; and the frailty myth, 128, 145, 156–57; Katherine Cole of, 193; and Kelli Anderson of, 142–43; readership of, 114, 126; reporting from, 4, 69–70, 114, 126, 140; and Shannon Bahrke, 37; and *Sports Illustrated Women*, 26,

114, 128; and sports-related injuries, 140; subscription rate of, 128; and U.S. Women's Soccer Team, 52; and women's coming out, 69–70; and women's sports leagues, 193
Sports Illustrated Women, 106, 114, 115, 146, 154–56, 264–65n44
Sports Illustrated Women/Sport, 67, 112–14, 150
Stephenson, Jan, 20–21, 59, 210, 280n39
Stokes, Louise, 163
Stone, Toni, 196–97
Stringer, C. Vivian, 11
Strong Women, Deep Closets (Griffin), 65
Strug, Kerri, 239
Summit, Pat, 116
Swift, E. M., 132, 186
swimming: and Black female athletes, 117; and Carin Cone, 190; and Chris von Saltza, 44; and Debbie Meyer, 170; and Donna de Varona, 190; female qualities of, 171; and Jenny Thompson, 25–26; and Katie Ledecky, 84; and Kornelia Ender, 173; and Michael Phelps, 136–37; and performance-enhancing drugs, 147–48, 173; and Shirley Babashoff, 147, 173; and swimmers, 45, 136–37, 147–48, 172–73, 190; and Title IX, 106; and women's college swimming, 102
Swoopes, Sheryl, 71, *113,* 258–59n44

Taurasi, Diana, 205, 206, 230
Temple, Ed, 43
tennis: and Alice Marble, 33; and All-England Lawn Tennis Club, 41; and Althea Gibson, 42–43, 58; and Amélie Mauresmo, 68–69, 71; and Andre Agassi, 35; and Andrea Jaeger, 61; and Anna Kournikova, 27; and Anne White, 33; and Australian Open tournament, 68, 254–55n67; and Battle of the Sexes, 54, 90, 91–93, 122; and

Bill Tilden, 54; and Black American Tennis Association, 43; and Bobby Riggs, 122; and Borg-Connors rivalry, 217, 218; and Chris Evert, 34, 46, 129, 213, 214, 215–18, 281n51; and Darlene Hard, 43; and equal pay, 214–15, 219; and Evert-Navratilova rivalry, 216–18, *216;* fans of, 91, 213, 220; and female athletes, 14, 23, 27, 32, 33, 34, 41–43, 91–92, 114, 128–31, 236–38; and first Battle of the Sexes, 91; and French Open's dress code, 35; and Gladys Heldman, 73, 214; and Gussie Moran, 33; and Helen Jacobs, 33; and Houston Astrodome, 91; and independent women's tour, 54; and Indian Wells Tournament, 219; and Jack Kramer's professional circuit, 5; and Jimmy Connors, 62; and Karol Fageros, 43; and Kim Clijsters, 29; and Lindsay Davenport, 68; and Martina Navratilova, 61, 62, 63–64, 69, 79, 129, 216–18; and men's tour, 65, 214–15, 216, 218–19, 225; and Monica Seles, 128–31, 133, 158; and Naomi Osaka, 137, 237–38; and Novak Djokovic, 219; number of sets of, 282n59; and Pam Shriver, 64–65, 69; and pay equity, 225; and players' emotions, 29–31, 32, 130; and professional sports organizations, 193, 218, 225; and Renée Richards, 73–74; and Rosie Casals, 73; and segregation, 265–66n53; and Serena Williams, 23–24, 29, 30–35, 41, 143–44, 145, 218, 219, 251n31; and sex chromosome tests, 73–74; and sexism, 242; and Shirley Bloomer, 43; and Steffi Graf, 37, 130, 231; and Suzanne Lenglen, 33; and table tennis, 5; and Taylor Townsend, 145; and tennis players, 45, 54, 73–74, 91–93, 122, 137, 143–44, 145, 218, 238, 251n31; and United States Lawn Tennis Association (USLTA), 42, 214;

tennis (*continued*)
  and United States Tennis Associa-
    tion (USTA), 73–74, 145; and U.S.
    Open, 30, 32, 73–74, 145, 213, 214, 215,
    219, 234; and Venus Williams, 24,
    34, 41, 42, 218, 219, 239–40, 281n49;
    and Williams sisters, 34–35, 41–42,
    218, 219; and Wimbledon, 33, 41, 62,
    79, 130, 145, 214, 237, 281n49; and
    women's outfits, 33–34, 35, 252n38;
    and Women's Tennis Association,
    30, 40, 69, 214, 218, 219, 225, 242,
    250n22; and women's tennis tour, 14,
    23, 24, 27, 41, 42, 43, 65, 68–69, 74, 91,
    129–30, 131, 141, 144, 145, 214, 215, 216,
    218, 234; and Zina Garrison, 144. *See
    also* Gibson, Althea; Hingis, Martina;
    King, Billie Jean; Riggs, Bobby; Wil-
    liams, Serena
Thomas, Debi, 175, 176, 177–78, 190
Thomas, Lia, 79–80
Thomashow, Amanda, 152, 153
Thompson, Jenny, 20, 25–26, 190
Tilden, Bill, 54
Time Inc., 1, 5, 6, 7, 115
Tinling, Ted, 33
Title IX: and access to education, 92–93,
    107–8; and arguments of Labinger
    and Bryant, 104–5; and Battle of the
    Sexes in tennis, 90, 92–93, 111–12, 122;
    and Black female athletes, 117, 118,
    119; and Brown University, 103–5, 123,
    124; challenges to, 101–4, 121, 123–24;
    and *Cohen v. Brown University*,
    104–5, 124; and College of William
    and Mary's programs, 102–3, 104; and
    equal access to resources, 106, 122,
    124; and equity for women, 13–14,
    92–108, 110–12, 113, 115–16, 117–18,
    120, 122, 124–25, 236, 245–46; and
    federal funds, 92–94, 101–2, 103, 107,
    111, 120, 124, 236; and federal law, 99,
    100, 101, 107, 108, 110, 112, 113, 115,
    120, 121, 123, 124; and female athletes,
    92–108, 110, 115, 116, 119, 122, 123,
    124–25, 127, 236, 240, 245–46; and
    football, 123; fortieth anniversary of,
    99, 100, 120, 122–23; and *Grove City
    College v. Bell*, 101–2; and high school
    and college levels, 101–9, 122, 123, 124;
    impact of, 98–99, 102, 111, 112, 124–25;
    lawsuits about, 100–101, 104–5, 124,
    263n21; and men's sports, 105–7; op-
    position to, 243; passage of, 12, 13, 92,
    93, 94, 99, 102, 106, 108, 110, 112, 165,
    235, 236, 240; and ponytail hair style,
    40; and quota systems, 104–5, 123;
    regulations of, 94, 95, 103, 108, 121,
    124; and scholarships, 118, 122, 123,
    124; and sports-related injuries, 14,
    125; and suit against Michigan State
    University, 100–101; and transgender
    athletes, 80; and U.S. Department
    of Health, Education, and Welfare,
    95–96; and U.S. Women's Soccer
    Team, 111; and Walter Byers, 94, 96;
    and white females, 117; and women's
    facilities, 124, 236
Torre, Pablo, 75, 77, 87
transgender athletes, 60, 73–80, 87–88,
    235
*Trouble with Blame: Victims, Perpetra-
    tors & Responsibility, The* (Lamb), 151
Tuchman, Gaye, 121
Tyson, Cicely, 41
Tyus, Wyomia, 169, 170, 274n21

United States: and American society,
    72–73, 80, 93–94, 96–97, 98, 101,
    161–62, 164, 165, 167; and Association
    of Boxing Commissions, 77; athletes'
    defections to, 189; and Atoy Wilson,
    177; Black Americans in, 167, 168–69,
    170, 177, 190, 265–66n53; and boycott
    of Moscow Olympics, 190; and Civil
    Rights Act, 93; civil rights in, 167, 190;
    and Civil Rights Restoration Act, 102;
    and competition with China, 178;

and competition with Russia/Soviet Union, 159–62, 164, 174, 189–90, 191, 229; Congress of, 123, 236; democracy in, 164, 165; Department of Education, 103, 117; and discrimination, 93–101, 102, 103, 120; Division of Girls and Women's Sports, 171, 191; and Eisenhower administration, 171, 191; and equal pay, 121, 192, 204, 205–6; and female athletes, 163–64, 165, 191; and the frailty myth, 126, 127–28; gay rights movement in, 87; and gymnasts, 239; and investment in women's sport, 165, 171, 191; and man on the moon, 161; mental depression in, 134–35; and Native Americans, 184–85; Navajo Nation in, 184; and Office of Civil Rights's role, 124; and Olympic teams, 159, 163; physical fitness in, 164–65, 191; and President Nixon, 173, 179; and protest of Smith and Carlos, 169–70; and relations with China, 179; and rights of trans people, 73, 80; and right to same-sex marriage, 72–73; segregation in, 163, 167; and soft power, 165; and the space race, 161–62; and the Sputnik satellite, 164; State Department, 168, 189; Supreme Court, 101, 102, 124; and track and field, 163–64, 165, 167, 169, 170, 190; and USA Gymnastics, 152; and U.S. Anti-Doping Agency, 146; and USA Swimming, 80; and U.S. Olympic Committee, 131, 167–68, 171, 191; and U.S. Women's Soccer Team, 220; and victim impact statements, 152; white privilege in, 118; and women's diving, 183; women's equality in, 92–93, 94, 117–19, 124; women's movement in, 121; and women's soccer, 108–12, 221, 222; and women's sports, 240; and World Cup soccer, 50, 109–12, 220–23; and World War II, 207. See also Title IX

United States Lawn Tennis Association (USLTA), 42–43, 214
United States Olympic Committee (USOC), 131, 168, 171, 289n49
United States Tennis Association (USTA), 73, 145
United States Women's National Soccer Team (USWNT), 10, 24–25, 52, 99–112, *111*, 206, 222

Vindication of the Rights of Women, A (Wollstonecraft), 9
Vonn, Lindsey, 137–38
von Saltza, Chris, 19, 44

Waddell, Tom, 54, 60
Wahl, Grant, 65, 88, 223
Walker, Alice, 119
Walker, Nefertiti A., 8
Wambach, Abby, 221–22
Wertheim, L. Jon, 27, 34, 42, 65, 70, 120–21, 134–35, 136, 137, 158, 224, 242, 250n22
Wheel within a Wheel: A Woman's Quest for Freedom, A (Willard), 9
White, Willye, 44–45, 58, 59, 163
Wicks, Sue, 70–71
Wie, Michelle, 212–13
Willard, Frances, 9
Williams, Linda D., 8
Williams, Serena: and anger, 29, 30, 31; and Australian Open, 143, *143;* and femininity, 23–24, 32, 34–35, 42, 47, 48; and Grand Slam tournaments, 218; hair styles of, 41, 42; health of, 35, 143–44, *143;* and motherhood, 35; as Sportsperson of the Year for *SI*, 47, 48, 52; tennis outfits of, 34–35, 254–55n67; as a tennis star, 218, 242, 244; Wimbledon victory of, 23; and women's muscles, 23–24; and women's rights, 4, 10
Williams, Venus, 24, 34–35, 41, 42, 218, 239–40. See also *Sports Illustrated*

Williamson, Nancy, 7, 9, 12–13, 55–56, 64, 88, 96–99, 101, 121, 127, 208, 244. *See also* sports; *Sports Illustrated*

Wind, Herbert Warren, 208, 210

Withycombe, Jenny Lind, 118

Witt, Katarina, 175–76, *175*, 178, 191

Wolff, Alexander, 40, 72, 103, 106, 107–8, 181–82, 183, 203, 204, 205, 206, 222, 279n30

Wollstonecraft, Mary, 9, 127

Women's Basketball League (WBL), 202

Women's National Basketball Association (WNBA), 40–41, 70, 193–94, 203–7, 221, 225–26, 226, 227, 234, 242, 258n41, 279n30

Women's Professional Golf Association (WPGA), 207–8

Women's Professional Soccer League (WPSL), 221

Women's Sports Foundation, 26, 32, 117

women's sports outfits, 33–38, 39, 42, 45, 51, 52. *See also* Navratilova, Martina; sports; tennis; Williams, Serena

Women's Studies International Forum, 60

Women's Tennis Association (WTA), 30, 40, 69, 73, 214, 218, 219, 225, 242, 250n22

Women's United Soccer Association (WUSA), 193, 220–21

Woods, Tiger, 212

World War II, 6, 36, 159, 163, 195, 196

Wright, Ben, 67

Wyrick, Waneen, 8

Yale women's crew team, 99–100, 122

Young, Iris Marion, 9

Young, Sheila, 100

Zaharias, "Babe" Didrikson, 49, 57, 154–55, 163, 165, 207, 208–10. *See also* golf; *Sports Illustrated*

Cultural Frames, Framing Culture

Institutional Character: Collectivity, Agency, and the Modernist Novel
Robert Higney

Walk the Barrio: The Streets of Twenty-First-Century Transnational Latinx Literature
Cristina Rodriguez

Fashioning Character: Style, Performance, and Identity in Contemporary American Literature
Lauren S. Cardon

Neoliberal Nonfictions: The Documentary Aesthetic from Joan Didion to Jay-Z
Daniel Worden

Dandyism: Forming Fiction from Modernism to the Present
Len Gutkin

Terrible Beauty: The Violent Aesthetic and Twentieth-Century Literature
Marian Eide

Women Writers of the Beat Era: Autobiography and Intertextuality
Mary Paniccia Carden

Stranger America: A Narrative Ethics of Exclusion
Josh Toth

Fashion and Fiction: Self-Transformation in Twentieth-Century American Literature
Lauren S. Cardon

American Road Narratives: Reimagining Mobility in Literature and Film
Ann Brigham

The Arresting Eye: Race and the Anxiety of Detection
Jinny Huh

Failed Frontiersmen: White Men and Myth in the Post-Sixties American Historical Romance
James J. Donahue

Composing Cultures: Modernism, American Literary Studies, and the Problem of Culture
Eric Aronoff

Quirks of the Quantum: Postmodernism and Contemporary American Fiction
Samuel Chase Coale

Chick Lit and Postfeminism
Stephanie Harzewski

American Iconographic: "National Geographic," Global Culture, and the Visual Imagination
Stephanie L. Hawkins

Wanted: The Outlaw in American Visual Culture
Rachel Hall

Male Armor: The Soldier-Hero in Contemporary American Culture
Jon Robert Adams

African Americans and the Culture of Pain
Debra Walker King

Against the Unspeakable: Complicity, the Holocaust, and Slavery in America
Naomi Mandel

I'm No Angel: The Blonde in Fiction and Film
Ellen Tremper

Visions of the Maid: Joan of Arc in American Film and Culture
Robin Blaetz

Writing War in the Twentieth Century
Margot Norris

The Golden Avant-Garde: Idolatry, Commercialism, and Art
Raphael Sassower and Louis Cicotello

Kodak and the Lens of Nostalgia
Nancy Martha West